PHYSIOTHERAPY

IN

DISORDERS OF THE BRAIN

)

E

E

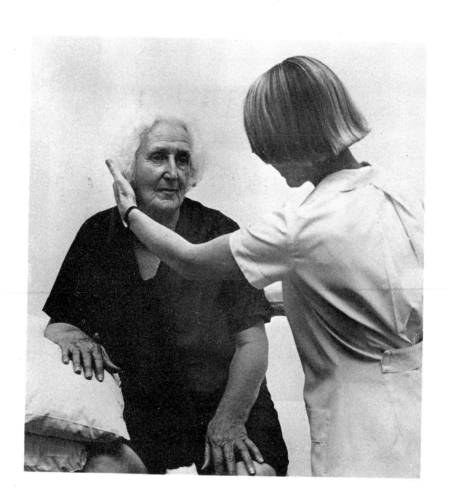

PHYSIOTHERAPY IN DISORDERS OF THE BRAIN

A Clinical Guide

by

Janet H. Carr, Dip. Phty.

Lecturer, School of Physiotherapy, Cumberland College of Health Sciences, Sydney.

and

Roberta B. Shepherd, Dip. Phty., F.A.C.P.

Senior Lecturer, School of Physiotherapy, Cumberland College of Health Sciences, Sydney.

Butterworth-Heinemann Ltd
Halley Court, Jordan Hill, Oxford OX2 8EJ

 PART OF REED INTERNATIONAL BOOKS

OXFORD   LONDON   GUILDFORD   BOSTON
MUNICH   NEW DELHI   SINGAPORE   SYDNEY
TOKYO   TORONTO   WELLINGTON

First published 1980
Reprinted 1983, 1985, 1987, 1988, 1989, 1990

ISBN 0 7506 0120 5

Printed in Great Britain by The Bath Press, Avon

PREFACE

This book has been written to help the clinical physiotherapist and the undergraduate recognise the problems resulting from brain disorder in adults and to give practical assistance in the treatment of these problems. There are three main themes throughout the book – the need for a problem-orientated approach to assessment and treatment, the need for an understanding of the processes involved in the relearning of motor skills by adults, and the need to understand the pathophysiological and psychological reasons for each patient's problems.

The authors' decision to illustrate the analysis of problems and methods of finding solutions to them has provided the design for the book. The first section is an introduction, providing an outline of nervous system development and the development of motor skill, and the process of aging. The second section describes the most common brain disorders seen by the physiotherapist, the problems which result and the main points in treatment. The third section and Appendix I are designed to be read in conjunction with the second section, in that the most common abnormalities of tone and movement control and particular treatment techniques are described in more detail. Some readers may find this format unconventional, but the authors hope the book will be found thought-provoking and a stimulus to further study in areas not always familiar to the physiotherapist.

ACKNOWLEDGEMENTS

For their valuable comments and suggestions we wish to thank Doreen Moore, Jon Leicester, Janet Clarke, Bill Shields, Jenny Harrison, Janet McCredie and Louise Mayne. We would like to thank Pat Greiner, Sue Ferris and Wendy Baguley for typing the manuscript, Eva Erdos for her help in obtaining literature, Penny Zylstra for the drawings and diagrams, and David Robinson and Joseph Hangya who took the photographs. We would also like to thank those patients whose photographs appear throughout the book.

In conclusion we would like to express our grateful thanks to the Principal of Cumberland College of Health Sciences, Dr. Jeffrey Miller, and the Council of the College, who granted us leave.

CONTENTS

Introduction

Physiotherapy for the brain-damaged patient has as its main objective the restoration of more normal function. The physiotherapist is involved in the treatment of problems of movement, but these problems, although they will vary with each patient, will always include some degree of sensory disability, emotional and behavioural difficulties, abnormalities of tone, difficulties with concentration, understanding and communication. The patient's functioning ability, in a very general sense, is disordered, and because of this, movement cannot be seen as isolated from mental processes or from environmental influences. The therapist should not, therefore, see herself as a dispenser of equipment and exercise, but as a potent force in the patient's environment, who can influence him towards the recovery of function, not only by providing an appropriate external environment, but also by stimulating and motivating his internal processes.

To have this effect the physiotherapist needs to understand a great deal about human function. She requires expertise in understanding normal movement, how learning takes place, particularly the learning of motor skills, the importance of motivation, and the importance to the patient of treatment goals clearly expressed and directly approached. Clinically, the therapist must develop observational ability, judgement, and the mental and physical skills which will enable her to move and guide the patient with subtlety, and to stimulate the response she wants from him.

In the past, there has been an emphasis on physical techniques as if they were an end in themselves. However, physiotherapy for the brain-damaged has entered a new phase, in which behavioural factors are assuming greater importance. Furthermore, physiotherapists are relating and applying the findings of physiologists, educational psychologists and bioengineers to therapy in an effort to improve movement by affecting the whole man.

While it is undoubtedly important to consider the methods available to the therapist for the treatment of patients, it may also be relevant to consider the therapist. It is probable that the therapist herself is a most important factor in determining whether or not the

1

patient develops his potential functional ability. Why are some therapists more successful with their patients than others? What attributes should be cultivated by therapists who want to work with the brain-damaged? The answer to these questions requires a more thorough investigation than is our intention in this book, but there are some points upon which it is interesting to ponder. The answers to both questions should probably make reference to the use of personality, of judgement and intelligence, the use of imagination and planning ability, and the ability to relate physically and emotionally to other people.

The use of *personality* includes the ability to impart confidence, to motivate, and to foster satisfying relationships. The ability to use imagination, to develop thinking skills, to reason logically, and when necessary laterally, while actually treating the patient, as well as when assessing him and planning his treatment programme, is essential if treatment is to be anything more than a stereotyped performance of a pre-planned and routine series of techniques.

Logical thinking is possible despite the frequent lack of basic premises such as knowledge of normal physiological and behavioural function upon which to build conclusions. Certainly, treatment of some of the movement problems seen in brain-damaged patients can be, at least in part, a simple logical exercise, involving an understanding of normal movement, assessment of the patient's function, evaluation of the key movement components which are missing or abnormal, and treatment which will help the patient recover effective function. If he does not improve, errors can often be traced back to poor understanding of normal movement, deficiencies in the initial assessment, defective judgement in evaluating the key problems, or to inappropriate or poorly performed treatment.

The ability to *think laterally* (de Bono 1967) offers the possibility of approaching a difficult problem from a different, non-logical point of view, in order to find a solution. This method of thinking may not come naturally to those brought up in the tradition of logical thinking, but its effectiveness in providing alternative solutions to problems for which there seems no logical solution, makes it a worthwhile mental skill for the therapist to cultivate.

If we consider Hudson's (1970) dichotomy of thinkers into convergent and divergent, we should question which type of thinker makes an effective therapist. Is it the convergent thinker who tends to be interested in the physical sciences, is conventional, usually ready to accept expert advice and frequently has a low opinion of himself? These people tend, according to Ellard (1974) to be more likely to want to exercise their authority over others in terms of reward or punishment. Or is it the divergent thinker, who has more artistic and biological interests, is more unconventional and interested in people, and is more likely to see situations involving other people as requiring solicitude or advice? The convergent thinker tends to have more set opinions than the divergent. The dilemma of the medical student, according to Ellard, is that with a tendency to be a converger, he is selected to be a scientist, but spends his working life in a humanity. The same could possibly be said of the physiotherapist.

Recovery of brain function. Little is known of what occurs in the brain following insult to a part of it. However it is probable that the damaged brain is capable of some reorganisation following head injury, stroke or surgery. Physical treatment aims at exploiting and stimulating this reorganisation and turning it to the most functional use. Denhoff and Robinault (1960) suggest that physical treatment develops the latent abilities of the individual. The editorial in the New Scientist (1975) says 'Recovery must depend in one way or another – through regrowth or reorganisation, or both – on undamaged areas of the brain taking over the function of the missing tissue. But it is clear that in order to do that they need as much help as possible from the remaining tissue; and, to be effective, the brain must have feedback from voluntary movement'.

Luria (1963) notes that reorganisation and adaptation can be observed in the higher vertebrates such as monkeys and man. He suggests that an essential condition of this is that the particular activity is necessary, that the greater the need the more automatically and easily will the reorganisation and adaptation be carried out. When part of the brain, 'a complex functional system', is damaged, restoration of function may take place by means of 'the intra-systemic conceptual reorganisation of the preserved links', or of new links which never before participated in the deranged functional system. This can usually be achieved by special training and practice which will eventually lead to automaticity of the particular function.

Raisman's (1969) findings indicate that part of the recovery may be due to the terminal endings of preserved cortico-spinal fibres and others forming new terminals which occupy denuded synaptic sites on the motoneurons. Gradually more of the motoneurons originally devoid of cortical innervation will regain it. 'Nothing is known of the factors stimulating the process and how training (use) appears to have a beneficial effect'.

Eccles (1973) postulates that changes in neuronal connectivity should be possible by the occurrence of microstructural changes in synapses, which may hypertrophy, bud additional synapses or even regress (Fig. 1). He links synaptic modification with learning, and suggests

3

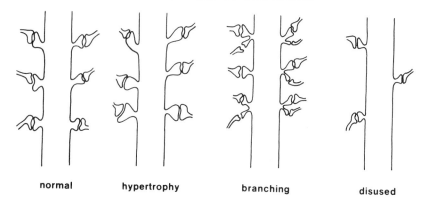

normal   hypertrophy   branching   disused

Fig. 1. *Plasticity of dendritic spine synapses. These drawings are intended to convey the plastic changes which are postulated to occur with growth and with regression (from Eccles, J. C. (1973)* The Understanding of the Brain. *New York, McGraw–Hill).*

that spine synapses on the dendrites of the pyramidal cells in the cerebral cortex and the Purkinje cells in the cerebellum, for example, are modifiable synapses concerned in the learning process. Certainly the effects of disuse on the spine synapses of pyramidal cells in the visual cortex have been shown in experiments with mice raised in visual deprivation.

Brodal (1973) suggests we must assume that 'intact fibres "take over" for the damaged ones', and suggests that 'remaining intact and functioning fibres establish new synapses where the destroyed fibres were previously active'. The studies of Wall and Egger (1971) support this assumption.

Although it is obvious that physical treatment, if appropriate to the patient's needs, helps him to recover useful function, there is a need for *the effects of treatment* to be investigated. Increased understanding would aid us in the development of more effective techniques and attitudes. This must be accomplished by clinical trials and research studies. Tinbergen (1974) stresses the importance to medical science of open-minded observation of 'watching and wondering', and he goes on to comment 'This basic scientific method is still too often looked down upon by those blinded by the glamour of apparatus, by the prestige of tests, and by the temptation to turn to drugs'.

Although methods of treatment should be as scientifically-based as possible, there is still an art in their administration to the patient. While the *science of physiotherapy* should deal with precise information gained by laboratory research, the *art of physiotherapy* involves the appreciation that we are dealing with human beings with their strengths, sufferings and anxieties. 'Scientists have learned that one cannot leave the observer out of the equation and the clinician knows one cannot leave the laboratory out of the clinic' (Schnell, Jenkins and Jiménez-Pabon 1964). In physiotherapy there is certainly a need to develop scientifically-based methods of assessment and treatment, but there is also a pressing need to study and develop the art of delivering them.

In an effort to describe treatment and to relate it to physiological, anatomical and behavioural principles, diverse *terminology* has developed which causes considerable confusion. As Eccles (1973) points out, a term may become practically useless if usage is too diverse. Terms used to describe treatment should be carefully considered for what they imply to others, whether to therapists, other health professionals, patients or relatives. As Basmajian (1975) has pointed out 'jargon has hindered rather than advanced the training of therapists in neuro-muscular facilitation – it has certainly frightened off scientists'. Goals and treatment should be described in everyday language, in terms of the function to be gained, which can be easily understood by the patient and his relatives, as well as by other health professionals.

The word *'transfers'* may be a good example of jargon. The therapist talks about teaching the patient to transfer from bed to chair. Unfortunately, the term implies passivity. It seems to have its origin in therapy in descriptions of the way a completely incapacitated patient can be lifted from bed to chair. However, it is also used to describe a patient learning to stand up from his bed and to sit himself down in his chair, activities which are not passive and which only require some guidance from the therapist. The trouble with the use of words whose meanings are passive is that they tend to encourage subconsciously a passive approach to treatment. The inexperienced therapist or nurse who knows she must teach 'transfers' to a patient following a stroke, may not consider that she has to analyse the task of standing up from a chair and to guide the patient as he actively performs the movement until he can stand up by himself. She is much more likely to do most of the work herself, passively transferring him from one position to the other.

Perhaps the most confusing words are the most ordinary ones and the ones which are used so frequently that no-one stops to think what they really mean and the impression they might give to others. An example of this is the word *'exercise'*. This is a familiar word in the physiotherapist's vocabulary, and it is time its use was revised. It infers methods of increasing strength and endurance, of keeping fit.

It is therefore appropriate in preventative health care programmes, in preparation for sporting activity and in the treatment of patients with musculo-skeletal problems who require to regain strength and mobility.

However, in the treatment of patients with dysfunction of the brain, with its effect on the mind as well as the body, physiotherapy is still confusingly described as consisting of passive exercises passing to assisted active, to active, to resisted active (Cohen 1971), or as 'mat exercises'. The latter term suggests a group of exercises done on a mat and says nothing of the functions to be improved or the goals to be attained. Treatment of a patient is sometimes described as involving 'mat exercises', 'activities of daily living' and 'gait training'. This gives no indication that each patient will have different problems and different functional needs. Furthermore it suggests a treatment 'routine'.

The methods used by therapists to enable patients to relearn movements following injury to the brain should not be directed towards improving strength but to improving function, which does not require strength so much as control. They involve complex interactions between therapist and patient, and involve the learning or re-learning of skills rather than the strengthening of certain muscle groups. They are a mental process as well as a physical process.

There is a tendency for therapists to seek out *recipes* or routines of treatment, although the great variability of patients and their problems makes this impossible. Treatment cannot be designed as a routine for particular diseases, but must be flexible and problem-solving, that is, designed around each patient's own individual problems.

Confusion also arises from the tendency to describe treatment by the use of *eponyms* (for example, 'Bobath' treatment, 'Rood' treatment) or phrases (for example, 'proprioceptive neuromuscular facilitation'). Both of these probably illustrate the desire for a prescribed routine of treatment complete within itself. Unfortunately, the contributions of the people whose names are involved are usually lost sight of in the general tendency to align oneself with one name or another. Furthermore, the inexperienced therapist could be forgiven for thinking these terms represent the only alternatives in treatment.

The mechanism by which improvement occurs following lesions of the brain is unknown, and therefore the reasons for the effectiveness of treatment designed to improve movement and function is uncertain. It is possible however that treatment which is directed toward the relearning of motor skills takes advantage of the brain's plasticity and is therefore potentially more effective than treatment directed

6

more peripherally by means of exercise programmes. It is probably reasonable to hypothesise, as does Ayres (1972), that the demands of the environment greatly assist the reorganisation of the brain after it is damaged. An important function of the therapist is to mobilise resources in order to provide an environment which is stimulating and motivating, which takes into account the effect of everything exterior to the patient, as well as the mechanisms within his body and his mind.

References

Ayres, A. J. (1972) *Sensory Integration and Learning Disabilities*. Los Angeles, Western Psychological Services.

Basmajian, J. V. (1975) Research or retrench. *Phys. Ther.*, **55**, 6, 607–610.

Brodal, A. (1973) Self-observations and neuro-anatomical considerations after a stroke. *Brain*, **96**, 675–694.

Cohen, B. S. (1971) Use of physical therapy in neurological disorders. *Maryland State Med. J.*, **20**, 12, 53–56.

de Bono, E. (1967) *The Use of Lateral Thinking*. London, Cape.

Denhoff, E. and Robinault, I. P. (1960) *Cerebral Palsy and Related Disorders – A Developmental Approach to Dysfunction*. London, McGraw-Hill.

Eccles, J. (1973) *The Understanding of the Brain*. New York, McGraw-Hill.

Editorial, *New Scientist* (1975).

Ellard, J. (1974) The disease of being a doctor. *Med. J. Aust.*, **2**, 318–323.

Hudson, L. (1970) *Frames of Mind*. London, Penguin.

Luria, A. R. (1963) *Restoration of Function after Brain Injury*. London, Pergamon.

Mellanby, K. (1976) Forecasting error. *Nature* (Lond.), 2627, 441.

Raisman, G. (1969) Neuronal plasticity in the septal nuclei of the adult rat. *Brain Res.*, **14**, 25–48.

Schnell, H., Jenkins, J. J. and Jiménez-Pabon, E. (1964) *Aphasia in Adults*. New York, Harper and Row.

Tinbergen, N. (1974) Ethology and stress disease. *Science*, **185**, 20–27.

Wall, P. D. and Egger, M. D. (1971) Formation of new connections in adult rat brains after partial deafferentation. *Nature* (Lond.) **232**, 542–545.

Section I

Chapter 1

The Development of the Nervous System

The study of embryology gives a rational explanation of the position and relationships of the structures found in the normal adult, thereby stimulating a more intelligent approach to the study of the anatomy and function of the nervous system.

Development 'involves a progression of changes that lead from an undifferentiated state to a highly organised and specialised functional capacity' (Timiras 1972). There are three fundamental processes involved in development (Hamilton and Mossman 1972) – *growth* meaning a quantitative increase in size and weight, *differentiation* meaning an increase in molecular and cellular complexity and organisation, and *metabolism* inferring chemical changes in the developing organism. Cell division is an essential part of the process of development whether this development is by growth or by differentiation.

PRE–NATAL GROWTH AND DEVELOPMENT OF THE NERVOUS SYSTEM

Pre-natal development divides into three main periods according to Snell (1972).

1. **Pre-embryonic** from fertilisation of the ovum to the formation of the embryonic disc with three germ layers (weeks 1–3).
2. **Embryonic** – a time of rapid growth and differentiation and of the formation of all major organs (weeks 4–8).
3. **Fetal** – characterised by growth and further development of organs and systems (weeks 9-term).

The Pre-Embryonic Period

Embryologists divide this period into four stages, maturation, cleavage, blastocyst and gastrulation. The first stage involves *maturation* of the male and female germ cells. Fertilisation occurs, usually in the Fallopian tube, when fusion of the two germ cells takes place. A zygote or fertilised egg is formed and a new organism begins its existence.

The term *cleavage* describes the next stage during which a rapid division of cells takes place. This converts the unicellular zygote into a multicellular organism called the blastocyst. By the time the zygote has reached the 12 to 16 cell stage (approximately 3 days) it has moved down the Fallopian tube. It consists of a group of centrally located cells and a surrounding layer of outer cells. The inner cell mass, called the *embryoblast* gives rise to tissues of the embryo itself while the outer cells form the *trophoblast* which later develops into the placenta.

The embryoblast and the trophoblast together make up the *blastocyst* (Fig. 2). The blastocyst already contains areas which are referred to as presumptive organ regions (Hamilton and Mossman 1972). At five days the free-moving blastocyst is thought to be transported to its site of attachment or implantation on the uterine wall. By eight days it is implanted (Fig. 2).

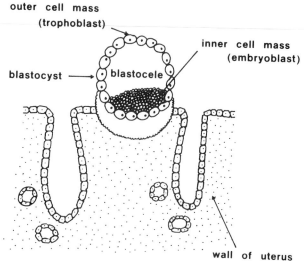

Fig. 2. *The attachment of the blastocyst to the uterine wall (implantation). (From Snell, R. S. (1972)* Clinical Embryology for Medical Students. *Boston, Little Brown & Co.).*

The process of *gastrulation* which follows will result in the establishment of three primary germ cell layers, the endoderm, mesoderm and ectoderm bringing the presumptive organs into the positions in which they will undergo their subsequent development (Hamilton and Mossman 1972).

However, in its first week the embryo is a bilaminar or two-layered cellular disc, consisting of two germ cell layers, one, the *ectoderm*, sitting on top of the other, the *endoderm*. During the third week the ectodermal cells proliferate at a great rate and many of them migrate towards the midline, giving rise to a prominence called the *primitive streak*. From this mass of cells arises the *mesoderm*, thus completing a trilaminar or three-layered disc of germ cells.

At the same time as the primitive streak is giving rise to the mesoderm, a solid cord of cells becomes evident. This is called the *notochord* (Fig. 3), from which will derive part of the axial skeleton. It

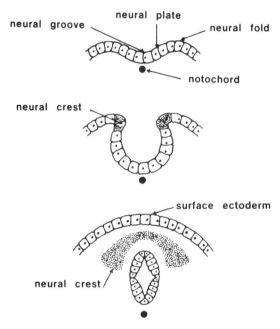

Fig. 3. *Section of an embryo showing the development of the neural tube and neural crest.*

will be replaced by the vertebral column as differentiation occurs.

By the end of week three, the ectodermal cells lying directly above the notochord have undergone a further thickening to form the *neural plate*, which is the basic structure of the nervous system. One day later the neural plate develops two lateral folds, and this modification of its shape allows the development of the *neural groove*.

The Embryonic Period

This period corresponds to the stage referred to by embryologists as *neurula*, during which the neural plate and axial structures of the embryo are elaborated. During weeks four to eight each of the three germ layers (ectoderm, mesoderm and endoderm) give rise to a number of specific tissues and organs (Fig. 4). By the end of this period the main organ systems have been laid down, and the major features of the external body form are recognisable (Langman 1969).

Cells forming the lateral margin of the neural plate form a strip of ectodermal cells called the *neural crest*. From these neural crest cells, neurons of the sensory peripheral nervous system and of the autonomic nervous system will be derived.

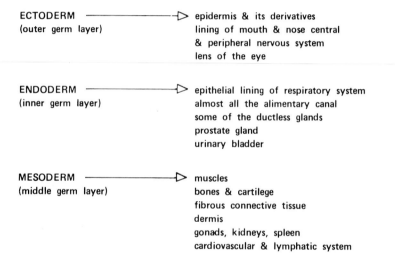

ECTODERM ⟶▷ epidermis & its derivatives
(outer germ layer) lining of mouth & nose central
& peripheral nervous system
lens of the eye

ENDODERM ⟶▷ epithelial lining of respiratory system
(inner germ layer) almost all the alimentary canal
some of the ductless glands
prostate gland
urinary bladder

MESODERM ⟶▷ muscles
(middle germ layer) bones & cartilege
fibrous connective tissue
dermis
gonads, kidneys, spleen
cardiovascular & lymphatic system

Fig. 4. *The specific tissues and organs which develop from each of the 3 germ cell layers.*

The neural groove deepens allowing the further development of the neural folds. By twenty-three days the neural groove is partly closed by fusion of the neural folds. Their complete fusion forms the *neural tube* which will develop into the brain and spinal cord. Its cephalic end dilates to form three primary brain vesicles, the prosencephalon or forebrain, the mesencephalon or midbrain and the rhombencephalon or hindbrain (Fig. 5). The remainder of the neural tube elongates and forms the spinal cord. Following closure of the neural tube, the neural crest forms two columns of cells each lying

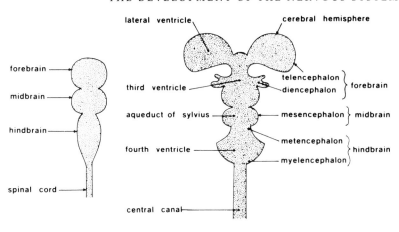

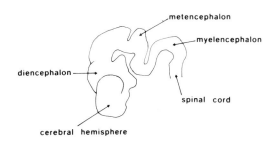

Fig. 5. *The cephalic end of the neural tube dilates to form 3 primary brain vesicles. The forebrain and hindbrain vesicles divide during week five. (From Snell, R. S. (1972)* Clinical Embryology for Medical Students. *Boston, Little Brown & Co.).*

adjacent to the dorsolateral aspect of the tube. Ultimately these neural crest cells will differentiate into the cells of the posterior root ganglia, the sensory ganglia of the cranial nerves, the autonomic ganglia, Schwann cells and others.

Adjacent to the neural tube are thirty-one pairs of *somites*. These are blocks of mesodermal cells which begin to differentiate in the fourth week into the cells which will form dermis, connective tissue, cartilage, bone and muscular tissue. The segmental arrangement of the somites forms the basis for the segmental innervation pattern of the spinal nerves, in that a pair of nerves is developed in association with each pair of somites.

15

The spinal cord

This is generally considered to be the most simply organised part of the nervous system. The thick layer of the walls of the neural tube is called the *neuroepithelium*. The neuroepithelial cells proliferate and their repeated division leads to an increase in the length and diameter of the neural tube. Cells form which are incapable of further division and these are called *primitive neurocytes*. These cells migrate to form a zone surrounding the neuroepithelial or mantle layer, which is actually the *primitive grey matter* (Fig. 6).

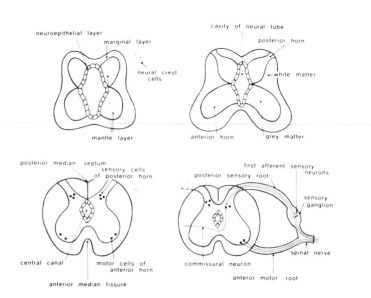

Fig. 6. *Different stages in the development of the spinal cord. The neural crest cells will form the sensory ganglion.*

The primitive neurocytes give rise to nerve fibres which grow peripherally and form a layer external to the mantle layer called the marginal layer. Their eventual white appearance, which will be due to the formation of myelin, will result in this layer being called the *white matter*. The addition of new primitive neurocytes to the mantle layer results in a ventral and dorsal thickening which will form the *anterior and posterior horns*. The nerve cells or neurocytes in the ventral thickening will become the *motor anterior horn cells*, and those in the dorsal thickening will become the *sensory posterior horn cells* (Fig. 6).

Continued growth leads to the formation of the *anterior median fissure* and the *posterior median septum*. The remaining lumen of the neural tube becomes the *central canal* of the spinal cord. Between weeks four to eight the spinal cord is the same length as the vertebral column (Fig. 16).

PROSENCEPHALON (Forebrain)		MESENCEPHALON (Midbrain)	RHOMBENCEPHALON (Hindbrain)	
TELENCEPHALON (Endbrain)	DIENCEPHALON (Between Brain)	MESENCEPHALON (Midbrain)	METENCEPHALON (Afterbrain)	MYELENCEPHALON (Spinal Brain)
cerebral cortex corpora striata rhinencephalon	epithalamus thalamus hypothalamus	corpora quadrigemina cruri cerebri tegmentum	cerebellum pons	medulla oblongata
lateral ventricles part of 111rd. ventricle	larger part of 111rd. ventricle	aqueduct of Sylvius	IVth Ventricle	central canal

Fig. 7. *Division of the forebrain, midbrain and hindbrain.*

The brain

During week five, the forebrain and hindbrain vesicles divide (Fig. 7), the forebrain vesicle into the telencephalon with *primitive cerebral hemispheres*, and the diencephalon, from which the *thalamic areas* will develop. The hindbrain vesicle divides into the metencephalon which will form the *pons* and *cerebellum*, and the myelencephalon or *medulla oblongata*. The wall of the developing medulla oblongata shows the typical organisation of the spinal cord, with the exception of the roof plate which helps make up the *choroid plexus of the fourth ventricle*. The motor nuclei of *cranial nerves* 9, 10, 11, 12, which originate in the medulla oblongata, develop earlier than the sensory nuclei but both have made their appearance by week 6. The mesencephalon shows no fundamental change in development.

The cavities which are the cephalic continuation of the central canal of the spinal cord, form the *lateral, third and fourth ventricles* and the *cerebral aqueduct of Sylvius*. The fourth ventricle is a direct continuation of the central canal of the spinal cord. The two lateral ventricles communicate with the third ventricle through the *interventricular foramen of Monro*. In the earliest stages the cerebrospinal fluid in the

17

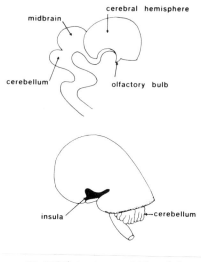

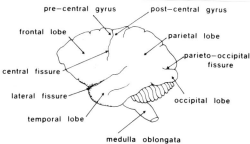

Fig. 8. *Stages in the development of the cerebral cortex. The hemispheres gradually envelop the midbrain and hindbrain.*

ventricular system is not continuous with that of the subarachnoid space.

The neuroepithelial cells proliferate as they do in the spinal cord, and cells for the mantle layer are produced. By the middle of the second month the mantle layer in the basal part of the hemispheres begins to increase in size. This bulge is called the *corpus striatum* because of its striated appearance. The gradual expansion of the cerebral hemispheres results in their overlapping the mid and hind brain (Fig. 8). The corpus striatum differentiates into two parts, the *caudate nucleus and the lentiform nucleus* (Fig. 9). This division is accomplished by an ever-increasing number of afferent and efferent

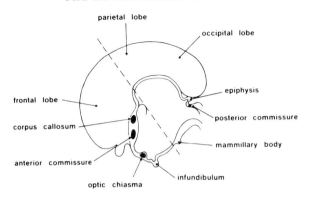

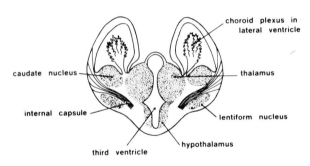

Fig. 9. *Section through the developing cerebrum.*

axons passing to and from the cortex of the hemisphere and breaking through the mass of the corpus striatum. The fibre bundle so formed is known as the *internal capsule*. The lentiform nucleus is divided later into the *putamen* and *globus pallidus*. This collection of nuclei is also referred to as the basal ganglia, although this term usually also includes the subthalamic nuclei and substantia nigra.

The brain now has a human appearance, and the adult form of cerebral development is well advanced. The central nervous system at this time constitutes twenty-five per cent of the whole body weight. The increasing expansion of the cerebral hemispheres results in the formation of the *frontal, temporal* and *occipital lobes*. It should be noted that the *parietal lobe* is not a lobe in the anatomical sense, but a part of the cerebrum which underlies the parietal bone. The three *meninges* (pia, arachnoid and dura matera) are distinct by the second month, as is the reticular system of capillaries which makes up the *cerebrovascular system*.

Nerve cell development

The fundamental structure of the nervous system 'is based upon the arrangement of nerve cells and their processes' (Ranson and Clark 1959).

After they have migrated into the mantle layer, the neuroblasts are relatively apolar, appearing rounded with no processes. As differentiation occurs, a fibre-like process grows out from opposite ends of each cell which is now called bipolar. A sprouting, which occurs following the regression of one of the processes, forms the *dendrites*, while the remaining process becomes the *axon* (Fig. 10). As further

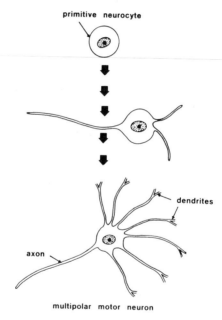

primitive neurocyte

dendrites

axon

multipolar motor neuron

Fig. 10. *Stages in the development of a multipolar motor neuron found in the anterior horn of the spinal cord.*

development occurs, the cell becomes an adult nerve or neuron. It should be noted that aggregations of cell bodies are referred to by the terms nuclei, ganglia and grey matter, and their fibres as tracts, pathways, funiculi, fasciculi, pedunculi, commissures and white matter, according to their arrangement within the nervous system.

In tracing the development of such nerve cells it is seen that the axons of, for example, a neuron in the posterior sensory horn of the spinal cord, penetrate the marginal layer (primitive white matter) where they ascend or descend to a different level. These *association neurons*, of which the brain and spinal cord are chiefly composed, are the means by which the central nervous system directs incoming inpulses to the appropriate outgoing pathways. The axons of the neurons in the anterior motor horn however, break through the marginal layer and form collectively the anterior motor root of the spinal nerve which will conduct motor impulses from the spinal cord to the muscles.

The mechanism by which a neuron grows out to its appointed place in the periphery (at the receptor or effector cell) is not understood. Szekely (1966) and others suggest that mechanical and chemical factors play a part. Certain nerve fibres are supposed to have selective affinities for their own projected pathways, and these affinities appear to depend upon mechanical guidance, biochemical guides along their route and biochemical properties within each neuron (Noback and Demarest 1975). The migration of cells from the neural crest (potential sensory ganglia) and basal plate (potential lower motor neurons) to the adjacent somites occurs early in development. As the somites differentiate into cells with specific functions (bone, cartilage, skin, muscle-forming) and begin their migration to form the various parts of the body, it appears that they maintain their connections with the neurons, and in this way the elongating nerve processes are 'towed' along to the periphery (Noback 1967). The potential of a peripheral nerve fibre to branch and grow in length is retained through life, as is seen in nerve regeneration following injury.

The spinal nerves, of which there are thirty-one pairs, are named and numbered according to the regions of the vertebral column with which they are associated. Anterior and posterior roots attach each nerve to the spinal cord. The anterior root describes the collection of axons of motor neurons in the anterior horns of grey matter. These neurons have developed from primitive neurocytes in the basal plates of the developing spinal cord. The posterior root describes the collection of axons of sensory neurons in the posterior root ganglion (Fig. 11). These neurons have developed from neural crest cells (Fig. 3).

The sensory part of the spinal nerve conveys to the central nervous system, impressions which are interpreted as temperature, touch, pressure, vibration, pain and proprioception. Dermatomes of the

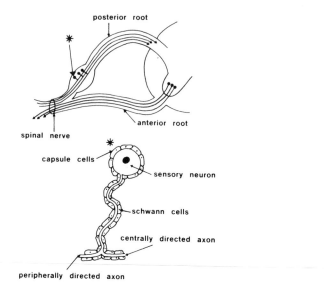

Fig. 11. *The structure of a posterior root ganglion.*

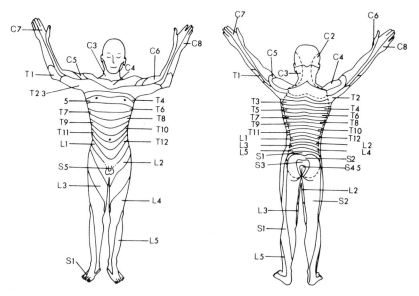

Fig. 12. *The arrangement of the dermatomes.*

trunk demonstrably correspond to spinal segments (Fig. 12), but the innervation of the limbs becomes more obvious when the embryology of the developing limb buds is considered (Fig. 13).

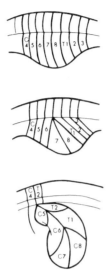

Fig. 13. *The developmental stages of the upper limb to illustrate the derivation of the segmental innervation of the limb. (From Ranson, S. W. and Clark, S. L. (1959)* The Anatomy of the Nervous System. *Philadelphia, Saunders).*

The autonomic nervous system

This part of the nervous system, which begins its development in the fifth week of embryonic life, includes the ganglia, nerves and plexuses through which the heart, glands, blood vessels and viscera receive their innervation. Connections are made at all levels of the nervous system, especially in the medulla, midbrain (hypothalamus), cerebral cortex, cerebellum and spinal cord.

Visceral function therefore, while more or less automatic, has powerful influences exerted upon it from high levels of the central nervous system. In this way, anxiety and excitement may interfere with digestive function, and Tibetan lamas may spend the night naked in the snow yet, because of their state of mind, suffer no drop in body temperature.

Blood supply to the brain

The brain receives its blood supply through four major arteries, two vertebral arteries and two internal carotid arteries (Fig. 14). These

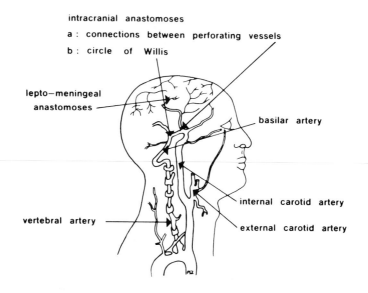

Fig. 14. *Anastomoses of the extracranial and intracranial cerebral circulation. (From Adams, G. F. (1974)* Cerebrovascular Disability and the Aging Brain. *Edinburgh & London, Churchill Livingstone).*

branch intracranially to form the main arterial channels for specific parts of the brain (Fig. 15). Anastomotic connections are extensive throughout the brain. By week six the reticular system of capillaries which comprises the cerebrovascular system is formed.

The Fetal Period

This period is characterised by rapid growth of the body with relatively insignificant advances in differentiation of the various tissues. The risk of malformation caused by environmental interference is no longer present by this period as the differentiation of organs is virtually completed.

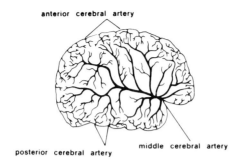

anterior cerebral artery

posterior cerebral artery

middle cerebral artery

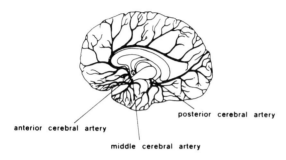

posterior cerebral artery

anterior cerebral artery

middle cerebral artery

Fig. 15. *The blood supply to the brain. Top–the arteries on the lateral surface of the cerebral hemisphere. Bottom – the arteries on the medial surface of the cerebral hemisphere.*

By the end of month six, the fetus has attained only twenty per cent of its future birth weight, the last three months therefore are characterised by rapid weight gains. Growth during this period is not equal for all parts of the body, and this difference in growth of various parts of the body extends from the fetus to the post-natal period and even until maturity. In other words, neither the fetus nor the newborn is a man in miniature (Wang 1968).

The spinal cord
As a result of the development of the limb buds and additional sensory and motor neurons at these levels, the cord becomes swollen in appearance forming the *cervical and lumbar enlargements.*

In month three, long ascending projectional tracts relay sensory

25

impulses to the brain and long descending tracts originating in the mid and hindbrain influence the spinal cord. In month five *corticospinal tracts* begin growing downwards from the motor cells of the cerebral cortex. In this way, during the course of its development, the spinal cord, once autonomous and independent, is placed under the control of the higher centres of the brain. The cervical portion of the cord begins to develop *myelin*, and the process extends both in a cephalic direction towards the brain, as well as in a caudal direction, the sensory fibres myelinating first. By the third month the spinal cord reaches the level of the third sacral vertebra. By the sixth month

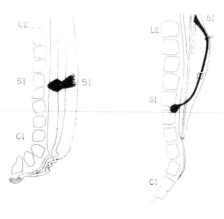

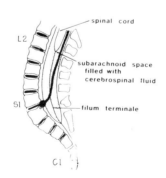

Fig. 16. *Successive stages in the development of the spinal cord showing the progressive obliquity of the first sacral nerve due to the differential growth of the spinal cord and vertebral column.*

it extends only as far as the first sacral vertebra as the vertebral column is growing more quickly than the cord (Fig. 16). At this stage the ascending posterior columns of white matter are myelinated, as are the descending vestibulo-spinal, reticulo-spinal and tecto-spinal tracts. By month seven the ascending spino-thalamic and spino-cerebellar tracts are myelinating. By the end of the fifth month the coccygeal end of the cord lies at the level of the first sacral vertebra. By term, it lies at the level of the third lumbar vertebra. Not until adult life does the cord lie at the level of the lower border of the first lumbar vertebra.

The brain

Both in the brain and in the spinal cord the two sides of the neural tube are connected by bundles of crossing fibres called commissures. Three of these are in the telencephalon and are called the *hippocampal commissure,* the *anterior commissure* and *the corpus callosum.* It is through the fibres of the corpus callosum that nearly all the regions of one hemisphere are associated with the corresponding regions of the other. In the fetus of five months it has attained the structure and shape characteristic of the adult. The *superior* and *posterior commissures* and *optic chiasma* develop in the diencephalon. By the eighth week, three main regions will have developed from the diencephalic part of the forebrain, the *epithalamus,* and *thalamus* and the *hypothalamus.* The

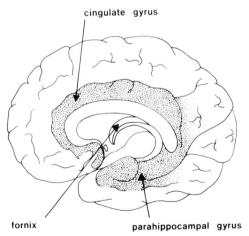

Fig. 17. *Medial aspect of the right cerebral hemisphere. Shading indicates the 'limbic lobe' of Broca which encircles the upper part of the brain stem.*

epithalamus is associated with the limbic system and includes the pineal body (Descartes' 'seat of the soul'). The *limbic system* (Fig. 17) mediates a variety of emotional, perceptual, hormonal and visceral responses involved in the individual's relationship with his environment. The *thalamus* has a major integrative function intercalating between many subcortical structures and the cerebral cortex. Most sensory impulses from sense organs are relayed to the thalamus before passing on to the cerebral cortex. The *hypothalamus* contains the highest integrative centres of the autonomic nervous system, regulating body temperature, endocrine glandular activity and the emotions.

The midbrain is little modified from the primitive neural tube (Fig. 18). However, by the twelfth week it serves to interconnect the fore and hindbrains. Eventually part of the midbrain differentiates into the nuclei of *cranial nerves 3 and 4*, and the *red nucleus, substantia nigra* and *reticular formation*. The midbrain ultimately contains the ascending sensory tracts such as the medial lemniscus and spino-thalamic

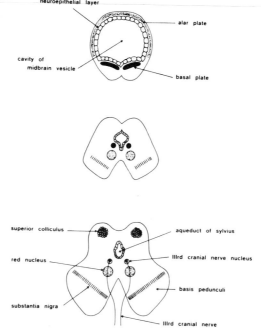

Fig. 18. *Stages in the development of the midbrain (From Snell, R. S. (1972)* Clinical Embryology for Medical Students. *Boston, Little Brown & Co.).*

tracts, descending extrapyramidal pathways and cerebellar connections. The *reticular formation* will develop into a central neural core extending from the medulla up through the pons and midbrain into the thalamus. Its functions will include the maintenance of arousal and the facilitation and inhibition of reflex activity. The facilitatory reticular formation is normally suppressed by the motor cortex, basal ganglia and cerebellum, whereas the inhibitory reticular formation needs to be driven into activity by these areas in order for it to exert an inhibitory influence over spinal cord reflexes (Eyzaguirre and Fidone 1975).

By week twelve the midline portion or vermis of the *cerebellum* and the two lateral hemispheres are recognisable. By week sixteen fissures are developing on the surface of the cerebellum and the characteristic appearance of the adult cerebellum gradually develops (Fig. 19). The cerebellum will function as a 'comparator' comparing

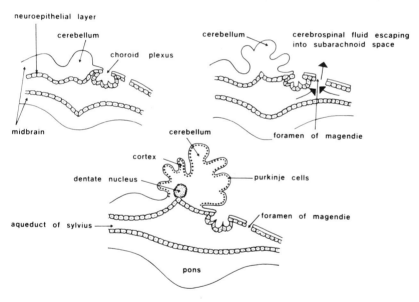

Fig. 19. *Sagittal sections through the developing cerebellum. (From Snell, R. S. (1972)* Clinical Embryology for Medical Students. *Boston, Little Brown & Co.).*

peripheral motor performance with motor command signals from the cerebral cortex. It will predict, judge and correct movements in order to ensure they are appropriate. The cerebellum is generally said to enrich the quality of motor performance by controlling the contractions of synergists and antagonists. Three small apertures are produced in the roof of the fourth ventricle, two lateral foramina (foramina of Luschka) and a median foramen (foramen of Magendie), which allow free passage of *cerebrospinal fluid* to the surrounding subarachnoid space.

In the final part of fetal life, the *cerebral hemispheres* grow so rapidly that a great number of convolutions separated by fissures and sulci appear on their surfaces. At birth the superficial layer of the cortex has a stratified appearance. This is due both to successive waves of cells from the mantle layer and to differentiation of the cortical cells. Specific cell types are found in different areas, pyramidal cells in the motor cortex, granular cells in the sensory cortex.

By week twenty-four *myelination* has spread from the spinal cord to the brain. This process is at first restricted to the fibres of the basal ganglia (corpus striatum), but gradually the pons, medulla and midbrain also show signs of it, although at term the brain is still largely unmyelinated. The descending motor fibres begin to undergo this process from week twenty-four, and it probably continues until at least two years of age. It appears that some nerve fibres do not complete myelination until puberty, or even middle adult life (Yakovlev 1960, Jacobson 1963).

The Process of Myelination

Myelination is the process by which nerve fibres in the developing nervous system become surrounded by a sheath that extends from just distal to the cell body to a point near the synapse. Most of the nerve fibres in the peripheral nervous system and central nervous system acquire myelin sheaths.

The process itself is little understood, but it is thought to involve, in the peripheral nervous system, the enveloping of a peripheral axon by a *Schwann cell* in a series of spiral laminations. This spiral lamination would account for the multilayer appearance of the myelin on investigation of a cross-section of a nerve (Fig. 20). The length of the Schwann cell provides limits to the length of the myelin sheath which therefore appears interrupted along its length by the nodes of Ranvier. There are no Schwann cells in the central nervous system but it is thought that their function in myelination is performed by *oligodendrocytes.*

Myelination confers upon a nerve fibre the properties of lowered threshold and increased conduction velocity, as well as the ability to carry repetitive impulses. The fact that non-myelinated fibres, which occur in the autonomic nervous system and in some pathways of the

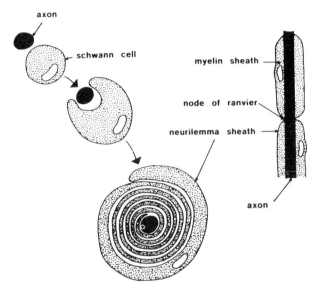

Fig. 20. *The process of myelination of an axon and a longitudinal section through a myelinated axon.*

brain and spinal cord, also conduct, makes the absolute dependence of the nervous system on myelin for conduction a subject for further research. The stability of myelin appears important, as is illustrated by the devastating consequences of its breakdown in a disease such as multiple sclerosis.

The relationship between myelination and the onset of nerve function has been the subject of many investigations. 'It may be that functional activity occurs before myelination' (Timiras 1972). Schulte (1969) suggests that myelination of axons together with arborisation (sprouting) of dendrites are the basic structural changes occurring in the course of nervous system development. Both myelination and arborisation have important functional implications. It is interesting in terms of the infant's development that at birth myelination of all the major sensory tracts is advanced in comparison with the beginnings of myelination of motor pathways.

Passage of an Impulse

Neurons conduct impulses from one point of the nervous system to another. They therefore make contact with each other, via their processes, across a *synapse*, and in this way one neuron can modify the activity of another neuron by a series of electrochemical phenomena, which are incompletely understood. The synapse consists of a *presynaptic membrane* and *post-synaptic membrane,* separated by an extracellular cleft. Adjacent to the presynaptic membrane are a number of small vesicles which appear to contain compounds which, upon the arrival of a nerve impulse (*action potential*), trigger off the excitation of a new impulse in the second neuron. Depending upon which substance is discharged the post-synaptic membrane will either be stimulated to produce an impulse or be inhibited from so doing (Fig. 21). An incoming impulse has a variety of pathways to

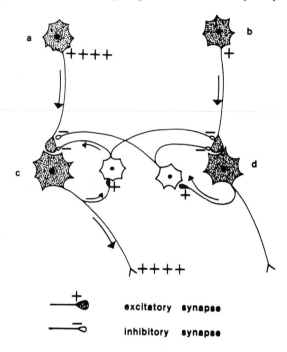

excitatory synapse

inhibitory synapse

Fig. 21. *Feedback inhibitory circuits utilising presynaptic inhibition. Inhibitory stimuli from neurons stimulated by axon collaterals of neurons c and d are sufficient to prevent d from firing but are not sufficient to prevent c from firing.*

take and one or more may be taken according to synaptic resistance which may vary from moment to moment. It is not necessary for every impulse entering by a given fibre to travel the same path within the central nervous system, nor produce the same result (Ranson and Clark 1959).

THE PRE-NATAL DEVELOPMENT OF FUNCTION (Fig. 22).

The cardiovascular and nervous systems are the first organ systems to function during embryonic life, and the embryo is said to enter upon the functional period of its development at the time when specific functions such as contraction of muscles and beating of the heart have their onset. This stage marks the beginning of the integration of the function of isolated units into total function, and the effect of function itself on the development of many organs and tissues is thought to be considerable.

Hamilton and Mossman (1972) describe three stages in the pre-natal development of function:

1. **Myogenic stage** when muscle fibres reach a stage of contractility on direct mechanical or electrical stimulation. This occurs a short time before the nerves supplying them can conduct impulses.
2. **Neuromotor stage** when direct stimulation of nerve trunks causes muscular contraction.
3. **Reflex stage** when reflex effects can be obtained by stimulation.

They point out that these three stages overlap to some extent. Some examples of the reflexes which can be elicited during the last stage are interesting to consider. By week fourteen, tactile stimulation of the face evokes responses which include rotation of the head, contraction of contralateral trunk musculature, extension of the trunk, extension of the upper extremity at the shoulder and rotation of the pelvis to the opposite side. By week twenty-two, tactile stimulation of the lips evokes a protrusion and pursing response. By week twenty-nine, tactile stimulation to the lips evokes an audible sucking response.

This reflex fetal stage is characterised by a lack of inhibition, which results in tonic and widespread reflex activity. It seems that the appearance of ordered sequences of performance in both time and space during later development is the result of the appearance of inhibitory mechanisms of an apparently central origin. During different stages of ontogenesis (development of the individual), functional maturation of the brain is said to begin in its reticular core and progresses towards the periphery or cortex (Bergstrom 1969). This can be seen in the early development of, for example, oral and respiratory control. The motor behaviour of the developing individual alters from tonic to phasic activity with the gradual appearance of inhibition.

	STRUCTURE	FUNCTION
WEEK 2	**Blastocyst** (future embryo & placenta) embedded in the uterine mucosa & begins its specific development.	
WEEK 3	Ectoderm thickens to form **neural plate**. Neural plate develops **neural groove**. **Neural crest** cells form. Neural groove deepens ————→ formation of **neural folds**.	
WEEK 4	Fusion of neural folds ————→ **neural tube**. Neural tube dilates ————→ **forebrain vesicle** **midbrain vesicle** **hindbrain vesicle** Remainder of tube elongates ————→ **spinal cord**. Neural crest cells differentiate into various sensory and autonomic ganglia.	Heart beats
WEEK 5	Forebrain & hindbrain vesicles divide. Their cavities form lateral, third & fourth **ventricles & aqueduct of Sylvius**. **Cerebral hemispheres** begin to expand.	
WEEK 6	**Thalamus** indicated. **Cerebellum** appears. **Cerebral commissures** appear Motor & sensory nuclei of **cranial nerves** 9, 10, 11, 12 originate in medulla oblongata. Capillary system formed (**cerebral vascular system**).	
WEEK 8	**Corpus striatum** differentiates into **caudate nucleus & lentiform nucleus**. **Lentiform nucleus** divides into **putamen & globus pallidus**. Expansion of cerebral hemisphere ————→ overlapping of mid & hindbrain. Formation of **frontal, temporal & occipital lobes**. Spinal cord same length as vertebral column. Development of **sense organs** progressing. **Meninges** (pia, arachnoid, dura matera) are distinct **Brain** has a human appearance.	First reflex arc functional. Reflex responses to tactile stimulation Irritation of upper lip ——→ withdrawal of head. Neck & trunk movement.
WEEK 10	**Corpus callosum** appears & connects R & L cerebral hemispheres. **Epithalamus, thalamus & hypothalamus** developing from forebrain.	Spontaneous movements observable & stereotyped. Tactile stimulation of lips ——→ swallowing movement

Fig. 22. *The development of the central nervous system and the prenatal development of function.*

34

WEEK 12	**Vermis & cerebellar hemisphere** recognisable. **Anterior commissure** develops and connects R&L cerebral hemispheres. **Taste buds** appear. **Inner ear** developing adult configuration.	Less stereotyped movements becoming more individuated. Movements increase in force. Mouth opening & closing. Chest muscles contract. Tactile stimulation of face $\longrightarrow$ head turning, contraction of contralateral trunk muscles, trunk extension, rotation of pelvis to other side.
WEEK 14	**General sense organs** (pain, temperature, deep pressure & tactile endings, chemical endings, neuromuscular spindles & neurotendinous end organs) begin to differentiate.	
WEEK 16	Characteristic folia of adult **cerebellum** gradually develop. 3 small apertures (F. of Luschka & F. of Magendie) appear $\longrightarrow$ **free passage of CSF** between ventricles & subarachnoid space. Cervical **spinal cord** developing **myelin.** **Cervical & lumbar enlargements** form.	Tongue movements. Abdominal muscles contract.
WEEK 20	Main components of middle & external **ear** have assumed adult form. **Pacinian corpuscles** appear. **Muscle spindles** in almost all muscles. **Golgi endings** & rudimentary **joint endings** present.	Effective but weak grasp. Protrusion & pursing of lips. Contraction of diaphragm. Sucking.
WEEK 24	**Myelination** in brain begins in **basal ganglia, pons, medulla, midbrain.** Spinal cord extends to SI vertebrae Posterior columns **myelinated.** Vestibulo - spinal, reticulo - spinal tracts **myelinated.**	Temporary respirations if born.
WEEK 28	**Cerebral & cerebellar connections myelinated.** Spino - cerebellar, spino - thalamic tracts **myelinated.**	Permanent respiratory movements established on birth. Eye sensitive to light. Maintained grasp. Olfactory perception.
FINAL 12 WEEKS	Differentiation of some **sense organs** completed. **Taste buds** reach functional maturity.	Reflex mechanisms for sucking, swallowing, well established.

Fig. 22. *Continued.*

The basic unit of neural activity is the simple reflex arc and this begins to function before the first observable spontaneous movements. However, it does not begin to function until the interneurons form the final synaptic connections between the afferent and efferent neurons (Noback and Demarest 1975).

The so-called 'simple' reflex arc is actually an 'abstraction' taken from the complex neural circuitry (Noback and Demarest 1975). It consists of a sensory receptor (muscle spindle or Meissner's corpuscle for example), an afferent (sensory) neuron which enters the posterior grey matter of the spinal cord, association, intercalated or internuncial neurons which lie completely in the grey matter of the cord, an efferent (motor) neuron in the anterior horn of the grey matter and an effector organ such as a muscle cell.

There are basically two theories as to the development of movement in the fetus. One concept (Coghill 1929 and others) suggests that initial mass activity occurs before any differentiation of movement occurs. The other concept (Windle 1944) suggests that simple reflex activity occurs and is built upon and integrated into more generalised movements.

POST-NATAL GROWTH AND DEVELOPMENT OF THE NERVOUS SYSTEM

At birth, growth and development of the nervous system are incomplete. The brain of the neonate is histologically immature, with the cells incompletely differentiated. No new nerve cells appear after the sixth month of fetal life, however, new connections can form between nerve cells. Sinclair (1973) comments that subsequent growth in the nervous system consists of an increase in the size of existing cell bodies, as well as enlargement, ramification and myelination of processes, and growth of specific connective tissues which support nerve material. A nerve cell can increase in mass up to 200 000 times. Fibres of the basal ganglia and those ascending from the spinal cord are the only ones to possess myelin sheaths at birth, although many fibres are in the process of myelination. In terms of myelination and function the main sensory fibres are therefore fairly well advanced, in contrast to the motor pathways. Myelination of fibres within the brain is largely a post-natal process, and is thought to continue into adult life.

Cerebral capillaries are much more permeable at birth than in adult life, and the blood-brain barrier develops during the early years of life. Hence, in infants with severe jaundice, bile pigments (serum bilirubin) can penetrate the nervous system and damage the basal ganglia causing athetosis, while a similar degree of jaundice in adults would have no direct effect on the nervous system. In the mature brain the blood-brain barrier allows only water, carbondioxide and oxygen to cross the cerebral capillaries with ease, which illustrates the difference between capillary permeability in the brain and elsewhere.

The brain is in fact much larger in proportion to body weight immediately following birth than it is in adult life. At birth it weighs about twelve per cent of the body weight. It doubles its birth weight in the first year and triples it by the age of five to six (Sinclair 1973). Its growth then slows up and the brain of the adult weighs only about two per cent of the body weight.

The cerebrum of the full term neonate is better developed posteriorly to the central sulcus than anteriorly, although the main features of the cerebral hemispheres are present. The cerebral cortex is only half its adult thickness, the extra thickness which occurs during the infant's development being due principally to an increase in size of nerve cells and the dendritic arborisation or sprouting of their processes. As the cerebral hemispheres develop, they progressively assume control over the lower centres of the brain and the spinal cord.

The period of rapid brain growth is sometimes called the 'brain growth spurt'. It begins in the fetal period, about mid-gestation, when the number of nerve cells found in the adult is already present except in the cerebellum, and it ends by the fourth post-natal year. Eighty-five per cent of this brain growth occurs post-natally. The growth spurt of the cerebellum takes place over a shorter period of time, starting its growth later but finishing it earlier than the rest of the brain (Dobbing and Sands 1973).

Following the marked acceleration in the growth of the central nervous system from birth to four years of age, there is a gradual levelling off in the pre-adolescent period. However, development of nervous tissue is not completed until after puberty, and perhaps not until later.

The onset of puberty coincides with maturation of the hypothalamus and some areas of the limbic and other cortical systems. Adolescence is a time of precarious emotional control and numerous behaviour changes. It is also characterised by the so-called 'adolescent growth spurt', with changes in the blood, in body shape and size, in height and in muscle strength. This growth spurt does not apparently include the central nervous system. The fact that it is preceded by a period of quiescence may be due to the necessity to postpone puberty in the human in order to allow time for the maturation of his complex brain (Sinclair 1973).

Maturity is characterised by functional stability and competence. Functional competence has 'several levels of integration, depending on the requirements of the organism at any specific age and the type and severity of the challenge to which the organism is exposed' (Timiras 1972).

Manifestations of progressive loss of cells within the central nervous system become noticeable shortly after adolescence. The special senses start to lose their acuity and range of performance. Hearing, for example, is at its most acute at the age of ten years.

The plasticity of the brain

It is said that the nervous system demonstrates the ability to be moulded by both external and internal influences, and that during certain periods of active growth and differentiation, it is particularly susceptible to changes in the environment. It appears that brain cells are capable of taking on new characteristics when the appropriate stimuli are received (Timiras 1972). Eccles (1973) suggests that we are still seriously underestimating the tremendous range of brain performance. Just as bones grow and are moulded by the demands of muscles and by weight-bearing, so also do neurons grow and become interconnected according to the chemical and electrical demands made on them.

Sinclair (1973) suggests that 'it is important in relation to learning to remember that, although no new nerve cells appear after birth, new connections can be formed between existing ones'. Eccles (1973) wrote 'the brain is a not a fixed action structure'. At its higher levels 'modifiability is the essence of its performance, as is evidenced by learning and memory...'. He goes on to say 'we have to think of the brain as being structurally plastic at the microlevel – some synapses being mature, others developing, others regressing'.

Certain African bushmen give their infants considerable experience of vertical antigravity postures by carrying them in a sling at the mother's side, or by holding them in sitting and standing on the lap (Konner 1972). These infants were advanced in sitting, standing up and walking, compared to the American sample described by McGraw (1963). Brody (1951) and White and Held (1967) have described the significant improvement in the rate of growth of visual exploratory behaviour and in visual attentiveness which follows an increase in handling of the infant.

It is probable (Timiras 1972) that stimulation is also important to the adult brain and that dendritic arborization and new connections between synapses occur when necessary. Timiras suggests that behavioural studies more than structural and biochemical data indi-

38

cate that plasticity of the central nervous system characterises later periods of development as well as those of infancy and childhood. In old age there is a decline in the ability of the central nervous system to make adaptive changes indicating a decline in its plasticity.

The Development of Movement

The development of movement in infancy reflects the gradual maturation of the brain, the assumption by the cerebral hemispheres of control over the more phylogenetically simple areas of brain stem and spinal cord. It is therefore not particularly relevant to a study of the treatment of an adult whose brain, although damaged, is mature.

Nevertheless, some aspects of movement development *are* relevant as they demonstrate the ways in which an infant practises and repeats the various components of a skill in preparation for learning the skill itself. They may form a useful guide to the way in which a brain-damaged adult may be helped to relearn the particular motor skills which he has lost.

For example, it is useful to understand how the infant practises the prerequisites for walking, how he prepares himself for the skill of walking. He must be given the opportunity to bear weight through his legs, then he practises shifting his weight and balancing laterally, backward and forwards (Fig. 23). Understanding this helps us to appreciate the most important prerequisites for walking and what the adult patient must practise if he is to be successful in learning to walk again.

Some therapists, however, have suggested that the use of what they call 'the neurodevelopmental sequence' should form a guide to the treatment of the adult patient. This neurodevelopmental sequence seems to be interpreted as meaning a progression through lying, prone, four point kneeling, upright kneeling, sitting and standing.

We would argue that as an infant's motor behaviour is merely a reflection of his immaturity, recreating this behaviour cannot be relevant to the adult. There is certainly no evidence to suggest that it is, despite the claim of some authors, that '. . . the performance of the developmental sequence should promote optimum recovery of purposeful movement' (Knott and Voss 1968).

There appear to be two misconceptions. The first is a misunderstanding of the effects of brain damage and of the brain's apparent capacity for recovery. Although an adult patient may demonstrate lack of balance control in sitting, this does not indicate neural immaturity. The therapist does not need to spend time stimulating activities developmentally less mature. She need only stimulate the

39

Fig. 23. *Transference of weight laterally is an essential pre-requisite for walking forwards.*

missing components of balance in sitting to trigger off this previously well-learned motor behaviour.

The second misconception is a lack of understanding of the way infants develop. Development of different functions overlaps. The infant does not perfect one skill before he goes on to the next. His practice of more advanced skills seems to improve his performance of earlier and 'simpler' skills. Nevertheless, one book on the care of stroke patients contains the suggestion that rolling from side to side 'should be completely mastered before continuing' with treatment (Johnstone 1976). This interpretation does not take into account the true complexity of the processes which make up development. There is no evidence to suggest that recreating the stages of infant motor development will enable the mature adult brain to re-establish functional competence.

It is possible that many patients are actually delayed or prevented from achieving their functional potential because they expend valuable time learning irrelevant activities. 'Following a developmental sequence encourages the ability to rise from a recumbent position to standing and walking via rolling, sitting, creeping on all fours, kneeling and standing . . .' (Peterkin 1969).

The development of movement has been described by many authors (Gesell and Ilg 1949, Sheridan 1968, Van Blankenstein, Welbergen and de Haas 1975, Illingworth 1970). All aspects of development, whether prehensive or locomotor, cognitive or behavioural, depend upon the development of certain basic factors such as head control, posture and movement against gravity and symmetrical and reciprocal movement as well as the inhibition of the unnecessary activity found in the child.

Head control is an important prerequisite for the development of many functions. Its development occurs in conjunction with extension against gravity, which progresses in a cephalo-caudal direction (Fig. 24). It allows communication to be established as the baby looks

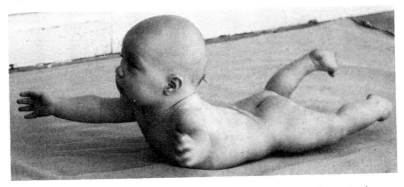

Fig. 24. *The stage at which head and trunk extension in prone is maximal.*

at his mother and begins to 'converse' with her. It allows the development of eye-hand control, and enables the infant to keep his head steady against gravity and to fix his eyes. It enables the development of balance reactions by which the infant is able to regain and maintain his balance against gravity. The development of both head and trunk control against gravity cannot be separated. For example, it is the development of lateral movement of the head together with lateral movement of the trunk which prepares him for the acquisition of the ability to maintain and regain his balance laterally. Without head control he cannot roll over (Fig. 25), sit up, eat or drink effectively, or vocalise clearly. As his head control develops so also does his ability to explore visually his surroundings.

Development of balance involves principally the development of

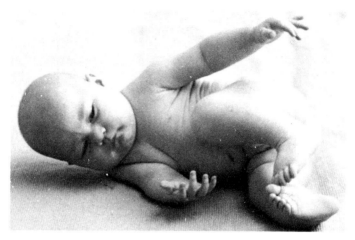

Fig. 25. *Rolling over, illustrating the development of head control, and the body righting on body reflex which enables the infant to rotate within his body axis.*

righting and equilibrium reactions and of the optical righting reflexes, and their integration with proprioceptive and tactile sensations. Righting and equilibrium reactions have been described by many authors (Magnus 1926, Rademaker 1935, Weiss 1938, Peiper 1963, Bobath and Bobath 1972).

Eyzaguirre and Fidone (1975) comment that the control of body equilibrium and orientation in space is one of the most important motor functions of the brain stem. The brain stem helps to maintain stability via what these authors call the 'body-orienting reflexes'. These reflexes are grouped according to where they arise, as labyrinthine, visual, proprioceptive or exteroceptive. In other words, sensory impulses from all these structures initiate the body-orienting reflexes or righting and equilibrium reactions. The vestibular system, of which the labyrinths provide the receptor function, maintains equilibrium, directs visual regard and preserves a constant head position, primarily by modifying muscle tone (Noback and Demarest 1975). The infant is developing his relationship with gravity from the time of his birth onwards. By five months he is developing equilibrium reactions in prone, and in supine by six months. As his parents hold him in sitting he begins to develop equilibrium reactions in this position. At first, head movement is more noticeable than trunk movement, but gradually movements of the head and trunk, combined with protective support on his hands, enable him to maintain the sitting position. By six months he is beginning to balance

Fig. 26. *The ability to maintain the sitting position is aided by widely abducted legs until the ability to regain balance is fully developed.*

forwards with his hands on the floor between his feet and is developing equilibrium reactions laterally (Fig. 26). By approximately eight months he is able to prop sideways with his hands on the floor beside him. By twelve months he can prop backward on his hands.

The baby is already standing up before he develops good control over sitting balance. He begins to develop equilibrium reactions in standing from the time when he first pulls himself to standing, and probably earlier, when he is held in the upright position by his parents. The development of equilibrium reactions in standing appears to add impetus to the development of equilibrium reactions in other positions, such as sitting and kneeling.

The fact that an infant does not appear to develop effective balance in a position until he is placed there or until he gets there himself is a point to consider in the treatment of brain-damaged adults. It is not uncommon to hear hospital staff comment that 'Mr. X is not ready to sit up yet, he has no sitting balance', without realising that he will not relearn sitting balance until he can experience balancing in this position with help.

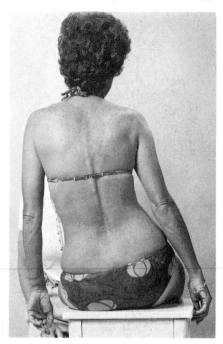

Fig. 27. *Normal equilibrium reactions demonstrated when the subject's weight is displaced laterally in sitting. Note the lateral flexion of the head and trunk with elevation of the pelvis.*

The time at which equilibrium reactions become fully developed is only vaguely understood. It is possible that in the average person they are never full developed, remaining a potential, the achievement of which depends upon the presence of other factors, such as co-ordination, sensitivity to certain stimuli, perceptual awareness, motivation, body shape and weight, and the absence of fear and anxiety. Sahrmann (1977) comments that movement at the body's centre of gravity triggers off a specific definable sequence of activity for stabilising the body and she suggests that this sequence of activity is probably unique to each individual.

There appear to have been few studies of balance reactions in normal adults. Nevertheless in observing the effects of being tilted off balance, certain predictable movements can be seen. These movements may vary in their range, speed, moment of initiation, according to many variable factors. They are illustrated in Fig. 27 to 29.

Fig. 28. *Normal equilibrium reactions demonstrated when the subject's weight is displaced laterally in standing. Note the lateral movement of the head and trunk.*

The development of the ability to move against gravity is an essential prerequisite to the development of **locomotion**.

From the time when he pulls himself to standing until he begins to walk, the child practises weight transference from one foot to another (Fig. 23), develops balance reactions in standing, and repeats the various combinations of movement which will enable him to walk.

He walks sideways around the furniture with only a minimum of support before he walks forwards. Walking sideways probably gives him practice in lateral weight transference, which is an essential prerequisite for taking a step forwards.

Functional use of his **hands** can be considered to commence when

45

Fig. 29. *Normal equilibrium reactions demonstrated when the subject's weight is displaced backward. Note the forward flexion of the trunk at the hips and the extension of the neck as the head moves forward.*

the infant can control the use of his eyes and his hands in combination. When the baby begins to sit, he requires at first that his hands be used for support, and there is little progress in development of prehension during this time. When tipped forwards the infant puts out his hands and weight-bears on them. This is called the parachute reaction or protective extension of the arms. When he no longer needs his hands for support he uses them to play, and his grasp rapidly develops from ulnar to radially orientated.

The development of thumb movement has been traced by Gesell and Halverson (1936). Its development from simple adduction to opposition with its component of abduction is closely related to the shift of functional dominance from the ulnar to the radial side of the hand.

The development of voluntary manipulation of objects is preceded by a range of activities which are practised separately and repeatedly. They appear to be exploratory, with the infant obviously concentrating hard on their performance, and they are probably an important part of the maturation of grasp, release and prehension. Manual dexterity develops as inhibition of inessential movements occurs.

Although during the first two years of his life the child has developed considerable manual dexterity there are some aspects of grasp and release which he cannot yet control. He still tends to approach objects with an exaggeration of finger movement, opening his hands too wide or closing them too firmly in grasping, and releasing objects with an exaggerated extension of fingers and thumb. This is called by Twitchell (1965) the avoiding response, but it also indicates that neither awareness of size of object in relation to hand nor inhibition of unnecessary activity are fully developed as in older children.

Similarly, the small child has a great deal to learn about the objects with which he is surrounded, and when he crushes an egg or a Christmas tree decoration, it is not only because he lacks the perception to control the strength of his grasp when he takes hold of the object, but also because he does not yet relate the object to its essential feature of fragility.

By his sixth year the child is further developing what Wynn-Parry (1966) terms the 'dynamic tripod' grasp, which involves the thumb, index and middle fingers. Co-ordination of this form of grasp will enable the child to progress his manipulative skills and will eventually enable him to write and draw with precision. For these functions he will also have to learn to stabilise his shoulder and elbow.

In the infant, **vocalisation** tends to be associated with movement. In the older child, speech is used to reinforce an action in playing, and speech to express an intention appears at all ages to aid concentration on a motor task. Luria (1961) gives examples of the reinforcement of action with speech.

The development of sensation
The newborn baby has some already highly developed senses. He is born with an intact peripheral sensory system (sense organs and afferent pathways to the brain), and with an intact, although immature, central mechanism in the brain. His first impressions of the world are through his touch receptors which are apparently highly

4

evolved. 'With neural mechanisms delicately attuned to receive stimuli from different kinds of environmental changes, both internal and external, and equally ready to initiate appropriate responses, man observes and listens, reacts, manipulates, and contemplates, storing within his own brain records of his experience' (Ranson and Clark 1959). Sensation therefore is subjective and unique to the individual.

Sherrington (1906) classified the sense organs into interoceptors, exteroceptors and proprioceptors. Gibson (1968) suggests that the term 'receptor' is ambiguous, implying on the one hand a passive mechanism that starts nerve impulses when touched off by a stimulus, but on the other hand, when used in reference to the eye, an active mechanism which accommodates itself to the possibilities of stimulation, which adjusts and explores.

The nervous system is continually being bombarded by stimuli from both internal and external sources. If this immense input were to be transmitted equally to conscious experience, life would become a constant torment. However, the nervous system can control this input so that on most occasions only the more relevant sensations are selected while the others are inhibited. Lance and McLeod (1976) suggest that this selectivity is the result of (I) adaptation of sensory organs which no longer respond after a certain period of stimulation; (2) presynaptic inhibition of adjacent nerve cells by active cells which ensure priority for the most relevant stimulus; (3) regulation by the motor cortex of synaptic transmission in the sensory nuclei which allows voluntary or involuntary suppression of sensory input; (4) the ability of the individual to concentrate on one sensation or thought or act in such a way as to cut out other sensations.

Purely anatomical and physiological considerations of the sense organs give little understanding of their relationship to function. Similarly, the sense organs cannot be considered in isolation from the rest of the nervous system, since their receptive function requires filtering and interpretation.

Interpretation by higher centres requires filtering, collection and collation of the received material, memory (storage and retrieval) of similar events, comparison and decision. Traditionally the receptive ınction and the passage of impulses to the brain is called *sensation;* organisation of the received information is called *perception*. The ıte is born with sense organs intact and a high degree of ıtiation in respect of some sensations, for example, touch. -, he has to develop the higher function of perception ˙e process of learning.

k at the sense organs in more detail.

The eyes. *Vision* allows the development of *visual perception,* which is the ability to perceive the world (colour, intensity of light-wave length, figure from background, perspective, form, depth, space and distance). Proprioceptive impulses arising from the intrinsic muscles of the eye give depth perception and dimension (Granit 1966). Vision allows the development of communication, through the development of eye to eye contact and reading and writing. Eye-hand contact is necessary for the development of skilled manipulative activities.

Many writers consider that motor activity is necessary for the development of perception. Held and Hein (1963), Held (1965) and Abercrombie (1970) describe its relationship to visual perception. Abercrombie comments that limitation of active movement retards perceptual development and inhibits overall intellectual ability. Vision is the primary source of sensation together with proprioceptive impulses and touch impulses arising from contact with the surroundings.

The eyes play an important part in the development of balance through the *optical (visual) righting reflexes.* These reflexes are not present at birth but begin to develop within the first few months. They are important in helping to align the body parts in space, that is, they contribute to the postural orientation of the head and body. They work with the labyrinths of the ears and the proprioceptors and exteroceptors to enable the body to maintain and regain equilibrium. They give sensory feedback on position in space, and position relative to other objects. They enable a check to be made on whether information from other organs (of touch and proprioception for example) is correct. As the result of their experiments some writers suggest that vision may be more important than proprioception in this regard. Vision is thus used to check movement and its direction. Gesell (1954) refers to the eye as functioning as a prehensory or manipulatory organ and called this the 'oculomanual prehensory apparatus'. Duke-Elder (1973) describes the mechanism of these righting reflexes in primates. When the head is moved from the prone to supine position, the eyes are turned up and down by the symmetrical control of the utricles (part of the labyrinth of the ear), over the superior and inferior recti. When the head is inclined to the left or right, the eyes roll towards the left or right, these movements being controlled by the saccules in the labyrinth. The eyes are therefore controlled in this function by the vestibular system, but they are also influenced by proprioceptive impulses from the recti muscles.

The ears. *Hearing* is not well developed at birth or for the first few days after birth, as the ear canals are filled with a gelatinous material.

Hearing is an important sensation in learning and in communication, when it has an essential relationship to speech. It is a means of allowing *auditory feedback*, which is a monitoring device giving information about the success or failure of our actions. The ears also provide a means of *vestibular feedback*, which help us monitor our position in space (our relationship with earth's gravitational pull) through the otoliths in the labyrinths, and is therefore essential for balance.

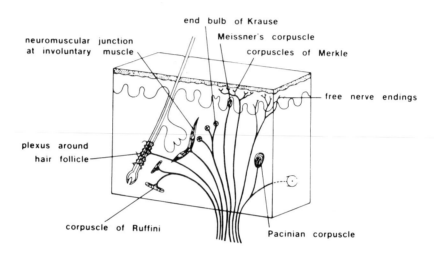

Fig. 30. *Nerve endings in the skin (From Noback, C. R. and Demarest, R. J. (1975) The Human Nervous System. New York, McGraw-Hill).*

Touch receptors in the skin (Fig. 30). These transmit information to the brain which will allow the discrimination of touch (recognition of objects, their shape and size, texture, recognition of two points of touch occurring at the same time). Recognition of direction of ¬ovement and position of body parts from pressure and touch gives ¬dback to reinforce information from proprioceptors and eyes. ¬rding to Ayres (1966), attention, perception and motor learning to depend upon the tactile system.
 ‵ of the fibres excited by light touch and pressure pass to the the posterior columns of the spinal cord (Fig. 31), synapsing ¬ile and cuneate nuclei. Second order neurons continue the ¬n of impulses (as the medial lemniscus) to the thalamus. neurons transmit the impulses on to the post-central

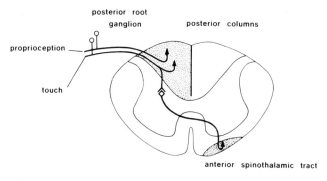

Fig. 31. *Diagram of a cross-section through the spinal cord showing the pathways taken by touch and proprioception.*

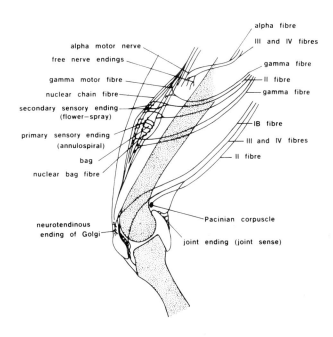

Fig. 32. *Nerve endings in voluntary muscles, tendons and joints. (From Noback, C. R. and Demarest, R. J. (1975).* The Human Nervous System, *2nd edition, New York, McGraw–Hill).*

gyrus of the cerebral cortex. Some tactile sensations appear to pass via the spinothalamic tract, and others via the spinocerebellar tracts.

Proprioceptors in muscles and joints (Fig. 32). These allow the recognition of pressure, stretch and traction, therefore of relationships between internal structures. This enables the detection of movement, the recognition of position in space of either a large or a small part of the body, plus recognition of direction of movement, and feedback as to whether direction of movement is appropriate to the function required (called kinaesthesia). These sensations appear to follow a similar route to the cerebral cortex as touch and pressure sensations (Fig. 31).

Perception is considered to be a function of the parietal area of the brain. Our understanding of this area has come almost entirely from studies of the results of lesions (Critchley 1953). The function itself is not clearly defined and 'perception' means different things to different people.

The terms 'perception' and 'sensory integration' are sometimes used synonymously, although some writers point out that perception is the *result* of sensory integration. Both terms imply the ability to store information and profit from experience. Perception is usually said to be one of the factors upon which cognition and intelligence depend (Singer 1968, Piaget 1969), and it probably cannot be separated from behaviour (Nathan 1969). The development of perceptuo-motor function progresses together with the gradual increase in the automaticity of movement, and lays down the foundation for the development of more complex motor skills.

The development of *laterality* and *directionality* is considered to be necessary for our ability to orient ourselves in space. Laterality is the term used to describe the preference for or superiority of one side of the body over the other in the performance of motor tasks. Directionality is the knowledge of left and right, up and down, before and behind. Its development allows us to recognise spatial dimensions and relationships. For example, we are able to recognise the relation- ship of a sleeve to a shirt which will help us to dress ourselves.

dy schema* (body awareness). The development of this percep-
nction depends to a great extent on movement (Frostig 1969)
ies particularly on vision and prehension. We plan our
ts towards a goal by knowing the parts of the body, how
and how they relate to each other, how the body relates to
ve must move around, through, under and over.

SUMMARY

In this chapter growth and development of the nervous system is briefly described in the pre-embryonic, embryonic, foetal and post-natal periods. The development of movement is discussed in relation both to the maturation of the brain and to the child's experiences. Various aspects of the infant's acquisition of motor skill are discussed for their relevance to an understanding of normal function. The authors also discuss the misconception that the sequence of movement development in the immature infant should be a guide to the treatment of brain-damaged adults.

References

Abercrombie, M. L. J. (1970) Learning to draw. In *Mechanisms of Motor Skill Development,* edited by K. J. Connolly. London, Academic Press.

Ayres, A. J. (1966) Interrelationships among perceptual-motor functions in children. *Am. J. Occup. Ther.,* **20,** 2.

Bergstrom, R. M. (1969) Electrical parameters of the brain during ontogeny. In *Brain and Early Behaviour,* edited by R. J. Robinson. New York, Academic Press.

Bobath, K. and Bobath, B. (1972) Cerebral palsy. In *Physical Therapy Services in the Developmental Disabilities,* edited by P. H. Pearson and C. E. Williams. Springfield, Illinois, Thomas.

Brody, S. (1951) *Patterns of Mothering.* New York, International University Press.

Coghill, G. E. (1929) *Anatomy and the Problem of Behaviour.* Cambridge, University Press.

Critchley, M. (1953) *The Parietal Lobes,* New York, Hafner.

Dobbing, J. and Sands, J. (1973) Quantitative growth and development of the human brain. *Arch. Dis. Childhd.,* **43,** 757.

Duke-Elder, S. (1973) *Systems of Ophthalmology,* vol. VI, 79–84, London, Henry Kimpton.

Eccles, J. C. (1973) *The Understanding of the Brain,* New York, McGraw-Hill.

Eyzaguirre, C. and Fidone, S. J. (1975) *Physiology of the Nervous System.* Chicago, Year Book Medical.

Frostig, M. (1969) *Move Grow Learn.* Chicago, Follett Educational Corp.

Gesell, A. (1954) *The First Five Years of Life.* London, Methuen.

Gesell, A. and Halverson, H. M. (1936) The development of thumb opposition in the human infant. *J. Genet. Psychol.,* **48,** 339–361.

Gesell, A. and Ilg, F. L. (1949) *Child Development.* New York, Harper and Row.

Gibson, J. J. (1968) *The Senses Considered as Perceptual Systems.* London, Allen and Unwin.

Granit, R. (1966) Sensory mechanisms in perception. In *Brain and Conscious Experience,* edited by J. C. Eccles. New York, Springer-Verlag.

Hamilton, W. J. and Mossman, H. W. (1972) *Hamilton, Boyd and Mossman's Human Embryology,* 4th edition. Cambridge, Heffer.

Held, R. (1965) Plasticity in sensory-motor systems. *Scient. Amer.,* **213,** 84.

Held, R. & Hein, A. (1963) Movement-produced stimulation in the development of visually guided behaviour. *J. Compar. Physiol. Psych.,* **56,** 872.

Illingworth, R. S. (1970) *The Development of the Infant and Young Child, Normal and Abnormal.* Edinburgh & London, Livingstone.

Jacobson, S. (1963) Sequence of myelinization in the brain of the albino rat. *J. Comp. Neurol.,* **121,** 5–29.

Johnstone, M. (1976) *The Stroke Patient.* London, Churchill Livingstone.

Knott, M. And Voss, D. (1968) *Proprioceptive Neuromuscular Facilitation,* 2nd edition. New York, Harper and Row.

Konner, M. J. (1972) In *Ethological Studies of Child Behaviour,* edited by N. C. Blurton-Jones. New York, Cambridge University Press.

Lance, J. W. & McLeod, J. G. (1975) *A Physiological Approach to Clinical Neurology.* London, Butterworths.

Langman, J. (1969) *Medical Embryology,* 2nd edition. Edinburgh & London, Livingstone.

Magnus, R. (1926) Some results of studies in the physiology of posture. *Lancet,* **2,** 531–535.

McGraw, M. B. (1963) *Neuromuscular Maturation of the Human Infant.* New York, Hafner.

Nathan, P. (1969) *The Nervous System.* London, Penguin Books.

Noback, C. R. (1967) *The Human Nervous System.* Tokyo, McGraw Hill.

Noback, C. R. and Demarest, R. J. (1975) *The Human Nervous System.* New York, McGraw Hill.

A. (1963) *Cerebral Function in Infancy and Childhood.* London,

H. W. (1969) The neuromuscular system and the re- of movement. *Physiotherapy,* **55,** 11, 145–153.

'69) *The Mechanisms of Perception.* London, Routledge &

Rademaker, G.C. J. (1935) *Réactions Labyrinthiques et Equilibre.* Paris, Masson.

Ranson, S. W. & Clark, S.L. (1959) *The Anatomy of the Nervous System.* Philadelphia, Saunders.

Sahrmann, S. (1977) Therapeutic exercise: past and future. *Paper delivered at 53rd Congress of A.P.T.A.* St. Louis, Missouri.

Schulte, F. J. (1969) Structure-function relationships in the spinal cord. In *Brain and Early Behaviour,* edited by R. J. Robinson. New York, Academic Press.

Sheridan, M. D. (1968) *The Developmental Progress of Infants and Young Children.* London, Ministry of Health.

Sherrington, C. (1906) *The Integrative Action of the Nervous System.* New Haven, Yale University Press.

Sinclair, D. (1973) *Human Growth after Birth.* 2nd edition. London, Oxford University Press.

Singer, R. N. (1968) *Motor Learning and Human Performance.* New York, MacMillan.

Snell, R. S. (1972) *Clinical Embryology for Medical Students.* Boston, Little, Brown & Co.

Szekely, G. (1966) Embryonic determinations of neural connections. In *Advances in Morphogenesis,* edited by M. Abercrombie and J. Brachet. Vol. 5. New York, Academic Press.

Timiras, P. S. (1972) *Developmental Physiology and Aging.* New York, MacMillan.

Twitchell, T. E. (1965) Normal motor development. *J. Amer. P. T. Assoc.,* **45,** 419–423.

Van Blankenstein, M., Welbergen, U. R. and de Haas, J. H. (1975) *The Development of the Infant.* London, Heinemann.

Weiss, S. (1938) Studies in equilibrium reactions. *J. Nerv. Ment. Dis.,* **88,** 150.

White, B. L. and Held, R. (1967) Plasticity of sensori-motor development in the human infant. *Child Develop.,* **35,** 349.

Windle, W. F. (1944) Genesis of somatic motor functions in mammalian embryos: a synthesising article. *Physiol. Zool.,* **17,** 47–60.

Yakovlev, P. I. (1960) Anatomy of the human brain and the problem of mental retardation. In *Mental Retardation,* edited by P. W. Bowman and H. V. Mantner. New York, Grune and Stratton.

Wang, H. (1968) *An Outline of Human Embryology.* London, Heinemann.

Wynn Parry, C. B. (1973) *Rehabilitation of the Hand.* London, Butterworths.

Further Reading

Bartelmez, G. W. and Dekaban, A. S. (1962) The early development of the human brain. *Contrib. Embryol.*, **37,** 13.

Held, R. and Freedman, S. J. (1963) Plasticity in human sensori-motor control. *Science,* **142,** 455.

Karczmar, A. C. and Eccles, J. C. (1972) *Brain and Early Behaviour.* Heidelberg, Springer.

Sheridan, M. D. (1975) *Children's Developmental Progress.* London, NFER Publishing Co.

Sperry, R. W. (1971) How a developing brain gets itself properly wired for adaptive function. In *Biopsychology of Development.* New York, Academic Press.

Chapter 2

The Process of Aging

What is the aging process and when does it begin? Neither of these questions can be fully answered. There have been many attempts at answers, but the attempts themselves raise many questions. Which of the anatomical and physiological changes are due to pathology and which to the process of aging itself? Which are due to disuse and which to misuse? The same question can be asked about the psychological changes reported. Which are due to pathology, which to socio-economic factors? Which to neglect and which to lack of love and stimulation? Are any of them due to the aging process itself? Is there such a thing as 'natural aging'?

It is interesting that the changes occurring in old age, called senescence, have been much less studied than the earlier stages of life, and that the psychological changes have been studied more than the physiological. That there are changes is an indisputable fact, but whether these changes are due to some inherent and inevitable tendency to age or whether they are due to misuse, disuse or disease, and therefore preventable or remediable, is as yet unsolved.

Aging, perhaps because of the too broad general use of the word 'geriatrics', is frequently regarded as a disease, rather than as one of the stages of life itself. The literature sometimes adds to the confusion by not making a clear distinction between the practice of *geriatrics* as the science of disease in the aged and its treatment, and the study of *gerontology* as the science of aging itself.

Normal aging has been little researched and is regarded as a taboo subject (Cameron, Stewart and Biber 1973) by many individuals. However, it is possible that a gradual shift in society's attitudes is occurring and that efforts are being made to reduce the fear of aging which exists in the community. 'The attitude of tacit acceptance of a debilitating old age is now being replaced by one that regards senescence as 'the subversion of function' the inevitability of which is open to question' (Timiras 1972).

A lack of understanding of the realities of old age has been one of the reasons why the aged person is regarded as a stereotype, despite the fact that his needs and life styles vary as much as in younger people. This is evidenced in the present day in the work force of many countries by compulsory retirement at sixty for women and sixty-five for men, an arbitrary demarcation between maturity and senescence which has little relevance to function, and by the tendency in some societies to isolate the aged into their own special groups where they have little contact with the real and active world. Davison (1969) considers that this rejection of the elderly may have something to do with the low social status of many of them. Recent literature seems to suggest that we rethink our modern, youth-oriented values. Certainly, our personal responses to the aged are conditioned to a large extent by the values of the society in which we live.

In society and family life there is a tendency to regard the aged as having certain predictable behaviours. Many of these so-called predictable behaviours, when they occur, are put down as due to increasing age which removes the necessity to search for a cause. In the health care environment, this stereotyping can result in errors of diagnosis, a negative view of the effects of treatment, and to unrealistic treatment programmes unsuited to the capabilities of the individual. There is a tendency for chronological criteria to assume more importance than biological or psychological criteria.

Just as abilities and functions vary from person to person in any age group, so in the older members of the community the decline in ability and function varies not only with the individual, but within that individual. It is probable that there are a number of factors, racial, climatic and environmental, which influence the rate of aging, as well as the inherited endowment of the individual. Genes are no doubt related to the potential for life span, but life style and environment appear to modify and shape the actual life span (Weg 1973a).

There have been a number of theories of aging and the time at which it starts, which range from those which suggest it begins at conception to the statement by the World Health Organisation that old age occurs at sixty-five. However, there appears to be a general agreement, in theory at least, that old age is descriptive of biological and psychological function rather than of chronology.

Some theories of aging
As Sinclair (1973) comments' theories of aging have far outstripped the available information'. He considers, and there are many who would agree with him, 'that the problems of old age are inextricably mixed up with the problems of growth'. Some have described aging as a consequence of the cessation of growth. Burch (1968) suggests

that many forms of aging result from a breakdown in the mechanism of central growth control; Curtis (1966) that 'aging is a deteriorative process which renders the organism more susceptible to disease, or less well able to withstand stress'. Others (Minot 1908, Weiss 1966, Sinclair 1973) have expressed the view that aging actually begins in the early stages of growth. In a sense, growth, development and differentiation continue throughout life and do not stop when the child reaches maturity. The aged who have had long lives with varied experiences show a high degree of differentiation. The continuation of the capacity to adapt and cope with stress determines the way in which aging individuals master the new tasks of later maturity and old age (Brody 1974).

The Effects of Aging on Body Systems and Function

In fetal life and early childhood, cell division or mitosis is of prime importance as a means of growth, except in the central nervous system. Mitosis persists through the early and middle years in order to keep cell numbers of tissues and organs in a steady state. The nerve cells, however, lose their mitotic ability when they develop from primary neuroblasts and they never divide again. With advancing years there is a gradual decline in the number of cells throughout the body.

A blunt recital of the anatomical and physiological changes occurring with increasing age can be misleading for two reasons. First, it is impossible in many cases to tell whether a particular change is due to 'natural' aging, misuse, disuse or pathology, and second, in the case of changes seen at autopsy, it is possible that some of these changes are due to artefacts induced at post-mortem. Furthermore, the presence of anatomical and physiological changes does not give much indication of change in functional ability. The process of aging, in the absence of pathology, 'is superimposed upon maturity imperceptibly' (Lawton 1965).

Provided all these points are kept in mind, it is useful to consider some of the findings. Most of them relate more to the behavioural and pathological aspects of old age than to the actual physical process of aging itself.

The nervous system

It can be postulated that aging of the central nervous system influences aging as a whole, but it seems certain that aging of the central nervous system will itself be affected by aging of other systems, in particular of the cardiovascular system.

59

It is said that the brain loses 10 000 nerve cells every day, which means that by the age of sixty-five or seventy about 20% of the total number of neurons present at birth have been lost. This nerve cell loss occurs in the cerebral cortex, basal ganglia, brain stem and cerebellum. Timiras (1972) points out, however, that other neurons seem to compensate for this loss, therefore the consequences are not as noticeable as would be expected. Gaitz (1972) considers that brain cell loss may eventually be reflected by disorientation for time, place, person and situation, memory loss, and decrease in the ability to calculate. It may also be reflected in loss of balance due to the decreased number of neurons in the brain stem, cerebellum and higher centres.

The actual amount of brain cell loss which results in obvious deficits in mental functioning differs from person to person, and is probably related to education, occupation and psychological, emotional and social adaptability. A protective social setting may obscure signs (Gaitz 1972). Tomlinson (1972) suggests that cortical neurons retain considerable reserves of intellectual capacity.

There is a general decrease with age in the response to certain environmental stimuli. For example, there is decreased hearing and decreased visual acuity. This may be partly due to impaired function of the receptor organs themselves. Speech becomes slower and less assured in old age, and this may be due to atrophy of the relevant part of the central nervous system, although it may also be due to a social environment which does not allow sufficient practice of speech. Discrimination of the various sounds involved in speech declines and this affects the ability to understand speech. This problem is especially evident where there is background noise. The presence of behavioural changes may indicate a decline in certain senses such as vision and hearing, as well as changes in the social environment.

There seems to be an increase in the threshold of cutaneous sensibility, which may be due to changes in collagen and in the elastic tissues of the skin (Timiras 1972) as well as to a decrease in the number of Meissner corpuscles in the skin. A gradual deterioration is seen in the temperature regulating mechanism which makes the aged less able to resist cold and heat, and to adapt to changes in temperature. There is an increase in the threshold of smell and taste sensation. Pearson (1928) describes impairment of tactile discrimination and vibration appreciation, and Howell (1949) reports impairment of pain and temperature discrimination. Agate (1970) comments that pain appreciation may vary from an almost complete lack of pain sensibility to extreme hypersensitivity.

Gutmann, Hauzlikova and Jakonbek (1968) describe changes

occurring in the intercellular relationship between nerve and muscle cell. They suggest that the motor endplates may suffer a random degeneration as age increases, leading to a muscle response which is similar to that following denervation. The functional result is muscle weakness. Many tendon reflexes are decreased or absent, probably because of the deterioration in the functional integrity of peripheral afferent fibres, which may be due to factors other than increasing age. Some degree of incontinence may occur if the autonomic nervous system loses some of its control over smooth muscle.

If motor endplates degenerate, it is possible that the muscle spindles undergo a similar change, which would result in decreased feedback to the central nervous system. This, combined with joint receptor degeneration which may take place in association with arthritic joint changes, would further interfere with feedback on body position and movement (Hasselkus 1974). This may explain the relative caution and slowness of movement seen in elderly people, as well as the deficiencies in balance. Often a lack of ability to adapt to the dark and a decreased perception of various levels of illumination shows itself in anxiety on entering a dark room from a light one. Positive Rombergism* is said to be present in some aged subjects (Sheldon 1960), and this would further account for difficulties with movement in the dark (Gaitz 1972). The presence of Rombergism, may also indicate the reliance placed on vision for external feedback on position in space.

Various changes in locomotion appear in the elderly and these are probably mainly due to neurological causes, although loss of musculo-skeletal flexibility and joint dysfunction will sometimes be factors. Many elderly people have an unstable, wide-based, almost ataxic walk, which Hasselkus (1974) puts down to trunk instability, cerebellar decline, proprioceptive, vestibular and visual loss. Trunk instability is associated with loss of muscle tone and strength, decreased flexibility of the trunk and neck, and therefore relatively ineffective equilibrium reactions.

After a long period in bed or after an illness, an apprehensive elderly person may attempt to walk with small toppling steps, with the feet either too far in front or too far behind the trunk. This is probably due to fear plus poor balance, and to sensory deprivation resulting from the period spent in bed. Elderly people in this situation should be prepared for walking by methods designed to stimulate their ability to maintain and regain balance in standing *before* they are encouraged to walk, as this will avoid the reaction of fear becoming established.

* Glossary

To be fully effective when balance is displaced laterally, balance reactions require lateral flexion of the trunk and neck, as well as limb movements (Figs. 27 & 28). Milani-Comparetti and Gidoni (1967) stress the importance of trunk movement in mature equilibrium reactions. Decreased strength and mobility in the trunk and neck interfere with equilibrium and are two of the causes of the poor balance frequently seen in the elderly. Poor condition of the feet, for example, deformities of the toes, corns, callosities, horny toenails, will all interfere with balance. Balancing in bare feet may also be difficult due to tenderness and hypersensitivity of the soles of the feet.

However, poor balance in the elderly may be compensated for by slowness of movement and hesitancy in performing antigravity functions, and should be understood as such, for equilibrium reactions can be improved, and slowness of movement and hesitancy are not essential accompaniments of aging.

The musculo-skeletal system

With increasing age, there is a steady decrease in the density of the long bones and vertebrae due to progressive loss of calcium. Height may be lost because of changes in the intervertebral discs and assumption of a relatively flexed posture. The continual gradual modification of the skeleton which has occurred all through life is part of the continuum of aging. Osteoporosis is characterised by porosity and rarefaction due to enlargement of bone canals and to formation of abnormal spaces. In the spine one or more vertebrae may collapse; in the long bones there is an increased likelihood of fractures. Calcification of the thyroid cartilage leads to alteration in voice, and to easily elicited fractures on handling of the neck (Walls 1970).

Biochemical changes occur in skeletal muscle fibres. As the fibres degenerate they are replaced by fat cells, so that, by the age of seventy, the total dry weight of, for example, the gastrocnemius, may be one third fat (Hasselkus 1974).

There is said to be a gradual decline in strength from thirty years of age onwards (Serratrice, Roux and Aquaron 1968), which may be due to other factors, such as disuse, as well as to the effects of age on the muscle fibres themselves. Sinclair (1973) suggests that a primary cause of senile changes in muscle is a partial failure of the trophic mechanism of the nerves which supply it. Voluntary or enforced inactivity, or a general malaise, may result in the loss of power seen in some older individuals. Some evidence points to a pattern of proximal muscle weakness with advancing age. There is also an increase in fatiguability which is most evident in the trunk muscles, including the muscles of the pelvis, shoulder girdle and neck. This interferes with movement which requires a stable trunk for fixation. However, some people preserve their muscle strength to a remarkable degree. Despite the loss of muscle fibres and the effects of disuse, exercise will apparently lead to an increase in the size of the remaining fibres. De Vries (1970) describes an exercise programme for sixty- to ninety-year-old men in which muscle strength was regained within six to eight weeks.

Decreased flexibility is a feature of increasing age. Stiffness in joints is caused by loss of elasticity in the connective tissues surrounding them. Loss of thoracic flexibility is due to the transformation of hyaline cartilage into calcified cartilage, which causes the ribs and sternum to lose their spring. There is decreased movement between the ribs and sternum, decreased lift of the ribs on inspiration and recoil on expiration.

Cardiovascular system

Changes in arteries due to age are difficult to distinguish from those caused by disease. Sinclair (1973) describes the heart muscle as degenerating with age. Certainly it appears that cardiac output is significantly reduced compared to that of the young adult, and therefore response to additional demands is reduced (Weg 1973b). Timiras (1972) comments that exercise in the elderly causes a marked acceleration in cardiac rate and an increase in blood pressure, and he suggests that limits are placed on the amount of muscular work that the elderly can perform by the circulatory demands of the exercised muscle.

Respiratory system

Loss of mechanical efficiency in the lungs, partly due to a gradual decrease in skeletal flexibility and alteration in the shape and capacity of the thorax due to postural changes, leads to less efficient air uptake, decreased ventilatory capacity and decreased total lung capacity. The main changes of function as reported by Weg (1973b) are decreased basal oxygen consumption, breathing capacity, residual lung volume and vital capacity.

The amount of oxygen that the blood takes up from the lungs and transports to the tissues decreases with age. This affects the body's response to exercise, as adequate blood oxygenation is a prerequisite for adequate muscle function.

Psychological factors associated with aging

It is possible that some of the personality changes which occur in the aging person are due to a reduction in sensory input from the eyes, ears, taste buds, nose and proprioceptors. This reduction may be due to the aging process, to disease, or to social circumstance. It is interesting that reduction in sensory input in experimental situations provokes psychological disturbances such as hallucinations, distortions of the body image and severe anxiety even in healthy young adults (Gaitz 1972).

Disengagement theory. It is postulated by some writers that some elderly people deliberately decrease their sensory input by refusing to go out and to socialise. This is called 'disengagement'. The theory is controversial, some considering that the need for emotional involvement with others becomes less intense with age. Havighurst, Neugarten and Tobin (1968) suggest that disengagement appears to be a process but that it proceeds at different rates in different people in different environments, and has different outcomes in terms of psychological well-being. Gaitz (1972) comments that 'social, economic and other problems stemming from the stereotyped responses of society to the aged may cause them voluntarily to withdraw and disengage from society, thereby further decreasing their sensory input and accelerating their mental deterioration'.

Emotional stress may initiate or aggravate physical ailments and together with a degree of debilitation may leave the person more susceptible to disease. It is not only the elderly who demonstrate this reaction to stress. They do, however, react more adversely than younger subjects to periods of hospitalisation, which has, amongst other things, a significantly adverse effect on speed of performance (Halberstam & Zaretsky 1966). Stewart (1975) comments that there is a greater motivation towards recovery in those people who are cared for in their own environment when they are ill, than in those who are institutionalised.

Similarly, where the elderly, for social reasons, are committed to institutional care in old peoples' homes, day hospitals or nursing homes, away from their own familiar surroundings and without family and friends, emotional and intellectual deterioration may occur rapidly. Davison (1969) describes custodial care as leading to a sometimes irreversible disintegration of personality due to loss of self-esteem and personal responsibility. These result from the relative absence of free choice and decision-making, which seem to be the patient's lot in institutional life. He cautions against staff developing over-protective attitudes towards their patients.

Intellect. Intellectual function in terms of conceptualising, judgement and verbal ability decreases very little if disease of the cerebral blood vessels is absent (Birren 1968).

The cognitive capabilities the elderly retain should be understood as well as the capabilities they lose. Decline may be a function of ill health or disuse of intellectual capabilities rather than of old age, in which case cognitive function can be enhanced (Gaitz 1972).

Learning. The ability to learn does not decline as much as has been supposed. We can see only the resultant performance, not the internal thought process. As Botwinick (1975) points out, poor performance may be due to poor motivation, lack of confidence or poor conditions for learning. However, when old people make errors in a learning process they tend to repeat them and find them difficult to overcome. Therefore, in learning a new task it is important for them to go slowly and deliberately so each step is assimilated correctly. Difficulty with short-term memory may in some older individuals interfere with learning, but many will adapt to this problem by using other methods to circumvent it (Heron and Chown 1967, Birren 1968). Improvement in performance in a particular learning task has been noticed to be associated with more time to respond to the stimulus. Most old people work best when allowed to go at their own pace, and this applies whether the task is mental or physical.

Factors in improved performance

It is probably true that human capabilities must be regularly used if they are to be kept at a high pitch of efficiency. The elderly will respond if suitable demands are made upon them, and they will deteriorate if none are made. Performance in the elderly, as with people in other age groups, is markedly improved by reinforcement, affection and a feeling of being wanted or necessary. However, it is interesting that society provides relatively few rewards for competence beyond a certain stage of life, when the social atmosphere changes to one of relative disregard and non-reward (Gaitz 1972).

Adaptation. Since the efficiency of the organism declines while the overall objectives of life remain the same, adaptation is necessary, and those individuals who adapt best demonstrate the signs of aging much later than those who adapt less well. Eventually increasing age tends to be accompanied by an increasing inability to adapt to the environment. Once more, how much this difficulty with adaptation is due to old age and how much to social and environmental influences is not clear. Welford (1962) describes what he calls 'load-shedding' as being an illustration of adaptability. To compensate for slowing of skilled activities, the elderly omit the less important details and devise new routines to improve the efficiency of their performance.

Brody (1974) and others have also emphasised the ability of the aged to compensate for specific losses of capacity and adapt to changing situations. Gaitz (1972) comments that concern with quantitative decline may mark the occurrence of qualitative changes, which represent attempts to adjust or cope. Welford (1962) reminds us that the life cycle is, after all, a series of interactions between man and his environment.

Reaction Time. It has been noted that speed of action falls off faster than physical endurance (Welford 1962). An increased time is needed to perform simple tasks. However, loss of speech is frequently compensated for by greater accuracy and attention to detail. Reaction time improves with practice, and psychological factors and information are important factors in this improvement. Rabbitt (1964) showed that elderly subjects are able to retain response levels whether they are given information to assist them in responding or not. However, given misleading information their response time became retarded considerably more than that of younger subjects. Similarly, the elderly take advantage of any opportunities for preparation before the response is required. They are reported to be cautious and to delay performance in order to maximise accuracy, and they become anxious if asked to perform a new task with insufficient preparation and at a given speed.

Pathology associated with aging

Many of the factors associated with old age predispose to disease, factors such as poor nutrition and loneliness.

Mental changes should not be assumed to be due to senile psychosis for they frequently have a physical cause which is reversible. Disorientation and confusion may indicate illness and be one of the first obvious signs. The elderly sometimes do not demonstrate pyrexia. For this reason increased respiratory rate and pulse rate may be a more reliable indicator of sickness. When elderly people are ill, a prolonged period in bed may precipitate mental deterioration.

Cardiovascular disease, cerebrovascular disease and cancer are the three commonest causes of death in the aged. Sokoloff (1966) suggests that cerebrovascular disease becomes the 'pacemaker' of the aging process within the brain. People with cerebrovascular disease may suffer postural hypotension, becoming dizzy or faint if they stand up too quickly. Johnson, Smith, Spalding and Wollner (1965) have reported, in patients whose problems are severe, an improved response to the assumption of an antigravity posture by repeated gradual changes in posture towards the upright.

There is a tendency to regard the elderly person with brain dysfunction as being incapable of responding to therapy, and therefore as not requiring treatment of any quality. This negative attitude stems as much from society's view that disability is an inevitable accompaniment of old age as from its lack of understanding of the adaptability and resilience of human nature. Many of the more serious problems of the stroke patient, for example, are the result of the attitudes of the people around him. There are many establishments in otherwise socially and economically developed countries where old people who have had strokes are cared for by people who have no understanding of the nature of their problems. A patient with oro-facial dysfunction is very likely to dribble his food. There are two remedies. He could wear a bib to keep his clothes clean, or he could have treatment specifically designed to improve his lip closure and swallowing. The latter procedures require little time and they are easily learned by nurses and therapists. They are also remarkably effective. The former remedy is more likely to be applied if the people caring for him regard old age as always associated with messy eating habits.

Too few staff in day hospitals and nursing homes appreciate the effects their institutions have upon elderly disabled people, or acknowledge that the patient's behaviour may be due to the institution as much as to old age.

Functional improvement could be enhanced in the elderly as in younger patients under conditions which are intrinsically rewarding. In other words a positive emotional response will promote more successful learning. One observation which can be made from a study by Halberstam and Zaretsky (1969) is that both aged and brain-damaged patients appear to have a similar learning potential to that of younger patients if time limits on performance are eliminated, if the emotional milieu is positive, and if the tasks are progressive and intrinsically rewarding.

Elderly brain-damaged patients seem to re-learn functional movements more easily and quickly when the movements are obviously relevant and meaningful. It also appears that the elderly re-learn movements more effectively when the movements are broken into their component parts then put together again, and when they are given time to practise. They learn better if their performance is monitored by the therapist's voice rather than from purely visual and proprioceptive feedback and they learn more easily if errors are avoided.

67

If the elderly have a positive place in the community, if they are encouraged to keep fit and healthy, then old age may not necessarily mean such a marked decline in function and happiness as it so frequently does. Therapists should be involved in planning preventative programmes for the healthy middle-aged and elderly, for 'activity and movement create the energy the body needs' (Gore 1974).

SUMMARY

In this chapter, some aspects of aging are described. In the health care field, negative expectations about the aged arise partly from anatomical studies which may be inaccurate and partly from behavioural studies which may demonstrate the effects of rejection, disuse, misuse or pathology on the aging person as much as any intrinsic 'aging' effect. The therapist should avoid generalisations about the elderly, and ensure that her assessment of an elderly patient finds out the real reasons for his problems rather than assuming they are age related. The authors recommend that health professionals take a more positive stance about the potential abilities of their elderly patients.

References

Agate, J. (1970) *The Practice of Geriatrics*. London, Heinemann.

Birren, J. E. (1968) Psychological aspects of aging: intellectual function. *Gerontologist*, Pt. 2, **8,** 1.

Botwinick, J. (1975) *Aging and Behaviour*. New York, Springer.

Brody, E. M. (1974) Aging and family personality: a developmental view. *Family Process*, **13,** 23–39.

Burch, P. R. J. (1968) *An Inquiry Concerning Growth, Disease and Ageing*. Edinburgh, Oliver Boyd.

Cameron, P., Stewart, L. and Biber, H. (1973) Consciousness of death across the life span. *J. Gerontol*, **28,** 92–95.

Curtis, H. J. (1966) *Biological Mechanisms of Aging*. Illinois, Thomas.

Davison, W. (1969) Relationships with geriatric patients. *Physiotherapy*, **55,** 6, 233–235.

de Vries, H. (1970) Physiological effects of an exercise training regimen upon men aged 52 to 88. *J. Gerontol.*, **25,** 325–336.

Gaitz, C. M. (1972) *Aging and the Brain*. New York, Plenum Press.

Gore, I. (1974) The meaning of ageing. *New Scientist*, 756–758.

Gutmann, E., Hauzlikova, V. and Zakonbek, B. (1968) Changes in the neuromuscular system during old age. *Exp. Gerontol.*, **3,** 141–146.

Halberstam, J. L. and Zaretsky, H. H. (1966) Rating reliability and affective value of words as a function of age and brain damage. *J. Gerontol.*, **21**, 529–536.

Halberstam, J. L. and Zaretsky, H. H. (1969) Learning capacities of the elderly and brain damaged. *Arch. Phys. Med. and Rehab.*, 133–139.

Hasselkus, B. R. (1974) Aging and the human nervous system. *Am. J. Occup. Ther.*, **28**, 1, 16.

Havighurst, R. J., Neugarten, B. L. and Tobin, S. S. (1968) Disengagement and patterns of aging. In *Middle Age and Aging*, edited by B. L. Neugarten. Chicago, University of Chicago Press.

Heron, A. and Chown, S. (1967) *Age and Function*. London, Churchill.

Howell, T. H. (1949) Senile deterioration of the central nervous system. *Brit. Med. J.*, **1**, 56–63.

Johnson, R. H., Smith, A. C., Spalding, J. M. K. and Wollner, J. (1965) Effects of posture on blood pressure in elderly patients. *Lancet*, **1**, 731–733.

Lawton, A. H. (1965) The historical developments in the biological aspects of aging and the aged. *Gerontologist*, **5**, 25–32.

Milani-Comparetti, S. and Gidoni, E. A. (1967) Pattern analysis of motor development and its disorders. *Dev. Med. Child Neurol.*, **9**, 625–630.

Minot, C. (1908) *The Problems of Age, Growth and Death*. London, Pitman.

Pearson, G. H. J. (1928) Effect of age on vibration sensibility. *Arch. Neurol. Psychiat.*, **20**, 482–496.

Rabbitt, P. M. (1964) Set and age in a choice response task. *J. Gerontol.*, **19**, 301.

Serratrice, G., Roux, H. and Aquaron, R. (1968) Proximal muscle weakness in elderly subjects. *J. Neurol. Sci.*, **7**, 275–299.

Sheldon, J. H. (1960) On the natural history of falls in old age. *Brit. Med. J.*, **4**, 1685–1690.

Sinclair, D. (1973) *Human Growth After Birth*. London, Oxford University Press.

Sokoloff, L. (1966) Cerebral circulation and metabolic changes associated with ageing. *Proceed. Assoc. for Research in Nerv. & Ment. Disorders*, **41**, 237–254.

Stewart, M. C. (1975) Motivation in old age. *Physiotherapy*, **61**, 6, 180–182.

Timiras, P. S. (1972) *Developmental Physiology and Aging*. New York, MacMillan.

Tomlinson, B. E. (1972) Morphological brain changes in nondemented old people. In *Ageing of the Central Nervous System*, edited by H. M. Van Praag and A. F. Kalverboer. Haarlem, De Erven F. Bohn N. V.

Walls, E. W. (1970) The anatomy of ageing. *Physiotherapy*, **56**, 12, 528–533.

Weg, R. B. (1973a) Aging and the aged in contemporary society. *Phys. Ther.*, **53**, 7, 749–756.

Weg, R. B. (1973b) The changing physiology of aging. *Am. J. Occup. Ther.*, **27**, 5, 213–217.

Weiss, P. (1966) Aging, a corollary of development. In *Perspectives in Experimental Gerontology*, edited by N. W. Shock. Illinois, Thomas.

Welford, A. T. (1962) On changes of performance with age. *Lancet*, **1**, 335–338.

Further Reading

Adams, G. F. and Hurwitz, L. J. (1974) *Cerebrovascular Disability and the Aging Brain*. Edinburgh & London, Churchill-Livingstone.

Ahammer, I. M. and Baltes, P. B. (1972) Objective versus perceived age differences in personality: How do adolescents, adults, and older people view themselves and each other? *J. Gerontol.*, **27**, 46–51.

Boyd, R. R. and Oakes, C. G. (1969) *Foundations of Practical Gerontology*. Columbia, University of S. Carolina Press.

Burnet, F. M. (1974) *The Biology of Ageing*. Auckland, Oxford University Press.

Cantela, J. R. and Wisocki, P. A. (1969) The use of imagery in the modification of attitudes toward the elderly. *J. Psychol.*, **73**, 193–199.

Eisdorfer, C. and Lawton, M. P. (1973) *Psychology of Adult Development and Aging*. Washington, Amer. Psych. Assoc.

Finely, F. R., Cody, K. A. And Finizie, R. V., (1969) Locomotion patterns in elderly women. *Arch. Phys. Med.*, **50**, 140–146.

Gore, I. (1973) *Age and Vitality*. London, Allen and Unwin.

Schaie, K. and Gribbin, K. (1975) Adult development and aging. *Ann. Rev. Psych.*, **26**, 65–98.

Toynbee, A. (1968) *Man's Concern with Death*. London, Hodder and Stoughton.

Chapter 3

The Relearning of Movement

An understanding of what is involved in normal movement, and of how movement (or motor skill) is learned is essential in the treatment of the brain-damaged patient. The adult who has suffered, for example, stroke or head injury, may no longer know *how* to move. His major need in terms of physical function will be to relearn those movements which he can no longer perform. It is the authors' opinion that those factors considered to be relevant to the *learning* of motor skill are also relevant to the *relearning* of skill by the brain-damaged patient.

A skill can be defined as 'any human activity that has become better organised and more effective as a result of practice' (Annett 1971). Motor skills are frequently divided into basic and complex. A complex motor skill may be a sport or professional skill, or a simple basic movement made more complex by the intention behind it. When a movement is said to be complex it usually means that it requires finer control, more concentration or more perceptual ability.

In the treatment of the brain-damaged adult, who must learn again how to perform the simple and complex tasks which he has learned throughout his life, the major factors in this learning (re-learning) process which are discussed in this chapter are the following:–

Identification of goal
Inhibition of unnecessary activity
The ability to cope with the effects of gravity and therefore to make balance adjustments while shifting weight
Appropriate body alignment
Practice
Motivation
Feedback and knowledge of results

Identification of Goal
Learning a motor skill involves two important factors which can be considered together. *What has to be learned must be identified*, that is, the

person has to be aware of the goal, and *the information has to be organised in the proper sequence to carry out the task* (Gagne 1962, Diller 1968). Ayres (1960) has suggested that neurological integration is enhanced when attention is directed away from muscular action and toward a purposeful goal.

In the treatment of the brain-damaged adult, the therapist should concentrate on making clear to him what must be learned, and on helping him to organise the movement to be learned by practising the components of the movement in their correct sequence. Practice of particular components of a motor function should be immediately followed by practice of the function itself. For example, to stand up from sitting, the patient must move his feet back under the chair, bend forwards from the hips with his head and thoracic spine in extension and when his weight is far enough forwards, he is ready to stand up.

The logic of this approach to the relearning of movement, in which the patient practises, with as much guidance and stimulation as he requires, the components of a movement which he either lacks or has no control over, is immediately apparent to most brain-damaged patients. The goal does not seem too far away, and the practice of these movement is seen as a preparation for function. In other words, the patient feels he is practising the movement he has lost, and not doing exercises or unrelated activities.

The patient also feels himself to be in a learning situation with some responsibility for this learning. Patients following stroke in particular respond well to this approach as it improves their self-esteem and their sense of having some control over their situation.

The Inhibition of Unnecessary Activity

This plays an important part both in the development of motor co-ordination in children and in the acquisition of skills in adult life. Motor learning in infancy is said to depend upon a continual refinement of the mass responses of the embryo and newborn (MacConaill and Basmajian 1969). There is electromyographic evidence of overactivity in the muscles of the young which serves no direct purpose in the performance of particular movements (Basmajian 1976). O'Connell (1958) points out that inexperienced or unskilled performers demonstrate more overflow into unnecessary muscles than skilled performers. Basmajian (1977) comments that it is necessary when learning a new skill that the many muscles which contract unnecessarily when one first attempts to produce the necessary response must be progressively inhibited. Blomfield and Marr (1970) suggest that movements are learned by the turning off of incorrect elemental movement. They explain the process in this way. A fast feedback loop to and from deep pyramidal cells via the pontine nuclei, intra-cerebellar nuclei and ventro-lateral nucleus of the thalamus, enables the pyramidal cells to check up on the effectiveness of the motor response.

Motor learning and control probably depend, therefore, more upon the progressive inhibition of undesired muscular activity or unwanted responses than on the activation of additional motor units (O'Connell 1972, Basmajian 1977). This is also necessary for the brain-damaged person who must learn again how to inhibit unnecessary activity.

The novice attempts to compensate for lack of skill by using greater strength. On the other hand, the skilled performer achieves far more by using less muscular effort in carrying out the specific activity. The brain-damaged patient, if not helped to do otherwise, will expend a great deal of energy in trying to move, and may never get beyond this point. In his treatment 'there should be a minimum expenditure of energy consistent with the ends to be achieved' (MacConaill and Basmajian 1969).

The fact that a skilled performer demonstrates less energy expenditure than one who is unskilled is probably due to a number of other factors associated with the elimination of unecessary muscular activity. These include the minimising of postural work by the development of more efficient balance and co-ordination and the modification of necessary movements to ensure they are of appropriate speed and direction (Shephard 1972).

Balance

Almost all our daily activities are performed under the influence of gravity. The major part of waking life is spent in protecting oneself from the effects of gravity upon the body. We occupy antigravity positions all day long, making continual automatic adjustments to ensure we maintain or regain our balance, since even the smallest movements tend to upset our carefully maintained equilibrium. These protective balance responses are considered to be a driving force in our lives, having survival value as well as enabling us to maintain our sense of dignity.

Balance reactions 'provide the "supportive" framework upon which many diverse kinds of motor behaviour can be built' (Shambes 1976). Kaluger and Heil (1970) point out that symmetry in the postural mechanisms and balance in the weight shift mechanism must develop for the child to be able to concentrate on perfecting complex motor skills. Gibson (1968) also suggests that for the basic orienting system to be effective as an information-gathering mechanism it must be symmetrical. The orienting system is considered to be important as a basic reference point for visual perception and the development of balance through the step by step experience of reaching out into the environment (Smith and Henry 1967).

Rood (1954) has stressed that an important factor in the development of motor skill is the necessity for stability in order to gain controlled mobility. Bobath & Bobath (1975) point out that postural reactions must be well developed and automatic for sensori-motor function to be effective. Ayres (1972) agrees that the postural responses must be developed but suggests it is not directly for the improvement of motor skill but for the enhancement of sensory integration at brain stem level. This, by aiding in the development of visual perception, for example, will enable motor skill to develop. She suggests that brain stem mechanisms must become integrated before higher cortical control can be established.

Balance is not static. It always involves small adjustments, whether actual observable movement or merely tonus changes. Holt (1975) comments that because gravity cannot be seen we sometimes forget its effect on everything we do. Maintaining the sitting position requires the ability, not just to stay there, but also to make small adjustments to the position as it is disrupted by movements of the head, the need for eye fixation and reaching out with the hand.

Body Alignment

Movement or motor skill, to be effective, must start from a particular postural and mental 'set', a state of readiness which involves the body parts being in appropriate alignment. Once movement has started, alignment must conform to the central programming for that particular movement. Hence, if we make a movement which feels awkward, the sensation of awkwardness comes either from a movement which started from the wrong 'set' or from a movement which did not conform to the brain's 'idea' of how it should have occurred.

One of the important aspects of the therapist's handling of the patient involves a constant monitoring of posture and movement. She observes abnormalities and makes adjustments as they are necessary. This is essential as one of the ways of giving the patient the normal postural set and it ensures that he has every possibility of experiencing normal sensory feedback. Adjustments are made in order to regain symmetry and normal weight-bearing alignment, to encourage relaxation of a tense elevated shoulder, to discourage an hyperextended knee, and so on. They may be very minor alterations to body alignment but such minor alterations will be essential for more normal movement.

Many aspects of the work of Alexander (1932), which has been described and discussed by the physiologists Sherrington (1951) and Coghill (1941), the writer Huxley (1937) and more recently by the animal biologist Tinbergen (1974), are relevant to physiotherapy.

Alexander suggested that misuse of the body musculature as occurs with, for example, too much sitting and too little walking, can disturb the entire system. When certain abnormal postures have become a habit, the brain receives signals from the musculature and skin which indicate that everything is normal when in fact it is not. This can be expressed another way by saying that we feel normal even if we are not. Bobath (1967) has used the same concept of abnormal or incorrect sensory feedback to explain the persistence of abnormal postures and movements in brain-damaged patients, and as a reason for treatment commencing early to avoid the 'imprinting' of abnormal movements.

Therapists who have treated patients with, for example, long-standing hemiplegia following stroke, appreciate the fact that one of the most difficult aspects of treatment is getting the patient to understand that what he feels as 'normal' is not, and that a different body alignment which feels strange is in fact normal and necessary to effective movement.

The person with an intact brain has similar experiences when he catches sight of himself in a mirror and finds that he is standing with rounded shoulders. If he tries then to straighten his shoulders and stand erect he feels 'different', not himself. He has to make a conscious effort to maintain that stance. When his concentration is on something else he will revert automatically to his usual poor posture.

The concept of central programming has been described by many authors. It is probable that the performance of movements is monitored by the brain at various levels of integration. In other words, the brain monitors movements and postures by checking feedback signals with expectation which results from previous experience.

Alexander, who was referring to people without brain damage, suggested a certain way of handling the body to enable the body musculature to function more normally. Tinbergen (1974) comments that 'It should not cause surprise that a mere gentle handling of body musculature can have such profound effects on both body and mind', and he goes on to say that 'Alexander treatment . . . is an extremely sophisticated form of rehabilitation, or rather deployment, of the entire muscular equipment, and through that of many other organs. Compared with this, many types of physiotherapy which are now in general use look surprisingly crude and restricted in their effect'.

Practice

Practice has a positive effect on motor learning only if it is guided and controlled. Practice of an inappropriate movement will have a retarding effect on learning.

Goodenough and Brian (1929) suggested that the amount of time to be spent in practice should not be recommended as, for example, daily or twice daily, but that instead the particular skill should be practised whenever unwanted movement habits are retarding progress. Singer (1968) suggests that shorter practice sessions with shorter rest periods extending over a longer period of time are most effective for the learning of certain motor skills.

As has been pointed out, an important factor in the relearning of movement appears to be that the learning process must have a recognisable goal. It is necessary that preparation for that goal should directly precede its practice in order to be relevant and that there is opportunity for the particular function itself to be practised, with guidance, in the most normal way possible. As Hellebrandt (1977) points out, tennis is not learned by hitting a ball against a wall. It is learned by practise of the game itself in its natural setting. In other words, if certain parts of a movement are practised, the patient should immediately attempt the entire movement, without the intervention of other activities.

For example, if a stroke patient is preparing for function in standing, treatment to improve his ability to stand is preferably done with him in this position. If he is having difficulty because he cannot control his knee in standing, he can learn this control in sitting with his leg extended (Fig. 145). The therapist gives approximation through his heel while the patient tries to control movement within the last few degrees of extension. This will give him the feeling of the control which he will need when he is standing. While the therapist stimulates extension she reminds the patient to think about how he feels so he will replicate this feeling when he stands up. He is immediately helped to stand and encouraged to maintain knee control while he bears weight through this leg and takes a step forwards.

Some components of a function are particularly essential to that function and practice of these components will enable the patient to perform the function itself. For example, to reach forward for an object in sitting requires the ability to shift weight and balance. If the patient has difficulty with balance in this position the therapist stimulates his ability to adjust his position by moving him about. She then takes advantage of his improved balance to enable him to practise reaching out for an object. Extension of the weight-bearing hip is an essential component in stepping forward with the other leg. If a patient cannot do this, that is, cannot shift his weight forward by extending at the hip, practice of this component either in standing or in lying will enable him to step forward more normally.

It has been observed that some patients who are asked to visualise the movement they are attempting and to think about its direction do better than other patients at relearning movement.

Mental practice, or conscious cortical control, is the act of sitting quietly and rehearsing in one's mind what one is trying to learn. The relationship between motor and mental activity has been described by Jacobson (1932) and Jones (1965) and more recently by Cardinall in 1977. There is electromyographic evidence of increased muscular activity during this mental practice. Cardinall suggests that 2 to 3 minutes practice at a time, done between treatment sessions, is sufficient, but stresses that mental practice is only suitable for patients who do not have communication or perceptual problems and who are able to understand the idea. Care should be taken that the patient understands the details of the task to be practised in order to avoid incorrect practice. Mental practice should not cause anxiety.

Motivation

Without motivation there is probably little ability to learn. We have to want to do what we are learning to do. The goal has to be worthwhile. It is probable that success is an important motivating force. Success is important in the early stages of learning a skill as it increases the person's level of aspiration.

Motivation can be provided by reward, by positive reinforcement using praise or an attitude of pleasure, by an understanding of the goals and by receiving immediate feedback of results. Praise as a direct reward is only effective if it is offered for the accomplishment of some specific desired behaviour. It loses its impact if given lightly, with no relationship to success. Therapists should consider the impact their words of praise may have upon the patient. Although one may want to praise a patient for his attempt at a movement, it is also important that he can relate certain words of praise, such as 'good' to success. In this way when his therapist says 'good' he will know that he has performed a movement correctly and that this is the movement he should repeat. 'Good' said without relevance is no aid to learning.

Belmont, Benjamin, Ambrose and Restuccia (1969) comment that the possibility of brain-damaged patients requiring 'unique motivating conditions for performance has received little consideration'. They go on to suggest that many stroke patients, for example, require more than the usual amount of personal contact in order to participate fully in their treatment programme.

Studies show that the brain-damaged tend to be unmotivated and relatively passive if left to practise on their own during rehabilitation. There may be a number of reasons for this, including poor memory, distractibility, brief attention span, perceptual dysfunction and boredom. It may also, however, indicate that the tasks to be practised alone have little meaning or relevance for the patient. Physical treatment which is ineffective may be so because it lacks motivating force by being not obviously relevant to the patient's needs, boring or not sufficiently difficult to need his concentration. It may also be due to the therapist's failure to feed back to the patient the correct information about the accuracy or otherwise of the function he is practising.

These days, when the tendency is to group patients together in large rooms, it is easy for health personnel to lose sight of the importance of privacy, and the different needs individuals of all ages and types have regarding this. It is easy also to become insensitive to the feelings of patients and their relatives. It is not only the patient who needs to be motivated towards recovery. His relatives and the community in which he lives, as well as the therapist, need to have similar motivation. The therapist's and relatives' positive approach to the patient's ability to return to a meaningful and happy life is one of the most important factors in treatment. 'Successful rehabilitation of a heavily disabled hemiplegic over many months depends less on physical methods . . . than on the conviction transmitted to the patient by a wise and experienced therapist that a return to home life, however restricted, is possible, that the will to continue the struggle counts more towards this than anything else, and that courage and best efforts are respected and admired' (Adams 1974).

Knowledge of Results and Feedback
These are important factors in learning or relearning movement. Feedback is derived from external sources via vision, hearing and skin receptors, and from internal sources such as the proprioceptors. A person knows whether or not his movement is successful either from his own sources or because someone gives him the information. However, as Bruner (1973) points out, feedback is not as simple as is sometimes thought. He suggests that it consists of 'internal feedback that signals an intended action within the nervous system', actually a feed-forward mechanism as it occurs prior to the other action,

'*feedback proper* from the effector system *during* action, and *knowledge of results* that occurs only *after* action has been completed'.

The neurophysiological mechanism behind the learning and execution of motor skills is not understood. For example, it has been assumed that the proprioceptors play an important part by providing feedback of position, movement and stretch, thus providing a monitoring system for the brain. This mechanism would depend upon the brain making a comparison of the intended movement with the efferent information it is receiving from the periphery. Not everyone, however, agrees that proprioception is a necessary factor in the acquisition of movement.

Lashley (1964), for example, suggests that sensory control is not active. Giving the example of piano-playing, he points out that the pianist's movements are too quick for proprioceptive feedback from limbs or visual reaction to the reading of the notes. He comments that a central nervous mechanism controls motor patterns by firing off 'with predetermined intensity and duration' or by activating 'different muscles in predetermined order'.

Taub and Berman (1968) demonstrated with spinal deafferentation of monkeys that peripheral inflow from receptors in the limbs is not required for the performance of complex movements. This appears to be in contradiction to the findings of Mott and Sherrington (1895), who performed spinal deafferentation on monkeys which resulted in the monkey's inability to move the deafferentated limb. As Jones (1974) points out, the Mott and Sherrington experiment, which is so often used to explain the necessity of proprioceptive sensation to movement, was a *unilateral* deafferentation, whereas the Taub and Berman experiment was *bilateral*. Taub and Berman explain the apparent contradiction by suggesting that the movements of one arm have an inhibiting effect upon the movements of the other, and that this effect is normally counteracted by the ipsilateral segmental afferent inflow. Therefore, if this inflow to one arm is abolished by a unilateral deafferentation, then the remaining active limb would have an inhibiting effect upon the movement of the deafferentated limb.

Taub and Berman go on to ask how an animal can learn to use a deafferented limb in the absence of vision, that is, how can it learn to repeat movements when it should not know where the limb is in space, whether it has moved and in what direction. They postulate that since knowledge and information of movements cannot have been conveyed over peripheral pathways, it must have been provided by a central mechanism. A central feedback system 'would return information concerning future movements to the CNS before the impulses that will produce these movements have reached the periphery'. Their experiments led Taub and Berman to consider the role of what they call 'central efferent monitoring' in learning.

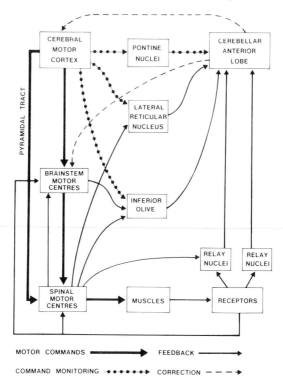

Fig. 33. *Some of the paths between the cerebral motor cortex, anterior lobe of cerebellum and lower motor centres with an interpretation of the function of these paths. The anterior lobe is assumed to correct errors in motor activity elicited from the cerebral cortex and carried out by command signals through pyramidal and extrapyramidal paths. The command signals are assumed to be monitored by the anterior lobe through paths relayed in the inferior olive and pontine and reticular nuclei. The spino-cerebellar pathways are assumed to serve as feedback channels which monitor the activity in lower motor centres and the evolving movement. (From Oscarsson, C. (1970) Functional organisation of spino-cerebellar pathways In* Hand-book of Sensory Physiology, *Vol. 2, edited by A. Iggo, Berlin, Springer-Verlag).*

Oscarsson (1970) describes internal feedback loops which connect cortex and cerebellum (Fig. 33) and suggests that these loops provide the mechanism by which voluntary motor signals from the precentral gyrus pass to the cerebellum to regulate balance, being in turn modified by input from the organs of balance in order that the appropriate motor command is generated.

Evarts (1971) comments that when sensory feedback is eliminated by deafferentation, 'feedback generated internally or by knowledge of results may be of critical importance in motor control'. He goes on to say that it is interesting 'to examine the extent to which new movements can be learned on the basis of knowledge of results and internal feedback', but with sensory feedback eliminated. Evarts uses the term 'internal feedback' in a similar way to Taub and Berman's 'central efferent monitoring'.

The concept that some form of central programming is essential in the control of movement has been put forward therefore by many authors, although the terms used vary. Sperry (1950) proposed that 'a corollary discharge of motor patterns into the sensorium may play an important adjustor role in the visual perception of movement along with non-retinal kinesthetic and postural influences from the periphery'. Von Holst and Mittelstaedt (1950) used the term 'efference copy' and 'reafference' in a similar way to 'corollary discharge'. MacKay (1966) asked an interesting question with a visual example. 'When the direction of gaze changes, the optical image moves over the retina. If the change is imposed on the eyeball from without, say, gentle pressure on the corner of the open eyelid, the visual world is seen to move. When the same change results from voluntary use of the eye muscles, however, no movement of the visual world is seen. What is it about voluntary control, we may ask, which makes this difference?'

Jones (1972) argues that central monitoring of motor outflow is a necessary condition for the accurate retention of voluntary movement, rather than muscle spindle firing. It is possible that 'the central nervous system may control the temporal sequence of muscle contraction through monitoring its own efferent outflow'.

The relationship between visual control and the acquisition of voluntary movement has been pointed out by Held and Hein (1963) and Held and Bauer (1967) in their experiments. Experiments have shown (Stelmark 1968 and Jones 1974) that techniques of augmenting proprioceptive input, such as resistance, may have little effect on accuracy of movement if verbal or visual knowledge of results is eliminated.

The heavy emphasis in much physiotherapy on the importance of proprioceptive inflow in the learning or relearning of movements is questioned by Jones (1974). He suggests that this theory of motor skill acquisition is inadequate, and that methods of physiotherapy to improve movement control may be ineffective if they are based upon the theory that proprioceptive feedback is essential to movement. He suggests that there is very little evidence for the belief that accuracy of movement control depends upon proprioception, and that experiments which claim to illustrate the necessity for proprioceptive feedback in movement control also involve procedures using visual and verbal feedback and presumably central feedback as well. He cites Taub and Berman's conclusions that in mammals 'once a motor programme has been written into the CNS, the specified behaviour, having been initiated, can be performed without any reference to or guidance from the periphery'. Taub and Berman point out that the fact that proprioceptive feedback often accompanies movement does not mean it is essential to the movement.

Speech is used by the therapist to provide *auditory feedback* to the patient, giving him information about the accuracy of the movement he is performing, and suggesting any alterations needed. The therapist also uses speech to stimulate and to guide movement. With brain-damaged patients the therapist must find the correct phrase to trigger off a motor response. The interpretation of the words that are used is important in all communication. A patient may not respond to a request when it is phrased one way but may respond when it is phrased differently. For example, 'push' may not elicit the appropriate response, while 'reach up toward the ceiling' may. It seems that with each individual certain expressions trigger off a motor response more automatically than others. Alteration in the tone of voice may also make a difference.

The patient may use his own speech (either internally or externally) to help him perform a movement (Luria 1961, Cotton 1974). This is often a very effective way of reinforcing movement, probably because it helps the patient concentrate on what he is doing, and because speech can be used to regulate movement.

If the patient is encouraged to look at the part which he is trying to move and in the direction in which he is to move, he may be stimulated to move more effectively by this use of vision and *visual feedback* to reinforce his motor performance. For example, following stroke and other brain trauma, hypotonia may be so severe that movement appears to be impossible. With guidance from the therapist combined with visual stimulation, the patient may be able to attempt a small part of a particular movement or at least gradually to assist in part of the movement.

For example, he is encouraged to look at his hand while he tries to reach forward with his arm. This visual stimulation helps him to concentrate his attention on movement of the limb, and reinforces his sensation of where he is in space and the direction in which he is moving.

Cognition

The role of cognition in learning motor skills has been discussed by several authors (Hellebrandt 1958, Leithwood and Fowler 1971). The aim of any motor learning is the ability to perform a movement with as little effort as possible, not having to concentrate on the way in which the activity is performed, thereby being free to give maximum attention to the goal being pursued. Complex cognitive processes are probably most involved in the initial learning period. As, gradually, the activity becomes more automatic, there is probably a continuous perceptual-cognitive monitoring until the activity requires reorganising, involving a return to more complex cognition.

Other Factors

In 1929 Goodenough and Brian described some other factors which they considered influenced successful performance of a skill. They are relevant to the relearning of movement also. They include:

Deterioration of performance may result from continuing practice in error.

There may be false associations of cause and effect. Not understanding the cause of error may result in taking inappropriate measures to correct the error.

Peculiar associations of meaning are frequently attached to certain verbal expressions, for example, 'try harder' may mean 'throw with great violence', 'push' may mean 'use all your force'.

Incorrect focussing of attention may occur in which, for example the person looks at his arm instead of at the goal when he is throwing a ball.

There may be frequent random changes in procedure without adhering to any one practice for long enough to develop control.

Emotional factors influence every learning situation. Stress, tension and anxiety, and of course other emotional states, appear to have their effects on movement, but in what way is not always clear. It seems that stress, tension and anxiety may promote, depress or not affect motor performance (Singer 1968). Research indicates that stress affects complex tasks in a different manner from simple tasks, both in learning and performance, disrupting the more complex tasks but sometimes facilitating the simpler ones.

Therapists are frequently concerned that treatment may be fatiguing, and undoubtedly the complaint of tiredness may sometimes be made by patients for various reasons, which may vary from the excessive use of effort or too long spent in one position or on one function, to a feeling of boredom or depression. The fact that elderly or brain-damaged patients do not necessarily become fatigued any more than anyone else should cause the therapist to consider what the reasons for apparent fatigue may be. If treatment is basically success-orientated, which it should be, each task which the patient is to attempt should be challenging but not overwhelming, and therefore should not cause fatigue or stress. The therapist should consider the effects of stress on performance and methods of promoting relaxation and preventing stress. It is not necessary to sit down or lie down in order to rest and relax. Tension is a state of mind which affects the entire body and a change in this state of mind will similarly affect the body.

The therapist should watch carefully for signs of tension or anxiety during treatment. It may be sufficient to draw the patient's attention to his physical/mental state, pointing out tense muscles and suggesting he relax them. The patient may indicate his tension or anxiety by an altered breathing rate or an increased depth of respiration. He may be able to reduce his tension by taking a few deep breaths with the emphasis on relaxed expiration and a feeling of letting go. This can be attempted in whatever position the patient is in, so that he understands relaxation as being part of movement and function and not something passive to be done in a·certain position.

For some patients however, training in special relaxation techniques will be useful and this may be done singly or in a group. The progressive relaxation techniques described by Jacobson (1929, 1964) or the techniques of Meares (1968) are probably the easiest to apply. Benson, Beary and Carol (1974) describe 'the relaxation response', the hypothesised central nervous system reaction underlying these altered states of consciousness, which include decreased respiratory and heart rate and decreased muscular tension.

There are some other factors to be considered in any treatment programme which has as its principle objective the relearning of movement. The therapist must develop her ability to impart both theoretical but particularly practical knowledge and skill to laymen as well as to professional health workers. She needs to be a motivator, stimulator and interpreter.

Treatment of the brain-injured patient requires considerable reinforcement throughout the day and there is a need for an emphasis on **consistency of goals** by therapist, nurse and relative. If relatives

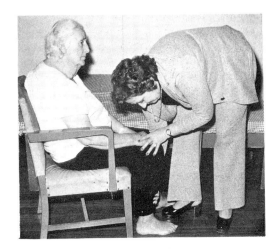

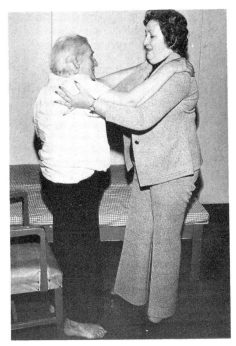

Fig. 34. *This woman quickly learns how to assist her mother following her stroke. As her mother improves she will reduce her assistance.*

85

understand his problems and the reasons why he has difficulty with certain functions, caring for him and living together will be easier. Their relationship will perhaps be closer because the relative will not only be a more understanding companion but will also be seen in a constructive role, not someone upon whom the disabled person becomes dependent but someone who is actively helping the patient become independent. A close relative should therefore be present at some of the treatment sessions, particularly in the early stages of rehabilitation (Fig. 34). Relatives who have been encouraged to help with treatment from the initial stages of the patient's rehabilitation develop familiarity with the handling necessary to help the patient move about, and this will help them cope when the patient goes home. Care is taken that the relatives are not made to feel totally responsible for progress, as this will increase anxiety and give rise to feelings of guilt if the patient's progress is slow. Griffiths (1970) describes well the ways in which the community can work together to aid in the rehabilitation of one individual. Carr and Shepherd (1979) illustrate ways in which relatives may stimulate movement.

Communication. Emotionally and physically the effective therapist's relationship with her patient is very close. This involves many factors including whether the therapist 'stands over' her patient or gets herself to the same level. This is one argument which the authors would use in favour of a low bed for adult patients in preference to a mat on the floor, which may result in the patient being, for at least some of the time, at a considerably lower level than everyone else, including his therapist. Perry (1973), following a survey of therapists, comments that only occasionally did they lower themselves to the patient's level. When they did the patient appeared to be more at ease and patient-therapist communication improved.

Mehrabian (1969), in discussing the significance of posture and and position in communication, comments that a higher percentage of eye contact between people communicating with each other is associated with more positive attitudes between them. Certainly, it is our experience that if the therapist makes an active attempt to engage in eye contact while within relatively close range of the patient, this not only is a method of communicating positive attitudes, but also aids concentration and orientation in space, and helps create a bond between therapist and patient.

The need for close physical proximity between therapist and patient results in considerable use of non-verbal methods of communication, such as touching, eye contact and facial expression, by which the therapist guides the patient's behaviour and by which the patient recognises such unspoken messages as encouragement, caring, approval and acceptance. Perry (1973) suggests that a therapist would be more effective in treatment if she was aware of her own non-verbal behaviour, and more understanding of its effect upon the patient. She suggests that such a potent tool should be used with understanding and adeptness.

Behaviour modification is a method of changing the overt behaviour of a person based on the phenomenon of conditioning, and it involves reinforcement, sequentialisation of tasks and individualised teaching methods. It has been described as successful in the learning of motor skills and speech (Kolderie 1971). Others such as Meyerson, Kerr and Michael (1967) have described its use in improving the typing skill of an eighteen year old boy with traumatic quadriplegia, and in teaching a seven year old cerebral palsied child to walk.

Unfortunately, many brain-damaged patients, but particularly stroke patients, are subjected to a form of modification of behaviour, which is not in their interests, as soon as they are admitted to hospital. In this environment, there are frequently strong pressures to be 'good'. Nursing staff may have the responsibility for keeping a large number of patients safe, clean, quiet and co-operative (Ullman & Krasner 1965).

Physiotherapists depend upon altering behaviour, reinforcing the desired response by verbal approval, smiling and positive physical contact, giving negative feedback when the patient's response is not correct. In many cases, one of the most effective reinforcers is the patient's knowledge of the extent of his improvement in the performance of a particular movement. Ayres (1960) writes that repetition without the subject knowing whether or not the movement is correct will not result in learning. 'It is only by being able to evaluate the results of a motor action that the central nervous system can make those permanent alterations that are known as learning'.

Mechanical aids

These are now a much less important modality in physical treatment of the brain-damaged than they used to be, and those which are necessary are becoming more sophisticated and more effective in improving function. In the past, aids for patients with neurological dysfunction were used to make up for lost function, and followed the same lines as aids for patients with musculo-skeletal disorders. They consisted of apparatus such as arm slings to support the hemiplegic arm, plaster splints to prevent contractures, foot splints to allow a plantigrade foot position and overcome the problem of an inactive anterior tibial muscle group. As aids to locomotion, therapists have given their patients crutches, walking sticks and quadripod or tripod sticks. Parallel bars have been used to assist the relearning of the movements of walking. Most of these aids originated in the days when neurological physiotherapy was mostly concerned with the musculo-skeletal sequelae.

Many therapists would now agree that the use of *parallel bars* has disadvantages in the treatment of the problems interfering with walking in brain-damaged patients. Bars are very supportive and protective. They prevent the patient from developing normal body alignment, the ability to shift weight and balance. They therefore prevent the development of confidence in standing. They encourage backward leaning which is a common problem in these patients who usually have difficulty shifting weight and remaining erect. They encourage weight-bearing through the hands when treatment should be emphasising bearing weight through the legs. They encourage the tendency to grasp and pull with the hands as a substitute for balance reactions. They encourage asymmetrical body alignment in those patients who already tend to be asymmetrical.

Similar comments can be made about the use of a *tilt table*. Although this is a very useful device for the spinal cord injured patient and for other patients for whom it provides an essential aid for standing, it is not necessary for most brain-damaged patients. It is a passive means of standing the patient and should only be used when there is no other possibility of the patient assuming the standing position more naturally. It discourages the redevelopment of balance and if it is not carefully used it encourages backward leaning.

The use of a *mirror* for helping the patient relearn certain points about function is contra-indicated in many patients with brain damage. When he looks in a mirror the patient receives a mirror image of himself in which function appears reversed. This adds to the confusion already present in many of these patients and, if used for a person with perceptual disorders such as apraxia, visual-spatial difficulties or confused laterality, it may increase his disability (Critchley 1950).

A more effective way of reinforcing the learning of movement in some patients may be the use of *videotape apparatus*. The patient can watch what he has been doing, which adds visual feedback to his other methods of monitoring his performance. It also enables him to use his cognitive abilities to reinforce learning especially if he has practised the movement mentally. The patient will also feel reassured that he is participating in his own treatment. Gonnella (1970) describes the use of *cine film strips* in teaching patients following orthopaedic surgery how to crutch walk.

Therapists are now exploring the possible therapeutic application of more active aids such as nerve stimulators which affect particular muscles, and biofeedback or sensory feedback apparatus which provides immediate information for the patient about his movements.

There have been several recent descriptions of the use of electrical stimulation to promote activity in single muscle groups in brain-damaged patients. Takebe, Kukulka, Narayan, Milner and Basmajian (1975) describe the use of a *peroneal nerve stimulator* in the treatment of hemiplegic stroke patients with inability to dorsiflex the foot and with no severe spasticity. However, they comment that a major problem was pain and only three of the nine patients tolerated treatment beyond a few days. Furthermore, although the ability to dorsiflex improved in some of the patients, there was not necessarily a carry-over into improved walking. Winter (1976) describes the use of *transcutaneous electrical stimulation* (TNS) in improving function in patients with multiple sclerosis and with hemiplegia following stroke. *Biofeedback therapy** is probably a more promising aid to the relearning of movement.

SUMMARY

The adult patient following brain-damage is in a learning situation. Certain factors such as identification of goal, inhibition of unnecessary activity, ability to cope with gravity, appropriate body alignment, practice, motivation, feedback and knowledge of results are discussed in terms of their relevance to treatment.

References

Adams, G. F. (1974) *Cerebrovascular Disability and the Ageing Brain.* Edinburgh and London, Churchill Livingstone.

Alexander, F. M. (1932) *The Use of Self.* London, Chaterston.

Annett, J. (1971) Acquisition of skill. *Br. Med. Bull.,* **27,** 3, 266–271.

Ayres, A. J. (1960) Occupational therapy for motor disorders resulting from impairment of the central nervous system. *Rehabil. Lit.,* **21,** 302–310.

Ayres, A. J. (1972) *Sensory Integration and Learning Disabilities.* Los Angeles, Western Psychological Services.

* Appendix 1

Basmajian, J. V. (1976) Electromyographic investigation of spasticity and muscle spasm. *Physiotherapy*, **62**, 10, 319–322.

Basmajian, J. V. (1977) Motor learning and control: a working hypothesis. *Arch. Phys. Med. Rehabil.*, **58**, 38–41.

Belmont, I., Benjamin, H., Ambrose, J. and Restuccia, R. D. (1969) Effect of cerebral damage on motivation in rehabilitation. *Arch. Phys. Med. Rehabil.*, Sept., 507–511.

Benson, H., Beary, J. F. and Carol, M. P. (1974) The relaxation response. *Psychiatry*, **37**, 37–46.

Blomfield, S. and Marr, D. (1970) How the cerebellum may be used. *Nature*, **227**, 1224–1228.

Bobath, B. (1967) Personal Communication

Bobath, B. and Bobath, K. (1975) *Motor Development in the Different Types of Cerebral Palsy*. London, Heinemann.

Bruner, J. S. (1973) Organisation of early skilled action. *Child Development*, **44**, 4, 1–11.

Cardinall, N. (1977) Mental practice. *Paper Delivered at 53rd Congress of APTA*. St. Louis, Missouri.

Carr, J. H. and Shepherd, R. B. (1979) *The Early Care of the Stroke Patient. A Positive Approach*. London, Heinemann.

Coghill, G. E. (1941) Appreciation: the educational methods of F. Matthias Alexander. In F. M. Alexander, *The Universal Constant in Living*. New York, Dutton.

Cotton, E. (1974) Improvement in motor function with the use of conductive education. *Develop. Med. Child Neurol.*, **16**, 637–643.

Critchley, M. (1950) The body image in neurology. *The Lancet*, Feb., 335–340.

Diller, L. (1968) Brain damage, spatial orientation and rehabilitation. In *The Neuropsychology of Spatially Oriented Behaviour*, edited by S. J. Freedman. Illinois, Dorsey Press.

Evarts, E, V. (1971) Feedback and corollary discharge: A merging of the concepts. *Neurosciences Research Proj. Bulletin*, **9**, 86–112.

Gagne, R. (1962) Military Training and principles of learning. *Amer. Psychologist*, **17**, 83–92.

Gibson, J. J. (1968) *The Senses Considered as Perceptual Systems*. London, Allen and Unwin.

Gonnella, C. (1970) Preliminary investigations into the effectiveness of programmed audio-visual instructions for patient motor activity. *Prog. Phys. Ther.*, **1**, 279–284.

Goodenough, F. L. & Brian, C. R. (1929) Certain factors underlying the acquisition of motor skills by pre-school children. *J. Exp. Psychol.*, **12**, 127–155.

Griffiths, V. (1970) *A Stroke in the Family*. London, Pitman.

Held, R. & Bauer, J. A. (1967) Visually guided reaching in infant monkeys after restricted rearing. *Science*, **155**, 718.

Held, R. & Hein, A. (1963) Movement-produced stimulation in the development of visually guided behaviour. *J. Compar. Physiol. Psych.*, **56**, 872.

Hellebrandt, F. A. (1958) The physiology of motor learning. *Cerebral palsy Review*, **19**, 9–14.

Hellebrandt, F. A. (1977) Motor learning reconsidered: A study of change. In *Neurophysiologic Approaches to Therapeutic Exercise*, edited by O.D. Payton, S. Hirt and R. A. Newton. Philadelphia, Davis.

Holt, K. S. (1975) How and why children move. In *Movement and Child Development*, edited by K. S. Holt. London, Heinemann.

Huxley, A. (1937) *Ends and Means*. London, Chatto and Windus.

Jacobson, E. (1929) *Progressive Relaxation*. Chicago, Universal Press.

Jacobson, E. (1932) Muscular phenomenon during imagining. *Am. J. Psychol.*, **49**, 677–694.

Jacobson, E. (1964) *Anxiety and Tension Control: A Physiological Approach*. Philadelphia, Lippincott.

Jones, B. (1972) Outflow and inflow in movement duplication. *Perception & Psychophysics*, **12**, 95.

Jones, B. (1974) The importance of memory traces of motor efferent discharges for learning skilled movements. *Develop. Med. Child Neurol.*, **16**, 620–628.

Jones, G. J. (1965) Motor learning without demonstration of physical practice, under two conditions of mental practice. *Res. Quart.*, **36**, 270–276.

Kaluger, G. and Heil, C. L. (1970) Basic symmetry and balance – their relationship to perceptual-motor development. *Prog. Phys. There.*, **1**, 132–137.

Kolderie, M. L. (1971) Behaviour modification in the treatment of children with cerebral palsy. *Phys. Ther.*, **51**, 10, 1083–1091.

Lashley, K. S. (1964) *Brain Mechanisms and Intelligence*. New York, Hafner.

Leithwood, K. A. & Fowler, W. (1971) Complex motor learning in four-year olds. *Child Development*, **42**, 781–792.

Luria, A. R. (1961) *The Role of Speech in the Regulation of Normal and Abnormal Behaviour*. Oxford, Pergamon.

MacKay, D. M. (1966) Cerebral organisation and the conscious control of action. In *Brain and Conscious Learning*, edited by J. C. Eccles. New York, Springer-Verlag.

MacConaill, M. A. and Basmajian, J. V. (1969) *Muscles and Movements. Basis for Human Kinesiology*. Baltimore, Williams and Wilkins.

Meares, A. (1968) *Relief Without Drugs*. London, Souvenir Press.

Mehrabian, A. (1969) Significance of posture and position in the communication of attitude and status relationships. *Psychol. Bull.,* **71,** 5, 359–372.

Meyerson, L., Kerr, N. and Michael, J. L. (1967) Behaviour modification in rehabilitation. In *Child Development: Readings in Experimental Analysis,* edited by S. W. Bijou and D. M. Baer. New York, Appleton, Century, Crofts.

Mott, F. W. and Sherrington, C.S. (1895) Experiments upon the influence of sensory nerves upon movements and nutrition of the limbs. *Proc. Roy. Soc., London,* **57,** 481–488.

O'Connell, A. L. (1958) Electromyographic study of certain leg muscles during movements of free foot and during standing. *Am. J. Phys. Med.,* **37,** 289–301.

O'Connell, A. L. (1972) *Understanding the Scientific Basis for Human Movement.* Baltimore, Williams and Wilkins.

Oscarsson, O. (1970) Functional organisation of spino-cerebellar paths. In *Handbook of Sensory Physiology,* Vol. 2, edited by A. Iggo. Berlin, Springer-Verlag.

Perry, J. F. (1973) Non-verbal communication during physical therapy. *Phys. Ther.,* **55,** 6, 593–600.

Rood, M. (1954) Neurophysiological reactions as a basis for physical therapy. *Phys. Ther. Rev.,* **34,** 9, 444–449.

Shambes, G. M. (1976) Static postural control in children. *Am. J. Phys. Med.,* **55,** 5, 221–252.

Shephard, R. (1972) *Alive Man.* Illinois, Thomas.

Sherrington, C. S. (1951) *Man on His Nature.* London, Cambridge University Press.

Singer, R. N. (1968) *Motor Learning and Human Performance.* New York, Macmillan.

Smith, C. U. and Henry, J. P. (1967) Cybernetic foundations of rehabilitation. *Am. J. Phys. Med.,* **46,** 379–467.

Sperry, R. W. (1950) Neural basis of the spontaneous optokinetic response produced by visual inversion. *J. Compar. Physiol. Psychol.,* **43,** 482–489.

Stelmark, G. E. (1968) The accuracy of reproducing target positions under various tensions. *Psychonomic Science,* **13,** 287.

Takebe, K., Kukulka, C., Narayan, M. G., Milner, M. and Basmajian, J. V. (1975) Peroneal nerve stimulation in rehabilitation of hemiplegic patients. *Arch. Phys. Med. Rehab.,* **56,** 237–240.

Taub, E. and Berman, A. J. (1968) Movement learning in the absence of sensory feedback. In *The Neuropsychology of Spatially Oriented Behaviour,* edited by S. J. Freedman. Homewood, Illinois, Dorsey Press.

Tinbergen, N. (1974) Ethology and stress diseases. *Science,* **185,** 20–27.

Ullman, L. P. and Krasner, L. (1965) *Case Studies in Behaviour Modification.* New York, Holt, Rinehart and Winston.

Von Holst, E. (1954) Relations between the central nervous system and peripheral organs. *Brit. J. Anim. Behav.,* **2,** 89.

Von Holst, E. and Mittelstaedt,H. (1950) Das Reafferenzprinzip. *Naturwissenschafte,* **37,** 464–476.

Winter, A. (1976) The use of transcutaneous electrical stimulation (TNS) in the treatment of multiple sclerosis. *J. Neurosurg. Nursing,* **8,** 2, 125–131.

Further Reading

Cross, K. D. (1967) Role of practice in perceptual-motor learning. *Am. J. Phys. Med.,* **46,** 1, 487–510.

Eccles, J. C. (1972) Possible synaptic mechanisms subserving learning. In *Brain and Human Behaviour,* edited by A. C. Karczmar and J. C. Eccles. Heidelberg, Springer.

Forward, E. M. and Hagadone, M. C. (1973) Sensory feedback and motor skills. *Phys. Ther.,* **53,** 6, 614–622.

Herman, R. (1970) Electromyographic evidence of some control factors involved in the acquisition of skilled performance. *Am. J. Phys. Med.,* **49,** 3, 177–191.

Welford, A. T. (1968) *Fundamentals of Skill,* London, Methuen.

Chapter 4

Assessment

Assessment bears a most important relationship to treatment, whether it be the initial assessment of a new patient or the continuing assessment throughout each treatment. Knowledge of where treatment should progress at each session comes from an understanding of the patient's present and immediate response. No treatment can be effective if the assessment is inaccurate.

Assessment has two principal functions apart from providing an aid to diagnosis. The first is to record the patient's initial status (what he can and what he cannot do) as well as his progress. To fulfil this function assessment must be as objective as possible and should consist of some standardised tests of measurement in which the patient's performance is measured against normative data and against his previous performances.

The second function is to act as a continuing guide to treatment, by giving the therapist information about the quality of the patient's performance, how he moves, what abnormalities interfere with movement.

There is considerable discussion at present over the form assessment should take. Should it be qualitative or quantitative? That is, should it describe *what* the patient can do or *how* he does it? Should it be subjective or objective? There is a need for physiotherapists to develop objective testing procedures and methods of recording *objective data*, and this should include the collection of data from normal subjects of different ages. On the other hand physiotherapists should also develop effective ways of recording their *subjective observations.*

Observation is a major part of assessment procedure. It is probably true to say that there is no other means which is so potentially accurate in the right hands. An experienced and observant therapist who understands the subtleties and variations of normal movement, and who will take the time to concentrate on each individual patient, will be able to assess his problems of movement with a fine degree of accuracy. This manner of carrying out an assessment can of course be criticised as being subjective, as it most certainly is, but there is an established place in all aspects of health practice for the subjective diagnosis or analytic opinion of the skilled practitioner. Its subjectiveness is only a problem if the practitioner is not skilled in her job.

Spence (1953) describes clinical observation as 'the craftman's skill in seeing quickly what he knows to be significant . . .'. He goes on 'It is the product not of guessing but of a sifted experience by which the significant is recognised with such rapidity that the steps or reasoning are not discernible to the uninitiated'.

Critchley (1953) comments that 'no simple system of marking can possibly replace the full and faithful recording in a descriptive fashion of exactly what the patient says and does under performance. Qualitative changes in behaviour can only in this way be given their true value'.

With any assessment it is important that the therapist knows what questions she wants answered. If she needs an objective, quantitative record of her patient's improvement, she uses a particular test. For example, if an ataxic patient narrows his walking base to a measurement which is nearer the norm for people of his age, weight and height, then this information is a specific indication of his improvement. It gives a figure for comparison. However, if the therapist wants to know how the patient is coping with his poor balance at home, then the most reliable information will be the subjective qualitative assessment of the patient in his own surroundings from a therapist, the patient himself and his relatives.

To answer these questions of 'how' and 'why' the therapist requires:–

the ability to *observe* in detail and with accuracy, to see at a glance how the patient performs a movement
an *understanding of normal functions* for comparison
the ability to *judge* the most essential missing or abnormal components of movement, which problems are primary and which are secondary.

Example 1:
This patient (Fig. 35) is having difficulty standing up from the bed.

Observation of his attempts (Fig. 36) shows that he is asymmetrical with his weight too far to one side, his weight is not far enough forward at his hips, and his feet are not properly placed. *Judgement* enables the therapist to place these points in order of importance, using her understanding of how a person normally stands up.

1. His feet must be in a position which will allow him to transfer his weight over them.

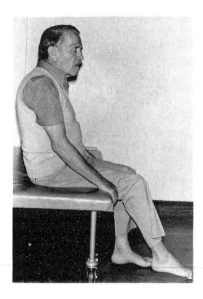

Fig. 35. *This man with Parkinsonism is unable to get from sitting to standing alone.*

2. His weight must be symmetrically placed, in other words he must be able to transfer it sideways.
3. He must transfer his weight further forwards by increasing the flexion at his hips while extending his spine and head.

Of course, she will know other relevant factors about the patient such as the presence of abnormal tone or sensation which will help her to understand why he has these difficulties.

The assessment of this function gives the therapist her theoretical guide to treatment for this particular problem. If her observation and judgement are correct, and she knows how to apply the appropriate treatment, the patient will soon be able to stand up with her guidance. Of course, as she proceeds with her treatment, she may find that there are certain other factors which interfere with parts of the movement. As she handles and guides the patient she constantly assesses his behaviour, and she must be flexible enough to respond to abnormalities in the most appropriate way, which can be illustrated by continuing this example a little further.

The therapist anticipates that he will have difficulty bearing weight through his right leg and changes her handling accordingly. She

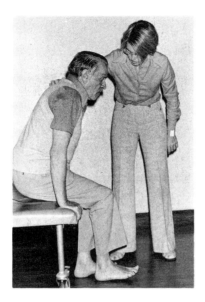

Fig. 36. *He is unable to shift his weight far enough forward at his hips, his feet are not properly placed and his weight is more on his left side than his right side.*

presses downwards through the right knee (Fig. 37) enabling the patient to transfer his weight evenly on to both feet (Fig. 38).

Another skill for the therapist to develop is the ability to *communicate* the results of her assessment to the patient and his relatives, and to other members of the health care team. The latter is done by various methods of recording and by discussion.

Recording assessment

There should probably be two types of written assessment. One which gives objective information about the patient's status at a particular time and which is intended for the communication of relevant information to those concerned with the patient's progress.

The second gives subjective information about all relevant aspects of the patient's function. It includes the initial analysis of function plus brief additions which are written down following each treatment session, describing the main changes in the patient's status, the

Fig. 37. *The foot is placed correctly and the therapist presses downward through his right knee at the same time as she shifts more weight on to that side.*

Fig. 38. *The therapist helps him shift his weight forward at the hips and he stands up.*

problems which have been concentrated on in treatment and the methods of treatment used. A form is probably an effective way of ensuring that certain details of function to be assessed are not omitted, but it has disadvantages in not encouraging the therapist to be flexible in her assessment. Details may vary but all written subjective assessments should include information about hand function, oral function, balance, sensation and tone, as well as general motor functions.

Assessment of function may also be recorded visually by video-camera or cine-camera (Bernstein 1967 and Atwater 1973). This enables visual records to be kept of the patient's movements and provides a record for comparison of the effectiveness of treatment and the patient's progress. They may be used as a means of passing on information to other health personnel involved in the patient's care enabling them to understand the therapist's criteria in treatment planning.

Still photographs are used by some clinicians. Holt, Jones and Wilson (1974) describe the use of a multiple sequential exposure camera which enables a series of eight still photographs to be taken at regular intervals with only one press of the exposure button.

Other methods suggested for analysing movements include the use of electromyographic telemetry (Battye and Joseph 1966, Joseph and Watson 1967, Basmajian 1974), light patterns (Apteker, Ford and Blech 1976), and strobe-light photography (Nelson 1976).

Assessment of Tone

The mechanism of tone is described in Chapter 11. As has been pointed out in that chapter, a state of tone is manifested throughout the body and not just in one group of muscles. To move passively the limb of a patient who is lying in the supine position will give some information about tone, indicating the presence of the clasp-knife phenomenon or lead-pipe rigidity, for example. However, a broader picture of tone and the effects of position and movement upon it, which is necessary for an understanding of the patient's problems and essential information for treatment planning, will emerge only gradually. Similarly, the testing of superficial reflexes and tendon reflexes may have some value in diagnosis but give little information on function. They will be performed by the neurologist as part of his diagnostic examination.

It is probably important to make a distinction between what can be called 'basic tone' and the effects of movement, anxiety, tension, effort, and position upon tone. Some patients who demonstrate obvious hypertonus when doing certain movements or when in certain positions may be found to have basically very low tone at other times. A stroke patient may appear to have a certain degree of spasticity, for example demonstrating abnormal movement synergies, yet may have basically low tone when at rest.

Methods of assessing tone
The therapist has three principal methods of assessing tone.

1. Observation of Movement
a) *Recognition of the abnormal synergies (patterns of movement) associated with spasticity.*
These abnormal synergies are noted throughout assessment as the patient performs certain movements and attempts certain tasks. Their presence reliably indicates hypertonus. These abnormal patterns will be apparent throughout movement. The patient, for example, may reach out for an object with his arm in internal rotation and pronation, and his wrist flexed and thumb adducted. Alternatively, abnormal synergies may be evident in associated movements in another part of the body, when the patient attempts a movement which is, for him, difficult and which requires effort. For example, in a hemiplegic patient, any resisted movement of the unaffected arm will be accompanied by an increase in tone in the opposite limbs (Fig. 85) in the abnormal pattern of spasticity. The value of noting these abnormal patterns in assessment and their inseparable relationship with spasticity has been stressed by Bobath (1966), and this method remains a most reliable indicator of spasticity of central origin.

In a patient with only a minor degree of hypertonus, abnormal synergies may only be evident when he performs difficult movements or when the situation involves some stress.

b) *Recognition of persistent or fluctuating abnormal movements and postures.*
The patient with Parkinsonism may demonstrate a persistent flexed posture, probably indicating an imbalance of tone between flexor and extensor muscle groups, often called flexion dystonia. Other patients with dystonia will demonstrate the persistent maintenance of bizarre postures (Fig. 103). Patients with intermittent spasms will demonstrate relatively sudden fluctuations of tone upon attempts at movement, particularly movement of the head.

100

2. Handling

This term is used to describe the physical relationship between the therapist and patient, as the therapist guides the patient in the performance of certain movements, assists him in others and sometimes passively moves him. The contact involved gives the therapist an accurate feeling of the patient's responses to movement, which she must compare with normal responses. She feels when the patient must move against the resistance of his hypertonus, or when he has insufficient tone to maintain a position or to control a movement.

The technique of *placing and holding the limb** (Semans 1967) is useful in that it gives the therapist information about the patient's ability to maintain a position against gravity. If tone is too low to allow any antigravity control the technique cannot be used. Throughout the test procedure she takes note of two aspects of the patient's response in particular.

a) *The 'feeling' of the limb.*
The normal limb offers no resistance to this movement and seems to offer assistance in that the limb can be moved easily. It also adjusts smoothly to change in direction and to removal of the therapist's hand. If there is resistance to the movement, tone is probably increased. If the limb feels heavy there is probably hypotonus.

b) *The appearance of the limb.*
The therapist observes the patient's attempts at holding the limb in various positions. If it cannot be held in one position without shifting either upwards or downwards it may indicate a degree of ataxia or athetosis with some hypotonus. Inability to hold the position without the arm shifting downwards may indicate some degree of hypotonus in the limb. The presence of spasticity may result in adduction of the shoulder and inability to maintain the arm position without associated movements.

Passive movement of a limb in a patient with spasticity may give a sensation of initial resistance followed by a sudden letting go (the clasp-knife phenomenon). In a patient with rigidity, the sensation may be one of constant and relatively equal resistance throughout the entire range of movement (lead-pipe rigidity). If tremor is superimposed upon rigidity, there is a jerky resistance to passive movement (cog-wheel rigidity).

3. Observation of the Effect of Tonic Reflexes

Patients with central lesions interfering with the control of the higher

* Appendix 1

101

centres over the brain stem may demonstrate the release of tonic neck reflexes and the tonic labrinthine reflex.* The influence of these reflexes may be minor and only evident in the position in which they are most readily elicited, or by the stimulus with which they are most easily evoked. In some patients the influence of these reflexes may be major, and effective movement may be interfered with or prevented. It is not necessary to test these reflexes specifically. It is usually sufficient to note their presence as the patient moves about.

Other methods of assessing tone

Tonic vibration reflex is suggested to have diagnostic significance as an objective test of tone (Hagbarth and Eklund 1969 and Hagbarth 1973). If a vibrator is applied, for example, to the elbow flexors in a normal subject, he will, despite the stimulation to his flexors, be able to overcome the vibratory effect and actively extend his arm. A patient with hypertonus, however slight, will be unable to overcome the vibratory effect and will not be able to extend his arm. This is a simple method of establishing the presence of hypertonus in a patient in whom it is not otherwise obvious. Others, including Spira (1976), suggest that an electrically induced reflex, the H reflex, may prove to be an effective method of measuring spasticity objectively, since it may represent a true reflection of the excitability of alpha motoneurons. However, there are considerable difficulties in its use.

Attempts have been made to grade spasticity numerically (Stitchbury 1975 and Goff 1976) with the intention of using such grading for various purposes, including the evaluation of treatment effectiveness. The *electromyograph* provides a means of measuring tone more objectively (Basmajian 1976). Norton, Bomze, Sahrmann and Eliasson (1974) describe an objective measurement system to evaluate the relationship between spasticity and rate of passive movement.

Assessment of Movement and Function

In assessing the movements and functions of adults with brain damage the therapist is concerned with three main factors:

1. The components of a function which are missing or abnormal and the effect of this on performance.
2. The effectiveness of the postural background to function, that is, the body's reaction to gravity.
3. The effect upon function of abnormal tone, involuntary athetoid or

* Glossary

tremorous movements, ataxic inco-ordination of movement and sensory dysfunction.

The therapist assesses those functions which can be considered to be the most commonly used and which form our principal everyday activities. These include sitting to standing, standing to sitting, walking, walking up and down steps, rolling over from supine to sitting on the edge of a bed, lying down again, reaching out with one arm, and hand function.

It may be useful to consider some of the major components to be observed in an *analysis of walking*. Weight is shifted laterally and forward on to one leg. The head and trunk shift laterally in the opposite direction. Flexion of the moving leg is combined with extension at the weight-bearing hip. (Weight is actually shifted forward by the extension at this hip). The knee of the moving leg flexes a few degrees as the hip flexes and weight is shifted forward. The knee is relatively extended when the heel hits the ground but it remains 'mobile' as weight is taken on that leg. This allows balance to be maintained during the phase when one leg must bear all the weight.

How many of these activities the therapist assesses depends on a number of factors, which may include the patient's opinion of his problems, her own initial impression of the patient as she talks to him, and her findings as she observes certain activities which are difficult. How much movement the therapist can assess also depends on how much the patient can do. He may be unable to do any movement on request. In this case the therapist notes his spontaneous movements and the position of his limbs as she communicates with him.

Assessment of such functions as dressing and other domestic and work functions is usually carried out by the occupational therapist, who will be aided in this by the physiotherapist's assessment of specific movements, which are the background to these functions. Assessment of oro-facial function and eating is described in Chapter 15.

As the patient moves about the therapist looks proximally to note head and trunk movement, his body alignment and general symmetry, ability to transfer weight, and more distally for signs of involuntary movement such as tremor, athetosis or chorea, and of ataxic inco-ordination and the effect of these on movement. She also notes whether he demonstrates any obvious signs of sensory abnormalities such as disorders of body image or tactile defensiveness.

In this period of observation, she has to make judgements about

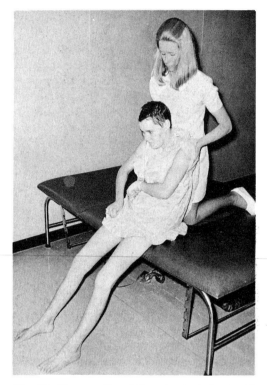

Fig. 39. *The rounding of the spine in sitting in this head-injured girl is secondary to her inability to flex her hips.*

which are the primary and which are the secondary problems. A patient (Fig. 39) may demonstrate a very obvious rounding of the spine when sitting. This, although it may be more obvious, is secondary to the inability to transfer weight forward by flexing the hips sufficiently in this position. Rounding of the spine in this case is compensating for the poor hip flexion.

As another example, a patient may mask his ataxia by holding himself stiffly (Fig. 91) and voluntarily limiting the amount of movement within his trunk, head and neck. It is obviously important for the therapist to establish whether the 'stiffness' of his movements is a primary or secondary problem. When she has judged that it is secondary to his problems of instability and poor balance, she will be able to plan a treatment programme which is appropriate.

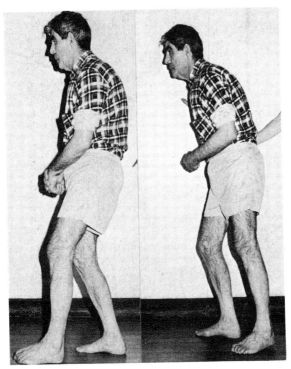

Fig. 40. *(a) This man with a left-sided spastic hemiplegia has difficulty stepping forward. Instead of flexing his hip he tilts his pelvis backward in order to take a step. He cannot extend his knees and the position of his pelvis makes it impossible for him to move his weight forwards by extending at his right hip.*
(b) He transfers weight to the right leg, bending forward over his right hip instead of extending it.

The therapist should understand normal movement and appreciate the basic components of which it is composed. She will then be able to see quickly which are the most significant abnormal components interfering with function and which are the most important missing components which are necessary for better function (Fig. 40). A brain-damaged adult who is not walking independently may not be doing so for a number of reasons. For example, an ataxic woman was found to be unable to stand alone. When she was stood up she showed a pronounced tendency to lean backward (Fig. 41).

105

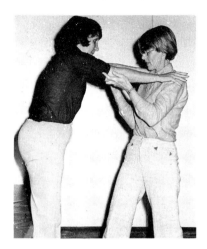

Fig. 41. *Elevation of the extended arms stimulates weight forward. It also prevents her from pulling down with her arms as she attempts to stand up.*

Whenever she was stood up by the ward staff she was always able to lean against the bed, or one of the staff would stand behind her to stop her from falling. In this way, backward leaning was actually encouraged and stimulated.

A treatment programme was commenced in which the therapist concentrated on encouraging normal body alignment. In standing the patient learnt how it felt to stand with her hips extended (Fig. 42). Treatment included the stimulation of balance using the technique of alternate tapping in standing and in walk standing with the body in normal alignment. All those who came in contact with her were instructed how to assist her to stand and walk, always helping her from in front and reminding her to extend her hips. The objective for the ward staff was never to let her lean backward. Three days later she was walking with minimal assistance, with her weight correctly aligned, indicating that the therapist's judgement of the major disability preventing her walking independently was correct. This example also illustrates the importance of the therapist sometimes concentrating on one particular and very specific problem.

It is important for the therapist to appreciate that a patient's failure to respond to treatment may be due to her inaccurate assessment of the problem. The result of treatment is, to a large extent, the result of assessment, and the therapist should go over assessment carefully if

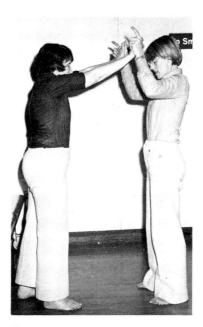

Fig. 42. *Further elevation stimulates extension of her hips and therefore more normal weight-bearing alignment.*

treatment is not effective, before she changes treatment or puts failure down to a poorly motivated patient.

Assessment of ataxia
Specific tests to indicate the presence of dysmetria or intention tremor include touching a finger to the nose, and a finger to the examiner's finger. Tapping of the thigh and alternate pronation and supination of the forearm will indicate if the patient has difficulty with the performance of rapid alternating movements. Signs of ataxia will be evident as the patient moves about and when his balance is tested (Fig. 93).

Hagbarth (1973) describes the use of vibration to elicit the presence of tremor and ataxic inco-ordination of movement when these are not obvious during the usual assessment. Stimulation of the tonic vibration reflex augments the effect of otherwise unobservable involuntary movements. Vibration in this case has diagnostic value.

Apart from these tests, the therapist will observe the quality of the

107

patient's movements, noting instability and in what part of the range of movement at a particular joint this instability is a problem.

Assessment of hand function

The assessment and improvement of domestic and vocational skills involving the hand is usually the province of the occupational therapist. However, it is essentially the physiotherapist's role to prepare the patient for such activities by ensuring that he has the background necessary for such skills (grasp and release in its many forms, control over objects of different size, weight and density).

Normal hand function is dependent upon such things as eye-hand contact and visual regard, stability and balance in sitting and standing, control over arm movement at the shoulder, elbow and wrist.

Hand function is assessed with the patient sitting at a table, on a chair which is of the appropriate height for him. He should be comfortable, distractions should be minimal, and his position should be as symmetrical as possible. The therapist notes the resting posture of his hands. The fingers are normally held in some flexion with the thumb opposed to the index finger.

Grasp and release. The patient is asked to pick up a number of objects of different sizes, shapes and weights and to put them down again. Accuracy of function, type of grasp and release and appropriateness of action are assessed.

Example: A patient following a mild stroke complained that he could not hold the steering wheel of his car without his grip slipping. On assessment he was found to be lacking control of grasp with the ulnar side of his hand. Further sensory assessment indicated that he also had some diminution in tactile awareness with this side of his hand. The result was that he did not automatically 'know' how firmly to grip the wheel through the various changes of position, and therefore his grasp was inappropriate to his needs.

Grasp is therefore observed through a range of activities which test radial and ulnar-side grasp, pincer grasp, whole hand grasp, lumbrical grasp, tripod grasp. Grasp is tested in relation to objects of different weight and density. Some patients have difficulty judging how firm their grasp should be. Earlier in this century, Head and Holmes (1911) described patients with difficulty appreciating compressibility. More recently Roland (1973) has described this inability to appreciate the force applied in a motor act as adynamaesthesia. It is a problem of hand function that otherwise is little described, yet it is very common.

Release is observed in relation to objects of different size. Many patients find it difficult to control. The spastic patient may only be

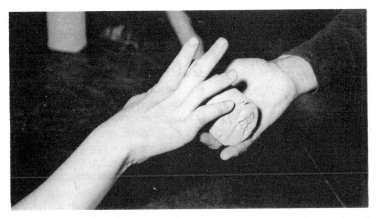

Fig. 43. *This girl with athetosis demonstrates an exaggerated extension of the fingers and thumb as she attempts to grasp an object. Note the flexion of the wrist.*

able to release with the wrist in flexion, a position which relaxes the tension in the finger flexors. The ataxic patient may show an exaggerated release because of difficulty controlling a fine range of movement. The athetoid patient demonstrates also a greatly exaggerated extension of the fingers as the hand approaches an object prior to grasping as well as on release (Fig. 43).

Patients with very minimal dysfunction who complain that they are clumsy frequently demonstrate grasping and releasing which is inappropriate to the object. This is sometimes combined with mild sensory disability of specific (e.g. tactile) or interpretive (e.g. stereognosis) type, or difficulty judging the compressibility of objects.

In testing grasp it is not sufficient to observe only one facet of its use. Pincer grasp, for example, may be adequate enough to enable the patient to pick up a pencil, but his inability to oppose the very tips of his thumb and index finger may only be evident when he is asked to pick up a pin. Similarly, he may demonstrate effective radial grasp using his thumb and index finger but be clumsy when applying this type of grasp to holding a pencil for writing. Whole hand grasp may be adequate for holding on to a towel in one position but inadequate if the towel is to be moved about.

The ability to hold an object through a range of arm movement should always be tested as well as the ability to hold the object with the arm stationary. Similarly, grasp and release should be assessed with the arm in different positions, including pronation and supination. Controlled movement may be possible if the hand is close to the body but impossible or difficult with the arm outstretched. Lack of control over the wrist in a radially deviated position or difficulty moving the wrist in the direction of radial deviation will interfere with fine control over grasp. Some patients have difficulty with grasp because it is not possible to maintain the thumb in the abducted position due to instability or lack of control over the carpo-metacarpal joint. These are reasons for hand dysfunction which can be easily overlooked.

The relationship between grasp and wrist position is important and should be noted. A patient who complains of mild disability may, because of an abnormal although imperceptible increase in tone, be unable to co-ordinate the appropriate amount of wrist extension with grasping of objects of certain sizes.

Tests for hand function described in the literature (Jebsen, Taylor, Trieschmann et al. 1969 and Taylor, Sand and Jebsen 1973) often tend to give information only about strength of grip. While it is no doubt true that the desire for objectivity in testing can be met by testing strength it is also true that maximum strength of grip is not the most important function of the hand, and is probably, for other than manual workers, one of the least important. Tests for hand function in brain-damaged patients which involve the testing of strength of grip take no account of the patient's ability to release which is just as important. The results of these tests performed on spastic patients in particular are bound to be misleading. A patient with spasticity of finger flexors may be able to grasp strongly, but with little or no ability to release. A positive result in this case does not indicate improvement but may indicate an increase in hypertonus. A better method of objective testing would be to time the patient's grasp and release of different objects.

Assessment of balance

Balance is influenced by a number of factors including emotional state, tone, body shape, size and weight, visual ability, and other factors such as supporting surface, age, joint integrity, pain and muscle strength. These innumerable variables make the accumulation of precise normative data a very difficult task.

The therapist gains important information about balance by watching the patient move about and whether he does in fact move at all. She notes whether he can move from one position to another, whether he can maintain a position against gravity. However, it is essential that his balance reactions are specifically analysed. For example, the therapist must know whether his head and trunk movement is appropriate when his weight is displaced (Fig. 44).

 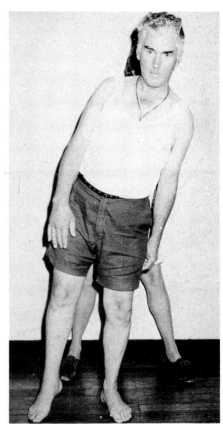

a   b

Fig. 44. *(a) Assessment of balance of a man with right-sided hemiplegia. Displacement of weight to the right shows lack of head and trunk lateral flexion. Note the excessive extension of the right knee.*
(b) Displacement of weight to the left shows lack of trunk lateral flexion and poor head lateral flexion.

Balance reactions are tested in sitting and standing. The head, trunk and limbs must all demonstrate the ability to move automatically in an appropriate way to restore the centre of gravity when the body weight is displaced and moved away from the midline (Figs. 27–29). Assessment of the patient's ability to adjust to shifting of weight *laterally* is particularly important (Shepherd 1979). It is necessary to note the presence of lateral flexion of the head and trunk (Fig.

111

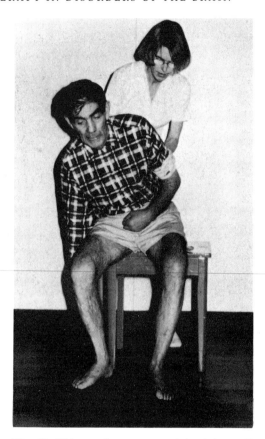

Fig. 45. *This man has very poor sitting balance. He has made himself more stable by spreading his legs apart because he has poor lateral flexion of the trunk. He is unable to regain his balance when his centre of gravity is disturbed.*

27). Trunk movement must be specifically analysed in terms of the patient's ability to depress the shoulder and elevate the pelvis as both of these are important components of the lateral flexion and one or other is commonly missing in brain-damaged patients (Fig. 45). Testing of the elderly must take into account their relative lack of trunk rotation and side flexion, otherwise this factor may be wrongly considered to be a problem resulting from the brain injury.

Protective extension of the arms is so much a part of balance reactions that they can be assessed to some extent together. The patient is tipped off balance forwards, backward and laterally against a wall (Fig. 46) in the standing position, or against the bed in sitting.

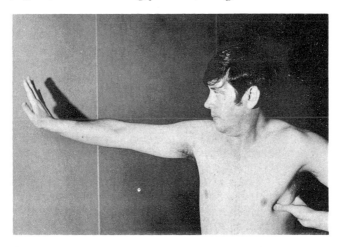

Fig. 46. *Assessment of protective reactions. This is also tested in a forward and backward direction.*

In assessment of balance reactions and protective extension of the arms it is also the automaticity and speed of response, its effectiveness, the excursion of movement and the time which elapses between the stimulus and the initiation of the response which are important.

Assessment of sensation

It must be emphasised that in testing sensation the therapist is testing the patient's perception of that sensation. This depends not only on the integrity of appropriate receptor organs, and of the peripheral and spinal cord pathways but also on the integrity of complex connections within the cerebral cortex. The patient's perception of a sensation is dependent upon his previous experiences. The perception of sensation is therefore very subjective and individual and we may all at times experience difficulty in communicating to others *exactly* what we feel, and sometimes we are not too clear whether what we feel is real or imagined.

Although much of the qualitative assessment of a brain-damaged patient is done informally, sensory testing is more formal and involves the patient in a situation in which he may feel himself on trial. The authors agree with Critchley (1953) when he cautions against an over-meticulous examination and suggests that the clinician avoids too many sessions devoted to sensory testing.

In order for the therapist to be sure of the accuracy of her assessment she must clearly explain and demonstrate each particular test to the patient, and establish with him the responses required. She must ask the appropriate question or give the necessary instruction clearly and briefly, making sure the patient can hear and understand. Where the tests require that the patient's eyes be closed, it is better to obstruct his vision with a card rather than to ask him to close his eyes voluntarily. Sensory testing will have to be modified for patients with verbal communication problems in order to avoid adding to the patient's frustrations. For example, in a test for stereognosis, if the patient is having difficulty naming the objects, he can be given a similar set of objects, so he can point to the one which corresponds with the one he is holding.

Pinprick, temperature and light touch. The function of the thalamus is to recognise these as crude sensations, but interpretation of the subtleties of discrimination and localisation is a higher cortical function. Light touch is probably the most important of these sensations to be tested in brain-damaged patients. It needs to be intact for the functions of two-point discrimination and stereognosis.

Pinprick is tested by touching the skin with a sharp pin.

Temperature is tested by using two test tubes, one filled with cold water and the other filled with hot water.

Light touch is tested by touching the skin with a piece of cotton wool. In each of these tests the speed of reaction should be noted as well as the ability to recognise the stimulus. All these tests are performed with the patient's vision obstructed. If the patient is hemiplegic, both sides of the body can be tested, giving the therapist a better idea of how he responds. The results of these tests can be recorded on a diagram.

During tests for light touch the therapist watches for signs of *tactile defensiveness*. This withdrawal on contact may also be noticed when the therapist touches the patient at other times during assessment or treatment. Although tactile defensiveness is usually only described in the literature in relation to children's problems, it may also be evident in adults following stroke or head injury. The therapist notes any other unusual reaction to touch. Patients with the so-called 'thalamic syndrome' may complain of severe pain on tactile stimulation.

Proprioception (kinaesthesia). Proprioception is the perception of the position of a joint and of movement of that joint. Joint position sense is tested in the thumb and fingers in the upper limb and at a larger joint such as the elbow or shoulder if the patient's response is poor, and in the great toe in the lower limb. The part is held in such a way as to minimise the number of tactile clues. The thumb, for example, is held at its lateral edges rather than antero-posteriorly. With the patient's vision obstructed, the thumb is moved into a position of flexion or extension, and the patient is asked whether he can feel the movement and whether the thumb is 'bent' or 'straight'. He should answer without hesitation.

The next three tests are tests for localisation and discrimination of stimuli.

Stereognosis. This term refers to the tactile recognition of common objects held in the hand, and to the recognition of different textures. Astereognosis or the inability to recognise common objects and differentiate textures could indicate central integrative dysfunction, but it will also be present where tactile sensation is absent or poor. Thus tactile sensation should always be tested prior to stereognosis.

The test is carried out in two parts. The subject is offered, with his vision obstructed, a selection of objects which he must name. They must be objects which are 'common' in that they would normally be easily recognised by him, for example, a key, coin, pen, ball. The object is placed in his hand and the patient can manipulate it although he must not use the other hand for assistance. An immediate attempt to do so indicates that the patient has a difficulty. If the patient is unable to manipulate the objects himself, the examiner can close his fingers over the object to allow him to feel its shape.

In the second part of the test, the subject is offered a selection of different textures which he could be expected to identify, for example, silk, velvet, emery paper. This test is carried out in a similar manner to the first part.

Two point discrimination. This refers to the ability to recognise two points applied simultaneously to the skin with vision obstructed. Normally this ability depends on the distance between the two points and this is crucial to the test. For example, normally two points can be recognised for any distance greater than 0·5 cm on the tips of the fingers, 1·5 to 2·0 cm on the palmar surface (Fig. 47), and approximately 6 to 7 cm on the trunk centrally above the shoulder blades. The distance between the two points is gradually increased to the point where they are perceived by the patient as two rather than as one. The test is most useful when applied to the hand, because this is one of the most sensitive parts of the body. It is performed by the examiner using a pair of calibrated dividers. The two points must be applied simultaneously and with as equal a pressure as possible.

Bilateral simultaneous tactile stimulation (sensory extinction). This

115

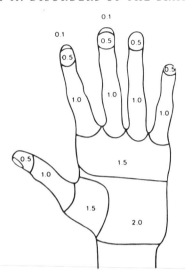

Fig. 47. *Average distance in cm at which two points can be recognised on the palmar surface of the hand with vision obstructed. (From Critchley, M. (1953)* The Parietal Lobes. *New York, Hafner.*

test enables the examiner to assess the presence of tactile inattention which causes the patient to be unaware of a part of the body and therefore fail to move it. The test for tactile localisation, which is the ability to localise the exact spot which has been touched by the examiner, should be performed first. It will not be present if light touch and pinprick recognition are absent. With the patient's vision obstructed, the examiner touches him lightly with the end of a pencil. The patient points to the spot touched. The test is then repeated on a corresponding site on the other side of his body. The examiner then touches corresponding sites on both sides of the body at the same time. *Tactile inattention* is present if the patient feels the touch when it is presented individually to each limb, but does not feel it on one side when both limbs are touched together. The patient with tactile inattention will not acknowledge the stimulus from the part of the body affected because the stimulus from the affected side of the body cannot compete with the stimulus from the unaffected side. This inattention applies not only to tactile stimuli but may also apply to vision and hearing.

Body schema*. Assessment of body schema is by observation of how the patient moves, how he dresses and from his conversation. The therapist notes, for example, whether he ignores one side of his body and space on that side. The patient may be asked to name body parts or point to body parts named by the examiner. The draw-a-man test demonstrates the patient's ability to express his concept of body schema. The psychological interpretation of this test is very specialised (Bach, Tracey and Huston 1971, Isaacs 1973). From the physiotherapist's point of view, it is interesting to note whether the patient omits part of the body. For example, a hemiplegic patient may draw a man with limbs only on one side (Fig. 48).

Fig. 48. *An example of a patient's drawing of his body in the early stages following stroke. Treatment will need to emphasise body parts, their relationship to each other and their position in space.*

Disorders of body schema are often present to some extent following brain lesions, particularly in the early stages. The therapist needs to anticipate and detect their presence, as they interfere with movement and give the impression of mental incompetence in the patient. The problems which arise may include denial of a hemiplegic limb (anosognosia*), finger agnosia (inability to recognise and name particular fingers), or unawareness of one side of the body (autotopagnosia*).

Difficulty with right-left discrimination should not be confused with unilateral neglect. It is tested by asking the patient to point to the left and right side of his body and of the examiner's body.

Motor praxis or motor planning. Assessment has been described for sensation and movement, and in this way the sensori-motor component of function can be evaluated. There is, however, the central mechanism of movement organisation which also needs to be considered in the assessment of brain-damaged patients. Movement requires a high degree of central organisation and it is not sufficient to have an intact peripheral sensory and motor system. This central organisation is called praxis*. Patients with defects in this organisation are said to have motor dyspraxia or apraxia, or difficulty with motor planning. They are unable to perform a task in the presence of adequate sensory and motor function, having understood the request.

An important part of the assessment of these problems consists of observation. The patient may appear clumsy, he may not be able to stand up when he is asked, although he may stand up to shake hands when the therapist enters the room. This indicates that automatic actions are possible but directed actions are not (*ideomotor apraxia*). He may lose his way when he is sent to another part of the department or ward (*lack of spatial organisation*). He may not be able to organise a sequence of movements (*ideational apraxia*) although he can do the different parts of the movement separately.

Some patients have difficulty with the interpretation of visual clues and their spatial organisation (*constructional apraxia*). With this difficulty a patient may demonstrate problems in dressing, putting his shirt on upside down or back to front. Constructional apraxia makes it difficult not only to dress but also to carry out organisational tasks such as setting a table for dinner. Frostig (1966) has described tests for constructional praxis. The therapist can perform two simple tests using a form board and a posting box.

The patient who, in the absence of aphasia, demonstrates difficulty writing, is said to have dysgraphia, in that he cannot organise the

* Glossary

118

individual elements of letters or words spatially or in sequence. This can be assessed by asking him to write his name and address, to copy letters and shapes.

Visual function. Visual impairment in the brain-damaged may result from lesions involving the eyes (reception), the optic radiation (transmission), or the visual cortex (appreciation). Damage to other areas of the cortex may interfere with visuo-spatial recognition. Visual disturbances are therefore extremely complex. Furthermore, they may be superimposed upon previously existing ocular disorders, especially in older patients. This latter point should be kept in mind as the patient may usually wear glasses. Visual function therefore may require the combined assessment of neurologist, speech pathologist, orthoptist, and ophthalmologist. This combined assessment will give the physiotherapist information about the presence of visual field defects, such as homonymous hemianopia, visual inattention, poor visual acuity, motor apraxia (involving eye movements), and visuo-spatial problems, such as agnosia for shapes, forms, numbers, faces, poor figure-ground perception, and problems with position in space.

It may be necessary for the physiotherapist to carry out simple tests herself for gross visual field defects and visual inattention.

Visual field defects. The examiner sits in front of the patient and asks him to look straight ahead at the examiner's nose. She covers the patient's right eye and moves her finger from behind the patient on his left side asking him to indicate when the finger enters his field of vision. The test is repeated to the other eye. Vision may be defective in a particular spot (scotoma)* in a particular part of the visual field, or in the same part of both visual fields (homonymous hemianopia).

Visual inattention. This is tested by presenting the patient with bilateral simultaneous visual stimuli. The examiner covers one eye at a time and asks the patient to indicate when he sees the examiner's finger. Once it is established that his vision is intact in this particular respect, two stimuli are then presented to the patient bilaterally and at the same time. If he only perceives one stimulus he is said to have visual inattention or extinction.

It is important that the presence of sensory disability is not used as indicative of poor prognosis in terms of the recovery of movement, rather than as a guide to treatment. Without doubt sensory dysfunction makes the relearning of motor skills difficult, but sensation and perceptual functions can be improved. Sensory awareness can be stimulated in very specific ways, but it is also stimulated by treatment

* Glossary

that gives the patient experience of movement and encourages him to concentrate on his sensory feedback.

Intellectual function (long and short term memory, abstract reasoning, orientation in time and place) may need to be assessed by a psychologist trained in intellectual assessment of the brain-damaged. Adams (1974) describes some tests which can easily be carried out by the clinician.

Assessment as a guide to progress

Assessment as a guide to *prognosis* has been discussed by many authors, including Marquardsen (1969) and Adams (1974), but, as we have seen, there are as yet no reliable tests. However, assessment of the patient's performance does provide the therapist with information about his *progress*. While he continues to improve his treatment sessions continue.

Once his progress reaches a plateau, the therapist must consider whether this is because no further improvement can be expected, or whether it indicates the need for a revision of treatment goals. This may be the time to call in a skilled colleague and to attempt to obtain a fresh view of the reasons for the patient's difficulties. If, however, it appears that no more progress seems likely at the moment, the patient may be discharged from treatment with a follow-up appointment in a month or three months.

Some general points about assessment

Adult patients whose movements are being assessed need to be appropriately dressed to enable the therapist to see details of movement without embarrassment to the patient. Assessment is carried out at the time most suitable to the patient, not when he is tired or under heavy sedation. The drugs taken by the patient should be considered by the therapist when she assesses his performance, otherwise she will obtain an unrealistic or false impression of his disability. Diazepam and other muscle relaxants, for example, affect tone, and therefore may result in an unrealistic picture of the real degree of hypertonus. They also slow down the patient's responses and give an incorrect impression of his ability to participate. Sedatives and hypnotics may also prevent him from concentrating and may result in his appearing incompetent or disorientated.

The therapist notes the patient's general appearance and more specific points, such as the condition of his skin, his respiratory function, his vital signs and any other physical signs which are relevant. She also notes whether he wears glasses, has a hearing problem or wears a hearing aid.

120

Although treatment and some forms of assessment are frequently carried out in a large room with other people present, specific forms of assessment which require more concentration should be carried out in a less distracting environment.

Perhaps one of the most important aspects of assessment, and the one which is sometimes overlooked, is the patient's own role in the assessment of his problems. This can be described in two ways. A patient with insight into his difficulties may be able to describe what *he* feels to be the major reason for a particular disability more accurately than the therapist, who should give the patient opportunity and encouragement to make this contribution. He may even devise tests for the assessment of his own capabilities. Samuel Johnson, for example, is reported to have tested his mental abilities (his 'reason') following a stroke by composing a prayer in Latin.

Relatives also will add considerably to the therapist's understanding of the patient by giving information about his previous 'drive', his adaptability and his mobility. They can indicate the amount of support to be expected from the community and give insight into the patient's confidence in his ability to lead a meaningful life when he leaves hospital (Suchett-Kaye, Sarkar, Elkan and Waring (1971). Information about such personality and social factors are important because they influence the patient's recovery following, for example, stroke or head injury (Ben-Yishay, Diller, Gerstman and Haas 1968).

Testing of muscle strength has little significance and may be misleading and inaccurate in the assessment of patients with brain damage. It is important to consider that these patients suffer from lack of central control over movement and not actual muscle weakness. Testing of muscle strength therefore gives no information which is useful for planning treatment or assessing progress.

Measurement of joint range similarly is of little significance. In patients with spasticity, for example, joint range measurement will not distinguish between limitation of movement caused by hypertonus and that caused by soft tissue contracture, and it is the latter that goniometry was designed to measure.

Assessment of the elderly
Chronological age is not necessarily a useful guide to the functional capabilities of aged adults, since the abilities of different individuals are extremely varied. The rate of aging varies with individuals and in different organs in the same individuals, so chronological and biological age are not synonymous. Peck (1968) and others have emphasised the need to use developmental rather than age criteria in looking at older adults.

If assessment of elderly people is to be accurate in terms of their real disability and effective in terms of a treatment plan, the therapist has to give careful thought to her own views about this age group. Errors are made through making inaccurate judgements or by having low expectations. An apathetic response to a suggested activity can be judged as due to the 'predictable' behaviour of the aged, and the fact that it may be due to poor nutrition or lack of motivation may be missed.

Similarly, there is always a risk that a problem may be attributed to old age when it is in fact a manifestation of a pathological state which is amenable to treatment. Adams (1974) describes an elderly patient who could not walk independently. When asked why not he replied that he could not see. He had bilateral cataracts which were subsequently successfully removed enabling him to walk.

The therapist should avoid judgemental statements to the effect that 'this man is *unco-operative* in assessment' or 'he is not *motivated* to get better' or 'he *will not do* what I ask' or 'he *cannot do* what I ask'. Vague allusions to motivation, lack of co-operation or apraxia give a false impression of the patient's problems, ensure that his reputation is ruined, and more important, prevents a thorough search for the reason for the problem.

Assessment of the elderly must take into account the problems of aging or arthritic joints, relatively diminished trunk movement, particularly in side flexion and rotation, the possibility of diminished sight and hearing, the tendency of some to deny the existence of pain and of others to over-react to it. The therapist needs to be sensitive to the old person's fear of being thought 'senile' or 'mad', which may cause him to hide his feeling that a hemiplegic limb does not belong to him. He should be encouraged to talk about these strange feelings and be made aware that the therapist understands them. The elderly need emotional support in an evaluation situation as they are frequently insecure and susceptible to stress at this time.

SUMMARY

Methods of assessing tone, balance, sensation and movement are outlined in this chapter. The close relationship between assessment and treatment is emphasised. The physiotherapist's assessment is both qualitative and quantitative and requires observational and judgemental skills and an understanding of the components of normal movement for comparative purposes.

References

Adams, G. F. (1974) *Cerebrovascular Disability and the Ageing Brain.* London, Churchill-Livingstone.

Aptekar, R. G., Ford, F. and Blech, E. E. (1976) Light patterns as a means of assessing and recording gait. Part 1. *Develop. Med. Child Neurol.,* **18,** 31–36.

Atwater, A. E. (1973) Cinematographic analysis of human movement. In *Exercise and Sport Sciences Reviews* 1, edited by J. H. Wilmore. New York, Academic Press.

Bach, P., Tracey, H. W. and Huston, J. (1971) The use of the self-portrait method in the evaluation of hemiplegic patients. *Southern Med. J.,* **64,** 12, 1475–1480.

Basmajian, J. V. (1974) *Muscles Alive. Their Function Revealed by Electromyography.* 3rd edition. Baltimore, Williams and Wilkins.

Basmajian, J. V. (1976) Electromyographic investigation of spasticity and muscle spasm. *Physiotherapy,* **62,** 10, 319–323.

Battye, C. K. and Joseph, J. (1966) An investigation by telemetry of the activity of some muscles in walking. *Med. & Biolog. Engineering,* **4,** 125.

Ben-Yishay, Y., Diller, L., Gerstman, L. J. and Haas, A. (1968) The relationship of impersistence, intellectual function, and outcome of rehabilitation in patients with left hemiplegia. *Neurol,* **18,** 852–861.

Bernstein, N. (1967) *The Co-ordination and Regulation of Movements.* Oxford, Pergamon.

Bobath, K. (1966) *The Motor Deficit in Patients with Cerebral Palsy.* London, Heinemann.

Critchley, M. (1953) *The Parietal Lobes.* New York, Hafner.

Frostig, M. (1966) *The Developmental Program in Visual Perception.* Chicago, Follett Educational Corp.

Goff, B. (1976) Grading of spasticity and its effect on voluntary movement. *Physiotherapy,* **62,** 11, 358–361.

Hagbarth, K. E. (1973) The effect of muscle vibration in normal man and in patients with motor disorders. In *New Development in Electromyography and Clinical Neurophysiology,* edited by J. Desmedt. Basel, Karger.

Hagbarth, K. E. and Eklund, G. E. (1969) The muscle vibrator – a useful tool in neurological therapeutic work. *Scand. J. Rehab. Med.,* **1,** 26–34.

Head, H. and Holmes, G. (1911) Sensory disturbances from cerebral lesions. *Brain,* **34,** 102–254.

Holt, K. S., Jones, R. B. and Wilson, R. (1974) Gait analysis by means of a multiple sequential exposure camera. *Develop. Med. Child Neurol.*, **16**, 742–745.

Isaacs, B. (1973) When a stroke patient draws a picture: a clue to disability. *J. of Geriatrics*, August, 37–41.

Jebson, R. H., Taylor, N., Trieschmann, R. B. *et al.* (1969) Objective and standardised test of hand function. *Arch. Phys. Med. Rehabil.*, **50**, 311–319.

Joseph, J. and Watson, R. (1967) Telemetric electromyography of muscles used in walking up and down stairs. *J. Bone Jt. Surg.*, **49B**, 774.

Marquardsen, J. (1969) The natural history of acute cerebrovascular disease. *Acta Neurol. Scand.*, **45**, Suppl. 38.

Nelson, A. J. (1976) Analysis of movement through utilisation of clinical instrumentation. *Physiotherapy*, **62**, 4, 123–124.

Norton, B. J., Bomze, H. A., Sahrmann, S. A. and Eliasson, S. G. (1974) Objective documentation of the relationship between spasticity and rate of passive movement. *Proceed. W.C.P.T.*, 416–422.

Peck, R. C. (1968) Psychological developments in the second half of life. In *Middle Age and Aging*, edited by B.L. Neugarten. Chicago, University of Chicago Press.

Roland, P. E. (1973) Lack of appreciation of compressibility. *J. Neurol. Science*, **20**, 51–61.

Semans, S. (1967) The Bobath concept in treatment of neurological disorders. *Amer. J. Phys. Med.*, **46**, 1, 732–785.

Shepherd, R. B. (1979) Some factors influencing the outcome of stroke rehabilitation. *Aust. J. Physiother.* **25**, 4, 173.

Spence, J. C. (1953) Methodology of clinical science. *Lancet*, **2**, 629.

Spira, R. (1976) Contributions of the H reflex to the study of spasticity in adolescents. *Physiotherapy*, **6**, 12, 401–405.

Stitchbury, J. C. (1975) Assessment of disability following severe head injury. *Physiotherapy*, **61**, 9, 268–272.

Suchett-Kaye, A. I., Sarkar, U., Elkan, G. and Waring, M. (1971) Physical, mental and social assessment of elderly patients suffering from cerebrovascular accident with special reference to rehabilitation. *Geront. Clin.*, **13**, 192–206.

Taylor, N., Sand, P. L. and Jebsen, R. H. (1973) Evaluation of hand function in children. *Arch. Phys. Med. Rehabil.*, **54**, 129–135.

Further Reading

Graham, O. (1975) Closed circuit television in assessment of disability following severe head injury. *Physiotherapy*, **61**, 9, 272–274.

Graybiel, A. and Fregley, A. R. (1966) A new quantitative ataxia test battery. *Acta Otolaryn. (Stockholm)*, **61**, 292.

Neuhauser, G. (1975) Methods of assessing and recording motor skills and movement patterns. *Develop. Med. Child Neurol.*, **17**, 369–386.

Section II

5 *STROKE*

6 *HEAD INJURY*

7 *PARKINSONISM*

8 *MULTIPLE SCLEROSIS*

9 *TUMOURS*

10 *INFECTIONS*

Chapter 5

Stroke

Cerebrovascular accident or 'stroke' is a term describing the sudden onset of neurological signs and symptoms due to a disturbance of the blood supply to the brain, including the brain stem, and resulting in temporary or permanent loss of function. The patient experiences a loss of motor function commonly on one side of his body (hemiplegia), and this may be accompanied by complete or partial loss of speech, disorders of oro-facial function, disorders of sensation and perception, and emotional disturbances. The neurological signs and problems of function depend on the extent and site of the brain damage and on the underlying condition of the brain.

Adams (1974) observes that the word 'stroke' refers to the rapidity of onset of signs and symptoms and not to the underlying cause. Cerebrovascular disease is the term used to describe the underlying factor in stroke, but it must be stressed that this is only the cerebral manifestation of what is usually a more general vascular disease which may include hypertension, arteriosclerosis, disease of the heart and great vessels, and variations in systemic blood pressure. The neurological signs and symptoms occur secondarily, because of the sensitivity and vulnerability of the brain to metabolic deprivation. The effect on the cerebral tissue depends on the degree and rapidity of the pathological process, the degree of obstruction, or the extent of the haemorrhage, the availability of collateral circulation, and the body's ability to regulate and maintain a consistency of blood flow to all areas of the brain. Subsequent damage may result from secondary extracellular oedema and swelling of the glial cells, causing further ischaemia.

The World Health Organisation's International Classification of Diseases (1971) lists a number of conditions under the heading 'cerebrovascular disease'.

Subarachnoid haemorrhage
Cerebral haemorrhage
Occlusion of pre-cerebral arteries
Cerebral thrombosis

Cerebral embolism
Transient cerebral ischaemia
Acute but ill-defined cerebrovascular disease
Generalised ischaemic cerebrovascular disease
Other and ill-defined cerebrovascular disease

Cerebrovascular accidents are most commonly seen in people over sixty years, but are seen with increasing frequency in younger age groups. They may be seen in children and young adults secondary to leukaemia, acute rheumatic fever, oestrogen-progestin therapy, congenital heart disease, mitral valve insufficiency, acute hypertension and congenital aneurysm or artery malformation.

Cerebral circulation
The cerebral circulation exists to supply oxygen and glucose to the brain and to remove carbon dioxide. It depends on the patency of the blood vessels, an effective collateral circulation, systemic blood pressure, a healthy heart, peripheral resistance, and normal blood composition. The blood is taken to the brain from the heart by four major blood vessels, the carotid and vertebral arteries (Fig. 14). They branch intracranially to form the main arteries (Fig. 15) which supply the specific areas of the brain. These vessels anastomose freely before entering the cerebral tissue, which explains why one or two vessels may be stenosed or occluded while the blood supply to the brain remains adequate.

Pathophysiology
Disturbance to the circulation of the brain may be caused by *stenosis*, *occlusion* of vessels, or by *rupture* of an artery. The most common underlying factor causing impaired circulation to the brain, arterial insufficiency or obstruction, is *atheroma* or fatty degeneration of the arterial walls. Circulation may also be impaired as a result of trauma, congenital malformation, inflammation of the vessels, or by a mechanical factor, such as pressure on vessels brought on by sudden rotation and extension of the head in the presence of degenerative changes in the cervical spine.

Aetiological factors causing atheroma are thought to be age (men over 45 years, and women over 55 years), a positive family history, excessive eating, drinking and smoking, raised blood levels of sugar, uric acid and lipids. The relationship between hypertension and atheroma is controversial (Adams 1974) and may be a more important factor in youth than in middle age (McKeown 1965) and in patients with ischaemic heart disease and diabetes mellitis.

The arterial supply may be impaired by *occlusion* caused by a dislodged atheromatous plaque, by thrombosis which may build up at an area of atheroma, by embolus, or by micro-emboli. The heart is the commonest source of emboli to the brain but they may also arise from lesions in the great arteries. If the embolus blocks a major artery, death may occur suddenly. Micro-emboli may repeatedly arise from a thrombus in a major vessel.

In *severe generalised cerebrovascular disease* a fall in blood pressure, or an alteration in the composition of the blood may result in neurological signs and symptoms. A fall in blood pressure may be caused by changes in posture, oversedation, haemorrhage or cardiac infarction. The composition of the blood may be altered in chronic respiratory disease, malnutrition and anaemia.

When hypertension and atheroma co-exist, hypertension probably assumes the dominant role in the cause of stroke, and may result in *cerebral haemorrhage*. The mechanism is uncertain but it is possible that micro-aneurysms in small arteries become weakened and bleeding occurs. There is a rapid outpouring of blood, which may become encapsulated and damage the surrounding brain tissue. It frequently enters the ventricular system. If the bleeding is considerable the patient may die immediately. The most common site of haemorrhage is in the internal capsule (Fig. 9), where the descending efferent fibres from the cerebral cortex and ascending sensory fibres of the thalamic radiation which pass from the thalamus to the cortex, are bunched together. The haemorrhage will damage or destroy some of these fibres. The next most common sites are in the thalamus, the parietal white matter and the putamen, followed by the cerebellum, then the pons. The effect of a haemorrhage in this latter site may cause such damage to vital structures that death may occur.

Following massive intracerebral haemorrhage, the surrounding brain tissue is compressed by the haematoma, and may be oedematous which causes distortion and shifting of the midline structures which may result in tentorial herniation.* Distortion of the blood vessels causes venous congestion and results in decreased blood to the brain and reticular system and, therefore, a further reduction of oxygen to the brain.

A subarachnoid haemorrhage, or a leaking of blood into the subarachnoid space, may be caused by a rupture of a cerebral aneurysm or angioma, or may be secondary to haemorrhage within the brain. Bleeding from an aneurysm or angioma is likely to re-occur. Treatment of haemorrhage from these two causes involves

* Glossary

bed rest and in some cases, surgical removal. Thirty per cent of patients with haemorrhage due to aneurysm die before reaching hospital.

A *subdural haemorrhage* may be chronic or acute. Blood may slowly exude from the subdural veins which are particularly fragile in elderly people. This extravasation may be associated with trauma which may only be very slight, or it may be associated with such conditions as alcoholism or liver disease. The lesion is superficial, and the neurological features are due to pressure on the brain from the subdural space. Aspiration of the resulting haematoma, through burr holes, is usually followed by a good recovery if diagnosis is quick and accurate.

The term *transient ischaemic attack* describes the occurrence of sudden, unpredictable, short-lived episodes of focal neurological deficit followed by recovery. These episodes result from carotid or vertebrobasilar artery insufficiency most commonly caused by atherosclerosis. They may also be caused by arterial abnormalities, or may result from sudden rotation and extension of the head in the presence of degenerative changes in the cervical spine, a fall in systemic blood pressure or a detached micro-embolus. Focal symptoms may include paraesthesia, dysphasia, dizziness or a feeling of 'weakness' in a limb or limbs. Some patients go on to suffer a major episode but some attacks cease due to increased collateral circulation. Adams (1974) suggests that the term 'reversible ischaemic neurological deficit' should be introduced to describe disturbances which last for more than twenty-four hours and sometimes up to three days followed by complete disappearance of the signs and symptoms of neurological deficit.

PROBLEMS FOLLOWING STROKE

The common problems seen in patients with hemiplegia following stroke are anxiety and fear, abnormalities of tone and of movement, disorders of sensation and its perception, disorders of communication and of oro-facial function, as well as behavioural changes and incontinence of bladder and bowel. The patient's entire functioning is therefore disturbed. He survives his stroke with problems which result from the lesion within his brain. The eventual outcome, however, will also to a large extent depend upon the attitude of the people with whom he comes in contact immediately following his stroke, how they view his problems, the quality of the treatment he receives, his personality and the support of his family and friends.

The problems which may be seen in patients following stroke vary from patient to patient. Some of the commonest are discussed below.

Tone

Immediately following stroke, tone is usually hypotonic but this is frequently a transient stage, and abnormal patterns of spasticity eventually develop to some degree. Hypotonus in the early stages frequently masks the onset of spasticity, and this can be demonstrated by a degree of hyperreflexia plus associated movements which are elicited by effort. The degree to which spasticity develops appears in the authors' opinion to be closely related to the type of treatment the patient receives, particularly to the amount of effort he is expected to use (see Chapter 12).

There may be some evidence of abnormal tonic reflex activity, such as release of the tonic labyrinthine reflex and asymmetrical tonic neck reflex but these are rarely severe enough to present the problem they do in other brain-damaged patients.

Sensori-motor Function

Problems of *movement and function* include an abnormal alignment of the body parts with asymmetrical posture and movement, an inability to shift weight and to move from one position to another, a loss of the normal postural background to movement, which results in an inability to adjust to alterations in the centre of gravity, and loss of the specific movement components of particular functions. These problems are further aggravated by the absence of any stimulus to move, by reduction in sensory input which results from his lack of movement as well as his sensory abnormalities, and by the loss of the memory of particular movements.

There may be partial or complete loss of particular *sensations and their perception,* in other words a failure of sensory impulses to reach the relevant areas of the brain from the various sense organs of skin, joints, muscles, ears, eyes and mouth. Light touch, pin prick, and temperature are usually recognisable, although the qualitative element may be only crudely appreciated. Lesions of the brain stem may result in hemianaesthesia and/or hemianalgesia on the contralateral or ipsilateral side depending on the site of the lesion. Subthalamic lesions sometimes result in spontaneous pain down the opposite side of the body. This thalamic syndrome results in considerable discomfort from touch stimuli to the skin and this discomfort usually causes some degree of depression.

Joint position and movement sense may be affected. *Joint position sense* is the recognition of movement, an awareness of its direction and of position in space. It is possible for a patient to recognise movement but be unable to recognise position and direction. These defects are more obvious distally than proximally. Loss of this sensation may have a devastating effect on the patient who may be unable to describe satisfactorily how it feels and how it affects him. Hodgins (1966) comments that despite this difficulty, members of the health professions assume that they can objectively understand and describe what the patient subjectively cannot. This may add to the patient's confusion and frustration, as Hodgins has illustrated for us with comments on his own problems following stroke.

Sensory functions which involve localisation and discrimination of stimuli such as stereognosis, two point discrimination and the ability to recognise bilateral simultaneous stimuli, may also be affected. These sensory functions are essential to effective use of the limbs.

Stereognosis is tactile identification of common objects and its absence is called astereognosis. It involves the recognition of the physical properties including texture as well as the nature of the object. Normally touch and vision both provide this information. Stereognosis requires a normal threshold for touch in the palm of the hand. It is not an inate ability but grows and develops through appropriate experience and can develop to great heights in musicians and in the blind or can be almost absent in the hand of the congenitally hemiplegic person. The recognition of objects is normally almost spontaneous in the adult.

Two point discrimination is the ability to recognise two points when simultaneously applied with vision occluded. When the two points are at a particular distance from each other, and this depends on the part of the body touched, the two points are felt as one. The most sensitive areas in the body are the lips, tongue, fingers and thumb.

Patients who disregard one stimulus over another if applied bilaterally and simultaneously are said to suffer *tactile inattention*. This disability causes the patient to be unaware of stimulation on his affected side, when this stimulus has to compete with a stimulus to the sound side. He is therefore unlikely to move the affected limbs. The ability to recognise both stimuli requires normal tactile localisation, that is, the patient has to be able to localise one spot when it is touched.

Perceptual problems, which are more complex than the recognition of individual sensations, may include disorders of right-left discrimination, *disorders of body image or body schema*. There are a number of manifestations of the latter. Critchley (1953), for example, tabulates nine types of disorder, pointing out that they are not clearly circums-cribed but fuse into one another. His list includes unilateral neglect, lack of concern over the existence of hemiplegia, denial of hemiplegia with delusions (anosognosia*), and loss of awareness of one body half (autotopagnosia*), which the patient may or may not be able to move. These are variously described as agnosias*. Agnosia may also develop as a secondary complication in patients whose immediate care lacks stimulation of bilateral symmetrical movement.

Although the patient may have adequate comprehension and sensory and motor function, he may demonstrate difficulty in per-forming a willed purposeful movement. This is called by the terms apraxia*, dyspraxia, or difficulty in motor planning. Apraxia may involve any movement. It is commonly seen in the lips and tongue. For example, a patient, asked to lick his lips, is unable to do so. However, a few minutes later he can be observed to lick them spontaneously while eating. Apraxia is usually associated with an inability to imitate movements.

Ideational apraxia is characterised by extreme absentmindedness and lack of purpose in various actions. For example, the patient may light a match and burn his fingers instead of lighting his cigarette. He can do the different parts of the action, pick up the match box, take out a match and strike it, but when he is asked to light the cigarette, he is unable to do so, or he will do something inappropriate, such as striking the cigarette on the matchbox.

Ideomotor apraxia is the inability to execute ideas. The patient may understand the purpose of an object but be unable to use it. For example, he may attempt to dress by putting his arm through the trouser leg.

Some patients demonstrate a particular disability when attempting to walk which persists beyond the early stages. This may be due to apraxia. The patient appears to have no idea about the movements required. He attempts to lift one foot without transferring weight on to the other one. He may move one foot forward and the other foot back. He may take little steps forward while leaving his weight backward. These problems may be very bizarre, and unfortunately it is easy for them to be thought of as a demonstration of senility or intellectual deterioration.

Some patients demonstrate what is called *constructional apraxia*, which has to do with the translation of an object from one spatial dimension into another. The defect is in poor conceptualisation of the spatial requirements of certain activities. For example, when the

* Glossary

patient attempts to write there is crowding and obliquity of the words. He will have difficulty with arithmetic, difficulty telling the time and orientating himself in space. He may complain of difficulty in sewing or in constructing a model.

In considering the *visual defects* following stroke it is necessary to distinguish between the patient's ability to see an object within his visual field and his visual perception of stimuli within the environment. The latter involves the recognition, discrimination and use of these stimuli. The hemiplegic patient may suffer one or both of these disabilities.

Patients with visual field defects are unable to see objects which lie within a particular part of the visual field which is that area we can see in front and to both sides of us while looking straight ahead. The patient does not always appreciate this loss in vision and therefore does not compensate by moving his head unless he is instructed to do so. Some patients rationalise the disability, suggesting their glasses need changing or the light is not good enough. This defect interferes with function considerably until the patient learns to compensate, and it causes spatial problems which will result, for example, in his bumping into doorways or missing utensils on his dinner tray. He will also have difficulty reading and writing across one line and back to the next. The words hemianopia or hemianopsia are used to describe the loss of half the visual field. *Homonymous hemianopia* describes the loss of half the field of vision on the same side of each eye, which means that objects are cut vertically.

A patient with *visual inattention* or visual field neglect will ignore visual stimulus on one side when simultaneous stimuli are applied to both sides in the presence of intact visual fields. Clinically the therapist will note that the patient pays inconsistent attention to the involved side.

Some patients have difficulty with *figure-ground perception* and are unable to distinguish a particular object from its background. This has a particular effect upon hand function and upon vision in general. A similar problem of discrimination may also be found in auditory perception. In this case the patient has difficulty distinguishing particular sounds from the background noise. The patient may appear to be deaf, lacking in comprehension or in concentration.

Visual perceptual problems may also include distortion of the perception of horizontal and vertical planes, and difficulty appreciating the three dimensional nature of objects. The patient may suffer from spatial disorientation. This may include a number of problems with regard to perception of space, the use of space and the concept of space. Other problems of vision and disordered body image will also cause problems with spatial perception and conception of space. The patient will have difficulty finding his way about, discriminating numerical symbols, telling the time, pointing to parts of his body or an object in space, difficulty visualising a mental picture of familiar people and things, and in understanding the meaning of up/down, in/out, front/back, and difficulty with certain tasks such as dressing.

There is a close relationship between sensations from both internal and external sources, memory and intellectual ability. Although they are always described separately, they cannot be isolated as they function together, enabling us to relate ourselves appropriately to our environment. Cognition and the ability to move result from their integration and both thought and movement are combined in communication.

There will also be a reduction in the amount and variety of sensory information and input, as well as abnormal sensory feedback which relays the sensations of the excessive amount of effort required to move, of abnormal body alignment and of asymmetrical movement. If this situation is allowed to persist secondary problems of perception will arise.

Communication

Patients following stroke frequently suffer some degree of communication problems, dysarthria, aphasia, loss of facial expression and gesture. *Aphasia* may be expressive or comprehensive, or, particularly in the early stages, both. To describe aphasia in such a way is to simplify loss a very complex function, which normally involves the use of symbols, reading and writing, memory and inner language. The patient will be unable to ask what is the matter with him or express his fears and despair. He may not be able to understand what is being said to him or he may be unable to appreciate that what he is trying to say is unintelligable to others. His attempts at communication so often result in frustration that he may quickly give up trying, which will further increase his social withdrawal. His frustration and despair is made worse if people talk over his head and do not include him in the conversation.

Apoplexy, as Hippocrates first described stroke, is the Greek word for 'strike down'. It is a very frightening experience for the patient and his relatives, and is naturally accompanied by feelings of frustration, despair, hopelessness, depression, anger, aggression, fear of the future and fear of eventual dependency on others. The patient in the early stages may be emotionally labile. This emotional incontinence (Fisher 1968) will result in outbursts of crying which are provoked by the slightest stimulus. The patient's emotional state will be even more precarious if he is also aphasic. Policoff (1970) points out that depression combined with speech disorders and emotional lability may simulate senile intellectual deterioration even when it does not exist.

Dementia, when it occurs, is a barrier to functional recovery and implies diffuse neuronal loss. Hurwitz and Adams (1972) point out that no single test reliably indicates its presence or absence, and suggest that the presence of 'an alert glint in the eye' may be the only means of assuming its absence.

Respiratory Function
In the very early stages following stroke, the patient may suffer some degree of respiratory dysfunction with poor lung expansion and risk of atelectasis and pneumonia. Poor lung expansion results from hypotonus and his relative immobility and will be aggravated by lying in the supine position. This position also encourages aspiration of fluids such as saliva and food. The patient may have only a weak cough and the threshold to stimulus may be high. Older patients have diminished expansion of the rib cage and this further aggravates the problem (Fig. 49).

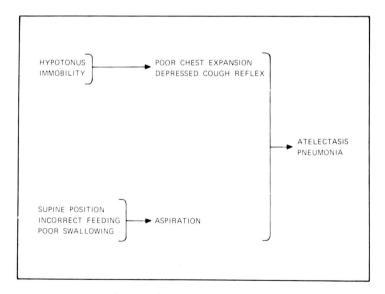

Fig. 49. *The predisposing factors in atelectasis and pneumonia.*

Oro-facial Function

Initially patients following a stroke may find it difficult to eat because of facial asymmetry, poor head position and oral dysfunction. Unilateral hypotonus around the face and mouth results in poor lip and jaw closure, and by involving the buccinator allows food to gather between cheek and gums. Tongue movements are ineffective or imprecise if the tongue itself is hypotonic, relatively immobile and too far forward in the mouth. Poor lip closure, ineffective tongue movement and sensory disturbances which diminish the patient's awareness of what is in his mouth result in poor swallowing, drooling and the risk of aspiration. This risk will be greater if the gag reflex is depressed.

Eating and vocalising are further complicated by poor co-ordination between respiration and oral function. Poor sensory awareness in the mouth may make it difficult to keep false teeth in position, which is where they must be if the patient is to re-establish proper eating and communication.

Nutrition

Oral dysfunction will initially cause an alteration in the patient's eating habits and diet. This, plus the staff's inability to understand or treat the underlying oral dysfunction, may result in poor nutrition.

The patient's nutritional status should be investigated if he is lethargic. He may have been under-nourished prior to his stroke.

Bowel and Bladder Function

Incontinence may be present in the early stage and in patients who are unconscious. Early assumption of the standing position and preparation for ambulation will usually overcome these problems. For this reason, incontinence should never be considered a contra-indication to weight-bearing in the erect position. In unconscious patients, catheterisation will be necessary, but where possible it should be avoided. The simplistic approach of indwelling catheter or repeated catherisations is detrimental to the patient's well-being and it provokes urinary tract infection (Policoff 1970).

A patient with communication problems cannot ask for a pan or bottle, and if he is unable to balance in sitting he will find it difficult and perhaps impossible to use a pan. These difficulties will add to his anxiety and loss of self-esteem. Hospitalisation can be a dehumanising experience and it is not helped by problems of incontinence broadcast to all within earshot when the nurse or therapist comments that 'Mr A. has wet the bed again'.

Sleep

Sleeping habits will also be altered during hospitalisation, and it is important to remember that a patient who appears drowsy and unable to co-operate or concentrate in treatment may have been given a sleeping draught in the early hours of the morning to help him sleep. Similarly, large doses of diazepam may make the objective of early standing and weight transference in preparation for walking impossible to achieve because the patient finds it difficult to concentrate and respond to handling techniques designed to stimulate antigravity activity. He may even find it a struggle to stay awake. Communication between the physician and therapist should solve this problem.

Attitudes

Related to all these problems is a frequent lack of understanding by the hospital staff of the patient and his needs. Once the stroke is over all but the most severely brain-damaged patients should begin to improve. It is difficult for staff to realise that once the vital signs are stable, the patient is not ill, and that to a large extent improvement of his problems is dependent as much on their attitudes as on their nursing care. Kottke (1974) has pointed out that 'deterioration is not an inevitable result of stroke'. In our experience lack of stimulation, both mental and physical, and an inability of staff to motivate the patient may result in the patient's deterioration. It has been hypothesised that social and sensory deficits which take place in the hospital situation result in behaviour which parallels that which is observed in sensory deprivation experiments.

The patient's early confusion may give the impression of dementia or senility, but its usual causes are fear, anxiety, speech disorders and the unfamiliarity of the surroundings. It may also be due to the disorientation which results from being horizontal. This type of confusion disappears when the patient assumes the vertical position in sitting or standing.

Many patients are also old and there is a tendency to underestimate their capacity in terms of mental fortitude and motivation. There is also a temptation to be more concerned with the patient's chronological age than with his pre-morbid capacity. Ullman (1964) has suggested that a proper understanding of him 'may make the difference between experiencing the patient as a confused old man or seeing him as a human being attempting to come to terms with an overwhelmingly stressful situation'.

140

MEDICAL AND SURGICAL MANAGEMENT

The initial stage following stroke may be equated with a medical and surgical emergency and requires co-ordinated and comprehensive care, which should be carried out in a special stroke unit (Drake, Hamilton, Carlsson and and Blumenkrantz 1973, Howard 1977). During this initial stage the patient may be unconscious or stuporous, and continual evaluation and supervision of his condition is essential in the first twenty-four hours in particular. Clinical features and past history may be the most important factors in distinguishing the type of brain lesion.

There are certain special investigatory procedures which may be instituted in order to determine the actual cause of the stroke. These may include cerebral angiography*, lumbar puncture*, echoencephalography*, exploratory burr holes*, isotope brain scan*, or computerised tomography*.

Surgery may include evacuation of a haematoma through a burr hole following haemorrhage. If investigations reveal a localised stenosis in one internal carotid artery, surgical removal of that part of the artery may be performed (thrombo-endarterectomy). If there is an aneurysm, excision may be performed with ligation of its parent arteries.

Adams (1974) summarises the principles of early medical management. He emphasises the importance of limiting brain damage by careful attention to the various systems of the body and by discovering any aetiology for which early or special treatment or investigations are required.

The objectives of medical therapy immediately following stroke are to improve the circulation of blood to the ischaemic area of the brain, to prevent thrombus formation, to reduce oedema, and to maintain blood pressure at the optimum level and thus promote adequate perfusion. The indications and contra-indications for administering hypertensive or hypotensive drugs is a complex medical problem. The value of anticoagulant therapy in cerebrovascular disease is not fully determined. It is probably useful following diagnosis of an occlusion caused by an embolus (Russell 1972, Walton 1975).

The period of bed rest varies with each patient. Complete bed rest in many cases is required for as short a period as forty-eight hours. If myocardial infarct has precipitated or followed a stroke, appropriate measures will need to be instituted and patients may require a longer period of bed rest than would be necessary following stroke alone.

* Glossary

For these patients, cardiac rehabilitation is combined with rehabilitation of the problems which follow the stroke.

PHYSICAL TREATMENT OF THE STROKE PATIENT

Rehabilitation must be active and positive and must be commenced early. It commences immediately the patient's stroke is completed, with handling which is designed to motivate him toward recovery, overcome his initial confusion, re-establish his relationships with the environment and help him relearn, in the most direct way possible, functions he has lost.

It is no doubt true that some physical treatment given to stroke patients is ineffective. Carr (1975) has emphasised that it is the *quality* of treatment given that is important. Treatment which is passive and inappropriate to the patient's needs will be totally ineffective in terms of the patient returning to the community. What is referred to in the literature as 'traditional' physiotherapy consists of treatment directed at the peripheral musculo-skeletal manifestations of the brain damage, commenced a few weeks after the stroke. This attitude takes for granted certain sequelae of stroke and fails to consider that some of them might be preventable. Aspects of rehabilitation essential for the learning of motor skills such as motivation, the presence of recognisable functional goals, stimulation of concentration and self-confidence, stimulation of sensory and perceptual functions, in other words the 'mental' aspects of rehabilitation, are ignored. Perhaps the strongest criticism of this attitude is that it probably, in our opinion certainly, produces many problems for the patient which do not have to develop and actually *prevents* him from reaching his potential degree of recovery. A recent Rehabilitation Study Group can still describe a therapeutic programme for stroke patients which consists of range of motion exercises, strengthening exercises, transfers, wheelchair activities and ambulation.

These attitudes do not take into account the suggested mechanisms of brain recovery following damage. It is possible that the dendrites of certain neurons may be relatively pluripotent in their capacity to form synaptic connections. This means that these cells may be capable of making new and different synaptic associations (Oppenheim 1971). Adaptive changes in their connectivity may then be brought about by functional activity (Jacobson 1969).

Another mechanism is the possibility of collateral sprouting. Wall (1975) suggests that intact axons may sense the presence nearby of denervated tissue and send out sprouts to occupy the vacated territory. He considers it is also possible that certain connections already exist in an inactive and ineffective form, that they mature and become effective as the dominant fibres degenerate.

Our experience with stroke patients over a number of years has indicated that the treatment we describe in this book is effective and relatively simple to carry out. Howard (1977), who reports thirteen years of experience on a special stroke unit, similarly stresses the importance of treatment being both early and aggressive. His evidence indicates that not only do more patients survive their strokes under this regime, but the quality of life of these survivors is greater than those treated by more passive means.

The advantage of a stroke unit is that the patient is cared for immediately after his stroke by nurses, therapists, medical and domestic staff all of whom have the same objectives. This ensures that for twenty-four hours of the day the patient is stimulated, treated, talked to, and listened to by people who understand his problems, and who go about solving them in a positive manner.

Howard, describing his own stroke unit, comments that when the patients are involved in interesting and competitive activities and stimulating treatment programmes all day, they sleep well at night without medication, they feel 'busy', they do not look sick nor are they treated as such. This is in marked contrast to so many day hospitals or nursing homes where the patients sit around all day with little to do, surrounded by staff who go about what they regard as custodial activities, often with great kindness, but with no idea of how these elderly patients are deteriorating in this atmosphere of passive entertainment and expectation of failure. Di Benedetto (1974) writes 'those placed in nursing homes and other wards tended to deteriorate. The paucity of mental stimulation and physical activity and the general lack of purpose and/or human gratification lead to regression'.

EARLY CARE

Care of the Unconscious Patient. Adequate ventilation and prevention of obstruction of the airway is essential in early care of acute stroke to ensure an adequate supply of oxygen to the brain and to eliminate the carbondioxide, to prevent retention of secretions, atelectasis and bronchopneumonia. This will involve regular and frequent turning and positioning in side lying, combined with vibrations to the chest, rib springing, postural drainage if indicated or if the patient is unconscious for a prolonged period, and if necessary some form of intubation and mechanical suction. Other nursing care

143

will involve the provision of adequate fluids, care of the skin and avoidance of urinary retention and bowel impaction.

Positioning. While the patient is unconscious or has to lie flat, he should be nursed in side lying with a pillow between his legs to prevent internal rotation, adduction and inversion of the affected leg when this leg is uppermost. The shoulder should be protracted and the arm relatively extended (Fig. 50). These positions will help to

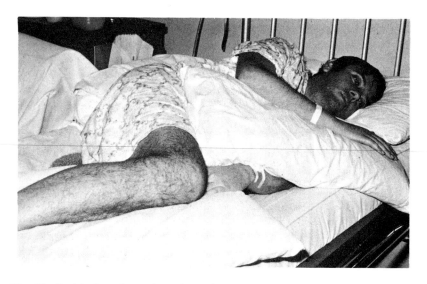

Fig. 50. *Positioning of a stroke patient who must lie flat in bed.*

avoid patterns of spasticity. Although this is passive it is probably a means of avoiding an early imprinting of certain habits of posture which may occur even at this early stage, when the patient is unconscious and therefore relatively immobile for twenty-four hours of the day. The use of a bed cradle is necessary to prevent the bedclothes pushing the foot into inversion and plantarflexion, and to allow the patient to move.

Stimulation of Function. The therapist should not wait for the patient to recover full consciousness before attempting to stimulate a response from him. She passively moves his arm giving him a goal for each movement. For example, 'I am taking your hand to touch your head'. She names the parts of his body as she moves his hand toward them and describes the movement, in an effort to make contact with him. The emphasis in these movements is on giving the

144

patient the sensory feedback of movement rather than on maintaining range of motion. The movements include taking the hand to the opposite shoulder, to the opposite hip, above the head to touch the bed, to his nose, forehead and mouth. The sensation of his own hand on his mouth sometimes stimulates a response from the patient when other movements do not.

Shoulder girdle movement, particularly protraction with approximation which may be combined with trunk rotation in side lying, will encourage the idea of reaching out.

Movement of the pelvis and the shoulder girdle, that is, rotation of the trunk in side lying, in the very early stages give the patient the idea of the movements required for rolling over. The ability to roll from supine to either side will be necessary in order to get up and sit over the side of the bed. Movement of the pelvis forward in side lying is also used to give the patient the feeling of the hip extension he will need when he stands and walks.

The patient will not always be able to perform movements on request. Therefore as his movements are guided and stimulated, he should watch and concentrate on the feeling of the movement and its goal. Brodal (1973), a professor of neuroanatomy, following his own stroke, described the effect on him. 'Subjectively it was clearly felt as if sensory information helped the patient to 'direct' the force of innervation through the proper channels . . . from introspection it appears however, that the subjective information about the movement to be executed, its range and goal is an essential factor'. He concludes that this effect is probably similar to the learning of all motor skills.

In order to encourage awareness of the affected side of the body and the space it occupies, the patient's activities should be directed toward this side. Food can be presented to him in this way and his relatives can be encouraged to talk to him from his affected side. In the very early stages his locker can be placed on this side to encourage him to transfer weight to that side as he reaches for his belongings. His bed and his chair can be placed so as to encourage him to look toward this side. Anderson and Choy (1970) comment that 'therapy specifically designed to overcome unilateral neglect of space and body and to re-orient the body in space has resulted in higher levels of achievement in the rehabilitation of stroke patients'.

Contact between eyes and hand, and the eyes and an object to be reached, should be established immediately as this is an important factor in the re-establishment of functional movement. It gives visual feedback which reinforces the learning process, and it stimulates awareness of body parts and their relationship to each other, and

145

spatial organisation, all of which are usually confused following stroke.

Vision is an important element in purposeful movement. It involves the hands, and the hands are involved to a greater or lesser extent in most functions. From her first contact with the patient, the therapist encourages him to make eye to eye contact with her. This helps him to concentrate and focuses his attention on her face, which is important in providing motivation and establishing communication.

Patients who have an homonymous hemianopia may need to be approached initially within their field of vision otherwise the therapist may find it difficult to encourage visual contact. However, the therapist should assist the patient to expand his field of vision by compensation, that is, by moving his head. Patients with the additional problem of denial or unawareness of hemiplegia will need to be constantly reminded, both verbally and by tactile and pressure stimulation, to turn their heads and use their vision.

Assessment of the stroke patient initially is informal. The most important point at this stage is that the therapist establishes rapport with the patient and with his relatives. She will gain an impression about his tone, sensory or perceptual disability, communication problems, oro-facial dysfunction and behaviour during the first treatment sessions. These areas of function will be assessed in more detail as she treats him over the next few days. The reader should refer to Chapter 4 for details of assessment.

SPECIFIC POINTS IN PHYSICAL TREATMENT

Stimulation of Weight Shift and Balance

All patients start to improve twenty-four to forty-eight hours following stroke unless there is some other complicating factor. The patient must be given the opportunity to learn to cope with gravity as soon as vital signs are stable, which is usually within the first couple of days. The fact of being in an antigravity position and having to make adjustments is an essential stimulus to the re-establishment of balance mechanisms.

The patient is assisted to sit over the side of the bed. The therapist encourages head and trunk side flexion to stimulate weight shift (Fig. 51) and to give him the feeling of weight-bearing on his affected arm.

In sitting he is encouraged to restore normal body alignment by transferring his weight from side to side and forward and backward with the therapist stimulating any missing head and trunk movements. This will enable him to sit alone. The next step in the

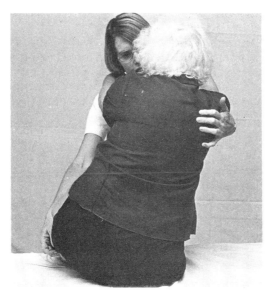

Fig. 51. *Practise of weight shift laterally in sitting quickly enables the patient to sit independently, as she feels confident in her ability to adjust her own position.*

restoration of effective balance is the stimulation of more automatic adjustments.

The patient's usual response when he is first assisted to sit or stand is to lean or fall toward the affected side with no control or stability. If balance is not stimulated he will compensate and adjust to the situation by shifting his weight to the unaffected side. He will abduct his legs which gives him a wide base of support and he will hold himself stiffly. This eventually becomes a habit and an established posture which is difficult to overcome. It will prevent the development of balance. Treatment designed to improve weight shift and balance develops the patient's confidence in his abilities. It instils in him a feeling for symmetry and normal body alignment and allows him to move.

Weight transference forward at the hips in sitting with head and trunk extension will prepare the patient for getting into standing. The therapist stimulates weight-bearing and weight transference on to the affected leg as the patient stands up. Pounding the heel on the floor increases the patient's awareness of his leg in space and helps him to stand up symmetrically (Fig. 52). The therapist assists by pulling the

147

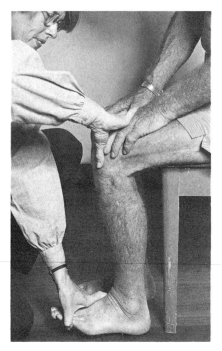

Fig. 52. *Pounding of the heel on the floor to increase awareness of weight-bearing.*

weight on to the affected leg as the patient stands up (Fig. 53). She must take care not to push the knee back as this will put him off balance. In order that the patient can stand erect, he must extend his hip (Fig. 53c) which will help him to control his knee.

The patient may need to rest his arms on the therapist's shoulders initially. This will stimulate weight transference forward at his hips in sitting and extension of his hips in standing. It helps to keep him symmetrical. Elevation of the shoulder girdle will help the patient to shift his weight laterally (Fig. 54), and will prevent retraction and depression of the shoulder girdle. It also give the patient some support. However, he will not learn to balance if he is held too much or if he pulls around the therapist's neck. Alternate tapping* will improve the patient's balance and enable him to stand and walk alone. Practice of walking backward and sideways will further improve his ability to shift weight and balance in the erect position.

---

* Appendix 1

148

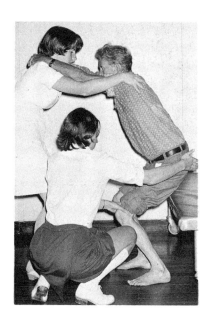

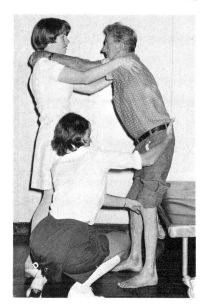

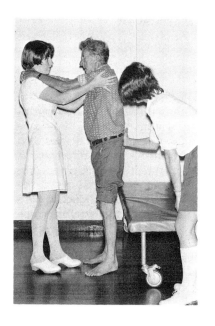

Fig. 53. (a, b) Pressure down toward his heel helps this man take weight symmetrically as he stands up. (c) He gains some control over his knee if his hip is kept in normal alignment.

Fig. 54. *Elevation of the right shoulder helps this woman to shift weight laterally on to the right leg.*

Stimulation of Weight-bearing

It should be noted that the presence of hypotonus is not a contra-indication to standing or bearing weight through a limb. Weight-bearing, which involves approximation to joint surfaces, should be practised with the joints in normal alignment. It stimulates muscular activity and control over the limb. The sensory stimulation which is applied to tactile, deep pressure receptors and proprioceptors combined with conscious attempts by the patient to think about the movement required helps to increase stability and stimulate movement. The use of conscious cortical control and mental practice helps the patient to concentrate on the particular components of a movement in order to relearn it.

When the patient first stands up, very early following his stroke, the most important components of standing to be stimulated include extension of the hip (Fig. 53c) in order that his weight-bearing alignment is normal, and the ability to shift his weight from one foot to the other. If he has difficulty gaining hip extension, it can be

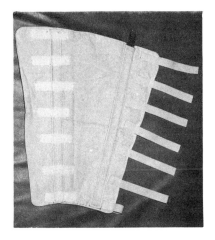

a

b

Fig. 55. *(a) A calico splint with two or three light metal struts and velcro straps.*
(b) The splint can be used for a few days to help the patient regain knee stability and to enable her to practise weight transference.

151

effectively stimulated in supine (Fig. 137). It is essential that following this practice of hip extension, the patient is assisted to stand and apply, in the standing position, what he has just learned.

If the knee is unstable, a *calico splint* (Fig. 55a) may be used to give the patient the feeling of weight-bearing (Fig. 55b). As it does not hold the knee rigidly in extension, it give the patient the opportunity to experiment with knee control without fear of falling. The therapist may also stimulate active control over knee extension by approximating through the knee with the patient in sitting or lying position (Fig. 145). Immediately the patient has some control in this small range of knee movement, he stands up again and practises bearing weight on the affected leg by stepping backward and forward with his unaffected leg. This early weight-bearing on the affected leg in standing will stimulate normal extension and the ability to walk, as well as prevent the development of spasticity. The ability to bear weight on the affected leg and step forward is very motivating for the patient who sees that he can take a step with weight on his affected side. **A limb load monitor*** is a useful device for encouraging weight shift on to the affected limb. It gives the patient auditory feedback as to the distribution of his weight.

It is important that the patient experiences early the reciprocal feeling of walking. It seems that the early stimulation of bilateral reciprocal and rhythmical movement stimulates the recovery of function. Experiments on animals have indicated this.

The therapist stands in front of the patient and guides his walking by helping him to transfer his weight as much as necessary and to keep his body in normal alignment. In particular, the therapist should explain to the patient that taking a step forward involves extending the hip of the standing leg. Although the therapist may have to guide and assist him a great deal at this early stage, practice gives him feedback of the semi-automatic movements of which walking is composed and helps to trigger off this previously well-learned activity. Walking facilitation is described in Appendix 1.

The patient must not be lifted, held or propped up, but should be given the opportunity to respond to stimulation. Although initially he can be assisted by resting his arms on the therapist's shoulders, as his balance improves, the therapist can stimulate his walking by guiding him from his shoulders. As soon as the patient can adjust his posture sufficiently to take a step alone the therapist withdraws some of her control so he can learn gradually to make adjustments on his own (Fig. 56).

* Krusen Research Centre, Philadelphia, Pennsylvania.

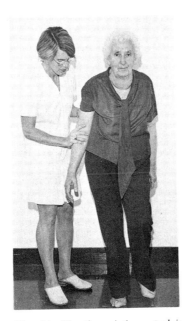

Fig. 56. *The therapist's control is gradually withdrawn. At this stage the patient needs only a little guidance which is given by elevating her arm. She will need to learn not to shift her weight so far to the right.*

Aids such as quadripod sticks and foot splints are not necessary for most patients following stroke. In the authors' experience, patients treated early in standing, in the way we have described, that is, with the emphasis on body alignment, weight-bearing, bilateral reciprocal movement and balance, develop sufficient control over walking to manage well without such aids.

If these aids are presented to the patient early, before he has a chance to develop some control, they probably *prevent* him re-establishing weight shift, balance and effective walking. The quadripod stick encourages asymmetry of posture and movement and discourages weight shift to the affected side (Fig. 57). Its use is inconsistent with the goal of stimulating recovery of function of the affected side. The walking which results is awkward and unstable. Attempts to walk in this unnatural way require considerable effort

153

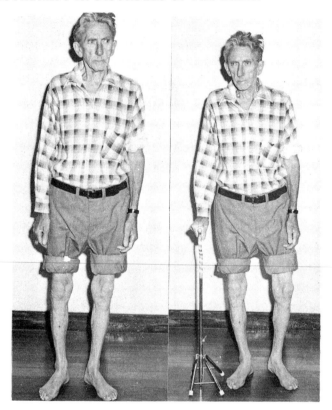

Fig. 57. *Note the effect of a quadripod stick on the standing posture of a man with left-sided hemiplegia. The stick encourages asymmetry and orientation away from the affected side.*

which increases spasticity. If a patient lacks confidence when walking in a crowd, he will get sufficient assistance by using an ordinary walking stick.

There are a few patients who will not benefit from treatment for various reasons such as inability to regain vigour or stamina after the stroke and loss of intellectual function. Unfortunately, it is doubtful whether these patients will walk safely even with apparatus and they will probably need a wheelchair for mobility.

The Prevention of Spasticity

Treatment as outlined, with its emphasis on the stimulation of balance reactions, normal weight-bearing alignment and the elimina-

154

tion of unnecessary muscular activity tends to minimise the development of spasticity. However, stimulation of movement of one part of the body must be carefully guided and controlled so as to prevent associated movements occurring in abnormal synergies elsewhere in the body. Certain factors such as cold, fear, effort, both physical and mental, and the assumption of an asymmetrical attitude, if not avoided, will stimulate an abnormal increase in tone.

As soon as the patient tries to move by himself he will find great difficulty. He will gradually learn to move using only the unaffected side of his body and this will involve great effort. This results from his lack of understanding of how to move and from his confused attempts to overcome his disability.

However, if he is discouraged from using inappropriate muscular activity and from moving in an asymmetrical manner, and if he is guided in the performance of movements until he can do them himself, he will quickly learn to move more effectively.

If the therapist does not, to some extent, restrict the tendency to over-activity of the sound side of the body in the early stages following the stroke, the limbs on this side will be used excessively and at the expense of the limbs on the affected side. This restriction of over-activity is probably an important factor in the prevention of the development of hypertonus and in allowing the patient to relearn symmetrical motor skills. It is interesting that Beck and Chambers (1970) report a similar result from their experiment in which animals were restricted from using the unaffected limbs.

Another factor influencing tone is anxiety. The therapist should aim to lower the level of anxiety and tension which is often found in these patients. It may only be necessary for the therapist to point out this increased tension to the patient, indicating his elevated shoulders of his stiff posture and suggest that he relax. Other patients may require special instruction in methods of relaxation. The prevention of spasticity is described in more detail in Chapter 12.

Although spasticity is not a major cause of dysfunction in those patients who are treated early in the way described in this book, the therapist will still be confronted by patients some time after their stroke who for various reasons have a marked degree of spasticity and probably some secondary soft tissue contracture. These patients usually require treatment which will inhibit the hypertonus in order to allow freer movement. For details of treatment to stimulate movement in patients with hypertonus, the reader should refer to Chapter 11.

Stimulation of Upper Limb Function

It is essential from the earliest stages of treatment to stimulate recovery of upper limb function.

Although control around the shoulder and shoulder girdle is necessary for most functions involving the arms, stimulation should not concentrate only on more proximal control, but should aim also to encourage return of muscular activity around the elbow, wrist and hand. Recovery does not occur from proximal to distal as is sometimes supposed. The patient may recover some isolated movements in his hand before he gains much muscular activity around his shoulder.

In supine, the therapist places the limb in various positions, in various ranges at different joints. She asks the patient to try to hold his limb or particular joints in certain positions, to move in and out of these positions, both eccentrically and concentrically. The patient will often recover isolated muscular activity around his shoulder with the arm elevated from 90° to 180° from his body. The therapist explores with the patient to find out where he can elicit activity, then encourages him to extend this activity. It is very often components of habitual activities which can be stimulated in this way.

The patient may find *mental practice* helpful as it enables him to practise particular movements of his arm when his therapist is not present. This type of practice is preferable to any physical practice in which the unaffected limb passively moves the affected limb.

Weight-bearing on the affected hand in sitting with the arm in extension and shoulder girdle elevated will stimulate extension throughout the arm and weight transference on to the affected side.

The therapist may need to direct how the patient uses his vision. For example, when he is attempting to weight-bear through his hand in sitting (Fig. 58), she not only makes him aware of his hand through tactile stimulation and pressure, she also gives him a functional goal, such as reaching toward the floor (Fig. 59).

Weight-bearing through the affected arm sideways and forward in sitting and standing (Fig. 60) stimulates extension of the arm with the shoulder in elevation, which is important for reaching out. It stimulates control around the shoulder. The early assumption of shoulder elevation in these positions and in supine and side lying (Fig. 61) prevents the development of secondary contracture of the soft tissues around the shoulder girdle, which is frequently the cause of a painful shoulder. It also helps the patient regain a sense of normal body alignment and position in space with his arms away from his body. As well as the patient's own attempts to elicit the necessary muscular activity, local stimulation of the triceps brachii and approximation

156

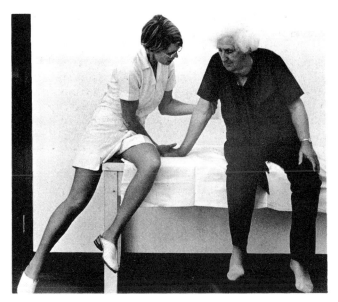

Fig. 58. *Weight-bearing through the hand stimulates extension of the arm and awareness of body parts. Weight must be shifted to the right side. Elevation of the shoulder facilitates this.*

through the arm will stimulate the idea of extension of the arm and will also inhibit the tendency to flexor spasticity. The patient must be discouraged from using inappropriate muscular activity.

Movement of the hand should never be neglected or put off until the patient has better shoulder control. The hand is normally accustomed to a great deal of sensory input. It is important that the patient receives stimulation to his hand which will prevent its neglect, and that he understands the necessity for concentrating on certain movements, particularly wrist extension, and attempted grasp and release with the wrist held in extension and radial deviation.

The patient with minimal disability following a stroke, but with some hand dysfunction, requires a careful assessement, and treatment which is very specific to the problems found. We stress this point because this type of patient may be neglected as his problems appear relatively minor. The reader should refer to Appendix 1 for some details of treatment.

A painful shoulder may be the result of poor handling of the patient or over-zealous practice of damaging movements by the patient himself. It may occur in the patient with spasticity around the

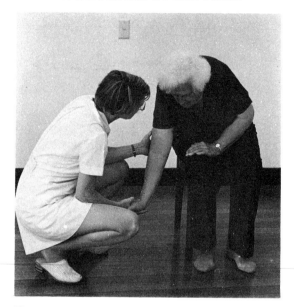

Fig. 59. *Reaching toward the floor. This encourages the woman to alter her centre of gravity.*

shoulder girdle as well as in the patient with a flaccid upper limb. In the latter case, the weight of the arm and the effect of gravity may cause stretching of the soft tissues around the shoulder joint and, eventually partial subluxation and pain on certain movements.

Spasticity of muscles attached to the scapula (rhomboids, trapezius, latissimus dorsi) may be present even when the upper limb is apparently hypotonic. This spasticity prevents the scapula from rotating and protracting when the arm is moved away from the body. The movement will therefore cause the head of the humerus to impinge upon the immobilised acromium process as it overlies the glenoid cavity. This type of trauma occurs frequently when the patient is pulled by his arm to sitting, or if he is attached to a pulley system with instructions to elevate the affected arm by pulling down with the other arm.

During all treatment involving movement of the upper limb constant attention should be paid to the relationship between the scapula and humerus. Similarly, when the patient with a hypotonic upper limb is sitting down, the therapist should ensure that his arm is supported with the shoulder slightly elevated and not left to hang unsupported (Fig. 62).

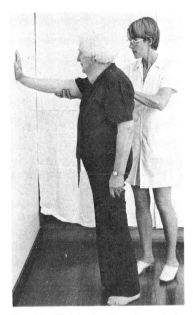

Fig. 60. *Weight-bearing through the arm in this position is stimulated early in treatment to encourage control around the shoulder girdle and stimulate awareness of the position of the arm in space.*

Arm slings are sometimes recommended. Unfortunately, they ensure that the arm is tucked away and forgotten, and they limit the sensory input to the arm and hand. The limb is held in a position of flexion which encourages the development of flexor spasticity and contractures. Although it is intended, in the case of the hypotonic arm, to keep the head of the humerus in the gleno-humeral joint, it is doubtful whether any sling does this. The very early and active stimulation of upper limb function is an important factor in preventing a painful shoulder and usually does away with the necessity for a sling.

A patient with disordered body image and denial of hemiplegia may need a sling at certain times in order to prevent damage to the neglected arm. However, emphasis in treatment with this patient should not be on the provision of a sling but on methods of improving the patient's perception of his limbs. Similarly, patients

159

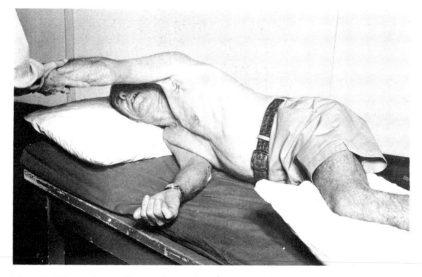

Fig. 61. *The patient will usually regain some control over muscular activity in side lying and supine. He is concentrating on trying to lower his arm slowly to the bed.*

with oedema of the arm may get some relief if the arm is not completely dependent, but again, oedema is not a problem in patients who have early stimulation of arm function. It is possible that sponge rubber under the upper arm (Bobath 1977) may be useful for some patients.

Establishment of Communication

Communication exists in facial expression, hand contact, eye contact tone of voice and gesture, as well as in speech and writing. It is essential for the development of a good relationship between therapist and patient. The inexperienced therapist, accustomed, quite unconsciously, to expecting certain behaviours from others in her communication with them, needs to appreciate that the unexpected behaviour of the aphasic patient is not the result of his being deaf, stupid or senile. Conversations and discussions in his presence should always include him, should acknowledge his presence and his importance, and demonstrate an awareness of him as a person, despite his inability to make the usual, expected contribution.

The speech pathologist, following assessment, will be able to explain the problems and give practical help to the patient, his relatives and all those involved in his rehabilitation, in an early

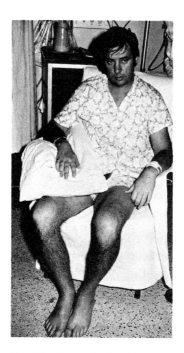

Fig. 62. *The patient's right arm is supported in sitting in order to avoid strain on the shoulder and to enable him to sit symmetrically.*

attempt to stimulate communication and prevent crisis situations. These would result in frustration for the patient which may discourage further attempts at communication on his part. However, the physiotherapist is often the first therapist to see the patient following a stroke and there are some general points she will need to consider.

From her first meeting with the patient, the therapist must develop an appropriate system of communication. The patient may be able to respond if he is given time to do so, and if the therapist spends time in establishing at least a yes/no response. Questions and comments should be phrased simply and slowly, using gestures and clues, such as pointing to objects, in order to help the patient understand. The responses required should need only a gesture, a nod, or a yes/no, instead of a complicated statement. Perseveration on words is discouraged as it quickly becomes a habit and prevents attempts at real communication. Patients whose jargon speech does not improve may

161

have to be advised to keep silent and another method of communication, drawing, gesture, writing, will have to be developed. It is a great relief for the aphasic patient to have someone understand his predicament, sympathise with his frustration, and who has the patience and time to attempt to get in touch with him.

Stimulation of Oro-facial Function

The organs of speech, eating and ventilation are to a large extent the same. Their functions are vital to respiratory function, nutrition, speech and well-being. Oro-facial dysfunction, which is distressing, potentially dangerous and embarrassing for the patient, responds well and quickly to appropriate treatment commenced within the first few days.

Oro-facial problems should be among the first problems to be treated, as success in these functions improves the patient's motivation, makes him feel more 'natural', and helps his relationship with others by improving his appearance. The effect on the patient and on everyone else of the rapid improvement which follows appropriate treatment is very marked in terms of his improved emotional state and in the changed attitudes of others toward him.

There are two important considerations in the early institution of oro-facial stimulation. A patient who cannot cope with food and drink will be fed by naso-gastric tube. This procedure prolongs his disabilities as he has no way of relearning the necessary movements. It gives him the appearance of an invalid, and is unpleasant. Naso-gastric tube feeding can be avoided in all but unconscious patients if the correct treatment procedures are instituted by the therapist and reinforced by nursing staff and relatives.

The other consideration has to do with the patient's self-image. Eating and drinking are important functions. They have cultural, developmental and social significance. Early restoration of the ability to feed oneself without dribbling food, choking or making a mess, has an important effect on the patient which is reflected in his early response to rehabilitation.

Treatment is designed to improve lip and jaw closure, facial expression, tone in the cheek, tongue movement and swallowing. It is performed with the patient in a sitting position, with his head in the midline. False teeth should be worn as soon as possible to prevent changes in the gums. Oro-facial dysfunction and details of treatment techniques are described in Chapter 15.

Patients who are emotionally incontinent or labile should be reassured that this will improve as control over movement improves.

162

Guidance in controlling respiration, particularly expiration, in order to co-ordinate breathing with speech and with eating will also help him gain control over explosive outbursts of crying. Similarly, vibrations to the thorax during expiration, which are useful for stimulating phonation, will also distract the patient and help him control these outbursts.

Importance of Relatives

A relative's help can be elicited during the early stages of treatment as this will help him to understand the patient's problems and how to cope with them. Relatives may be able to communicate with the patient better than a stranger, certainly initially until rapport and trust have developed. He may be more disorientated in the presence of strangers than with relatives, so it will be helpful and reassuring for him to have them present whenever possible. Some immigrant patients revert to their mother tongue immediately following a stroke, and contact may have to be made with the patient in this language initially.

If the patient is looked after at home following his stroke or if he goes home before he is fully independent, his relatives should understand how to handle him to allow him to develop independence and how to stimulate his mental and emotional capacities (Griffiths 1970, Carr & Shepherd 1979).

The overall objectives in treatment are toward independence in home, working life and recreation. Nevertheless, relatives need practical help in preparing for the patient's homecoming. An initial home visit will help in planning for necessary assistance in alterations and additions (such as height of bed, provision of rails in the bathroom) and will give the therapist information about the skills the patient will need in order to cope with existing arrangements. Follow-up home visits will ensure that everything goes as smoothly as possible.

One of the factors important in recovery is undoubtedly the patient's degree of *motivation*. His premorbid personality and his inner drive and adaptability, will affect his ability to cope with this new situation, and the degree of family support and the attitude of those around him will profoundly influence his motivation. The patient needs to make short-term achievements to reassure himself that he can improve. It is probably true that nothing succeeds like success, and this applies to patient, relatives and therapist. Success gives the patient confidence in himself and in his therapist's ability to deal with his problems.

Sexual Problems

These problems following stroke are rarely discussed, probably because the patients are in late middle age and old age. Nevertheless, for physical and emotional reasons these problems certainly exist. Frankel (1967) comments that most sexual disturbances are symptoms of emotional difficulties in any age group. Counselling may be necessary if these problems cause emotional conflict between the patient and his spouse.

Home Life and Employment

The possibility of returning to work depends on many factors, such as the type of employment, the employer's interest, the degree of physical handicap, the availability of transport and the adaptability of the patient. For example, a fitter and turner who was unable to return to his former position because of poor manipulative skills, returned to the same firm in a supervisory capacity.

Early in the patient's rehabilitation, his employer may be contacted and then kept informed of his progress. The occupational therapist will introduce into his treatment psychomotor testing and simple tasks appropriate in terms of his occupation. Training centres attached to rehabilitation departments are effective in increasing the patient's endurance as well as in improving skills. The occupational therapist and physical therapist may work out a programme to prepare him for a special skill required for his employment. Some patients will need placement in a sheltered workshop.

This aspect of rehabilitation should not be overlooked in those who have retired. The patient will need advice and training which is appropriate for looking after himself at home, and for his pastimes, whether they be gardening or bowls. The housewife also will need particular help as she may have to cope with many different tasks including the care of children.

When the patient lives alone, careful planning and help from community resources will make the patient's living at home as pleasant and safe as possible.

Physiotherapy as described helps improve the patient's concentration, attention span, short term memory and integration of sensation by providing a suitable learning environment. Ayres (1966) has commented that treatment designed to influence motor function cannot avoid effecting *perceptual processes*. As the therapist stimulates the patient to move she should consider this effect, in order to prevent secondary perceptual problems such as the development of agnosia with respect to the affected side, and in order to treat any specific perceptual problems which exist. It is generally accepted that perceptual development in children depends on planned and purposeful activity. The practice of purposeful activities in adult patients will similarly result in some improvement in perceptual function.

In the treatment of the stroke patient, *goals* must be realistic, purposeful and credible to the patient as well as sufficiently difficult to present him with a challenge. They should concern the functions with which the patient is himself concerned. Most patients will want more than anything else to be independent in dressing, toileting, eating and walking, and the fact that the therapist has designed his treatment to enable him to do these things should be immediately obvious to him.

Goals should be consistent. Once the patient can walk with guidance from the therapist, she should help him to walk part of the way to the occupational therapist and not put him in a wheelchair to transport him there. Similarly, when the occupational therapist has spent time helping him to dress independently she should make sure the ward staff know which clothes he can put on by himself so he will not be passively dressed each morning.

Movement must become automatic or semi-automatic to be effective. Granit (1972) comments that 'even those movements which we regard as voluntary are largely automatic'. An important factor in *progressing treatment* is that the therapist, having started by guiding and stimulating the patient's movements, gradually decreases her guidance, and stimulates automatic responses from him.

From the patient's point of view, treatment progresses from his early state of confusion, through the stage when he must concentrate hard on relearning movement, and eventually to the point when he can respond automatically without conscious thought when he is moved by the therapist and when he attempts a particular functional goal. Adams (1974) points out that normally the cerebral activity concerned, for example, in walking, is subcortical and even visual perception is unnecessary if the person is confident that the pathway ahead is clear. After a stroke, however, a high level of cortical activity is required 'to interpret error and devise correction to maintain appropriate levels of comprehension and concentration, and to cope with apprehension, discouragement and other emotional aspects'.

SUMMARY

This chapter briefly describes the pathophysiology of stroke, common problems which may occur and physical treatment of these problems.

Eventual outcome to a large extent depends upon the attitudes of the people with whom the patient comes in contact early following his stroke, how they view his problems and the treatment he receives. The possible mechanisms of recovery of brain function are briefly discussed. The authors' clinical findings indicate that certain factors in treatment (the early stimulation of balance in sitting and standing, the avoidance of associated movements and guidance in the relearning of familiar motor skills) results in a return of muscular activity in those muscles required for functional movement rather than into abnormal muscle synergies. The marked spasticity found in many stroke patients may be as much due to inappropriate treatment and the patient's experiences as to the actual brain damage.

References

Adams, G. F. (1974) *Cerebrovascular Disability and the Aging Brain.* Edinburgh and London, Churchill Livingstone.

Anderson, E. K. and Choy, E. (1970) Parietal lobe syndromes in hemiplegia. *Am. J. Occup. Ther.,* **24,** 1, 13–18.

Ayres, A. J. (1966) Interrelation of perception, function and treatment. *J. Am. Physical Therapy Assoc.,* **46,** 74.

Beck, C. H. and Chambers, W. W. (1970) Speed, accuracy and strength of forelimb movement after unilateral pyramidotomy in rhesus monkeys. *J. Comp. Physiol. Psychol. Monograph,* **70,** 1–22.

Bobath, B. (1977) Personal communication.

Brodal, A. (1973) Self-observation and neuro-anatomical considerations after a stroke. *Brain,* **96,** 675–694.

Carr, J. (1975) Reappraisal of the early treatment of hemiplegia in adults. *Aust. J. Physiother.,* **21,** 4, 151–154.

Carr, J. and Shepherd, R. (1979) *The Early Treatment of Stroke. A Positive Approach.* London, Heinemann.

Critchley, M. (1953) *The Parietal Lobes.* New York. Hafner.

di Benedetto, M. (1974) Optimal care for the severely involved stroke patient. *Rehabil.,* **91,** 27–35.

Drake, W. E., Hamilton, M. J., Carlsson, M. and Blumenkrantz, J. (1973) Acute stroke management and patient outcome: the value of neurovascular care units. *Stroke,* **4,** 933–945.

Fisher, C. M. (1968) in *Cerebral Vascular Disease,* edited by J. F. Toole, R. G. Siekert and J. P. W. Lisnant. New York, Grune and Stratton.

Frankel, S. (1967) Sexual problems in rehabilitation. *J. Rehab.,* **33,** 19–20.

Granit, R. (1972) Constant errors in the execution and appreciation of movement. *Brain,* **95,** 649–660.

Griffiths, V. (1970) *A Stroke in the Family.* London, Pitman.

Hodgins, E. (1966) *Having a Stroke and Getting Over It.* New England Journal of Medicine.

Howard, B. E. (1977) A practical approach to care of the acute stroke patient. *Paper given at the 53rd National Congress* of the A.P.T.A. St. Louis, Missouri.

Hurwitz, L. J. and Adams, G. F. (1972) Rehabilitation of hemiplegia: indices of assessment and prognosis. *Brit. Med. J.,* **1,** 94–98.

Jacobson, M. (1969) Development of specific neuronal connections. *Science,* **163,** 543–547.

Kottke, F. J. (1974) Historia obscura hemiplegiae. *Arch. Phys. Med. Rehabil.,* **55,** 4–13.

McKeown, F. (1965) *Pathology of the Aged.* London, Butterworths.

Oppenheim, R. (1971) Discussion in *The Biopsychology of Development,* edited by E. Tobach, L. A. Aronson and E. Shaw. New York, Academic Press.

Policoff, L. D. (1970) The philosophy of stroke rehabilitation. *Geriatrics,* **25,** 99.

Russell, R. R. (1972) Clinical effects of cerebrovascular disease. In *Scientific Foundations of Neurology,* edited by M. Critchley, J. L. O'Leary and B. Jennett. London, Heinemann.

Ullman, M. (1964) Disorders of body image after stroke. *Am. J. Nursing,* **64,** 10, 89.

Wall, P. D. (1975) Are connections stable in the adult mammalian brain? In *Sensory Physiology and Behaviour,* edited by R. Galun et al. New York, Plenum Press.

W.H.O. (1971) Cerebrovascular Disease: Prevention. Treatment and Rehabilitation. *Wld. Hlth. Org. Techn. Rep. Ser.,* 469.

Walton, J. N. (1975) *Essentials of Neurology.* 4th Edition. London, Pitman.

Further Reading

Bogardh, E. and Richards, C. (1974) Gait analysis and re-learning of gait control in hemiplegia patients. *Proc. W.C.P.T. 7th International Congress,* 443–453.

Diller, L. (1969) Perceptual and intellectual problems in hemiplegia – implications for rehabilitation. *Med. Clinics of N.A.,* **53,** 3, 575–583.

Hagen, C. (1973) Communication abilities in hemiplegia: effects of speech therapy. *Arch. Phys. Med. Rehabil.,* **54,** 454–463.

Hyman, M. D. (1972) Social psychological determinants of patients performance in stroke rehabilitation. *Arch. Phys. Med. Rehabil.*, **53**, 217–225.

Isaacs, B. and Marks, R. (1973) Determinants of outcome of stroke rehabilitation. *Age and Aging*, **2**, 139.

Isaacs, B. (1976) The place of a stroke unit in geriatric medicine. *Physiotherapy*, **62**, 5, 152–154.

Leche, P. (1972) Speech therapy and the treatment of cerebrovascular disease. *Proc. Roy. Soc. Med.*, **65**, 85–88.

Lehmann, J. F., De Lateur, B. J., Fowler, R. S., Warren, C. G., Arnold, R., Schertzer, G., Hurka, R., Whitmore, J. J., Masock, A. J. and Chambers, K. H. (1975) Stroke: does rehabilitation affect outcome? *Arch. Phys. Med. Rehabil.* **56**, 375–381.

Leiper, C. (1971) The left hemiplegic: discrepancies between actual and presumed capabilities. *Physiotherapy Canada*, **23**, 4, 159–162.

Lerner, S. (1971) Lack of movement efficiency in C.V.A. patients with perceptual dysfunction. *Physiotherapy Canada*, **23**, 2, 59–63.

Shepherd, R. B. (1978) Re-learning of movement in brain-damaged adults. *Paper delivered at the 8th International Congress of the World Confederation for Physical Therapy*, Tel Aviv. In press.

Shepherd, R. B. (1979) Some factors influencing the outcome of stroke rehabilitation. *Aust. J. Physiother.*, **25**, 4, 173

Stockmeyer, S. (1978) Hemispheric specialisation. *Paper delivered at the 54th American Physical Therapy Association Annual Congress*, Las Vegas.

Chapter 6

Head Injury

There have been increasing numbers of people sustaining head injuries in recent years and these injuries have progressively become more severe and complex. Accidents as a cause of death occupy first place in the group below 44 years of age (Walker 1971), and fourth place in all age groups. Of these accidents, head injury implicates 70%, and of this group 60% are due to road accidents. The other common causes of head injury are industrial and sporting accidents, attempted suicides, and accidents at home.

TYPES OF HEAD INJURY

Head injury may occur as a result of a direct blow to the head, or the head may be injured indirectly from an impact to other parts of the body. Direct injury may be blunt or penetrating.

A direct blow may be due either to the impact of an object upon the non-moving or slower moving head (such as a blow to the head in boxing or an object falling on the head), or may be due to the moving head being decelerated by a non-moving or slower moving object (such as the road in a fall from a motor cycle). An indirect injury may result from extreme extension and flexion of the head and neck in a road accident or from a fall on the buttocks. This indirect impact seldom causes severe head injury.

Blunt injuries, or acceleration-deceleration injuries as they are sometimes called, commonly result in multiple injuries of the body as well as widespread brain damage. The impact may cause scalp injuries, deformation of the skull with or without fractures, or depressed fractures which may lacerate and perforate the dura mater and brain. Movements of the brain within the cranium and changing pressure throughout the brain may together provide the cause of concussion, intracranial haemorrhage or cerebral contusion and laceration, both of which may lead to haemorrhage at several levels.

Gurdjian (1971) describes the mechanism of injury to the cranio-cerebral mass as being compression of the tissues which pushes them together, tension on the tissues which pulls them apart, and shearing or sliding of tissues over other tissues. All three can occur together or in succession. Experiments suggest that shearing strains as the brain moves about in the skull do the most damage and account for some of the severe injuries associated with widespread degeneration of the white matter (Jennett 1970).

The cranio-cerebral mass can also be penetrated by an object such as a bullet or sharp weapon. The skull can be crushed by compression forces.

Due to the relative mobility of the brain within the skull, a brain injury can occur opposite the site of trauma. This is called a contrecoup lesion (Fig. 63).

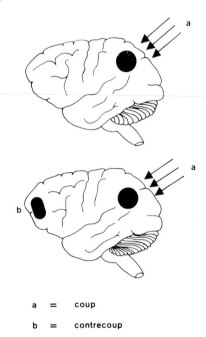

a = coup

b = contrecoup

Fig. 63. *Brain damage may occur opposite the site of trauma – a contrecoup lesion. (From Jamieson, K. (1971) A First Notebook of Head Injury. London, Butterworths).*

It is sometimes difficult to decide whether presenting neurological signs directly result from a head injury or whether they were prompted by some other cause, such as a cerebrovascular accident,

170

epileptic fit or spontaneous subarachnoid haemorrhage. For example, it may be difficult to determine whether the patient fell because he had a stroke with loss of movement, whether he fell and injured his head, or whether his relatively minor fall combined with cerebrovascular disease or hypertension precipitated a haemorrhage or thrombosis.

PREVENTION

It is beyond the scope of this book to do more than express the need for prevention of the initial injury with its devastating effect on the intellectual, physical and emotional well-being of the injured and their families.

However, one aspect of prevention, which requires considerable emphasis for those involved in caring for the head-injured patient from the moment of injury, is the prevention of a 'second accident' and of secondary brain damage due to hypoxia. A second accident may occur at the roadside or may be due to faulty handling of a fracture, for example, a fracture of the cervical spine. Secondary brain damage due to hypoxia, and even death, may result from aspiration of vomitus or blood or from relatively minor thoracic injuries.

Hence, it is important to stress the need for careful handling and observation. Intelligent recording, from the time of injury, of the patient's state of consciousness, that is, his level of alertness, type of response, and of his neurological status, and any changes in these, is most important. In this way factors which may lead to secondary brain damage can be quickly recognised and treated.

Management of the head-injured patient involves large numbers of people from different disciplines, and this necessitates the need for a 'common language' and 'understandable communications' in recording changes in consciousness and neurological state. 'The emphasis should be on recording what is seen and describing what actually happens rather than attempting an interpretation to be fitted into a box number or a single word' (Gibson 1971b). Words such as 'stupor', for example, mean different things to different people and are better avoided.

Multiple Injuries

The problems arising from severe head injury are often further complicated by the presence of multiple injuries to the rest of the body. The increased difficulty in the management of such complex injuries is illustrated by a series described by Hitchcock (1971b). In this series of nearly 8000 patients, 64% of those with multiple injuries died.

It is obvious that multiple injuries must complicate the handling of these patients. Walker (1971) points out that they interfere with the cerebral reparative process by impairing the function of systems normally maintaining cerebral haematosis. Approximately 50% of head-injured patients have some damage to the rib cage and underlying organs which may result in flail chest, lung contusion, pneumothorax, or haemothorax. Cervical spine involvement is seen in approximately 10% of cases (Walker 1971). Other injuries include fractures of the extremities, spine (with or without spinal cord injuries) and pelvis, craniofacial injuries, rupture of abdominal viscera and peripheral nerve injuries.

It is important that those in contact with the patient from the moment of injury should look out for and report any bruising or tenderness, as there is considerable difficulty in diagnosing injury in the unconscious or confused patient who is unable to assist by describing his symptoms.

Injury to the Skull

Skull fractures are painless, and because the greater part of the skull is devoid of muscle, there is no associated muscle spasm to aid diagnosis. However, most skull fractures are diagnosed following routine post-accident x-ray.

Not all head injuries are accompanied by fractures of the skull. Lewin (1966) has pointed out the fallacy of the popular lay concept that a fractured skull is always serious, whereas a head injury without a fracture is relatively mild. In other words, the severity of head injury cannot always be judged by the presence or absence of a fracture. It is the extent of the brain injury which is of first importance. Nevertheless, the presence of a skull fracture is some evidence of the severity of the initial blow.

Certain fractures, such as those which are compound or depressed, may require surgery. Such fractures carry a risk of complications, because of their position and the extent of displacement. These complications may include infection and epilepsy.

Mechanism of Brain Damage

Injury may occur directly to the nervous tissue of the brain itself, to the blood vessels or to both. Secondary damage may occur as a result of such factors as hypoxia, autolysis*, cerebral oedema, infection, intracranial haemorrhage and haematoma (Fig. 64).

	LOCAL EFFECTS	DIFFUSE EFFECTS
PRIMARY	CONTUSION LACERATION	NEURONAL CONCUSSION FIBRE SHEARING
SECONDARY	HAEMATOMA INFECTION	SWELLING HYPOXIA

Fig. 64. *Mechanism of brain damage. (From Jennett, W. B. (1970)* An Introduction to Neurosurgery. *London, Heinemann).*

Concussion is a state of unconsciousness immediately following head injury. Its cause is not fully understood. Jamieson (1971) says that it is only seen in acceleration-deceleration accidents. He suggests that there is evidence of diffuse damage to nerve cells and fibres occurring at the time of head injury. Lance and McLeod (1975) suggest that it is a transient loss of consciousness caused by sudden movement, or arrested movement, of the brain within the skull. Rotation of the cerebrum on the brain stem at the midbrain produces a shearing strain across this junction (Fig. 65) which temporarily inactivates the reticular formation. The reticular formation is particularly susceptible to mechanical disruption as it is composed of numerous synapses. Traction forces may cause a conduction block across these synapses which may last for varying periods of time. Brain and Walton (1969) suggest that it is doubtful whether any physiological or anatomical distinction should be drawn between concussion and more prolonged states of unconsciousness resulting from head injury.

Concussion is always accompanied by some degree of retrograde and post-traumatic amnesia*. The duration and depth of concussion and the period of post-traumatic amnesia are sometimes helpful in assessing the severity of the head injury.

* Glossary

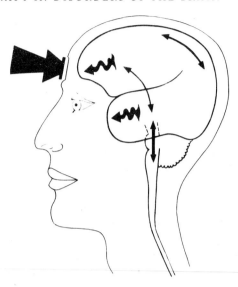

Fig. 65. *Unlike most animals, man's brain stem joins his cerebrum at a right angle, so accelera-tion – deceleration tends to rotate the cerebrum around its junction with the midbrain, stretching all the fibres across this junction, i.e. causing injury to brain stem structures. (From Martin, G. (1974)* A Manual of Head Injuries in General Surgery. *London, Heinemann).*

Contusion and laceration. 90% of contusions and lacerations are said to occur in relation to the rough and sharp bony structures within the skull (Jamieson 1971). Contusion is a bruising of the brain immediately beneath the injury. Laceration is a tearing of the tissue which can either be produced in a similar way, or from a penetrating wound, or in a contrecoup position. Severe contusion is usually accompanied by oedema resulting in cellular anoxia and dysfunction.

Intracranial haemorrhage may occur as a result of laceration. It may develop within the brain itself or on its surface. Contusion causes multiple small intracerebral haemorrhages and occasionally more extensive bleeding. Haemorrhages are referred to as subarachnoid, subdural, extradural or intracerebral, according to their location. Secondary haemorrhages may occur due to displacement of the brain. This displacement may result from raised intracranial pressure due to oedema, or from a space-occupying lesion such as a haematoma.

174

Subarachnoid haemorrhage. Bleeding into the subarachnoid space is quite common following head injury. The patient complains of headache, neck stiffness, nausea which may be accompanied by vomiting, and photophobia. He may become irritable. Positive Kernig's sign* may be elicited. If the haemorrhage is uncomplicated, the patient remains in bed for a few days and them commences gradual mobilisation.

Extradural haemorrhage is bleeding from an injured artery or vein into the extradural space produced by the dura being stripped from the bone. The vessel injured will depend on the site of the trauma. The bleeding and pooling of blood causes further stripping of the membrane. The resultant haematoma causes cerebral compression. The clot must be evacuated as soon as possible and the haemorrhage arrested. Extradural haematoma can follow a relatively minor head injury and may be fatal if undiagnosed and untreated.

Subdural haemorrhage is bleeding into the subdural space with subsequent clot formation. It often accompanies severe contusion and laceration of the brain. Blood may be found on one or both sides of the brain and is often mixed with cerebrospinal fluid. Cerebral compression results from and is in relation to, the size of the haematoma, which takes on space-occupying qualities. Compression may be relieved surgically but subsequent progress will depend on the extent of the injury to the brain.

Intracerebral haemorrhage. Multiple small haemorrhages may occur within the brain itself and may form a haematoma.

Infection is an important complication following head injury, although less common now due to better surgical care and chemotherapy. Infective cranial and intracranial complications may include infected scalp wounds, osteitis of the cranium which is rare, meningitis, infective thrombophlebitis, and intracranial abscess, which may be subdural, extradural, or intracerebral. Meningitis is seen most commonly following an injury which is accompanied by a tear of the dura, particularly when this results in leakage of cerebrospinal fluid from the nose or ears, which provides a ready access for infection.

Brain Oedema. Focal oedema (an increase in extracellular fluid) may develop around an area of contusion or haemorrhage. More generalised oedema, without evidence of contusion or laceration, may occur in a widespread fashion.

Normally autoregulation of the cerebral blood flow provides the brain with glucose and oxygen, protects the blood-brain barrier

* Glossary

against mechanical stress and thus protects the brain from oedema. The blood-brain barrier may be opened up by concussion or hypercapnia which alter autoregulation of the cerebral blood flow. The barrier opening follows capillary dilatation and increased pressure. Cerebral oedema may thus result from raised capillary pressure and capillary permeability which is caused by loss of autoregulation (Rapopart 1975).

Oedema causes an increase in intracranial pressure, brain compression, venous congestion, cellular anoxia and dysfunction. It may cause cerebral displacement, which can have disastrous effects upon the basal ganglia, hypothalamus and brain stem. Space-occupying lesions combined with oedema may cause tentorial herniation[*].

Hypoxia. Increased intracranial pressure combined with aspiration of vomitus, blood or secretions, and circulatory shock due to blood loss associated with multiple injuries, cause severe changes in the blood and cerebrospinal fluid. Maloney (1971), Le Roux (1971), Gibson (1971a), McGuire (1973) and others emphasise that many patients with head injury die or may suffer permanent secondary brain damage because of cerebral hypoxia. Hypoxia is a feature of all thoracic injuries. Flail chest, pneumothorax and haemothorax all interfere with oxygenation of the blood. At a later stage, lung collapse, bronchopneumonia and pulmonary oedema may also cause hypoxia.

There is clinical and experimental evidence (Loudon, Brueggemann and McLaurin 1975) which suggests that the brain damage may directly cause damage to the lungs. It is possible that it is the hypoxaemia of the brain, which is the initial event in the cycle, which causes lung pathology. Parham, Ducker and Redding (1975) suggest that the lung pathology following brain trauma can be divided into three categories

1. mechanical insufficiency
2. acute pulmonary oedema
3. subacute respiratory distress syndrome.

This latter term includes many types of interstitial pulmonary congestion which may occur at varying times after the injury and which are not due to heart failure.

Following brain injury the sympathetic nervous system causes a constriction of pulmonary venules. Persistance of the constriction causes pulmonary oedema. Eventually respiratory failure may occur because of the vicious cycle which ensues. This includes pulmonary

* Glossary

176

capillary damage, closure of small airways and hypoxaemia.

Cerebral compression may be caused by raised intracranial pressure due to a space-occupying haematoma regardless of its site, by focal oedema combined with contusion, or by generalised oedema if it is sufficient to produce displacement of the brain. Compression, if unrelieved, can cause irreversible brain stem damage and even death. It must be remembered that the mature cranium is incapable of expansion, unlike the immature cranium of the infant, and when pressure within it is increased there is a point when the brain must move. In other words, there is a shift or herniation of the brain, either beneath the falx, through the tentorium, or through the foramen magnum. This will result in grave neurological signs related either to direct compression of the brain stem, to compression of one of the cranial nerves, or to the vascular supply to the brain.

Signs and symptoms of cerebral compression may include an increase in blood pressure as the intracranial pressure rises, a slowing of the pulse rate and of the respiratory rate. Breathing deepens and may become stertorous. Either local or general neurological signs may become evident. Focal pressure may result in aphasia or homonymous hemianopia which will become obvious in the conscious patient. Worsening hemiplegia, and pupillary changes such as inequality of the pupils or dilatation of one pupil on the side of the haematoma, may also be signs of cerebral compression. In the later stages, pressure on the brain stem will result in decerebrate rigidity. Papilloedema* may be seen but mostly as a later manifestation.

Any deterioration in the patient's level of consciousness and type of response is the most significant and reliable sign of compression. Hence the necessity for careful recording of what the patient can do, how he reacts and the position of his limbs. The conscious patient may complain of a worsening headache and become restless and irritable. Restlessness and irritability may be observed in the semiconscious patient. Increasing compression is more difficult to diagnose in the severely head-injured patient who is deeply unconscious or who has not had a period of consciousness. The importance of observation and a neurological baseline for comparison is obvious.

Immediate surgical intervention, usually exploratory burr holes*, is necessary to relieve pressure. These may be preceded by appropriate neurological investigations such as computerised tomography.*

Abnormal postures. Particular postures are demonstrated experimentally in animals following clear ablation procedures. At a certain level of ablation, the animal demonstrates a decerebrate posture in

* Glossary

177

which all four limbs show a considerable increase in extensor tone. The extensor hypertonus of decerebrate rigidity is due to the unleashing of the facilitatory reticular formation which generates extensor tone plus the loss of the inhibition normally executed over extensor tone by the inhibitory reticular formation. As the brain stem is important for postural control which is largely due to extensor activity, the extensor bias is to be expected. Eyzaguirre and Fidone (1975) comment that the sloth whose postural control, because he hangs in trees, has a flexor predominence, demonstrates a flexor bias following decerebration.

At a higher level of ablation, the animal demonstrates a decorticate posture in which the forelimbs show an increase in flexor tone and the lower limbs an increase in extensor tone. The terms 'decerebrate' and 'decorticate' are sometimes used to describe the posturing of human patients with lesions of the brain.

The head-injured patient, following widespread and diffuse damage to the cerebral hemispheres with changes within the brain stem, and as a result of supratentorial herniation, may demonstrate a posture similar to that in decerebrated experimental animals. The legs are extended, adducted and internally rotated, the feet are plantar-flexed and inverted, the arms are extended and internally rotated, with the wrist and fingers flexed (Fig. 66). The trunk is extended and the head retracted, sometimes to the extent of opisthotonus. Other patients demonstrate a posture similar to that called decorticate in which the arms, instead of being extended, are flexed and internally rotated. Decerebrate posturing may occur in 'attacks', in response to a stimulus or spontaneously. It is usually associated with fluctuations in pulse rate, blood pressure, temperature and respiration which may result in considerable respiratory embarrassment.

Traction to the brain stem may result in damage to the long descending pyramidal and extrapyramidal tracts and to the ascending sensory tracts. This damage to the extrapyramidal tracts will be one of the causes of the hypertonus seen following head injury.

The release of abnormal reflexes such as the tonic labyrinthine reflex* and the asymmetrical and symmetrical tonic neck reflexes* may occur in these patients.

Epilepsy is an important complication following head injury. It may complicate recovery following a depressed fracture when there is penetration of the dura, following post-traumatic amnesia of more than 24 hours or associated with focal cerebral damage from intracranial haematoma. Jennett (1970) says that focal fits are more

* Glossary

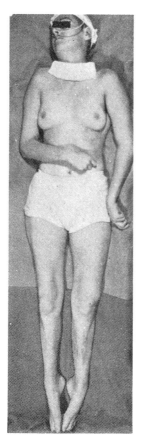

Fig. 66. *Decerebrate (left side) and decorticate (right side) posturing.* (From Lewin, W. (1966) *The Management of Head Injuries.* London, Baillière, Tindall and Cassell.)

common in the early stages than general fits and should be observed carefully. Epilepsy may occur within the first week. However, late epilepsy may occur several years after the initial head injury.

Hydrocephalus may result from a block in the cerebrospinal fluid pathways over the surface of the brain. Insertion of a ventricular-atrial shunt may be necessary to relieve pressure.

179

Admission to Hospital

Briggs (1975) divides head-injured patients admitted to hospital into three broad groups:

1. Those with severe injuries requiring treatment to save life or prevent irreversible damage.
2. Those with less severe injuries but with a high risk of developing life-threatening complications.
3. Those with apparently minor injuries admitted for observation.

Physiotherapists will be involved in and concerned with treatment of patients in the first two groups for varying periods of time, working with the medical and nursing staff to ensure as far as possible the quality of survival.

PHYSICAL TREATMENT OF THE HEAD-INJURED PATIENT

The head-injured patient presents a considerable problem of management. Preservation of life and prevention of secondary brain damage are the first priorities in the emergency treatment of the head-injured and multiply-injured patient. Care of these patients involves the expertise of a wide range of health professionals.

Skilled and forward-looking care in the immediate stage can prevent many subsequent disabilities, a fact which must not be overlooked in the urgent concern to save life (Hitchcock 1971b). The quality of recovery, not only immediate survival, should be in the minds of all who care for the patient from the time of his accident.

When the patient is first seen it is impossible to forecast the extent of his recovery with any accuracy. Some authors classify the severity of head injury in relation to the degree of orientation found in the patient or to the extent of post-traumatic amnesia, but these are probably unreliable parameters. Others consider the length of coma to be a prognostic guide. Of those who are in a coma for more than one month, 20% will return to work, 60% will survive in varying degrees of unemployable disablement, and 20% will die (Martin 1974). Final rehabilitation of the severely head-injured patient may take up to two years or more.

EARLY CARE

Unconscious patients following head injury will preferably be nursed in a neurosurgical or specialised head injury intensive care unit. However, where the patient is admitted will depend upon the site of the accident, the presence of suitable facilities in close proximity and his condition. He may be admitted to an intensive care unit or to the general ward of a small country hospital.

Consciousness is a state of awareness in which the subject is capable of perception (Lance and McLeod 1975). The reticular activating system in the brain stem is considered to be the area of the brain which is responsible for arousal and maintenance of consciousness. Depth of consciousness is gauged by the person's response to painful stimuli, speech, touch and pressure. Impairment or *loss of consciousness* may be caused by severe and diffuse damage to the cerebral cortex, and damage to the midline structures of the thalamus and midbrain involving the reticular formation. This damage may occur directly or indirectly, by means of cerebral compression, reduction of blood flow or its oxygen content, or from shearing or tearing during injury. Unconsciousness following head injury is transient unless followed by death, and may last from a few hours to several months.

It is preferable that the head-injured patient in these early critical stages should be treated by a therapist with considerable expertise in acute respiratory care and an understanding of the relationship between respiratory and brain function.

Some General Points about Early Care

The airway. Provision of a clear airway, adequate ventilation of the lungs, plus adequate perfusion 24 hours a day is essential in the management of the head-injured at this stage. The patient is nursed on a firm surface in a semi-prone position or on his side. The semi-prone position in particular is important in the prevention of aspiration of vomitus and blood, and in preventing the airway from being blocked by the tongue. Secretions are mechanically aspirated from the mouth and nose frequently. Leakage of cerebrospinal fluid via the nose is a contra-indication to nasal aspiration because of the risk of infection.

Hypoxia may cause further damage to the brain and prevent or slow down recovery of damaged but viable brain tissue. Adequacy of ventilation is estimated by the measurement of tidal volume, respiratory rate, $PaCO_2$ and PaO_2 levels, while adequacy of perfusion is estimated by pulmonary artery pressure, systemic blood pressure, pulse rate and cardiac output.

Positioning. The patient is usually nursed undressed to make nursing and other important procedures easier, to help prevent pressure areas, and for easier observation. He is nursed without pillows on a firm surface. The bed may need to be elevated to reduce intracranial pressure. However, some authors stress that elevation of the patient's head is usually ill-advised as it contributes to venous congestion and cerebral oedema.

A special bed, from which the ends can be removed to allow easy access for mechanical suction and ventilation is preferable. These beds are easily moved, have protective sides and can be tilted. The patient will need a pillow between his legs and another for the support of his arm in an attempt to prevent abnormal reflex activity and posturing. Special care must be taken in positioning a patient with a tracheostomy, or with endotracheal intubation so that he may be suctioned easily. Care must be taken also in positioning the tube from the respirator to make sure it does not kink.

Tube feeding. When unconsciousness persists and until automatic swallowing is re-established, the patient is fed via a nasogastric tube. This method of feeding may be accompanied by bowel disturbances, but is preferred to intravenous feeding which, if prolonged, results in electrolyte inbalance. It is important to remember that the patient can still vomit and aspirate even when tube fed. Prolonged tube feeding and unconsciousness may eventually result in weight loss and poor nutrition.

The unconscious patient will require turning every two hours for 24 hours in the day. This will help prevent pressure areas and pooling of secretions in the lungs. Positioning and turning may be complicated by the presence of other injuries.

Observation. In some units patients are connected to multi-monitoring units which produce electroencephalograms and electrocardiograms, record intracranial pressure and the level of carbon-dioxide in the blood. They also give warning of cardiac arrest and apnoea. This type of automatic monitoring sometimes proves unreliable in restless patients (Obrador 1971) and it requires expert knowledge for accurate interpretation.

Briggs (1975) emphasises the dependency of the patient on the skilled care of the nurse and physiotherapist and quotes Potter (1964) 'Special knowledge and quality in nursing care may be the deciding factor between life and death of a patient'.

As well as the recording of vital signs (rate and type of respiration, pulse rate and blood pressure) the importance of observation and recording of levels of alertness and response to stimuli, of the size and reaction of the pupils, and of the posture and movement of the limbs and trunk, must be emphasised. Changes in these three areas, may be of great importance in the recognition of deterioration or of improvement. McLaurin and Ford (1964) and Hitchcock (1971a) have suggested that emphasis on autonomic function is generally of less importance than that of conscious level, pupillary reactions and posture.

Other information to be recorded includes temperature, signs of bruising or tenderness, observation of colour, and focal seizures or more generalised fits.

The Skin. Prolonged unconsciousness combined with immobilisation in bed are always precipitating factors in the development of pressure areas. Prolonged pressure has a deleterious effect upon the skin. Added to this, extreme catabolic responses are frequently seen following head injury (Briggs 1975). The most important prophylaxis is frequent and regular turning combined with careful positioning, with special observation and care to areas which are particularly susceptible to damage. Bladder and bowel incontinence add to the risk of skin breakdown. These patients require a urinary collection device or catheterisation.

Nursing the patient on a sheepskin or ripple mattress is effective in reducing the effects of pressure, especially when frequent and regular turning is difficult because of injuries. Sheepskin boots are useful in preventing pressure areas on the heels. Foam rubber rings are probably of little benefit. They often cause pressure elsewhere, and are usually bandaged on, thus preventing easy observation of the skin.

When associated injuries require treatment by splint, plaster or traction, special attention to prevent skin breakdown will be necessary. Brisk, firm rubbing of the at-risk area of skin with a piece of ice produces a local erythema and seems effective in preventing the effects of pressure (Goff 1969).

The Eyes. Damage to the eyes may result from direct injury, or through dessication or trauma to the insensitive conjunctivae in the unconscious patient, or through injury to the facial nerve. This latter causes a lower motor neuron paralysis and results in an inability to close the eye. This may lead to conjunctivitis or to overflow of tears resulting from excessive secretions or obstruction of the lacrimal passage. Some form of artificial closure of the eyelid may be necessary but certainly the eye must be covered. It is most important to note that abrasion of the open eye in the unconscious patient may result in corneal ulceration leading to blindness. Damage to the optic nerve, to the cranial nerves supplying the muscles of the eyes, or to the vision-controlling centres in the brain may result in loss of vision, nystagmus, double vision or visual field defects such as scotoma* or hemianopia.

* Glossary

Temperature. A disturbance of temperature control may result from damage to the thermostatic mechanism in the hypothalamus resulting in hyperthermia. It is essential to keep the temperature as normal as possible. Elevation of the body temperature diminishes the recuperative power of the damaged brain (Loew 1971). To reduce the temperature the patient is sponged with cold water, covered with ice cold wet sheets with a fan directed on to him, or nursed with bags of ice applied to his naked body.

Other factors such as meningitis, bronchopneumonia, urinary tract infection or wound infection may also result in a raised temperature which is usually accompanied by sweating.

Relatives. The relatives of patients with head injuries will need help, support and explanation from the moment of injury until final rehabilitation. They will need to understand that they should try to establish contact with him even though he appears unconscious and unable to respond. The need for these early attempts at contact with the patient must be explained to the relatives, so they will not feel foolish carrying on a monologue. Patients can frequently recall these early attempts at communication and comment during their later rehabilitation of the reassurance they gained. Relatives are able to help stimulate and assist the patient to re-orientate himself, by bringing in familiar photographs and by telling the therapist of his interests.

As the patient begins to regain consciousness, relatives will need help in understanding and trying to cope with his perseverant and possibly regressive behaviour, emotional instability, aggression, irritability and poor concentration. These changes in behaviour may be aggravated by communication problems and be easily misunderstood. In the early stage, some of these problems, for example poor concentration and inability to co-operate in treatment, may be wrongly attributed to intellectual impairment. Many of these problems improve with time, proper understanding and insight into the reasons.

Methods of ensuring adequate ventilatory function

Injury to the chest wall may include rib fractures, flail chest or tissue loss. The lungs may be contused, ruptured or be the site of a haematoma. The oesophagus or diaphragm may be ruptured. The heart and great vessels may be damaged. The trachea or bronchi may be fractured, compressed or obstructed. Aspiration of vomitus, blood or a foreign body, such as teeth, may occur. The swallowing reflexes may be depressed. The respiratory centre itself may be depressed following injury to the brain stem.

All these complications of head injury may progress to or be aggravated by infection, sputum retention, pulmonary fat embolism, haemothorax, pneumothorax, hypo- or hyperventilation, pulmonary or bronchial oedema developing into atelectasis and broncho-pneumonia. The patient with head injury may have previously suffered from a chronic thoracic disease and this will add to the difficulty in management.

Artificial airways

Some means of ensuring a clear airway is necessary in the uncon-scious head-injured patient.

An oro-pharyngeal airway (Guedel's tube) may be used to facilitate pharyngeal suction by providing a clear pathway to the pharynx, to prevent the catheter from being bitten and to prevent the tongue from falling backward and obstructing the airway.

Endotracheal intubation may be indicated in certain circumstances, for example, where there is difficulty maintaining a clear airway by an oro-pharyngeal tube, as an emergency measure in a cyanosed patient, during transportation of a patient who is deeply unconscious and whose prognosis is uncertain. In other words, it may be necessary for patients who require mechanical assistance to breathe and frequent mechanical suction. It may be inserted through the nasal passage or mouth.

Ulceration and laryngeal damage may occur if the tube is left in situ for too long, and in long term care, tracheostomy will be the preferred method of ventilation.

It is generally considered that except in a real emergency trache-ostomy should be preceded by endotracheal intubation. It then becomes an elective procedure, and can be performed with an endotracheal tube in place.

Tracheostomy may be indicated in certain circumstances, for example, for patients who have a flail or crushed thorax, a fractured jaw with severe facial injury, cervical spine injury, in patients who remain deeply unconscious for some time following a severe head injury, for patients with a chronic thoracic disease or where there is disturbance of bulbar function and spasm of the glottis. In other words it may be necessary in patients who have an obstruction of the upper respiratory tract, in patients who require mechanical assistance to breathe, in patients who require frequent mechanical suction, and to prevent aspiration of vomitus, blood and secretions.

The complications following tracheostomy may include infection, surgical emphysema, pneumothorax, tracheal stenosis, tracheo-oesophageal fistula and haemorrhage.

A cuffed tube, either endotracheal or tracheal, will be necessary for most patients. The cuffed tube is designed to provide a good seal between the trachea and the tube. It is used to prevent air from escaping around the tube when positive pressure ventilation is being used, and to prevent vomitus and secretions from the mouth from entering the bronchi in patients who do not have a swallowing reflex. A tube with a soft pressure cuff which moulds to the trachea and adjusts to the pressure within it is used in preference to the older style of tube. The latter requires a greater pressure on a smaller surface to provide an adequate seal and therefore tends to cause ulceration and stenosis of the trachea. The cuff is deflated for a few minutes every two hours to avoid ulceration and stenosis. Mechanical suction of the mouth and pharynx must be performed before and while the cuff is deflated to prevent the patient from aspirating. Care must be taken in inflating the tube so as to ensure the right amount of inflation to create a seal while avoiding over-inflation which adds to the risk of ulceration. A patient with a cuffed tube is unable to speak because it prevents air from passing over the vocal cords.

Humidification and warming of the inspired gases through a nebuliser is essential to prevent drying and crusting of secretions since the normal mechanism of humidification in the upper respiratory tract has been bypassed.

Assisted ventilation and drainage will be necessary when there is increasing ventilatory effort caused by decerebrate posturing or thoracic injury, increased respiratory rate resulting in hyperventilation or depressed respiratory rate resulting in inadequate ventilation and carbondioxide retention. It is also indicated when there are signs of rising intracranial pressure, in the hope that the early correction of hypoxia and control of the respiratory rate may minimise the extent of tissue destruction.

Intermittent positive pressure ventilators are used to inflate the lungs or assist inspiration. Expiration is passive although some machines do have a negative phase which may sometimes be used to assist circulation. When intermittent positive pressure is used to ventilate the patient, the gradient for venous return from the peripheral parts of the body to the right side of the heart is reduced, therefore hindering venous circulation. Hence the use of a negative pressure phase in the machine's expiratory cycle may be recommended by the anaesthetist. A patient who requires mechanical assistance to breathe should never be left unobserved. Ventilators are used in which tidal volume, respiratory rate, airways pressure and inspired oxygen levels can be set with reasonable accuracy, and regulated according to pulmonary and blood gas function.

Physiotherapy

Physiotherapy is commenced as soon as the airway is established in order to ensure that the lungs are kept fully expanded and that stasis plus retention of secretions is prevented. Effective physiotherapy ensures a clear airway, prevents lung collapse, reduces the arterial CO_2 level and ensures adequate oxygenation of the blood, and hence the brain. Methods of treatment include regular and frequent turning, correct positioning, regular mechanical aspiration, rib springing, percussion and vibration to the thorax. Postural drainage may be possible after the first 24 hours but this will depend on the patient's condition. It is usually contra-indicated in the presence of cerebral oedema and raised intracranial pressure. Postural drainage may have to be discontinued temporarily following surgery, or investigative procedures such as lumbar puncture or encephalography.

Mechanical suction will be required at least until the patient regains consciousness, in order to remove secretions from the respiratory passages and ensure a clear airway. Suction is indicated before and after the patient is turned from one position to another, and whenever breathing can be heard to be obstructed by secretions. Airways obstruction by secretions must also be suspected if the patient's colour changes or if he becomes restless. Suction will elicit the cough reflex unless the patient is deeply unconscious or has a brain stem lesion with depressed activity of the respiratory centre.

A soft catheter of the correct size for the patient's airway is introduced into the pharynx through the mouth, the oro-pharyngeal tube or via the nasal passages. This latter will be contra-indicated when there is leakage of cerebrospinal fluid from the nose, and in the presence of facial injuries.

If there is an endotracheal tube or a tracheostomy tube the catheter is introduced into the trachea via the tube. A sterile technique is essential. Care must be taken during suction to avoid damage to the delicate membranes of the nose, to the pharynx, trachea and carina, and to prevent the introduction of infection.

In patients who require mechanical ventilation, the ventilator is disconnected momentarily to allow suction to be performed. The oxygen-air supply must not be disconnected for too long and some patients will require hand ventilation with a bag breathing device prior to and interspersed with suction.

When coughing is ineffective or absent the lungs can be hyperventilated manually by means of an oxygen-inflation unit or anaesthetic bag which is attached to the tracheostomy or endotracheal tube and which produces a maximal expansion of the lungs when compressed. The pressure is released to coincide with expiratory overpressure and

187

vibration by the physiotherapist. The procedure is repeated rhythmically until the secretions are discharged into the trachea from whence they can be suctioned. This method of clearing the airway is used in conjunction with positioning, each area of the lungs being treated in turn with emphasis on re-expanding any area of atelectasis.

Decerebrate posturing restricts movements of respiration. Hypertonus around the shoulder girdle will also restrict respiratory movements. The supine position increases the resistance to diaphragmatic expansion and increases the tendency towards extensor hypertonus and these factors together with the risk of aspiration provide good reason for avoiding this position.

Some physiotherapists are using treatment procedures which produce reflexive, involuntary respiratory movement. These can be performed on the unconscious patient as they do not require the patient's co-operation. They are based on techniques which cause co-contraction of the abdominal muscles as described by Rood. Bethune (1975), who describes these techniques, considers that the results, which include deeper respiration, improved respiratory pattern and an apparent increase in the level of consciousness are remarkably consistent, although the mechanism is little understood.

All methods of treatment will have to be modified in patients with complicating thoracic injuries. The frequency of treatment and the exact nature of it will be dictated by the signs and symptoms as they present. Observation of thoracic movement and rate of respiration, auscultation, radiographs and blood gas levels will assist the therapist to assess the frequency and methods of treatment required. Noisy or difficult breathing or asymmetrical thoracic expansion needs to be investigated immediately. The causes may be obstruction of the airway by secretions, or obstruction of the tube, which may be either encrusted or too long. If it is too long it will enter the right main bronchus, obstruct the left bronchus and prevent expansion of this lung. Co-operation between the therapist and the nurse is essential in timing these physical procedures with other care.

Methods of Ensuring Joint Integrity and Muscle Length

Prolonged unconsciousness following head injury is usually accompanied by hypertonus and frequently by decerebrate posturing and abnormal tonic reflex activity which may eventually result in contractures of muscles and soft tissues (Fig. 67). These problems may be aggravated by faulty positioning of the patient by inexperienced staff who do not understand the significance of hypertonus and abnormal

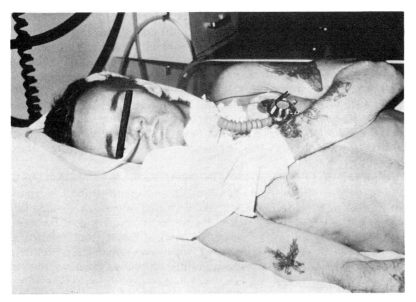

Fig. 67. *Prolonged and persistent abnormal posturing may result in contracture.*

postures, and who do not use the appropriate methods for minimising their effects.

The difficulty in positioning a head-injured patient with other injuries such as limb fractures and severe abrasions aggravates the tendency for contractures to develop. However, contractures may also occur because of the severity and longevity of rigid posturing which causes great difficulty in positioning the patient satisfactorily. Noxious stimuli may cause an increase in hypertonus and unfortunately the head-injured patient frequently has painful or uncomfortable procedures administered to him.

There is evidence in experimental animals constantly confined to a certain postural set that structural changes eventually develop in the proprioceptors themselves. If these structural changes occur in humans, they may explain some of the difficulties experienced in caring for the long-term rigid patient. Changes in muscle spindle morphology and alteration of receptor sensitivity in the muscle spindles of the shortened muscle occur when a joint is held in an extreme position for a sustained period (Eldred, Bridgman, Kano, Sasaki and Yellin 1967).

During the stage when the patient must be confined to bed, the

189

likelihood of contractures developing can be lessened. To do this it is necessary to minimise the severity of hypertonus and abnormal posturing *throughout the body*. Care must be taken not to stimulate fusimotor activity which is highly sensitive to cutaneous stimulation. This is accomplished by *positioning*, which inhibits primitive and pathological neuromuscular activity, by *careful handling* with a minimum of inappropriate stimulation, and by facilitation and encouragement of *movement*. As soon as the patient is sufficiently conscious he should be sat on the edge of the bed and stood up, as weight-bearing through the limbs assists in preventing contractures.

Positioning

The patient is positioned in side lying or semi-prone, as these positions, because they are less likely to elicit abnormal tonic reflex activity, make hypertonus easier to control. A pillow placed between slightly flexed legs prevents the leg from adducting and internally rotating and the foot from inverting, a position which may stimulate extensor spasticity in the lower limb. Calf muscle contracture must in particular be prevented as it is a major barrier to early weight-bearing. The arm is supported on a pillow with the shoulder girdle protracted and elbow extended.

In patients who must be nursed in supine because of complicating injuries, such as a fractured femur which has not been immobilised by internal fixation, positioning of the knee in some flexion will help to control extensor hypertonus and calf muscle contracture.

Movement

At the stage when the patient is unable to respond actively, either volitionally or automatically, passive movements performed by the therapist are the only means of movement possible. It is probable that the 'passive movements to maintain full range of joint mobility' referred to in the literature, if performed with no regard for the presence of hypertonus, are ineffective or dangerous. It is doubtful whether a passive movement can be performed in full range in the presence of severe hypertonus without resort to potentially danger-ous stretching. Overzealous stretching, particularly around the elbow joint, may lead to inflammation or tearing of the muscles followed by calcification and bone formation in muscles, tendons and ligaments, and this is particularly likely to occur in patients who are not responding to pain. Sudden stretch is known to stimulate the stretch reflex and increase tone in hypertonic muscles, and should also be avoided.

Eldred *et al.* (1967) comment that temporary reversal of an abnormal posture is unlikely to influence receptor sensitivity once muscle spindle morphology has altered. The limb will therefore regain its abnormal position after passive movement. The most effective means of preventing contractures appear to be positioning and avoidance of uncontrolled stimulation.

Passive movements will aid in the inhibition of hypertonus if the emphasis is initially on movement of proximal parts of the body (Figs. 68 & 69). When free movement has been gained proximally, the therapist moves the patient's hand to touch various parts of his body, various objects and different textures. She moves his lower limbs,

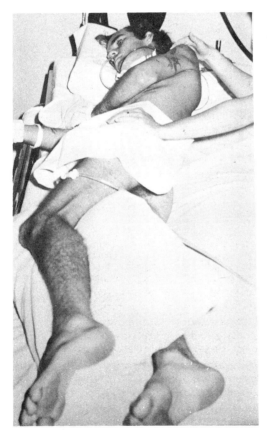

Fig. 68. *Rotation between pelvis and shoulder helps to inhibit hypertonus.*

191

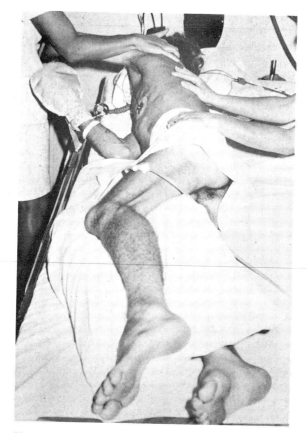

Figure 69. *Protraction of the shoulder girdle and extension of the arm in external rotation will further inhibit hypertonus.*

concentrating on flexion and extension of the knee with the hip extended, holding the foot in dorsiflexion and eversion (Fig. 70).

These movements are done two hourly when the patient is turned. Care is taken while moving a limb to check that the movement is not stimulating associated movements in the rest of the body. The therapist must also be careful where she places her hands so as not to stimulate hypertonus. For example, if she places her hand in the palm of the patient's hand she may stimulate flexor spasticity in the whole of the upper limb.

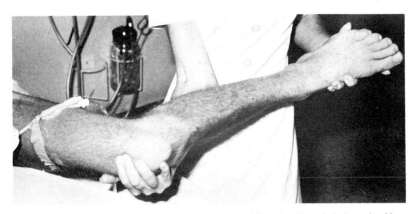

Fig. 70. *Knee movement with the hip extended and foot dorsiflexed. It is preferable to hold the foot on the dorsal surface to prevent stimulation of extensor hypertonus.*

Nurses caring for these patients need a clear understanding of the necessity for the means of inhibiting hypertonus by positioning, proximal movement and avoidance of uncontrolled stimulation. They should understand that inhibition of tone throughout the body will help prevent the development of local contracture.

The limbs should not be restrained unless this is essential. Most forms of restraint increase tone throughout the body by applying intermittent stretch to hyperactive muscle spindles. For this reason, footboards, sleeping boots and cock-up splints are contra-indicated in these patients. Inflatable plastic splints may be useful in inhibiting flexor hypertonus of the upper limb and may eliminate the need for restraint by keeping the patient's hands away from his face. However, if flaccid paralysis is present, as a result of damage to a peripheral nerve, for example, some form of splinting to prevent contracture and deformity may be necessary.

The use of drugs such as diazepam, oxazepam or nitrazepam to relieve hypertonus may be useful, but they also depress consciousness, making assessment of the patient more difficult and masking signs of deterioration or improvement.

LATER CARE

The difficulties encountered in discussing the treatment of the head-injured stem from the great variety of problems with which these patients present and the dissimilarity of one patient from another. Treatment depends on accurate assessment and upon the physiotherapist's ability to solve problems.

193

It is the authors' intention in this part of the chapter to point out some of the most important details of physical treatment for these patients. For more detail about the treatment of specific problems, the reader should consult the previous chapter and Section III.

The stage of improving consciousness may be a difficult one for all concerned in the patient's rehabilitation. His behavioural responses and neurological status may vary from day to day or more frequently. Those caring for him must give consideration to the restoration of his sense of dignity by talking to him as a person, by considering his feelings during conversation around his bed and by ensuring that he is appropriately dressed. Relatives and staff will need help in acknowledging his behaviour as a manifestation of his brain damage rather than as intentional. This will require more effort when the patient's appearance and behaviour is unpleasant, disturbing, regressive and so unlike his former self. It is worthwhile remembering that many of the procedures carried out on the unconscious and semi-conscious patient are unpleasant and perhaps this is one reason why the reaction of some patients is an aggressive, denial response.

As the patient returns to consciousness, the emphasis in physiotherapy changes. As soon as possible he must be stimulated to relearn the functions he has lost and the therapist should ensure that he is involved in his treatment by insisting on his participation and by careful, easily understandable explanations of what is happening.

Probably the most important objectives of rehabilitation at this stage are to provide sufficient stimulus to motivate the patient, to stimulate automatic antigravity reactions, to stimulate sensory integration and perception, and to help him relearn the movements he can no longer perform.

Problems Affecting Function and their Treatment

The problems affecting function will vary according to the areas of the brain affected and to the extent to which they are damaged. Treatment is largely in the hands of the physiotherapist, occupational therapist and speech pathologist at this stage.

It is doubtful whether any therapist, treating the head-injured patient with his widespread and changing problems, can expect to follow a preconceived treatment plan. She must be continuously alert and sensitive to changes in his level or responsiveness and in his emotional and neurological state. She must also be adaptable and imaginative enough to be able to alter the emphasis and the details of her treatment so as to work toward restoring his motor skills and his mental equilibrium.

The therapist should observe for and attempt to control any behaviour which makes treatment difficult or impossible, or which results in negative attitudes from those who come in contact with him. It is possible to manipulate the consequences of these behaviours in order to modify or change them. Take, for example, a young head-injured patient who laughs uncontrollably at any stimulus, this laughing always being accompanied by marked extension of the jaw. This behaviour should not be reinforced by others laughing with him, drawing attention to him, or stopping their demands upon him. The laughing should be ignored where it is inappropriate and positive verbal or other reinforcement given to him for appropriate behaviour. In this particular example, positive reinforcement may be given whenever the patient keeps his mouth closed.

Oro-facial and respiratory dysfunction

There should be an emphasis in early treatment on overcoming the problems of oro-facial and respiratory dysfunction. The establishment of normal swallowing, unassisted breathing, effective coughing and communication by facial expression, gesture and speech is essential if the patient is to resume more normal function.

All patients following head injury will have some degree of communication difficulty. Some, however, will also have specific speech and language problems, such as aphasia. Oro-facial problems may include inability to swallow, poor lip and jaw closure, an aversion to certain textures in the mouth, inability to chew, and abnormal reflex activity such as a bite reflex and a hypo- or hyperactive gag reflex. Facial asymmetry may be present due to loss or cortical control or due to a facial nerve palsy.

Once the patient can breathe unaided for several minutes he is disconnected from the ventilator for short periods. He requires reassurance as tension and anxiety may precipitate respiratory distress. He needs constant supervision when he is first taken off the ventilator. These periods of unassisted breathing are gradually increased in duration and frequency.

Normal speech and eating are dependent upon the normal control of inspiration and expiration. Patients who have had both nasogastric and tracheostomy tubes in situ for a period of time need to re-develop co-ordination of respiration, speech and eating once these tubes are removed. Prolonged tube feeding is associated with deprivation of oral sensation and results, for example, in reduction of the sensations which are necessary to stimulate swallowing.

When it is time for these tubes to be removed it is usually easier if one tube is removed before the other. For example, removal of the nasogastric tube first allows the patient to re-establish swallowing control. When his tracheostomy tube is removed he can then re-establish breathing control without so much risk of aspiration. He will also need to re-develop his ability to co-ordinate respiration with speech.

Assumption of an antigravity position such as sitting helps to stimulate lung expansion, coughing, swallowing and eating as well as communication.

The patient who is unable to sit alone because of severe extensor hypertonus (Fig. 71) or extensor spasms, may be more easily controlled and may develop more control himself if he sits astride a roller or on a chair with his hips flexed, weight forward and arms on a table

Fig. 71. *This girl following head injury is unable to sit because of extensor spasticity which prevents her from flexing her hips.*

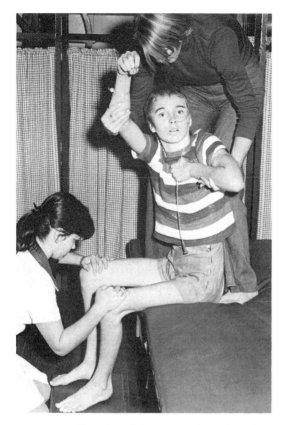

Fig. 72. (a) *Elevation of the arms and rotation of the trunk with feet on the floor inhibits spasticity and allows flexion at the hips.*

(Fig. 72). This will stimulate head control and vision. It will be simpler for him to control his respirations and vocalise, and he will also be able to re-develop eating and drinking skills. He will feel more symmetrical and his head will be in an effective position for eye contact and communication with the therapist or relative.

Abnormalities of sensori-motor function

Hypotonus may be present in the early stages. It is often transient, developing ultimately into some degree of constant or fluctuating hypertonus. A generalised hypotonus may, however, remain, associated with *ataxia*.

197

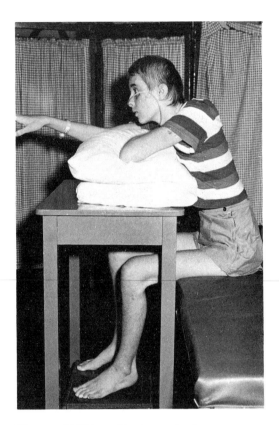

Fig. 72. *(b) This enables her to sit alone.*

Hypertonus, which is a common problem following head injury, is usually distributed throughout the trunk, head and limbs in a quadriplegic manner, but frequently one side is more affected than the other or one side has tone of a different quality from the other. This asymmetrical involvement may give the appearance of a hemiplegia.

Some patients demonstrate an abnormal degree of generalised flexion which has a tendency to increase when the patient is disturbed. This apparently primitive behaviour may be accompanied by perseverant whimpering noises.

If the tonic neck reflexes* and the tonic labyrinthine reflex* are

* Glossary

198

released from cortical control, movement and posture will be affected by head position. Effort, whether mental or physical, will cause associated movements in abnormal synergies of spasticity which also interfere with attempts to regain function.

Tremor may be present either as an intention, action or resting tremor. Cerebellar ataxia and rarely, athetosis, may be seen by themselves or in combination with hypertonus.

Abnormal tone and movement and abnormal postural reactions will interfere with attempts to re-establish function by affecting head control and visual regard, balance, weight transference, weight-bearing, symmetry, normal body alignment and the particular combinations of movements that go to make up motor skills. At no point however, can sensori-motor function be considered as separate from cognitive and behavioural functions such as concentration, comprehension, communication, social behaviour, reasoning ability and conceptualisation.

As soon as the patient's level of consciousness improves, sitting out of bed should commence. At this point emphasis in treatment will be on stimulating balance and movement in sitting and standing, that is, on stimulating movement in positions which are most relevant. The assumption of these positions has a number of positive effects on the patient. As they are positions in which we normally spend our waking day, the patient is given a feeling of normality even when he has not yet achieved the ability to control the position himself. They help his readjustment to more normal movement and provide motivation. They stimulate him to be more alert than he would be in either supine or prone when he would tend to drift off and lose concentration. These positions enable the therapist to stimulate eye contact and head control and encourage the use of the optical righting reactions which help him to align himself with his surroundings and to re-establish his automatic responses to alterations in his centre of gravity. *The assumption of upright positions and early activity* in these positions aids the patient in regaining control over his bladder, and helps prevent an excessive increase in hypertonus.

As soon as possible the patient should be taken out of the ward into a treatment area. At first it may be necessary to transport him on a trolley but as soon as he is beginning in treatment to practise weight shift in sitting, he should be transported in a wheelchair. Again, in this sitting position he will receive stimulation from his environment with less tendency toward lethargy, and he will be practising maintaining and regaining head and trunk control. A broad strap around the trunk will allow the patient who lacks sufficient balance or who has extensor spasms to travel safely in a chair.

Many head-injured patients are young adults and experience of movement on a ball (Figs. 121, 122) or on air mattress provides a stimulus to *vestibular function* by stimulating automatic balance responses from the limbs, trunk and head. The patients will often practise controlling their movement on the ball by themselves, and because such activity is fun, they learn to appreciate the value of free and unimpeded movement. It is interesting that patients given such experience of movement rarely demonstrate a marked degree of hypertonus.

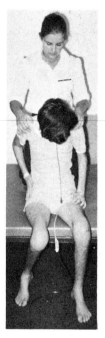

Fig. 73. *This girl following head injury is unable to sit.*

Postural adjustments and the ability to move about are stimulated in sitting and standing by encouraging *weight transference* forward and laterally and weight-bearing through the hands (Figs. 73 and 74) as well as through the feet. As soon as the patient can transfer weight laterally and forward in standing he is ready to take steps and start walking. It is important that *walking* is stimulated early in treatment in order to give him the feeling of the rhythmical and reciprocal movements necessary. The use of a tilt table to enable the patient to

Fig. 74. *Weight-bearing through the hands in this manner encourages lateral weight shift and awareness of position of head in space and improved body alignment.*

201

be put in the standing position is sometimes suggested. However, this method of standing is passive and does not encourage the re-establishment of normal active standing. It may have some use for certain patients who are difficult to control. However, it is preferable for the patient to stand up in a more natural way, via the sitting position, with the therapist giving him as much guidance and assistance as necessary to make the change of position possible. Two therapists may be required at first and it is a good idea for the occupational therapist and physiotherapist to work together at this point.

Stimulation of movement may be limited by *contractures*, the most common being flexion of the elbow, wrist and fingers, and plantar-flexion and inversion of the foot. The latter is usually the most serious and it can prevent early weight-bearing and walking. Treatment methods directed at inhibiting hypertonus throughout the body, including reflex inhibiting movement patterns* and the stimulation of balance reactions* may result in a gradual increase in range at these joints, the degree of actual muscle shortening sometimes being confused with hypertonus. Real shortening of the tendo Achilles may, however, be considerable and will need to be corrected, preferably by weight-bearing inhibitory plasters* (Figs. 146 and 147), or if necessary by tenotomy.

It is futile to try to separate the problem of contracture and treat it separately from the total picture of movement disability. Many contractures, particularly of the upper limb, gradually improve as the patient is stimulated to move about. It is therefore important that treatment does not concentrate on the contracture so much as on stimulating functional movement.

Treatment, since it is aimed at restoring function, should consist of movements which are goal-directed and which therefore have some meaning for the patient. Exercise programmes, which are not based on the particular problems of the individual, may have no meaning for these patients in terms of regaining lost skills. They are less likely to trigger off a response from the patient's damaged brain. Valuable time is lost when the patient has to expend his limited attention span on exercises which have no functional goal immediately apparent to him. In addition, exercise programmes are usually directed at increasing strength and are therefore irrelevant to the head-injured patient whose movement problems do not arise from muscular weakness but from loss of cortical drive, and perceptual and emotional dysfunction.

Following head injury the patient may suffer partial or complete

* Appendix 1.

loss of one of the special senses such as hearing, vision or taste. Tactile and proprioceptive sensations may be altered. Commonly there is loss or alteration of the integration of sensations manifested by such perceptual disorders as astereognosis, loss of two point discrimination, visual agnosia, disorders of body schema and visuo-spatial disorders. Apraxia or inability to motor plan is also seen in some patients.

Perceptual dysfunction is probably always the cause of considerable problems in the first few months following head injury. Much of it may be secondary to the deprivation of stimuli and the lack of experience of movement which the patient suffers during the early stages. Treatment of all head-injured patients should include activities which stimulate in particular an awareness of body parts and their relationships, and orientation in space. Movement itself enhances both sensation and sensory integration.

Hearing loss or impairment either from the head injury itself or as a pre-morbid state must not be confused with receptive aphasia, and defects in hearing must eventually be thoroughly investigated.

The therapist must watch for any signs of *visual problems*. These may include double vision (diplopia), nystagmus and visual field defects, all of which will interfere with the patient's responsiveness and motivation, and his ability to regain symmetry, head control, visual regard and optical righting. For example, a patient with double vision may attempt to keep one eye closed, may close both his eyes or may constantly hold his head in a position which enables him to focus. He may need to have his affected eye covered during treatment. The orthoptist, following her assessment, will be able to suggest ways of improving and stimulating his vision.

As well as specific sensory deficits and the problems resulting from reduced sensory input, there will also be problems which arise as a result of the sensory feedback from abnormal movements and abnormal tone. The patient's sensory experiences during the period following his head injury have been on the whole unpleasant and unnatural, and may be one of the reasons for some patients' apparent desire to be left alone. A form of tactile defensiveness may be evident, the patient removing himself from certain forms of stimulation. This usually responds well to techniques which desensitise and condition him to accept the sensations.

Behavioural disturbances. These may include drowsiness, confusion, irritability, outbursts of rage, depression, anxiety, aggression, apathy and lack of volition, poor concentration, memory loss, egocentricity, hyperactivity, impulsiveness and dementia. Some of these disturbances may manifest themselves in regressive, inappropriate and perseverant behaviour which needs to be channelled into more purposeful activity. Certain behaviour, such as sudden bursts of rage, are thought to be related to the patient's pre-morbid personality. Social workers and psychologists will be helpful in guiding relatives and other health professionals in coping with these difficult behaviours. However, psychiatric referral may be necessary for some patients.

These behavioural disturbances will affect his home and social life and may eventually be the most difficult of the problems with which he and his family will have to cope. In the long term they may affect his employment possibilities or schooling, and they may develop into psychiatric disorders.

Needless to say, the therapist requires to be understanding, patient, firm, imaginative and adaptable in deflecting the patient's antisocial behaviour into channels appropriate to her aims and his requirements.

Some General Points about Rehabilitation

The word 'rehabilitation' means different things to different people. It should infer that the patient is to be rehabilitated to the maximum of his ability and not just to within the limits of his disability. Therefore, it is necessary that the physiotherapist does not assume recovery has been reached just because the patient is so much better than his immediate post-injury state. The outcome of rehabilitation of these patients can only be assessed in terms of the home, social, occupational, and medical status of the individual. Acceptance and adjustment by the patient and his family may depend upon a change of values. Jennett (1972) comments that 'judgement about outcome is apt to have a large subjective component . . . a different view of recovery may be taken by the patient himself who knows only how *well* he was *before* injury, by the doctor who knows only how *bad* he was *after* injury, and by the family who know something of both'. Walker (1972) suggest that the degree of adjustment may relate more to the quality of the original brain than to the severity of the injury or the clinical impairment.

Where a patient may appear to lose interest and fail to improve, the therapist should not assume that recovery has ceased but should try to establish the reasons for this situation. For example, inappropriate treatment will cause boredom through being too easy, or frustration through being meaningless or too difficult. External stimuli may be interfering with his concentration and he may benefit from being treated for a while in a quiet atmosphere. A young male patient may benefit from being treated by a male therapist. Many patients benefit from swimming programmes which also stimulate mental functions and the ideas incorporated into the Halliwick method (Reid 1976) seem particularly useful.

Anxiety and tension, whether generated by the health professionals, the relatives, the patient himself or by other patients, should be avoided as far as possible. It is important that not only the patient but his relatives also should be involved in, and have explained to them, all changes in care whether it is the first time he is sat up or the first time he is taken out of the ward.

The patient should go on an outing or go home for a weekend as soon as possible. Home visits should be made by the therapist before and after he goes home, before in order to plan for his return, some time after to make sure that he and his relatives are coping satisfactorily. It seems very important that the first major step forward into home and social life is as successful as possible. Relatives require considerable support at this time and must have access to whatever help is necessary. Lack of this help will lead to considerable anxiety and stress within the family.

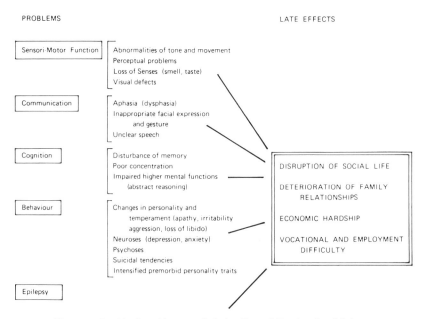

Fig. 75. *Residual problems and their effects following head injury.*

Families and patients are too often left with little recourse to help once the patient is discharged, or once rehabilitation is said to have been completed. It is important that he is reassessed at some period following discharge, with further treatment or advice given for any physical, social or emotional problems which have appeared since discharge. This period of reassessment is also an opportunity for the social worker to check that there is no further financial, placement or employment assistance to be suggested.

The Late Effects of Head Injury

Some of the residual problems and their effects are summarised in Fig. 75. These late effects are important factors in the social, economic and family life of the individual. Poor manipulative skills combined with intellectual slowness may be the most irritating residual problems experienced by the patient and his relatives. Epilepsy is often one of the most inhibiting factors in terms of employment and family acceptance.

Planning for future employment of the head-injured patient should begin as soon as possible. The occupational therapist introduces into the treatment programme appropriate job-orientated tasks. Over the period of rehabilitation, assessments of his physical function, behaviour, intellectual function and motivation are made. The settlement of brain-damaged patients can be considered under six headings–

return to former employment
return to modified former employment
placement in alternate employment
referral for retraining
placement in a sheltered workshop
unemployable

Some authors (Hooper 1967 and Briggs 1975) consider that financial compensation and impending settlement can be a possible bar to full rehabilitation. Others, find that disability benefit by itself does not influence employment. One of the most important considerations in the planning for employment is the patient's mental state. Negative factors include the lack of facilities for retraining, the long wait for placement, the small number of sheltered workshops and the level of unemployment of the fit and well. Availability of transport frequently presents a problem. Dresser, Meirowsky et al. (1973) and others have shown that the degree of emotional stability and pre-injury mental endowment have a considerable effect upon future employment probability.

SUMMARY

In this chapter the mechanism of brain damage following head injury is described briefly. The need for an understanding of the relationship between respiratory and brain function is emphasised in an outline of the care of the unconscious head-injured patient. Some of the common problems and the major objectives of rehabilitation are discussed with particular reference to the quality of this rehabilitation in order to prevent the sequelae of disuse and deprivation.

References

Bethune, D. (1975) Neurophysiological facilitation of respiration in the unconscious adult patient. *Physiotherapy Canada*, **27**, 5, 241–245.

Brain, R. and Walton, J. N. (1969) *Brain's Diseases of the Nervous System*. pp. 979–987. London, University Press.

Briggs, M. (1975) Management of patients with head injuries. *Physiotherapy*, **61**, 9, 266–268.

Dresser, A., Meirowsky, A., Weiss, G., McNeel, M., Simon, G. and Caveness, W. (1973) Gainful employment following head injury *Arch. Neurol.*, **29**, 111–116.

Eldred, E., Bridgman, C. F., Kano, M., Sasaki, Y. and Yellin, H., (1967) Changes in muscle spindle morphology and discharge with alterations in muscle status. In *Neurophysiological Basis of Normal and Abnormal Motor Activities*, edited by M. Yahr and D. Purpura. New York, Raven Press.

Eyzaguirre, C. and Fidone, S. J. (1975) *Physiology of the Nervous System*. Chicago, Year Book Medical.

Gibson, R. M. (1971a) Technical factors, equipment and time, In *Head Injuries. Proceedings of an International Symposium*. Edinburgh and London, Churchill Livingstone.

Gibson, R. M. (1971b) Early Management of the multiple injured patient with particular reference to the head injury. In *Head Injuries. Proceedings of an International Symposium*. Edinburgh and London, Churchill Livingstone.

Goff, B. (1969) Excitatory cold. *Physiotherapy*, **55**, 11, 467–468.

Gurdjian, E. S. (1971) Mechanisms of impact injury of the head. In *Head Injuries. Proceedings of an International Symposium*. Edinburgh and London, Churchill Livingstone.

Hitchcock, E. (1971a) The role of the nurse in the diagnosis and treatment of head injuries. In *Head Injuries. Proceedings of an*

International Symposium. Edinburgh and London, Churchill Livingstone.

Hitchcock, E. R., (1971b) Summary of emergency care of head and multiple injury. In *Head Injuries. Proceedings of an International Symposium.* Edinburgh and London, Churchill Livingstone.

Hooper, R. C., (1967) Rehabilitation in head injuries. *Proc. W.C.P.T.,* 93–103.

Jamieson, K. (1971) *A First Notebook of Head Injury.* London, Butterworths.

Jennett, W. B. (1970) *An Introduction to Neurosurgery.* London, Heinemann.

Jennett, W. B. (1972) Some aspects of prognosis after severe head injury. *Scand. J. Rehab. Med.,* **4,** 16–20

Lance, J. G. and McLeod, J. W. (1975) *A Physiological Approach to Clinical Neurology.* London, Butterworths.

Le Roux, B. T. (1971) Thoracic trauma. In *Head Injuries. Proceedings of an International Symposium.* Edinburgh and London, Churchill Livingstone.

Lewin, W. (1966) *The Management of Head Injuries.* London, Bailliere, Tindall and Cassell.

Loew, F. (1971) Pathophysiological basis for the management of head injuries. In *Head Injuries. Proceedings of an International Symposium.* Edinburgh and London, Churchill Livingstone.

Loudon, R. G., Brueggemann, M. W., and McLaurin, R. L. (1975) Respiratory pattern and compliance changes after experimental head injury. In *Head Injuries. Second Chicago Symposium on Neural Trauma,* edited by R. L. McLaurin. New York, Grune and Stratton.

McGuire, J. (1973) The early treatment of the head injured patient. *South African J. Physiother.,* **29,** 1, 4–7.

McLaurin, R. L. and Ford, L. E. (1964) Extradural haematoma. *J. Neurosurg.,* **21,** 364–371.

Martin, G. (1974) *A Manual of Head Injuries in General Surgery.* London, Heinemann.

Maloney, A. F. J. (1971) The fatal head injury and some neuropathological observations. In *Head Injuries. Proceedings of an International Symposium.* Edinburgh and London, Churchill Livingstone.

Obrador, S. (1971) Organisation of head injury care in the hospital. In *Head Injuries. Proceedings of an International Symposium.* Edinburgh and London, Churchill Livingstone.

Parham, A. M., Ducker, T. B. and Redding, J. S. (1975) In *Head Injuries. Second Chicago Symposium on Neural Trauma,* edited by R. L. McLaurin. New York, Grune and Stratton.

Potter, J. M. (1964) *The Practical Management of Head Injuries*. London, Lloyd-Luke.

Rapoport, S. I. (1975) Blood-brain barrier, permeability, autoregulation of cerebral blood flow and brain oedema. In *Head Injuries. Second Chicago Symposium on Neural Trauma*, edited by R. L. McLaurin. New York, Grune and Stratton.

Reid, M. (1976) *Handling the Disabled Child in Water*. Birmingham, Association of Paediatric Chartered Physiotherapists.

Walker, A. E. (1971) General survey of head injury problems. In *Head Injuries. Proceedings of an International Symposium*. Edinburgh and London, Churchill Livingstone.

Walker, A. E.(1972) Long term evaluation of the social and family adjustment to head injuries. *Scand. J. Rehab. Med.* **4**, 5–8.

Further Reading

Ford, B. (1976) Head injuries – what happens to survivors. *Med. J. Aust.*, **1**, 603–605.

Gordon, E. (1972) Controlled ventilation in the management of patients with severe head injuries. *Scand. J. Rehab. Med.*, **4**, 21–25.

Katsurada, K., Yamada, R. and Sugimoto, T. (1973) Respiratory insufficiency in patients with severe head injury. *Surgery*, **73**, 2, 191.

Luria, A. R. (1975) *The Man with a Shattered World*. London, Penguin.

Mitchell, A. R. K. (1971) Psychiatric consequences of head injury. *Occupational Therapy*, **34**, 2.

Muller, G. (1975) Scales of gravity in head injury. *Scand. J. Rehab. Med.*, **7**, 84–90.

Williams, M. (1972) The psychological testing of patients with head injuries. *Occupational Therapy*, **34**, 2, 21–24.

Wilton, N. M. (1975) Psychiatric sequelae of head injury. *Aust. J. Physiother.*, **21**, 3, 101–103.

Chapter 7

Parkinsonism

It was James Parkinson (1755–1824) who first described, in 1817, the 'shaking palsy' which bears his name. Parkinson's disease is now classified as one of a group of disorders comprising the Parkinson syndrome, the result of pathological processes which damage the extrapyramidal system, and which share some of the common features of rigidity, tremor, bradykinesia and postural instability. It is usual to distinguish between idiopathic Parkinson's disease (paralysis agitans) and symptomatic Parkinsonism due to known causes.

Over the last fifteen to twenty years a change in the understanding of the pathogenesis and treatment of Parkinson's disease has followed new concepts of biochemical and physiological function. These include the discovery that the amount of chemical transmitter substance, dopamine, is depleted and its formation decreased in the neostriatum of patients with the disease. If this deficiency can be counteracted by dopamine replacement therapy (L-dopa) the symptoms are relieved. Prior to these relatively recent developments, Parkinson's disease was thought to have an unremitting course and to be of an intractable nature.

The signs and symptoms of Parkinsonism may appear following *intoxication* with carbonmonoxide, manganese or methyl bromide, or may be associated with the use of such *drugs* as phenothiazine or reserpine. In these latter cases the signs are usually reversible following a reduction in the dosage of the drug. Involvement of the basal ganglia by a *tumour* may give rise to signs of Parkinsonism, and *compression of the midbrain* may result in tremor and rigidity.

Arteriosclerotic Parkinsonism The patient with Parkinsonism due to vascular changes usually gives a history of little strokes. There is usually circulatory atheroma of the basal ganglia and internal capsule. The full picture of Parkinsonism is rarely seen in these patients, and it is often associated with dementia.*

In this form of Parkinsonism there are usually signs of *bradykinesia* and *hypokinesia*, progressing to *akinesia*. *Rigidity* is atypical in that it

* Glossary

210

does not have the plasticity usually associated with parkinsonian rigidity. Instead it feels to the examiner as if the patient is actively resisting the movement, the whole limb stiffening in response to contact. This phenomenon is called gegenhalten. Critchley (1931) observed that this arteriosclerotic rigidity is more obvious in the limbs than in the trunk, in the proximal rather than the distal segments of the limbs and in the legs more than in the arms. Tremor is hardly ever seen. Pseudobulbar palsy* is often present, combined with the emotional problems of uncontrollable laughing and crying. Other changes may be present which are typical of degeneration, such as the re-emergence of the primitive sucking and palmarmental* reflexes.

Encephalitic Parkinsonism is seen in some patients following encephalitis lethargica, a disease thought to be due to a neurotropic virus which causes pathological changes in the grey matter of the midbrain and substantia nigra.

The Shy-Drager Syndrome is associated with long-standing postural hypotension and may be aetiologically related to Parkinsonism (Adams 1974). The initial symptoms are those of autonomic insufficiency such as dizziness, syncope and fatiguability, but the symptoms progress to rigidity, bradykinesia and tremor.

Idiopathic Parkinson's Disease is a degenerative disorder and the most common cause of the Parkinson syndrome. It may appear in the third or fourth decade, and when it does, it may be a sequel to encephalitis, although there may be no history of encephalitic illness (Lance and McLeod 1975). However, it is more commonly seen in the second half of life, commencing between the ages of 50 to 65 in males, who are affected more frequently and at a slightly earlier age than females. Diagnosis is made on the basis of clinical examination.

Clinical Features and their Pathophysiology

There is still no agreement as to the actual localisation of the pathological changes in Parkinsonism, but it is considered to be a disease of the extrapyramidal system. Pathological studies indicate the presence of generalised cerebral changes which are similar to those of senility. The globus pallidus, substantia nigra and various brain stem areas contain the most severe changes including cellular degeneration. The most constant finding is a loss of cells from the posterior part of the substantia nigra. Lance and McLeod (1975) comment that it 'appears to be a system degeneration involving

* Glossary

central pathways which deploy dopamine as a neurotransmitter'. Dopamine is a transmitter in the neural pathway which starts in the substantia nigra and terminates in the caudate nucleus and putamen after penetrating the globus pallidus (Fig. 76) and its concentration

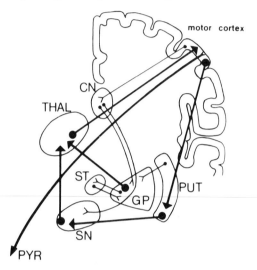

Fig. 76. *The connections of the basal ganglia: Thal: thalamus, CN: caudate nucleus, PUT: putamen, SN: substantia nigrea, ST: subthalamic nucleus.*

has been found to be reduced in the basal ganglia themselves. Bradykinesia, tremor and rigidity are the so-called classical features of Parkinson's disease.

Bradykinesia is a slowness in initiating and performing movement and is independent of the amount of rigidity. It is frequently described as a 'poverty' of movement, whereas the term *akinesia* is used to describe the complete inability to initiate a willed movement. There is a diminution or loss of spontaneous and automatic movements (Fig. 77) and this can be observed in such features as an expressionless face, lack of blinking, reduced arm swing in walking and difficulty in getting out of a chair. The patient is relatively immobile but he is not necessarily weak. It has been found in animal experiments that depletion of dopamine within the brain causes both akinesia and rigidity (Steg 1972).

Tremor. There are two types of tremor which may be seen in Parkinson's disease, an exaggerated *physiological or action tremor,* which has a frequency of 6 to 12 cycles per second, and a *resting or*

212

Fig. 77. *Poor balance in standing. This man is unable to stand independently.*

alternating tremor, which has a frequency of 3 to 5 cycles per second. It is not clear with any accuracy what causes the tremor. McLeod (1971) comments that 'lesions placed in the substantia nigra and other parts of the basal ganglia have always failed to produce tremor in experimental animals'.

The *resting or alternating tremor* may affect any part of the body, but it more often begins in the upper limb. It may spread to involve all four limbs, jaw, tongue and head. It disappears when the patient is asleep or truly at rest and relaxed, and becomes more obvious when he is tense or anxious, or in a stressful situation. It may disappear during voluntary movement but more commonly it is replaced by an *action tremor*. However, 'it is not clear whether one tremor mechanism is a continuum of the other' (Lance and McLeod 1975). Most patients demonstrate an action tremor, which, in conjunction with rigidity is responsible for the cogwheel phenomenon.

Parkinsonian rigidity is a form of hypertonus. It differs from spasticity in several ways (see Chapter 11). The flexor muscles of the upper and lower limbs and trunk are more affected than the extensors. The clasp-knife phenomenon is not present and there is resistance to passive movement in both the agonist and antagonist muscle groups, this resistance being felt throughout the entire range with the exception of the first few degrees. Phasic muscle reflexes are within normal limits. However, there is an increased response to stimulation of the tonic vibration reflex, probably because the static component of the tonic stretch reflex is enhanced rather than the dynamic component (Lance and McLeod 1975). This form of hypertonus has a lead-pipe quality, the so-called lead-pipe rigidity. As mentioned above the effect of tremor superimposed on this rigidity changes its quality, and passive movement demonstrates the cogwheel phenomenon. It is not absolutely certain what causes the plastic rigidity found in Parkinson's disease, but present evidence favours the hypothesis of hyperactivity of the alpha motoneurons. However, it is possible that there is also increased gamma motoneuron activity particularly in the early stages of the disease.

Patients with Parkinson's disease tend to develop eventually a flexion dystonia in which the body is held in a flexed posture, because of the inappropriate relationship between flexor and extensor muscle groups. Although this flexed posture appears constant, there may not be much resistance to passive extension of the body. Alpha motoneuron activity probably dominates at this stage. A transient inability to initiate walking, referred to as 'freezing', is probably due to the co-contraction of both agonist and antagonist muscle groups, and some observers consider this is a manifestation of flexion dystonia (Andrews 1973). Freezing is also seen on attempts to initiate other activities.

Problems of Function

The classical features described above of bradykinesia, rigidity and tremor lead to problems of movement and function, which include disorders of the regulation of posture and of balance, and disorders of oro-facial function.

Onset is usually insidious and it is often difficult for the patient to give an exact history of when he first noticed any problems. *Early signs* may include a tremor, a passivity which affects the whole patient but which may be more noticeable in his expressionless face, or a failure to swing one arm when walking. He may complain of aching and stiffness in the affected limbs. Usually both sides of the body are affected, perhaps one side more than the other. In the initial stages only one side may demonstrate problems.

The patient is rarely, if ever, referred to the physiotherapist at this early stage, although patients seen by the authors have demonstrated signs of impaired balance and other disorders of functional activity which would respond to physical treatment. Involvement of postural reactions (righting and equilibrium) tend to be referred to in the literature as a later manifestation of Parkinson's disease, possibly because they are not often tested in the early stages, which may be partly due to a poor understanding of the importance of postural reactions to normal movement.

Sensation is not affected in these patients, but many of them complain of pain, stiffness and aching of muscles and joints. Sensory feedback is probably reduced and abnormal, particularly after years of rigidity, bradykinesia and tremor.

Autonomic disturbances may include urgency of micturition, flushing of the skin and uncomfortable sensations of heat sometimes accompanied by sweating. The excessive salivation often referred to may well be the result of poor oro-facial function with difficulty in lip closure and a heightened threshold to swallowing. It seems that these patients require a greater stimulus to set up the swallowing mechanism than is provided by the presence of saliva. This, together with poor tongue movement and lip closure, seems to be the principal cause of dribbling.

Behavioural disturbances. Patients with Parkinson's disease are often depressed and frustrated. Most people are familiar with the disabilities associated with the disease and consider it to be 'incurable'. Fortunately, the outlook is much more positive for many patients since the advent of replacement therapy.

The patient may have considerable insight into his problems and understanding of his functional difficulties. If he is still enjoying an active working life when the disease is first diagnosed he will be concerned about the future for himself and for his family, about the possibility of losing his job and about what he is sure will be years of gradual deterioration.

Lack of spontaneous facial expression and gesture during conversation and social contact often result in misunderstandings, and may be the cause of some of the patient's feelings of frustration and isolation. Severe resting or action tremor and difficulties with eating and drinking are socially embarrassing.

Although dementia may accompany the arteriosclerotic form of Parkinsonism, there seem to be differences of opinion as to whether or not intellect is affected in patients with idiopathic Parkinson's disease. The main difficulty in assessing intellect in these people is the absence of suitably designed tests for the elderly and disabled. Intelligence tests demand either verbal or manipulative skills and are on the whole designed for children and young adults. Signs of decline in memory and working ability may be due to a number of factors, such as poor communication, social isolation, inactivity, frustration in attempting fine manipulative tasks and depression.

Therapists are often surprised by the degree of understanding and insight their patients demonstrate. The therapist who can establish good rapport with her patient will often find her evaluation of his problems will be greatly facilitated by his understanding and by an intellectual astuteness which is in marked contrast to his passive and uninterested appearance.

Problems of movement result from rigidity, tremor and bradykinesia and cause varying degrees of functional disability. The patient tends to develop a flexed posture with little head movement. In sitting, his weight is usually too far back (Fig. 35) and he tends to sit very still, lacking spontaneous adjustments such as the weight shifting and fidgeting observed in normal subjects. He has difficulty in getting from sitting to standing because of his problem in initiating weight transference forwards at the hips and in placing his feet far enough under him to enable him to shift his centre of gravity sufficiently to stand up. When he attempts to sit down again he is unable to adjust to the necessary transference of weight and may collapse into the chair. Alternatively, he may not be able to get more than halfway down to the chair without, as one patient described it, pushing down hard as if against some force.

In standing and walking his weight may be too far back and he has to tilt his trunk forwards (Fig. 80). This presents a threat to his balance. He tends to walk with short shuffling steps and a wide base (marche à petit pas). When he wants to turn around, he does so in one piece, taking small steps instead of rotating his body. He has difficulty walking around objects and negotiating doorways. He has difficulty initiating movements, and once he has started he may not be able to stop. It appears as if he is somehow committed to the movement. He lacks rotatory movements, particularly of the trunk, which may be one of the reasons for the loss of associated arm swing when walking. If he loses balance backward he tends to take little steps backward (retropulsive walking). If the loss of balance is forward, he tends to take little steps forward (propulsive or festinant walking). He gives the impression at these times of trying to catch up with his feet. If he has to stop quickly he may lose balance.

Manipulative skills are considerably reduced, because of rigidity and bradykinesia, and may be further hampered by an action tremor. His fingers are flexed at the metacarpophalangeal joints and the thumb is adducted. The patient has difficulty with bathing, dressing and eating, and to some extent, with all activities involved in looking after himself. His handwriting becomes very small with cramped letters, and he has difficulty with other functions which involve the performance of rapid alternating movements.

The normal postural background to movement as well as movement itself may be severely disturbed. The patient may have great difficulty in changing his position or adjusting to even the smallest displacement of weight. He lacks the spontaneous head and trunk righting and spontaneous movements of the arms and legs necessary to regain his balance when his weight is displaced. Protective reactions of his arms may be absent.

Many of the movement difficulties experienced by the patient stem from disorders of balance, as most functional movements, including those which may primarily involve the hands, require the ability to control balance and to shift one's centre of gravity.

Oro-facial dysfunction. The most striking features are usually the patient's expressionless face and lack of spontaneous alteration in expression and gesture during conversation. The presence of a resting tremor involving his jaw, alternate protrusion and retraction of his tongue, and constant head movements, are other obvious manifestations of oro-facial dysfunction. Poor lip and jaw closure and tongue movement result in difficulty swallowing and eating, and these are added to by difficulty in getting the food to his mouth, by poor sitting balance and lack of head movement.

Reduction in spontaneous eye movements combined with infrequent blinking result in a staring appearance of the eyes. He finds it difficult to follow a rapidly moving object, and eye convergence is impaired. Poor phonation and articulation (dysarthria) result in a monotonous hesitant voice which lacks volume and which may be no more than a whisper. These, together with his lack of gesture and immobile face, make communication very difficult and frustrating, and sometimes impossible.

Thoracic expansion is considerably reduced by rigidity, flexed posture and bradykinesia. This affects the co-ordination between respiration and speech and respiration and eating. It also lowers his vital capacity, and affects endurance.

Medical and Surgical Management

Medical management consists principally of *replacement therapy*. The transmitter substance, dopamine, which is depleted in the basal ganglia, does not pass the blood-brain barrier, therefore, its precursor, L-dopa, is administered. L-dopa appears to be much more effective than any drug previously used. Improvement following its administration is particularly noticeable in the bradykinesia, but is also seen in the rigidity. Its effect is less predictable in reducing tremor, although in time the tremor does reduce in some patients.

There is said to be an improvement in 70 to 80% of patients taking L-dopa, and cessation of dosage because of side effects is necessary in only 10% of patients (Selby 1971). Therapy is given orally and can be commenced at any stage of the disease. Some patients do not respond immediately, others show an immediate and dramatic improvement.

Side effects, which occur in only a small percentage of patients, may include hypotension, dyskinesia, or drug-induced involuntary movements such as choreoathetosis, psychic reactions such as nocturnal hallucinations, cardiac dysrhythmias and gastrointestinal disturbances such as nausea, vomiting and anorexia. All of these side effects may be minimised by a reduction in the initial dose, careful supervision and gradual increments in the dosage. Gastrointestinal disturbances tend to subside if the L-dopa is taken on a full stomach. L-dopa in combination with carbidopa is said to cause fewer gastrointestinal disturbances.

There are no absolute contra-indications for L-dopa therapy, but it may not be appropriate in patients with severe dementia associated with Parkinsonism, ischaemic heart disease or cardiac arrhythmias. Patients with arteriosclerotic Parkinsonism receive smaller doses initially, with response to treatment being evident in ten to fourteen days. Adams (1974) reports that although the effects on this type of Parkinsonism are not as dramatic as in younger people the patients 'have a sense of well-being, and evidence of more liveliness, interest and animation'.

It is not known with certainty whether L-dopa affects the natural history of the disease or whether it relieves the symptoms without affecting the long-term deterioration.

Stereotaxic surgery for Parkinson's disease involves the making of a lesion in the ventrolateral nucleus of the thalamus and sometimes in the globus pallidus. There are many limitations to the use of surgery in the treatment of this disease, but it may still have a place in combination with L-dopa therapy. Marked improvement may be seen in the rigidity and in the tremor, but bradykinesia is not affected at all and the tremor may return.

PHYSICAL TREATMENT

The emphasis in physical treatment for patients with Parkinsonism has changed since the advent of replacement therapy. The patients who need physiotherapy fall broadly into two categories. The first group are those whose control over movement and stability are poor following the reduction of rigidity and bradykinesia brought about by replacement therapy. The second group are those who cannot tolerate this therapy or those for whom it has little effect.

Prevention

Unfortunately, the patients in the latter group are frequently only referred for physical treatment when they already have severe disability, when contractures, dystonia, reduced vital capacity and endurance are so severe that the effects of treatment must be very limited. Physical treatment in the prevention of disability is still not widely understood or practised. There is sometimes the feeling expressed that the patient is not 'bad enough' for physiotherapy.

Early physical treatment depends on the patient's particular difficulties but will also take into consideration the probable progression of disability which will develop over a period of time. In general, treatment will consist of advice to the patient on ways of maintaining extension of the body against gravity, preventing loss of mobility and establishing a routine which will enable him to have good thoracic mobility with an effective vital capacity. The maintenance of thoracic expansion will be easier if generalised extension against gravity can be maintained. The reduction of respiratory efficiency and the poor exercise tolerance seen in patients whose disabilities have progressed over a long period of time are due in large part to the gradual flexion of the trunk, which prevents thoracic expansion.

Physiotherapy will not alter the progress of the disease itself, but it will prevent the patient from developing, to a disabling extent, the secondary effects on the aging musculo-skeletal system of disuse and inactivity, as well as improve his subjective feelings of well-being. It is interesting that some patients seen in the early trials of replacement therapy showed signs of improvement but their general debility and the severity of their contractures were so devastating that they were not able to take advantage of it and improve their functional abilities without orthopaedic surgery. This situation represents a failure of preventative health care.

In general, the therapist's objectives in the early stages of Parkinson's disease are to maintain the patient's general well-being and prevent the secondary effects of disuse and inactivity, therefore enabling him to benefit to the greatest possible extent from replacement therapy or neurosurgery.

Physiotherapy Combined with Drug Therapy

Relief of bradykinesia, rigidity, and a feeling of well-being as a result of replacement therapy may not be followed by a spontaneous increase in mobility. A patient who has spent a number of years with gradually decreasing activity may have lost the feeling of how to move or even the urge to move. He may no longer be able to make the spontaneous movements necessary for regaining balance because he has had no practice. He will have diminished endurance and tolerance of activity and probably a limited view of his ability to accomplish effective movement.

Following replacement therapy the patient may experience a different feeling of postural instability compared with the instability he experienced as a result of rigidity and bradykinesia. Replacement therapy provides the possibility of improving movement and posture but physical therapy is required for a short period to help the patient adjust to his new situation and to enable him to make full use of his new capabilities. A similar situation frequently exists after stereotaxic surgery.

Some General Points in Treatment

The patient is assessed and his problems evaluated following the general principles outlined. Treatment will concentrate on the restoration of more normal body alignment, with weight being borne in the midline on extended hips rather than backward. The therapist will *stimulate balance reactions* to give the patient the feeling of how to regain balance and regulate these movements. He may need to be surprised by what he can accomplish. Treatment will also aim to improve his ability to *initiate movement,* to *move rhythmically and bilaterally,* and to *increase the excursion of all movements,* particularly rotation and extension.

The major cause of limited movement may be tremor, bradykinesia or rigidity, or a combination of all three. There is no specific technique which decreases tremor, apart from ensuring that the patient understands the importance of relaxation and freedom from anxiety, effort and stress, all of which tend to increase tremor in most patients. Weight-bearing through a tremorous limb will sometimes cause a temporary reduction in tremor. Stress, effort, anxiety and tension should all be avoided during treatment as they increase the patient's tendency to 'freeze'.

Fig. 78. *Facilitation of the rhythmical, reciprocal movements involved in walking.*

Fig. 79. *Stimulation of rhythmical walking using two sticks.*

221

Movement to be functional needs to be rhythmical and bilateral and therefore involves the entire body. The patient with Parkinsonism has little sense of the rhythm of movement because his activities are so limited. Rhythmical movements involving rotation are stimulated from the shoulders, arms or pelvis, and in both sitting and standing (Fig. 78). This gives the patient the feeling of freedom of movement even if it is done passively to begin with, and the rotation decreases the rigidity to some extent.

Rhythm and freedom of movement in walking can be stimulated by speech either by rhythmically emphasised words or by counting. Walking is facilitated* from the shoulders, or by the therapist walking side by side with the patient with emphasised stepping movements and rotation of the body. Arm swing and rotation are stimulated with two sticks operated by the therapist (Fig. 79). The initially passive movements of the arms encourage more rotation of the trunk and consequently larger steps. Pieces of paper on the floor add visual stimulus for walking with longer steps. Walking over obstacles will encourage weight-bearing on one leg, a more purposeful step and more confidence in walking.

Parkinsonian patients frequently have a low opinion of their abilities, and improvement during treatment sessions needs to be demonstrated to them in ways which have meaning for them. For example, one patient at the end of a treatment session was delighted to find she could catch a ball when it was thrown to her. Another woman took up ballroom dancing again when her confidence in standing improved. In her treatment sessions, music was used to help her to regain some sense of initiating rhythmical movement and this, together with some improvement in her balance, gave her the confidence she needed.

The technique called rhythmic initiation, which is described by Knott and Voss (1968) can also be used to improve initiation of movement. It is particularly effective in initiating sitting to standing, a movement which Parkinsonian patients frequently find difficult or impossible. The patient, who should be sitting symmetrically, is helped to move his feet back under the chair. He can rest his arms on the therapist's shoulders or at her waist which will help him to extend his trunk and head and stimulate the transference of weight forward (Fig. 38). The therapist transfers his weight forward and backward, flexing and extending his hips in a rhythmical manner several times until she feels some freedom of movement. She helps him to move his head into extension or flexion until he is doing this automatically.

* Appendix 1

Gradually as movement becomes freer his weight is transferred further and further forward, and the patient is asked to join in the movement with the therapist. When the weight is far enough forward and the therapist feels the patient is ready to stand, she asks him to do so and assists and guides him with the movement.

Knott and Voss suggest the use of resistance once the patient is moving freely, but in our experience the technique is more effective in giving the patient increased freedom of movement if it is done without resistance. Many patients with Parkinson's disease feel as though they are always struggling against resistance or are weighted down in their attempts to move, and they enjoy the feeling of increased mobility and the conversion of this into functional achievement. The same technique can be used for sitting down again.

Parkinsonian patients tend toward a generalised flexion of the trunk, head and limbs, although they sometimes are able to extend the neck to compensate for a very flexed thoracic spine. This flexion is usually combined with some asymmetry, as one side is usually more affected than the other. In sitting the patient may counteract his extreme flexion by leaning backward at his hips, which gives the impression that he is falling backward, and indeed his balance will usually be very poor in this position.

Activities which encourage weight transference combined with the appropriate head and trunk movement will lead to an improvement in the patient's ability to regain his balance when his centre of gravity is disturbed, as will the methods of improving the initiation and rhythm of movement described above. All activities in an antigravity position should *emphasise normal alignment of the body* and avoid any tendency to lean backward (Fig. 80).

Prone lying is sometimes suggested to improve extension as theoretically it is one position from which a general extension can be encouraged. Unfortunately, prone is rarely a comfortable or a practical position for the elderly, and even a fit elderly person will demonstrate a greatly reduced ability to extend the trunk in this position. If the patient has already some anatomical limitation of extension in his trunk, hips and shoulders he will be completely helpless in prone. Emphasis throughout treatment on extension of the hips in standing and flexion of the hips in sitting will enable more trunk extension. Elevation of the arms will give the patient the feeling of a generalised extension (Fig. 81).

The patient may require treatment for specific difficulties in the use of his hands. His treatment programme will include methods of improving those functions which enable prehension to be more effective, such as increased trunk extension, extension and elevation

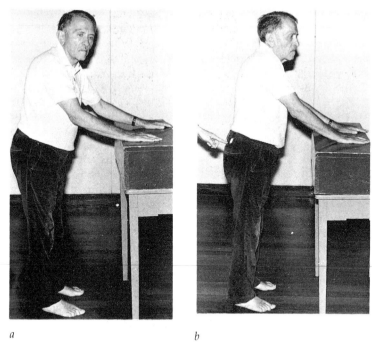

a   b

Fig. 80. (a) *This man's body is poorly aligned because of the flexion at his hips.* (b) *Practise of extension of his hips improves body alignment.*

of his arms and improved balance and eye-hand contact in sitting, as well as treatment for specific hand function difficulties.

Oro-facial function

Oro-facial problems cause particular difficulty, frustration and embarrassment. Many of these patients have become used to being left out of conversations because their responses are slow, and the therapist may need to give considerable encouragement to the patient and allow him time to respond. She should make use of her own facial expression and variations in tone of voice to stimulate more spontaneous communication.

The patient should be encouraged to take a deep breath before he speaks in order to increase the volume of sound and the number of words to a breath. Over-pressure applied to his thorax on expiration in sitting will improve his thoracic expansion and practice of deep breathing at home may *improve his vital capacity,* which will in turn improve his phonation. Elevation of the arms will increase trunk

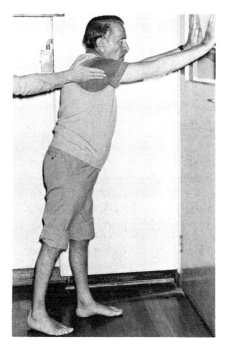

Fig. 81. *Improved extension and body alignment with arm elevation.*

extension and therefore facilitate better thoracic expansion. The therapist encourages the patient to make sounds on expiration. Vibration of the thorax alters and increases the tone and volume of vocalisation. This gives him experience of different sounds and helps him vary the tone of his voice and he will therefore speak more intelligibly and effectively. This approach to his vocal difficulties is more effective than a direct approach in which the patient consciously practises consonants and vowels. This is likely to cause anxiety, which, combined with the effort entailed, may cause him to 'freeze'.

Vibration to the tongue with the therapist's finger may improve articulation and swallowing by stimulating tongue movements (see Chapter 15). A more extended posture will make eating and drinking easier. Lip and jaw closure, chewing and swallowing are also stimulated by methods described in Chapter 15.

Relatives

An understanding of the patient's problems and the reasons for his movement difficulties, rather than mere acceptance of them, will

225

enable relatives to work out their own ways of helping the patient and of stimulating him. They need to be aware of any improvement which occurs so they will allow the patient to perform for himself what functions he can. They can be taught the technique of rhythmic initiation to use if he cannot get up from sitting. The same technique used to stimulate trunk rotation will enable them to help the patient get out of bed in the morning if he has difficulty with this movement. This can be done in supine by rolling the flexed legs from side to side, or in side lying by rolling the top part of his body.

Many patients with Parkinsonism demonstrate improved function and experience a feeling of well-being as a result of physical treatment. Patients who show marked improvement in tone and movement following surgery or replacement therapy, will gain better control over balance, posture and function if they also have physical treatment. The ideas described in this chapter need to be co-ordinated into an appropriate treatment programme which makes use of and builds on any improvement as it occurs.

SUMMARY

In this chapter the group of disorders which shares the common features of rigidity, tremor and bradykinesia, their pathogenesis and treatment are described. The effects on function which result from these clinical features are discussed in terms of problems of movement, balance, behaviour, communication and oro-facial function. Emphasis in treatment is on the prevention of unnecessary disability and on the stimulation of balance reactions, the initiation of movement, the increased excursion of movement with more normal body alignment and the improvement of vital capacity.

References

Adams, G. F. (1974) *Cerebrovascular Disability and the Aging Brain.* Edinburgh and London, Churchill Livingstone.

Andrews, C. J. (1973) The influence of dystonia on the response to long-term L-dopa therapy. *J. Neurol. Neurosurg. Psychiat.,* **36,** 630–636.

Critchley, M. (1931) Neurology of old age. *Lancet,* **1,** 1221–1230.

Knott, M. and Voss, D. E. (1968) *Proprioceptive Neuromuscular Facilitation.* New York, Harper and Row.

Lance, J. W. and McLeod, J. G. (1975) *A Physiological Approach to Clinical Neurology.* London, Butterworths.

McDowell, F. H. and Markham, C. H. et al (1971) The clinical use of levodopa in the treatment of Parkinson's disease. In *Recent Advances in Parkinson's Disease*, edited by F. H. McDowell, and C. H. Markham. Oxford, Blackwell Scientific Press.

McLeod, J. (1971) The pathophysiology of Parkinson's disease. In Symposium on Parkinson's Disease. *Aust. & N.Z. J. of Med. Suppl. 1* **1**, 119–23.

Selby, G. (1971) A preliminary report of Australian trials with L-dopa. *Aust. & N.Z. J. of Med., Suppl. 1,* **1**, 48–56.

Steg, G. (1972) Biochemical aspects of rigidity. In *Parkinson's Disease* Vol. 1, edited by J. Siegfried. Berne, Huber.

Further Reading

Andrews, C. J., Burke, D. and Lance, J. W. (1973) The comparison of tremor in normal, Parkinsonian and athetotic man. *J. Neurological Sciences* **19**, 53–61.

Di Scipio, W. J. (1971) Combined behaviour therapy and physical therapy in the treatment of a fear of walking. *J. Behav. Ther. and Exp. Psychiat.,* **2**, 151–152.

Parkinson's Disease and the Parkinsonian Syndrome. (1970) London, Roche Products Ltd.

Stefaniwsky, L. and Bihowit, D. (1973) Parkinsonism: facilitation of motion by sensory stimulation. *Arch. Phys. Med. Rehabil.* **54**, 75–77.

Chapter 8

Multiple Sclerosis

Multiple sclerosis is a demyelinating disease causing widespread degeneration of the central nervous system. It is one of a group of demyelinating disorders which include acute disseminated encephalomyelitis, and which have broadly similar pathological changes. Little is known of the exact aetiology and pathogenesis of these disorders and it seems unlikely that the same process causes the myelin destruction.

In temperate zones multiple sclerosis is probably the most common neurological disease affecting young adults. It affects women more than men, and is most frequently seen in women in the 30 to 40 age group and later in men. It may, however, occur at any age between 10 and 50 years.

The disease is usually progressive over a period of 20 years, and usually results in severe disability. There is, however, a proportion of relatively mild cases with few or no problems after many years. In the more acute cases, progress can be rapid, resulting in incapacity in one or two years, and death from urinary tract infection or broncho-pneumonia. The disease does not always involve the central nervous system in a generalised distribution, and may present in middle age, for example, as a focal spinal cord disturbance.

The demyelination occurs in plaques or patches within the white matter of the brain and spinal cord. These plaques are often seen in perivenous or periventricular distribution. Occasionally they are seen in the grey matter.

The cause of multiple sclerosis is still unknown despite extensive research. It has never been reproduced experimentally in animals and diagnosis still depends on the history and signs of the disease over a period of months or years, because there is no specific investigation to confirm or refute the diagnosis.

The disease is characterised by remissions and relapses. The remissions are rarely complete and may last for either a long or short period. In some patients they never occur.

Epidemiology and Aetiology

Epidemiology has probably contributed more to the understanding of multiple sclerosis in recent years than to any other discipline in medicine (Millar 1971). The distribution of multiple sclerosis has been examined by many authors and may be summarised as being high in temperate climates, particularly in Northern Europe and North America, and rare in the tropics. It attacks white races principally, although it has been known to affect negroes living in Europe and North America.

The hypothesis which recognises environmental factors as a cause of multiple sclerosis is supported by the geographic distribution. Leibowitz, Kahana and Alter (1973) divide the possible causative factors into two groups, the geoclimatic, for example, temperature and amount of sunshine, and the socio-economic, for example, standard of living, diet, air pollution, urbanisation and industrialisation.

The results of a survey of patients with multiple sclerosis in Israel showed that the disease was common among immigrants from Europe, and rare among immigrants from Afro-Asian countries. The prevalence of multiple sclerosis in native born Israelis was as high as in European immigrants (Leibowitz, Kahana and Alter 1973).

Another writer (Dean 1972) hypothesises that in countries where the disease is rare, early contact with the causative agent, probably a virus, protects the population by making them immune. In other words, the causative factor may be common where the disease is rare, the inhabitants achieving an immunity through early exposure. This may explain why age is a factor in the incidence of multiple sclerosis in immigrant populations. In South Africa there is a high incidence of the disease in immigrants from Northern Europe, but only in those who emigrated after the ages of 15 or 16 years. It is only a quarter as common among English-speaking white South African born people, and only one eleventh as common among the Afrikaans-speaking white South African born, who, as a whole, have closer contact in childhood with the black population and have a lower standard of hygiene than the English-speaking population.

Other theories have been put forward in an attempt to discover the cause of this disease. One of these suggests that there is a deficiency of polyunsaturated fats and a disturbance in lipid metabolism, which causes an alteration in the blood-brain barrier allowing toxic agents to cross. Another theory questions whether the cause could be a slow viral infection such as measles (Sutherland 1977) or an auto-immunology to myelin basic protein (Adams 1972). In a number of patients, approximately 60 to 70% according to Millar (1971) and Sambrook (1975), the gammaglobulin content in the cerebrospinal fluid is raised, but this is not conclusive as it is also raised in cases of neurosyphilis, encephalitis, acute polyneuritis and cerebral tumour. This may be a result of myelin breakdown rather than a cause. It is also suggested as possible that genetic factors may predispose certain individuals to the disease, but little is understood about this. There is strong evidence that, whatever the cause, the disease is acquired in childhood even though the symptoms do not appear until later (Millar 1971, Kurtzke 1972). It is thought that myelination is not completed until puberty, and it is interesting to consider that minor attacks of demyelination in childhood could possibly be repaired.

Pathophysiology

Multiple plaques of *demyelination* and *gliosis* of varying age are seen throughout the white matter of the cerebrum, cerebellum, brain stem and spinal cord. The plaques vary in size from a pin head to approximately two to three centimeters in diameter. The peripheral nerves are not affected unless the position of an area of demyelination interrupts their emergence from the brain stem or spinal cord. The most common sites are the grey-white boundary in the cerebrum, periventricular regions, cerebellar white matter, optic nerve and cervical cord, and they often appear to be centred around small blood vessels particularly the venules (Adams 1972).

Demyelination is a disintegration of the myelin sheath caused by an inflammatory and destructive process, the axons being partly or completely denuded. The axons themselves are preserved initially. This differs from Wallerian degeneration, in which axonal degeneration accompanies the myelin sheath break up. This initial preservation of axons may account for the remissions of symptoms which take place (Kraft and Wessman 1974). The final pathological process involves destruction of the nerve fibres followed by gliosis which is called sclerosis. Secondary degeneration above and below the lesion does not appear to occur, therefore the degenerative patches remain isolated. Function of the neuron is initially impaired but eventually there is complete interruption of nerve impulses.

The question of the possibility of functional *remyelination* in the central nervous system still remains unanswered and problematical. There have been reports of incomplete remyelination activity in experiments with rats (Leibowitz 1966). Nevertheless, evidence at present suggests that the axons in the central nervous system cannot be effectively remyelinated.

230

Gliosis is an increase in neuroglial tissue. Neuroglial tissue takes the place of the connective tissue found in other systems. There is much speculation about this reaction in multiple sclerosis. Adams (1972) summarises in the following way the stages in the development of the sclerotic plaque. There is early hyperplasia of the neuroglia, lipid phagocytosis during which the myelin lipids are degraded, fibril formation and finally complete sclerosis.

Adams concludes that 'the primary attack in multiple sclerosis is directed against the myelin sheath itself, the oligodendrocyte, or the vascular endothelium. Damage to the oligodendrocyte would be expected to impair myelin maintenance, while damage to the vascular endothelium would allow a hypothetical agent to enter from the blood and attack either the myelin sheath or the oligodendrocyte'.

Drug therapy

While aetiology remains unclear and because of the possibility of spontaneous remissions, treatment and evaluation of its effectiveness is difficult and must rely on empirical evidence.

The use of steroids has been widely practised, but some (Sambrook 1975) suggest that there is still no evidence to indicate that they influence the eventual outcome of the disease, although they may accelerate the onset of a remission when given during an acute relapse. Steroids are sometimes combined with an antiserum such as antithymocyte globulin (A.T.G.). The rationale for this is to destroy some of the cells producing antibodies which act against nervous tissue. Clinical trials using immuno-suppressant drugs are still progressing.

Drugs such as baclofen and diazepam may be useful in the reduction of hypertonus. Too large a dose of either may make the patient drowsy or too hypotonic to move. Where severe flexor and adductor spasms are present due to spinal cord lesions, intrathecol phenol may reduce hyperreflexia sufficiently to allow the patient to sit more comfortably in a wheelchair and to be nursed more easily.

CLINICAL MANIFESTATIONS

The clinical signs and symptoms of multiple sclerosis reflect the site of the involvement and its intensity. Lesions may be present well before the clinical onset, and these lesions may already involve many and random parts of the nervous system.

Clinical onset may be characterised by a single focal lesion which almost always remits. This focal lesion may be a blurring of vision, or a feeling of numbness and tingling in a limb. Remission may be followed by further relapses with gradually increasing neurological deficit. This situation of remissions and exacerbations continues in varying degrees throughout life. However, the onset of signs and symptoms may be followed by a steady deterioration.

Prognosis is impossible because of the variability of the disease, and because of the lack of any reliable diagnostic test. It may be related to the age of onset. McAlpine (1961) followed a group of 241 patients with a diagnosis of multiple sclerosis over ten years and found that 33% were completely unrestricted in their activities and many of those who were disabled to some extent were able to lead an active life.

The effect of the diagnosis on the patient and his family will be one of considerable distress. Their knowledge of the disease and its consequences will initiate fears for the future which are unlikely to be dispelled by a search through the texbooks or conversations with others. Therefore, when considering the problems and management of these patients we must see them within the context of this distressing, disabling and progressive disorder and its effects upon the patient, his social and vocational life, and his family.

We will not describe all the clinical manifestations associated with multiple sclerosis. The reader should refer to the chapters on hypertonus, hypotonus and cerebellar ataxia. However, there are a number of features which occur particularly often, and these are described briefly below.

Sensory signs and symptoms, such as paraesthesia of a limb or of the face, with numbness and tingling, may be the first clinical signs. Involvement of the posterior columns of the cord results in disordered position and movement sense, vibration sense and touch. Pain and temperature sense may also be affected. Due to the unpredictable nature of the disease, sensory problems may affect one arm, one leg, one side of the body or all four limbs.

Visual disturbances may be an early sign of the disease. They may result from retrobulbar neuritis or demyelination of the optic nerve. There may be blurring or dimming of vision in one or both eyes. Some patients lose the sight of one eye or suffer double vision (diplopia)*. Nystagmus is often seen and may accompany other signs of cerebellar dysfunction. Visual field defects, although sometimes seen, are uncommon.

Other senses may be involved, such as taste and smell. Hearing defects are rare. Perceptual dysfunction, indicating lesions within the parietal area of the brain may also occur.

* Glossary

Disorders of tone and movement occur according to the part of the central nervous system involved and may change as the disease progresses. It is possible for a patient to demonstrate at an early stage in the disease a certain amount of hypotonus with predominantly cerebellar symptoms, which, as the disease progresses, are overlaid by spinal cord hyperreflexia and hypertonus of central origin.

Other signs of involvement of the cerebellum and its connections, include intention tremor, dysmetria and dyssynergia. These result in loss of postural stability and of the normal smooth control of movement, including the movements of speech which becomes scanned and explosive.

Involvement of the vestibular tracts will result in transient or persistent **vertigo**. Vertigo may be defined as an illusion of movement in the person's relationship with his environment. It is caused by imbalance between the vestibular input from each side or by conflict between visual, proprioceptive and vestibular information when one is inappropriate to the others. It may be accompanied by vomiting and a feeling of dizziness, or a sense of motion with inadequate reason.

Involvement of the cranial nerves or higher centres may result in disorders of facial expression, ptosis*, dysarthria and oral problems including impaired swallowing.

Hypertonus of supraspinal origin, with hyperreflexia and extensor plantar responses, may occur in any distribution throughout the body. It will be accompanied by associated movements in abnormal synergies and loss of cortical control over movement.

Disturbances of proprioception, of cerebellar control, and of tone will all interfere with **balance**, and equilibrium reactions will either be abnormal or inappropriate. Loss of cortical control over movement, poor sensory feedback and abnormal tone will also interfere with functional movement. The patient will have difficulty, for example, transferring weight, remaining erect in antigravity positions, and using his hands.

In the past **behavioural and intellectual impairment** have been paramount in any discussion of problems, but more recent literature seems to indicate that these disturbances are being seen in a different perspective. As Sambrook (1975) points out 'depressive illness is common in society today and patients with multiple sclerosis are not immune to it'. Fritsch (1972) comments that 'some behavioural patterns are constitutional'.

It is interesting to refer to the results of a series of psychological

* Glossary

tests which were administered to a group of patients with a conformed diagnosis of multiple sclerosis, who were paired with subjects with normal brain function. The results showed that patients with multiple sclerosis did poorly in all tests that required motor performance. Only mild deficits, if any, were present in stored verbal information and comprehension, and they showed relatively mild impairment in tasks requiring abstract reasoning and logical analysis. The authors of this study, Reitan, Reed and Dyken (1971), hypothesised that the inconsistencies in the literature with regard to intellectual and cognitive impairment may, in part, be due to the nature of the tests used. These tests had been shown to reflect inconsistent deficits in patients with other types of cerebral disease or damage.

However, most physical disability is associated with emotional changes and patients suffering from this disease are not excluded. The progressive nature of the disease, the age of onset, the unknown prognosis and possible eventual dependency, and the epilepsy which is present in a small percentage of cases, in themselves are sufficient reason for a wide variety of behavioural disturbances. There may be depression, euphoria which is often associated with denial of illness, anxiety, antisocial behaviour, passive aggression, loss of libido and sexuality, irritability and emotional lability with frequent and wide changes of mood. In some patients, behavioural disturbances may deteriorate into terminal dementia, delusions and paranoia.

Involvement of bladder and bowel functions is common. The bladder may be hypertonic which results in frequency and an urgent desire to micturate, or hypotonic with retention and overflow. Sphincter control may be lost or impaired.

Family problems may include anxiety, fear of the future, feelings of guilt following emotional upsets, and feelings of inadequacy. Financial problems, in terms of loss of income, cost of transport to hospital for treatment or to work will cause further anxiety and real burdens. A parent or spouse of a severely disabled person may come to regard himself as a nurse's aide, with resultant strain on personal relationships. As many of these patients have young families, problems of child care and the need for domestic help may also arise.

Some patients, whose clinical signs present in middle age or later and are only slowly progressive, suffer minimal functional problems. Others, who develop clinical signs early in life and whose disease is rapidly progressive, quickly develop severe problems which interfere greatly with their lives. In whatever category a particular patient belongs, it is important that the therapist listens carefully to the patient's opinion of which problems interfere most with his life because even apparently insignificant problems may not be so to the patient.

PHYSICAL MANAGEMENT

Almost any manifestation of neurological disorder can be observed in these patients. Extreme variability occurs not just from one patient to another but also in the same patient at different times. A therapist responsible for a patient with multiple sclerosis must be skilled in neurological assessment and treatment. The wide-ranging and variable nature of the problems which arise illustrate very well the need for thorough assessment, good judgement in deciding the major problems which interfere with function and a problem-solving approach to treatment.

Below are some general suggestions about the patient's management in an attempt to give an overall picture of the way in which a therapist may approach the problems and work out solutions.

The most important *objective* of medical and physical management of a patient with this progressive disease is to enable him to remain with his family and to lead a fulfilling and happy life for as long as possible. The ability to remain at work is important for most people and this must be another important objective for those who are responsible for the patient's management.

Management must always be in terms of what is best for the patient and his family. It is not difficult, when confronted with the complexity of a patient's problems, to lose sight of this most obvious fact.

One of the problems faced by the therapist in the management of patients with this disease is the tendency for them to be referred for physical treatment when they are already severely disabled. The reason for this has to do with a misunderstanding of the roles of physical and occupational therapy and has unfortunate ramifications. This late referral results in the hospital-based therapist seeing only those patients who have been admitted with urinary tract or respiratory infections, or for surgery to pressure areas. In other words, they see only those patients at the depressing end of the spectrum. Therapists therefore, tend to have a negative view of both the disease and its effects and treatment.

This situation may result in a negative, hopeless attitude toward the patient and his treatment which will in turn have an adverse effect upon him and upon his confidence in his own ability to benefit from treatment. It has been observed (Ritchie Russell and Palfrey 1969, Davies 1975) how well these patients respond to treatment if it is given within the positive atmosphere which surrounds patients with traumatic spinal cord injuries. The positive approach engendered by the enthusiastic therapists who tackle the problems of the spinal cord injured also has a positive effect upon the multiple sclerosis patient. As Davies (1975) points out, the approach of therapists who deal with spinal cord injured patients tends to be very different from that of therapists who treat patients with multiple sclerosis. It is probable that these two groups of patients, who tend to share the same age group, may both benefit from combined treatment sessions. This is preferable to the young multiple sclerosis patient being treated, as he so often is, with elderly patients with whom he feels nothing in common, or in special treatment centres, where he will be in a group of patients who demonstrate the varying stages in the progression of the one disease.

The therapist must encourage neurologists and general practitioners to refer patients for early physical evaluation. This early assessment certainly does not imply that the patient need spend periods attending regularly for treatment sessions. However, early assessment enables the therapist to plan with the patient methods of keeping fit, active and mobile. This may consist of pleasurable activities such as swimming. He may require specific and intensive treatment for brief periods designed to minimise the effects on function of new or worsening symptoms, or he may need assistance with the organisation of his home life and employment.

The main advantage of this early contact with the patient is undoubtedly the *prevention of problems which will arise from inactivity and disuse,* and the minimising of the effects of new lesions upon function. However, early contact also gives the patient and his relatives a person to whom they may go for advice about the difficulties with function which may arise from time to time. The therapist through her understanding of movement and the composition of tasks and activities may be the person best equipped to give this advice.

The tendency in some physiotherapy literature to divide physical management into treatment and functional activity seems particularly illogical in the context of multiple sclerosis, as it suggests divisions which do not really exist in the practical situation. Physical management consists of the prevention of functional disability as far as this is possible, and, where it already exists, it aims to improve function.

The therapist, having determined in her assessment the major problems of function, must find out the reason for these problems. Treatment will then emphasise ways of overcoming them. For example, it may be necessary to improve sensory awareness, to stimulate balance and control against gravity, to improve symmetry and body alignment, to inhibit hypertonus, to alter the height of a wheelchair, or to provide the necessary apparatus to improve function.

The problems interfering with function must be analysed careful. in order to use the most appropriate treatment technique. Cryotherapy* may be useful as an inhibitor of spinal-induced spasms. Where this hyperreflexia involves principally the lower limbs and is accompanied by severe loss of functional movement, a programme of exercises designed to strengthen movement of the upper limbs and trunk may be necessary to facilitate the use of crutches or wheelchair. Where hypertonus and poor motor function is principally of supraspinal origin which may involve the body in a hemiplegic or quadriplegic distribution, methods of inhibition, such as reflex inhibiting movement patterns*, may be used in combination with methods of stimulating movement. Strengthening exercises will be inappropriate in this case as resisted activity tends to cause a generalised and difficult to control increase in tone.

Many patients demonstrate symptoms of hypertonus arising from both supraspinal and spinal lesions and in these cases it is necessary to concentrate on those problems which most interfere with function. Movement problems are frequently further complicated by symptoms of cerebellar ataxia, or by loss of some sensory function.

Cerebellar ataxia with dysmetria may be the cause of problems of hand function in a patient whose lower limbs are mainly affected by spasms. His treatment programme will include methods of improving symmetry, balance and stability in sitting, because these are necessary for effective hand function. It will include methods of reducing hypertonus as well as methods of improving stability around his trunk and shoulder girdle, in order to develop more effective reaching out and manipulation.

In the case of patients with a rapidly progressive form of the disease, it is important to maintain the patient's ability to stand. This may be accomplished by certain apparatus, such as leg corsets (Fig. 55) or calipers, but the latter are not very practical for most patients. The tilt table is a particularly effective and comfortable aid to standing for these patients, and may help to prevent contracture. It may be used to enable the patient to use his hands. If modified, it gives support while leaving the patient to exercise some control over his balance.

Rest and fatigue. Rest is usually indicated during a relapse. Otherwise, it should be as much a part of the patient's daily life as it should be for everyone else. It is possible that too much emphasis is placed on not tiring the patient during treatment sessions. Of course no physical treatment should place the patient at the point of

* Appendix 1

exhaustion, but physical fatigue within normal limits for the individual will respond to periods of rest.

It is probable that apparent fatigue caused by feelings of frustration, failure, or a negative attitude are much more detrimental to the patient. When a patient complains of being tired, the therapist should consider carefully what the reasons may be. He may have been expected to continue practising the one skill for too long without a rest, he may not have slept the night before, or he may have had an emotional upset with his family before attending for treatment. On the other hand, he may be bored with his treatment, not understanding the relevance of the programme to his problems. This situation may be improved either by a more thorough explanation of the reasons for particular treatment, or by introducing activities which do seem relevant and which are also good fun.

Exposure to heat, either local or general, has an enervating effect on most people, with a reduction in energy, and this effect should be considered in planning a treatment for the multiple sclerosis patient.

Exercise programmes. Ritchie Russell (1966) reported the development of a programme of rest and exercise for patients in the early stages of multiple sclerosis. The programme involved two or three periods of rest every day for ten to twenty minutes, with a period of stressful exercise designed to increase the circulation around the spinal cord and brain stem. The results over a period of four years were encouraging, but patients had great difficulty in maintaining their motivation to continue the programme if they experienced a significant improvement soon after they commenced it. The difficulty with any preventive programme stems from lack of motivation in patients who have little disability. For this reason, home programmes in these early stages which stress swimming and modest sporting activity are probably more realistic and therefore more likely to be carried out.

The Halliwick system of organised swimming clubs for people of varying disabilities, is a valuable recreational activity, improving motivation and providing pleasure, improving breathing control and keeping the patient active. Similarly, an organisation such as Riding for the Disabled provides another form of recreation which has similar benefits.

Diet. A special diet containing polyunsaturates has been recommended by some (Swank 1970), but there is no clinical evidence of any improvement in the outcome of the disease. However, patients who are overweight have greater difficulty in moving about, and if they are also immobile, they are more difficult to nurse effectively, and weight loss is usually recommended.

Emotional lability. Speech disorders are often combined with persistent crying which makes communication with the patient particularly difficult and prevents speech therapy and other treatment from being effectively instituted. Brookshire (1970) describes a treatment programme devised to eliminate persistent crying behaviour in a multiple sclerosis patient with a severe articulation disorder. He comments that in general the literature about emotional lability in the brain-damaged suggests that such behaviour is a neurological sign and beyond the control of the patient. Brookshire points out that '. . . . emotional behaviours which appear to be organic in nature may have or acquire functional value for the patient. If such behaviours result in attention, sympathy, termination of demands made upon the patient, and so forth, the frequency of the behaviours will be maintained or increases, because they are followed by favourable consequences.' Emotional behaviours are therefore modifiable by means of their consequences. Treatment for this patient involved positive reinforcement of a response which was incompatible with the undesired crying behaviour.

Pregnancy. Millar (1971) considers that the overall progression of the disease is probably unaffected by pregnancy. However, patients are usually warned that pregnancy may initiate a relapse and prospective parents will need to consider the physical and emotional strains of caring for young children. Sambrook (1975) probably makes an important point when he says that 'an over-cautious attitude to having a family only generates in the patient's mind a gloomy outlook on the future rather than creating a fuller life'.

Bladder and bowel management. In the rehabilitation of the spinal cord injured patient, much time, emphasis and effort goes toward the prevention of a permanent indwelling catheter or frequent catheterisation with their attendant risks of infection. Effort directed at achieving the same objective should be an integral part of the management of the multiple sclerosis patient. Unfortunately, catheterisation is often thought of as inevitable for these patients.

A hypertonic bladder may be treated with anticholine drugs such as pro-Banthine which reduce the activity in the detrusor muscle. Millar (1971) suggests that the skilful use of diuretics may reduce the necessity for micturition during the night.

A hypotonic bladder may respond to surgery of the bladder neck, which enables easier emptying and reduces the residual volume of urine (Millar 1971, Sambrook 1975). Routine manual expression performed every two hours helps prevent bladder distension. Activity and mobility, particularly in the upright position, aids in the prevention and management of incontinence.

If bladder incontinence cannot be controlled by routine expression, drugs or surgery, an appliance will be necessary. A urinal attached to the penis and thigh is the most satisfactory for male patients. The problem is more difficult in female patients, but new varieties of absorbent pads are proving relatively useful. Elphick (1970) suggests that pants without a crotch gusset make it easier to change incontinence pads. If catheterisation is unavoidable, a self-retaining catheter appears preferable to daily catheterisation as it has less risk of infection.

Vertigo is usually provoked by sudden head movement. The patient may attempt to cope with it by fixing his eyes on a stationary object and by keeping his head still which causes muscle tension. If vertigo is severe he may not be able to move. Treatment commences with the patient fixing his eyes on a static object and slowly moving his head. When he can do this without vertigo, treatment is progressed to more rapid head movements, slow head movements with eyes closed, then rapid movements with the eyes closed. When the patient can tolerate this without vertigo other movements can be introduced.

Treatment of the severely disabled. There are two important points to keep in mind in considering the disabled chairbound or bedridden patient. The first concerns the need to keep his general condition as satisfactory as possible, attempting to prevent pressure areas, contractures, and retention of pulmonary secretions. The second concerns the need to aid his relatives in caring for him.

Periods of standing each day, if necessary assisted by a tilt table, will help to prevent contractures and pressure areas, improve bladder and bowel control, and act as an emotional stimulus. Erect standing must be encouraged before the patient becomes dependent on a wheelchair. Once he has developed even relatively slight contractures of his hip and knee flexors, standing even in a tilt table may be uncomfortable, and because of mechanical malalignment of the trunk on the limbs, will predispose to further distortion.

The need to prevent contractures cannot be stressed enough. Contractures, especially of the hip and knee flexors and calf muscles, are painful, make it difficult for the patient to be comfortable, discourage attempts at turning and therefore initiate the development of pressure areas. Eventually, the combination of pressure areas and contractures may make sitting in a wheelchair extremely uncomfortable, and therefore lead to a further decrease in the patient's activity.

As well as periods of standing, techniques which reduce tone, including drug therapy, and cryotherapy if he can tolerate it, will help prevent contractures. Ice baths may give the patient relief from hypertonus, particularly spasms, and may enable him to move more

240

freely. Cryotherapy has only a temporary effect on hypertonic muscles but may make the patient feel better, especially if it is followed by standing. However, the most important factors in the development of contractures are position, that is, alignment of the limbs, and gravity.

Once contractures have occurred, surgery, which must be followed by physical treatment, will probably be necessary to correct them. However, it must be done early and result in improved function, otherwise, if it is left until no function is possible, it inflicts unnecessary pain and emotional strain on the patient. Weight-bearing inhibitory plasters* may be successful in correcting contractures if they can be combined with standing. Significant sensory loss may contra-indicate the use of this form of splinting.

In helping the patient in and out of bed, wheelchair or chair, and on and off the lavatory, relatives, nurses and therapists should encourage him to do as much of each movement himself as is possible with their assistance. It often seems easier to lift him bodily, but although it will be slower when he tries himself, it may give him some feeling of independence and the activity will help to keep him mobile. The therapist teaches relatives and nursing staff how to encourage the patient's involvement in these movements.

If the patient can no longer help himself, equipment, such as an hydraulic hoist, may be useful, both to relieve relatives and nursing staff from the strain of moving him about, and to enable the patient to feel less of a burden. A battery-operated wheelchair will give some freedom to a patient who can no longer operate a hand-driven chair.

There are other aids which will eventually be necessary for many patients, and they include the provision of a fixed or hand-held shower, with a chair to sit on, a bath seat, a raised lavatory seat, rails in the bathroom, and a bed of the most suitable height to enable the patient to help himself.

The wheelchair must be the right size for the patient so that he obtains sufficient support and is comfortable. The foot plates should be of the correct height to enable his feet to rest on them in the plantigrade position to aid in the prevention of contracture of the calf muscles. Eating utensils may need to be modified to enable the patient to feed himself. Small alterations to clothing will help the patient dress and undress himself (Macartney 1973 and Reich 1976). His chair, table, desk, or work bench may require alterations to allow him to use them effectively. If he is in a wheelchair, ramps will need to replace steps, and rugs will need to be removed from the floor to

* Appendix 1

241

allow him to move about with less effort. Special devices will enable him to use the telephone and drive a car. Some families will know themselves what help they need and what appliances are necessary. Others will need guidance from the physiotherapist, occupational therapist or social worker.

A bedridden patient requires frequent and regular turning and careful positioning. Sheepskin, ripple mattresses, or water beds will add to his comfort and contribute to skin care. A bed cradle is essential to keep the weight of the bedclothes from his feet. It is necessary to encourage the patient to communicate with his companions and participate as much as he can in the world around him.

Assistance required for the family of a severely disabled person may include domestic help, care of children, financial assistance, professional counselling, organisation of outings for the patient if his family has no car, and organisation of social activities for him. If necessary, arrangements may be made for the admission of the patient to a residential centre while the family goes on holidays. The gradual emergence of community-based health care services in some countries is making more realistic the objective of enabling the very disabled person to stay at home with his family.

Whether the patient with multiple sclerosis is treated by one therapist or whether his treatment is in the hands of a rehabilitation team, it is essential not to lose sight of the importance of

the prevention of unnecessary disablement, and

the maintenance of maximal functional ability.

With such complex and changeable problems, it is easy, especially where a number of health care personnel are involved, to lose sight of these objectives, and omit from the total programme treatment for some of the problems which are most important to the patient and his family. It has been observed by Aldes (1967) that 'those on a total rehabilitation programme maintain a high level of well-being, experience fewer exacerbations, and are able to maintain their functional level'.

SUMMARY

In this chapter the epidemiology, pathophysiology and the problems associated with multiple sclerosis are discussed. The problems are usually complex and diverse as they may result from lesions in one or many parts of the brain and spinal cord. Some general suggestions about the management of these patients are made, including the need for early contact in order to help the patient to remain as fit, active and mobile as possible.

References

Adams, C. W. M. (1972) *Research on Multiple Sclerosis.* Springfield Illinois, Charles C. Thomas.

Aldes, J. H. (1967) Rehabilitation of multiple sclerosis patients. *J. Rehabil.,* **33,** 10–12.

Brookshire, R. H. (1970) Control of 'involuntary' crying behaviour emitted by a multiple sclerosis patient. *J. Communication Disorders,* **3,** 171–176.

Davies, P. M. (1975) A physiotherapist's approach to multiple sclerosis. *Physiotherapy,* **61,** 1, 5–6.

Dean, G. (1972) On the risk of multiple sclerosis according to age at immigration. In *Multiple Sclerosis Progress in Research,* edited by E. J. Field, T. M. Bell, P. R. Carnegie. Amsterdam and London, North Holland.

Elphick, P. (1970) *Incontinence.* London, Disabled Living Foundation.

Fritsch, M. (1972) Possibilities in the medical treatment and rehabilitation of severely handicapped patients suffering from multiple sclerosis. *Proc. XII World Congress Rehab. Int.,* 473–476.

Kraft, A. M. and Wessman, H. C. (1974) Pathology and etiology in multiple sclerosis. *Phys. Ther.,* **54,** 7, 716–720.

Kurtzke, J. F. (1972) Migration and latency in multiple sclerosis. In *Multiple Sclerosis Progress in Research,* edited by E. J. Field, T. M. Bell, P. R. Carnegie. Amsterdam and London, North Holland.

Liebowitz, S. (1966) Immunological reaction in the central nervous system. *J. Roy. Coll. Physicians,* **1,** 85.

Liebowitz, S., Kahana, E. and Alter, M. (1973) The changing frequency of multiple sclerosis in Israel. *Arch. Neurol.,* **29,** August, 107.

MacAlpine, D. (1961) The benign form of multiple sclerosis. A study based on 241 cases seen within three years of onset and followed up until the tenth year or more of the disease. *Brain,* **84,** 186–203.

Macartney, P. (1973) *Clothes Sense for Handicapped People of All Ages.* Disabled Living Foundation, London.

Millar, J. H. D. (1971) *Multiple Sclerosis: A Disease Acquired in Childhood.* Springfield Illinois, Charles C. Thomas.

Reich, N. (1976) Clothing for the handicapped and disabled. *Rehab. Literature,* **10,** 290–294.

Reitan, R. M., Reed, J. C. and Dyken, M. L. (1971) Cognitive, psychomotor and motor correlates of multiple sclerosis. *J. of Nervous and Mental Disorders.,* **153,** 3, 218–224.

Ritchie Russell, W. (1966) Disseminated sclerosis – rest and exercise. *Medical News* supplement, January 14.

Ritchie Russell, W. and Palfrey, G. (1969) Disseminated sclerosis – rest and exercise therapy – a progress report. *Physiotherapy* **55,** 8, 306–310.

Sambrook, M. A. (1975) Medical management of multiple sclerosis. *Physiotherapy, 61,* 1, 2–4.

Sutherland, J. M. (1977) Aetiology of multiple sclerosis. *Med. J. Aust.* **1,** 237–238.

Swank, R. L. (1970) Multiple sclerosis: twenty years on a low fat diet. *Arch. Neurol.* **23,** 460.

Further Reading

Block, J. M. and Kester, N. C. (1970) Role of rehabilitation in the management of multiple sclerosis. *Mod. Treat.,* **7,** 5, 930–940.

Burnell, S. F. (1974) Western domicilliary care service. *Aust. J. Physiother.,* *20* 1, 29–32.

Dix, M. R. (1974) Treatment of vertigo. *Physiotherapy,* **60,** 12.

Mandelstam, D. A. (1975) *Incontinence: A Very Common Complaint.* London, Disabled Living Foundation.

Chapter 9

Tumours

An intracranial tumour is a space-occupying lesion within the skull of neoplastic or chronic inflammatory origin. The site and nature of the tumour determines the mode of onset and clinical features. It may have an insidious onset as in a slow growing meningioma, or a rapid onset as in a medulloblastoma. The majority of intracranial primary tumours are known collectively as gliomas. Metastatic tumours are the second most common variety.

Glioma
These tumours arise from neuroglial cells which constitute the supporting tissue of the nervous system. Those most commonly encountered are the astrocytomas, glioblastomas and medulloblastomas. They are all infiltrative tumours which makes complete surgical removal difficult and they tend to reoccur. A glioma may leave intact the nervous tissue which it infiltrates. Astrocytomas are generally slow growing and relatively benign. Glioblastomas are extremely malignant and are usually seen in adults of middle age. Medulloblastomas are rapidly growing malignant tumours of infancy and childhood. Some authors classify all gliomas as astrocytomas and grade them from I to IV, grade I being the least anaplastic and malignant, grade IV the most.

Meningioma
Meningiomas do not usually invade the brain, but tend to compress it. Many of these tumours are related to the bones of the skull. They are essentially benign and are often successfully removed by surgery, followed by complete recovery, the site of the tumour determining the surgical accessibility (Jennett 1970). They are more common in women than in men.

Metastatic tumour
These tumours are most commonly secondary carcinomas arising as blood-borne metastases from tumours in other sites. Secondary cerebral tumours are usually rapidly growing and multiple.

Neuroma (neurilemmoma, neurofibroma)

The most common intracranial neuroma is a circumscribed tumour found on the acoustic nerve. Symptoms include deafness and vertigo. Surgical removal is often possible if the tumour is detected early.

Vascular tumour

Small *angiomatous malformations* (simple tumours composed of blood vessels or lymphatic vessels) may erupt and result in a subarachnoid haemorrhage.

Haemangioblastomas are cystic tumours most commonly found in the cerebellar hemispheres. These are often familial and are associated with malformations in other parts of the body.

CLINICAL FEATURES

All cerebral tumours, because of their space-occupying qualities and because of the rigidity of the skull, will usually give rise to an increase in intracranial pressure, which is characterised by headache, vomiting and papilloedema*. Increased intracranial pressure may also give rise to mental symptoms, for example, impairment of memory, intellect and behaviour, and disorientation in time and space.

The symptoms of raised intracranial pressure may be combined with progressive focal symptoms which depend upon the site of the tumour, for example, aphasia, cerebellar dysfunction, visual defects, spastic hemiplegia or epilepsy. Focal symptoms are caused by degeneration of nerve cells, pressure interfering with the blood supply and resulting in anoxia of the brain, or they may be due to toxic products. Diagnosis and localisation of the tumour depends on clinical examination, history of illness, and neurological investigations.

MANAGEMENT

Treatment consists of surgery, radiation and drugs. However, the susceptibility to damage of the surrounding parts of the brain places limitations on their use (Jennett 1970).

Following surgery careful observation for any signs indicating formation of a clot or deterioration will include any change in conscious level, alteration in movements of the limbs, size and reaction of the pupils, or a rise in blood pressure, and a fall in pulse rate. The patient is usually nursed from side to side. He may have ventricular drainage if there is suspected blockage of the circulation of the cerebrospinal fluid, lumbar drainage if pressure is high, an

* Glossary

intravenous drip, and a nasogastric tube. Depressed consciousness and a depressed swallowing reflex predispose to aspiration. In this case, the patient should be nursed in the semi-prone position to prevent aspiration of oral secretions, fluids and vomitus and to prevent the tongue from falling back and blocking the airway.

The patient will require two hourly turning and positioning. Particular attention to positioning will be necessary if there are any signs of hypertonus, to prevent the limbs from being held in the abnormal patterns of spasticity. A bed cradle will prevent the weight of the bed clothes from pushing the feet into plantarflexion.

The semi-conscious or unconscious patient will require physiotherapy to the chest to keep a clear airway, to provide adequate oxygenation of the brain and prevent atelectasis and bronchopneumonia. This will include postural drainage when necessary and, if the patient's condition allows, vibrations, assisted breathing and coughing. The physiotherapist will see the patient pre-operatively to explain to him the importance of keeping a clear airway and to assess his neurological function. Mechanical suction may be necessary to stimulate the cough reflex and to remove secretions. Some patients may require tracheostomy and intermittent positive pressure ventilation (see Chapter 6).

Early mobilisation following surgery is important. The patient may be able to sit out of bed within 24 to 48 hours, and is usually able to dress and leave the ward in approximately ten days. Assessment of the patient will indicate what problems of movement and function are present. The reader should refer to Section III and Appendix I for details of the treatment of these problems.

SUMMARY

This chapter gives a brief description of some of the commonest intracranial tumours. Physical treatment will depend on accurate assessment of each patient.

References

Jennett, W. B., (1970) *An Introduction to Neurosurgery*. London, Heinemann.

Chapter 10

Infections

The central nervous system, its meningeal coverings and its peripheral component, the spinal cord, may be invaded by infective agents like any other part of the body. These infective agents may include bacteria, viruses, spirochaetes and parasites. Whereas some bacterial infections may be part of a widespread disease process affecting the whole body, certain viruses called neurotropic viruses, have a predilection for nervous tissue. In general, infective agents produce an inflammatory response within the nervous system.

Below is a brief outline of some infections of the central nervous system and their effects.

Bacteria

Bacteria may enter the central nervous system as a result of a fracture of the skull, particularly when this is complicated by a penetrating wound or by tearing of the dura mater. When this tearing is caused by a fracture of the skull, organisms may spread to the meninges from the nasopharynx. There may be a direct spread of bacteria from a middle ear infection, paranasal sinusitis, osteomyelitis of the spine or skull, or from infections elsewhere in the body. The most common bacterial infections result in meningitis, intracranial thrombophlebitis and intracranial abscesses.

Meningitis is an inflammation of the meninges of the brain and spinal cord. Most cases are due to pyogenic infection or to tuberculosis if meningitis of viral or parasitic origin are excluded. The common symptoms are headache of a 'bursting' character (Brain and Walton 1969) with pain radiating into the neck, down the back and into the limbs. Vomiting may occur. Neck stiffness is present due to spasm of the neck extensors and head retraction. A positive Kernig's sign,* photophobia and mental confusion may occur. Localised meningitis may produce epilepsy or hemiplegia. Diagnosis is by lumbar puncture and examination of the cerebrospinal fluid. Treatment of meningitis depends on the isolation of the involving organ-

* Glossary

ism, the possibility of removing the source of infection and the sensitivity of the organism to particular chemotherapy. Some patients may have residual problems, for example, epilepsy, deafness, blindness or spasticity resulting from permanent damage to the nervous system.

Intracranial abscess may be extradural or subdural, or more commonly in the brain itself. There is usually some degree of irregular pyrexia and headache, vomiting, bradycardia, and sometimes papilloedema,* which indicate raised intracranial pressure. The patient may become drowsy and stuporous. Focal neurological signs depend on the situation of the abscess and may include aphasia, hemiplegia, visual field defects or ataxia. Treatment consists of antibiotic therapy and neurosurgery. Many survivors have residual problems of ataxia or spasticity, and suffer from headaches or epilepsy.

Neurotropic viruses

Neurotropic viruses attack the neurons, that is, the grey matter of the central nervous system. They are responsible for acute anterior poliomyelitis, various forms of encephalitis and encephalomyelitis. Other viruses, which are not normally neurotropic, such as mumps and glandular fever, may attack the central nervous system giving rise to an encephalitic or meningitic illness.

The idea of 'slow virus' infections has aroused interest in recent years. *Kuru,* a progressive disease occurring in natives of New Guinea, causes cerebellar ataxia initially, and appears to be due to a neurotropic virus. It seems to be closely related to scrapie, a chronic neurological disorder of sheep, the signs of which do not appear until at least nine months after innoculation (Brain and Walton 1969, Walton 1975). Some researchers consider that multiple sclerosis may be due to an unidentified 'slow' viral agent.

Acute anterior poliomyelitis. The virus attacks particularly the anterior horn cell of the grey matter of the spinal cord, the cells of the nuclei of the motor brain stem and sometimes the cerebral cortex. The virus is thought to enter the body via the alimentary canal or via the nasopharynx particularly after recent tonsillectomy. It apparently enters the nervous system via the peripheral and autonomic nerves (Walton 1975). It is almost unheard of now in countries in which Sabin oral vaccine is used.

The virus causes a meningitic illness and a proportion of cases develop flaccid paralysis of a lower motor neuron type along with

* Glossary

fever, severe muscular pain and tenderness. The distribution of muscle weakness is variable but any muscle or muscle group may be involved. Where the nuclei of the brain stem are involved there may be respiratory paralysis and/or paralysis of the facial, pharyngeal, laryngeal and lingual muscles.

Some nerve cells may be only temporarily affected, but others are destroyed which results in permanent muscle weakness and paralysis. Wallerian degeneration of the axon occurs throughout the entire length of the nerve fibres of the cells involved.

Encephalitis is an inflammation of the brain. If it also involves the spinal cord it is known as *encephalomyelitis*.

Encephalitis lethargica (sleeping sickness) is probably due to a neurotropic virus. The principal pathological changes are seen in the mid-brain and substantia nigra. It reached epidemic proportions in the decade following its appearance in 1915, and is rarely seen now. In its original form the disease had an acute onset with headache, disturbances of sleep rhythm and visual abnormalities. It had a high death rate and those who survived were left with varying degrees of disability. Behavioural disturbances were often very severe and a large percentage developed encephalitic Parkinsonism in the chronic stage even up to twenty years after the acute illness.

Other forms of virus encephalitis and encephalomyelitis which are due to neurotropic viruses include Japanese type B, St. Louis, Russian spring-summer, equine (U.S.A.) and Murray Valley (Australia) varieties in which the virus is carried by a mosquito or a tick. All levels of the nervous system may be affected and severe inflammation is always observed in the brain stem, basal ganglia and the white matter of the hemispheres. All these viruses cause an encephalitic illness characterised by headache, fever, a period of confusion, stupor or severe coma, rigidity, spasticity or tremor of the limbs. Mortality can be as high as 60% in epidemics. Some patients recover completely, while others show signs of permanent intellectual and physical disability.

Herpes simplex virus may cause an encephalitic illness in all age groups. The illness is characterised by coma, high temperature and features suggesting a lesion of one temporal lobe, such as fits and hemiplegia. It is often fatal.

An acute **disseminated encephalomyelitis** can follow vaccination against smallpox, innoculation against rabies and influenza, or it can complicate chicken pox, measles, German measles and rarely scarlet fever, or it may appear spontaneously. Viral encephalitis and encephalomyelitis involve the grey matter principally, whereas the principal pathological change in acute disseminated encephalo-

250

myelitis involves the white matter, with perivascular demyelination of the brain and spinal cord (Walton 1975). The onset and clinical picture of the illness is extremely variable, and treatment is essentially symptomatic. Some patients will die, some will recover completely. Residual clinical manifestations may include spasticity, ataxia, mental defects, epilepsy and changes of personality.

Spirochaetal infections
The most common spiral micro-organism to invade the central nervous system is the spirochaetal agent of syphilis. As a result of modern chemotherapy, this micro-organism is less likely to affect the nervous system. Tabes dorsalis (locomotor ataxia) is a variety of neurosyphilis in which there is inflammation of the posterior root ganglion with secondary involvement of ascending nerve fibres in the posterior columns of the spinal cord.

Guillain-Barré syndrome
Guillain-Barré syndrome (acute idiopathic polyneuropathy) is included under the heading of infections although there seems to be no actual agreement on its classification, aetiology and pathogenesis. The syndrome describes a condition involving the spinal nerve roots, peripheral nerves and sometimes the cranial nerves resulting in motor, sensory and occasionally autonomic disturbances. It is characterised by an acute onset and rapidly developing paralysis which may involve the respiratory muscles and muscles of swallowing as well as the muscles of the trunk and extremities. It may follow an acute infection and is sometimes known as acute post-infective polyneuritis. It may also arise spontaneously. The first symptoms may be headache, vomiting, pyrexia, pain in the back and limbs, and neck stiffness.

The condition is characterised by demyelination followed by remyelination in the recovery stage, but recovery is seldom complete. It may involve an inflammatory response of an allergic type or a hypersensitivity in which the nerves are attacked by lymphocytes or an unidentified virus (Walton 1975).

The motor weakness which is of a flaccid lower motor neuron type is usually symmetrical. It may affect all four limbs and the trunk simultaneously and it may begin in the lower limbs and spread upward to include the facial muscles. The muscles of swallowing can be affected with the inherent danger of aspiration of fluids, saliva, vomitus or food. Superficial and deep reflexes are usually depressed and the plantar responses are flexor if present. Sensory symptoms include loss of position sense, numbness, tingling, feeling of pins and needles, and pain and tenderness especially in the calves. Sensory symptoms may be more pronounced distally, although there are some cases in which there is very little demonstrable sensory loss apart from paraesthesia. Sphincter control may be impaired. There may be spontaneous remission and complete recovery in a few months. There may be remissions followed by relapses, or recovery may be very slow and incomplete.

Treatment with ACTH or cortisone is considered by some to be effective, while others do not consider they have any effect on the natural history of the disease. Immunosuppressive agents have been given with marked success.

AN OUTLINE OF PHYSICAL TREATMENT

The reader should refer to the chapters in Section III for details of the physical treatment of the specific problems which may follow infections of the brain.

Although the physical treatment of lower motor neuron lesions is not within the scope of this book, outlined below are some points about the approach to the management of the treatment of patients with lower motor neuron paralysis. This may help to make clear the fact that when the pathophysiological mechanisms underlying problems of function are different, the emphasis in treatment must be different.

For example, in these patients, whose main problems interfering with function are *muscular paralysis or weakness*, strengthening of muscles is necessary to improve functional capabilities. This is accomplished by techniques which hypertrophy the muscle fibres still innervated and which stimulate the sprouting of collateral nerve fibres. These strengthening techniques are a major part of treatment, in marked contrast to the treatment of patients with disordered brain function.

In patients with acute lower motor neuron lesions, rest is essential in the acute paralytic stage as there is some evidence that physical activity or localised trauma in the pre-paralytic and acute paralytic stage predispose to severe paralysis.

Physical treatment involves gentle passive movements within a pain free range and without too much handling of the tender muscle bellies. Light splints may be necessary particularly when there is unopposed muscular action, to prevent over-stretching of muscles and contractures. The patient is nursed on a firm mattress with a bed cradle to prevent the weight of the bed clothes from pushing the feet into plantarflexion.

During the paralytic stage the patient's respiratory function is observed regularly and if there are signs of involvement of the muscles of respiration, function is measured day and night. A vitalograph is used to indicate when artificial ventilation is necessary. The patient is also observed for any signs of bulbar paralysis which will lead to aspiration of saliva, food, fluids or vomitus.

Once the stage of recovery begins, active physical treatment within the limits of comfort is commenced. Improvement in muscle power may continue over a period of six months to two years.

Active treatment includes methods of assisting movement where necessary, and as soon as possible, methods of stimulating and strengthening movement. Resistance may be applied manually or by using gravity, water, or apparatus. Muscles are stimulated to contract both isotonically and isometrically in specific techniques, such as the techniques of PNF described by Knott and Voss (1968). These techniques are directed toward a particular muscle or muscle group. Activities which stimulate automatic movement and improve endurance, agility and co-ordination are also introduced.

Residual problems may include permanent muscle weakness or paralysis, muscle wasting, fasciculation, contracture, deformity and trophic changes.

SUMMARY

This chapter gives a brief description of the commonest infections which may affect the central nervous system. Although physical treatment of lower motor neuron lesions is not included in this book, some points in management are briefly outlined to emphasise the importance of considering the pathophysiological mechanism causing particular problems when planning treatment.

References

Brain, R. and Walton, J. N. (1969) *Brain's Diseases of the Nervous System*. London, Oxford University Press.

Knott, M. and Voss, D. E. (1968) *Proprioceptive Neuromuscular Facilitation*. 2nd. edition. New York, Harper and Row.

Walton, J. N. (1975) *Essentials of Neurology*. 4th Edition. London, Pitman Medical.

Section III

Chapter 11

Hypertonus

The terms spasticity, spasm, rigidity and dystonia are used clinically to describe the increased tone (muscular activity) found in many different disorders of the brain involving the basal ganglia, the subthalamus, and the cerebral cortex with its extrapyramidal outflow. They are used clinically to describe the *quality* of tone.

The distribution and the quality of hypertonus are probably related to the site of the lesion as well as to its extent but at the present time there is no clear explanation of this. This term *spasticity* is used to describe hypertonus resulting from a lesion of the cells in the cerebral cortex and their extrapyramidal projections. *Rigidity* is descriptive of a severe state of spasticity as well as of the hypertonus due to lesions of the basal ganglia as seen in Parkinsonism. *Dystonia* is used in a similar context but also describes the particular quality of hypertonus found in those basal ganglia disorders which result in athetosis. *Spasm* usually refers to fluctuations of tone as occur in conjunction with athetosis, and also to the hyperreflexia which follows spinal cord lesions.

Hypertonus may exist at birth or develop in the postnatal period as part of the syndrome called cerebral palsy. It may become evident over a period of time in a degenerative disease such as multiple sclerosis or Parkinson's disease, or as the result of a tumour. It follows a period of transient hypotonus following a cerebrovascular accident or a head injury. The underlying presence of hypertonus during the stage of transient hypotonus can probably be demonstrated by the preservation of tendon jerks in some patients at the stage when the limbs appear hypotonic to clinical examination (Lance and McLeod 1975), and by the presence of associated movements in abnormal spastic synergies (Bobath 1970). In certain lesions of the brain, hypertonus may occur in conjunction with athetosis or ataxia. In some cases hypertonus co-exists with hypotonus. Denny Brown (1966) pointed out that a muscle group can be both spastic and flaccid. It is also possible for a patient to demonstrate hypertonus in one part of a limb and hypotonus in another.

In this chapter the characteristics of hypertonus associated with lesions of the brain and its effect upon movement and function will be considered and methods of treatment aimed at diminishing hypertonus and improving function will be described. The problems associated with spinal-originating hypertonus in terms of patient problems and therefore of treatment, are different from those associated with central-originating hypertonus, and are not considered in this book.

PATHOPHYSIOLOGY AND CHARACTERISTICS OF HYPERTONUS

The physiological differences between the various clinical manifestations of hypertonus are not completely understood. Rushworth in 1960 said that 'the fundamental disorder of physiology which determines the difference between the Parkinsonian plastic type of rigidity, the statuesqueness of the dystonias, and clasp-knife spasticity is not entirely clear'. Even the word 'tone' is of uncertain meaning.

Clinically, *'muscle tone'* is used to describe the feeling of resistance and assistance felt by the clinician as she moves a limb through a range of movement, and to describe her observations of the posture of the head, trunk and limbs as the patient moves, or holds a limb against gravity. Some clinicians, however, prefer to talk of 'postural tone' in order to clarify the point that a state of tone is manifested throughout the body and not just in one group of muscles.

In the presence of hypertonus the clinician feels a *sensation of increased resistance* as she moves the limb. This resistance occurs throughout the entire movement, or through the beginning of the movement in the presence of the clasp-knife phenomenon. She also observes the posture of head, trunk and limbs during movement, when the patient is holding a limb against gravity and when he is at rest. These postures will involve *abnormal* and *asymmetrical alignment* of head, trunk and limbs and may demonstrate the effects of tonic neck and labyrinthine reflexes. *Associated movements* in abnormal synergies will be seen especially if movement involves effort.

However difficult it may be to distinguish physiologically between the various types of centrally originating hypertonus, we can assume that they probably all result from different mechanisms by which the brain stem is released from control by higher centres.

Spasticity

This form of hypertonus results from a lesion of the motor cortex or its extrapyramidal outflow which normally exercises a major control-

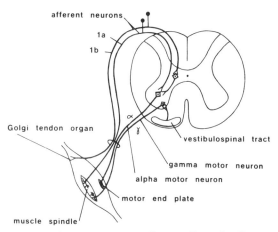

afferent neurons

1a

1b

Golgi tendon organ

vestibulospinal tract

gamma motor neuron

alpha motor neuron

motor end plate

muscle spindle

Fig. 82. *The monosynaptic reflex arc. Group la afferent fibres from the muscle spindle synapse directly with alpha motoneurons in the anterior horn, whose axons cause the muscle fibres surrounding the spindle to contract. The alpha motoneuron is inhibited via an interneuron by group 1b fibres from Golgi tendon organs. The gamma efferent system is regulated by descending motor pathways, one of which, the vestibulospinal tract, is illustrated.*

ling influence over brain stem activity. Spasticity therefore is a clinical manifestation of abnormal tone resulting from disordered supraspinal control over the stretch reflex arc (Fig. 82). Normally, tone is maintained at a level which is appropriate for movement and stability by a regulated interplay between the inhibitory cortico-reticulospinal (extrapyramidal) tract which accompanies in close anatomical relationship the corticospinal (pyramidal) tract throughout its course, and the facilitatory pontine reticulospinal and lateral vestibulospinal pathways (Fig. 83). It is probable that many other influences are directed at the stretch reflex arc by longloop reflexes involving the basal ganglia, brain stem and cerebellum. A failure of what is apparently a complex regulating system results therefore in abnormal excitability of dynamic fusimotor (gamma) neurons and skeletomotor (alpha) neurons, and perhaps of static fusimotor neurons as well (Ashby 1973).

This disordered supraspinal control may occur in lesions involving any part of the cortico-reticulospinal tract from the cells in the cerebral cortex, areas 4 and 6 and their projections, through to their terminations in the spinal cord.

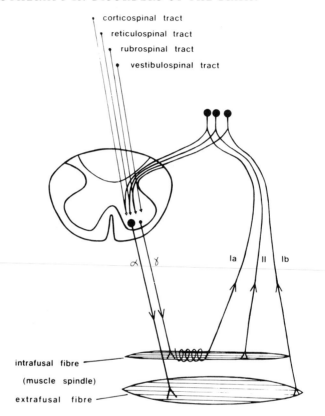

corticospinal tract
reticulospinal tract
rubrospinal tract
vestibulospinal tract

Ia   II   Ib

intrafusal fibre
(muscle spindle)
extrafusal fibre

Fig. 83. *Efferent pathway to extrafusal and intrafusal muscle fibres. The alpha motoneuron innervates the extrafusal muscle fibres and the gamma motoneuron the muscle spindle. Group 1a afferent fibres from the muscle spindle synapse with the alpha motoneuron to form the afferent limb of the stretch reflex arc. Group 11 afferents have sensory receptors in the muscle spindle and group 1b in the Golgi tendon organs. (From McLeod, J. G. (1971) Pathophysiology of Parkinson's disease.* Aust. New Zeal. J. Med. Suppl., 1, 1, 19.)

Differences between spasticity of spinal origin and spasticity of central origin. Total transection of the spinal cord will cut off the nervous system below the level of the lesion from the controlling influences of the brain, thus allowing unrestrained spinal cord activity and preventing functional movement. The patient demonstrates a state of hyperreflexia which resembles in some ways the hyperreflexia of spasticity and rigidity seen in lesions of the brain. However, in complete spinal cord lesions, the cessation of inhibitory control over the spinal cord, normally exerted from the brain stem through the dorsal reticulospinal tracts, results in the release of flexor reflexes. These reflexes are not released to the same extent in any lesion above the brain stem, as the intact pathways from the reticular formation will still be maintaining their inhibitory control over the flexor reflex afferents. Furthermore, the pathways from the vestibular nucleus will still be carrying facilitatory impulses to the motoneurons of the extensor muscles (Ashby 1973).

The myotatic reflex behaviour of muscles which are spastic as a result of a cerebral lesion is shown by Herman and Mecomber (1971) to be different from the behaviour of muscles which are spastic as a result of spinal cord lesion. They studied the effects of varying rates of stretch, with or without vibration, imposed upon these muscles, and also their agonist-antagonist (reciprocal innervation) relationships. Their findings suggested that the primary endings of spastic muscles in paraplegia are not as sensitive either to the rate of stretch or to vibratory stimuli as hemiplegic spastic muscles. The authors considered that the differences in reciprocal innervation may be due to dissimilarities in feedback from the muscle receptors.

The differences between spastic paraplegic and spastic hemiplegic muscles have also been described by other authors, including Norton, Bomze, Sahrmann and Eliasson (1974). Herman, Freedman and Mayer (1974) report their study of the effects of passive stretch. In the hemiplegic spastic muscle, passive stretch resulted in extreme tension. Marked hypertonus led to postural shortening of the antigravity muscles with displacement of the joint. The reflex activity radiated to the synergists but the increase in tension in these muscles was not as intense as in those being stretched. Paraplegic spastic muscles, however, demonstrated a varied response to passive stretch. Following spinal shock, stretch induced comparatively little tension and frequently elicited generalised flexor or flexor-extensor movements of the lower limbs.

The pattern of spasticity in lesions above the brain stem is usually extensor in the lower limbs, and flexor in the upper limbs, sometimes called a decorticate posture, and, less commonly, extensor in both upper and lower limbs, called a decerebrate posture. These terms are sometimes used clinically because of the similarity of these postures to the postures seen in experimental animals. However, the latter relates to certain precise levels of lesion, which are not replicated in man as the result of a brain lesion.

The patient with spasticity of central origin demonstrates postures and both volitional and automatic movements which are stereotyped and in *abnormal synergies*. The head, trunk and limbs are in abnormal alignment. The most commonly seen synergies involve the antigravity muscles, in a pattern of depression and retraction of the shoulder girdle, flexion, adduction, internal rotation of the shoulder, flexion of the elbow, wrist and fingers, pronation of the forearm, and adduction and flexion of the thumb. The lower limb is extended, internally rotated and adducted, with inversion and plantarflexion of the foot. The pelvis is elevated and retracted (Fig. 84). These patterns are not

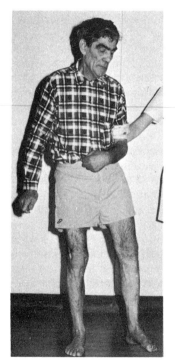

Fig. 84. *Abnormal flexor synergy of upper limb and extensor synergy of lower limb with obvious trunk involvement. Note the retraction of the left side.*

always as well defined as this infers, however most patients will demonstrate some element or variation of them.

These synergies may involve all four limbs (quadriplegia) or two limbs on the same side (hemiplegia). The trunk is substantially involved because of the trunk and girdle attachments of the spastic limb muscles.

Spasticity is accompanied by hyperactivity of the stretch receptors which is demonstrated by increased resistance to stretch. This increased resistance is demonstrated by clonus, the clasp-knife phenomenon, increased phasic tendon reflexes, abnormal tonic vibration reflex, and by the presence of tonic neck reflexes. Associated movements are easily elicited and take place in the abnormal spastic synergies. As well as these manifestations of extrapyramidal dysfunction, the spastic patient demonstrates another abnormal reflex, Babinski's sign, which is symptomatic of damage to the pyramidal tract.

The clasp-knife phenomenon is demonstrated by initial resistance to passive movement of a limb which is followed by a sudden relaxation of this resistance, not unlike the sensation experienced when one opens a clasp-knife. This phenomenon may be found in either the upper or lower limb but is more commonly noticed in the lower limb, particularly in the quadriceps muscle. Burke and Lance (1973) comment that in many patients the limb remains hypotonic once it has passed beyond the clasp-knife point. As soon as the knee is extended again the initial resistance is repeated.

It is considered by some (Granit 1970) that the mechanism may be as follows. An initial stretch to the quadriceps, for example as the knee is passively flexed, stimulates the hyperactive stretch receptors in the muscle, causing an initial resistance. Continued stretch to this resistance stimulates the Golgi tendon organs which have a high threshold to stretch, but which, once they fire off, inhibit muscle spindle activity. The result is immediate relaxation of the extensors and usually contraction of the antagonistic group. Lance and McLeod (1975) comment that this explanation becomes less satisfactory as more is understood about the Golgi tendon organ (Stuart, Mosher and Gerlach 1971).

Clonus is another manifestation of the hyperactivity of the stretch receptors. It is demonstrated clinically by applying a gentle stretch to the spastic muscle, which responds with regular repeated sharp contractions, the reflex arc being discharged at the rate of 6 to 7 muscle twitches a second (Lance and McLeod 1975). It is most evident in the calf muscles, and may be elicited when the patient places the ball of his foot to the ground, thus applying a moderate stretch to the calf. In a patient who has a plantarflexed foot as part of the abnormal posture of his leg, the ball of the foot will always touch the floor first. This stimulates more extensor hyperactivity and if clonus is present this adds to the difficulty he has in weight-bearing.

The fact that clonus can occur is considered to be due to the in-parallel relationship between the intrafusal and the extrafusal muscle fibres. The stretch to the muscle causes the hyperactive spindles to fire off. This results in a muscle contraction which takes the tension off the spindle. The spindle ceases firing, the muscle relaxes and is therefore put under tension again, so the sequence is repeated. Sustained clonus is mostly a manifestation of a lesion of cortical motoneurons and their connections. However, brief episodes of clonus are sometimes found in anxious, tense people.

The tonic vibration reflex represents the result of vibration of muscle spindles which induces activity in group Ia afferents, thus acting as a sustained stretch stimulus (Eklund and Hagbarth 1966). The response to vibration varies in patients with spasticity as it does in normal people according to the frequency and amplitude of vibration, and whether vibration is applied to muscle tendon or belly.

The tonic vibration reflex cannot be elicited after complete spinal transection in muscles innervated below the level of the lesion (de Gail, Lance and Neilson 1966, Gillies, Burke and Lance 1971). This seems to indicate that this reflex is somehow dependent upon supraspinal pathways.

Hagbarth (1973) reports that muscles which are spastic as a result of a cerebral lesion frequently respond more briskly to vibration than relaxed muscles in normal subjects. In addition, the reflex has a more abrupt onset in spastic muscles. Hagbarth describes how vibration over the palmar surface of the wrist in a patient with spasticity caused not only wrist flexion and pronation but also flexion of the elbow and adduction of the arm. This illustrates the stereotyped way in which spastic muscle groups must contract together in a total synergy. The reflex is damped down in the early stage following stroke.

The tonic vibration reflex can be inhibited voluntarily by a normal person, but patients with spasticity resulting from cerebral lesions have been found to be unable to do this (Hagbarth and Eklund 1968). This is probably because the reflex arc is maintained in a hyperactive state by lack of corticoreticulospinal inhibition.

Babinski's sign is also referred to as the extensor plantar response. In a normal adult, a flexion movement of the great toe occurs upon stimulation of the lateral side of the sole of the foot. In the presence of a pyramidal tract lesion the great toe will extend. Extension of the toe upon this stimulus occurs in normal infants as part of an immature total flexion or flexor withdrawal response, in which the entire leg is flexed, abducted and externally rotated, and the foot dorsiflexed away from the noxious stimulus. As the infant's brain matures the primitive responses, such as this total flexion, become more controlled, and the Babinski sign is no longer evident. As it is mediated through the first sacral segment, the sensory pathways from the lateral sole of the foot to the spinal cord must be intact.

Associated movements. These are movements which accompany a motor function but are not involved in it and are not necessary for its performance. Riddoch and Buzzard (1921), referring to what they called 'associated reactions', described them as 'automatic activities which fix or alter the posture of a part or parts when some other part of the body is brought into action by either voluntary effort or reflex stimulation'. Brunnstrom (1970) describes associated movements as 'reflex tensing of muscles and involuntary limb movement'. The terms overflow and synkinetic movements are also used synonymously.

The developing child demonstrates a gradual inhibition of associated movements as his brain matures. Nevertheless, they can be seen in normal adults during the performance of a task which is new and as yet unlearned.

In patients with hypertonus these associated movements are more easily elicited. They occur on movement particularly if it involves effort (Fig. 85), and even on such involuntary actions as sneezing and yawning. They may occur on an emotional stimulus, and can be stimulated by the desire to move or speak. Their influence on the patient's function and on his recovery of function is frequently considerable.

Associated movements occur in the abnormal synergies which are typical of hypertonus. Hence Bobath (1970) stresses their importance in as an indication of spasticity in the assessment of tone and in the treatment of patients with hypertonus, particularly those patients who are apparently hypotonic.

When the stimulus ceases, tension remains in the muscles then gradually subsides. These movements may occur in patients who have no voluntary movement, as well as in patients who have. They may be strong enough to prevent any functional activity, or they may interfere with a voluntary movement at some point during its performance.

It should be noted that the position of the head may have an effect upon the extent and distribution of associated movements. This probably indicates the effect of the asymmetrical and symmetrical tonic neck reflexes, or the tonic labyrinthine reflex. For example, a patient with left-sided spasticity, when asked to squeeze a ball in his unaffected hand, may demonstrate that flexion spasticity is more easily elicited in his left arm when his head is turned to the right. In

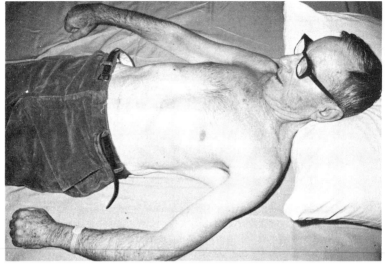

a

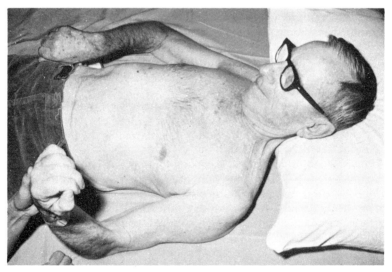

b

Fig. 85. (a) The patient at rest demonstrates spasticity which is seen in the retraction of his right shoulder and flexed wrist.
(b) When he is asked to move against resistance he demonstrates associated movements. On the right side muscular activity is seen in the abnormal spastic synergy.

266

the same patient extension may be more easily elicited in this arm when the head is turned to the left.

It appears that the strength of associated movements may vary according to whether the brain lesion is recent or old. Patients with old lesions and residual flexor spasticity usually demonstrate a strong flexion response in the upper limb. This may be due to the fact that over a period of time patterns of spasticity tend to become established.

Lack of cortical drive. Sahrmann (1977) points out that a major dilemma confronting the therapist lies in trying to separate the problem of weakness from the problem of hypertonicity. Her studies of the upper limb indicate that spasticity is not confined to flexor muscle groups, but is more evident in these muscles in man because of our upright posture. She considers that both flexors and extensors suffer a diminished cortical drive due to the extrapyramidal brain lesion, and that difficulty contracting the muscle group (elbow extensors) antagonistic to the more hypertonic group (elbow flexors) is due to this lack of cortical drive as well as to difficulty in relaxing the flexors after voluntary effort. This is particularly true if stretch reflexes are providing additional input. Bobath (1959) has suggested that spasticity of a particular muscle group may inhibit activity of the antagonistic group and that this may be the reason for the apparent muscle weakness which occurs in the antagonistic group. 'The weakness . . . of the extensors of the arm is relative and in direct proportion to the inhibition imposed upon them by their spastic antagonists'. Eklund, Hagbarth, and Steen (1969) suggest that most observers would probably be in agreement.

The Effect of Spasticity on Movement

In the presence of severe spasticity, the repertoire of movement is very limited because the patient's activity is dictated by his spasticity. As these spastic movements are not functional the patient may be incapable of any effective movement. In patients whose spasticity is relatively mild, movement will be possible but more skilled activities will be imprecise, and balance and protective responses will not be effective.

The spastic patient *lacks the ability to balance,* that is, to adjust automatically to any alteration in his centre of gravity. His balance reactions are either absent, abnormal or ineffective by being too slow in response or inappropriate. He frequently lacks the head and trunk movements appropriate to balancing.

Associated with his problem of balance is his *difficulty in shifting*

267

weight, an essential element in all function and not just in moving from one position to another. In order to transfer weight and balance it is necessary to be able to bear weight with the limbs and trunk in their normal weight-bearing alignment (Fig. 138).

The patient's *posture is asymmetrical* (Fig. 84). The muscles of the trunk, shoulder and pelvic girdles are involved in the abnormal synergies, and this involvement causes considerable interference with all function which then must be attempted from this abnormal alignment of the body.

The patient is *unable to select the movement components appropriate for particular functions.* For example, when he is walking he may not be able to extend the knee and dorsiflex the foot while his hip is in flexion (Fig. 40). He may be unable to maintain his wrist in extension while flexing his fingers to grasp an object. All activities require combinations of movements at various joints, performed automatically or semi-automatically by muscles which have fine interactions with each other, and the spastic patient is incapable of these variations.

Rigidity

Lesions of the basal ganglia and the subthalamus, such as are typified in Parkinson's disease and certain choreic disorders, usually result in rigidity, as do some lesions of the cerebral cortex, in which rigidity is clinically a severe manifestation of spasticity. The basal ganglia, subthalamus and cerebral cortex act to control the facilitatory reticular formation of the brain stem with its powerful antigravity mechanisms. Therefore lesions in these areas may result in the partial release of the reticular formation from their control.

Rigidity is fundamentally the same phenomenon as spasticity, as they both result from overactivity of uncontrolled brain stem mechanisms. However, they are clinically demonstrated in slightly different ways.

There are various types and degrees of rigidity. The patient who has been spastic for a long period demonstrates an unchanging hypertonus which may be described by the clinician as rigidity. It is this severe hypertonus of long-term origin which gives the appearance of muscle shortening, and in fact, the long-term result of unrelieved rigidity, wherever the lesion, will be actual contracture.

The rigidity of Parkinsonism is characterised by its 'lead pipe' or 'plastic' quality in which both flexor and extensor muscle groups are involved. There is an approximately equal sensation of resistance to passive movement throughout range of movement in both directions,

268

in contrast to the clasp-knife effect of spasticity. Passive movement may demonstrate the cogwheel phenomenon, in which there is an alternate increase and decrease in resistance to the movement. This may be the result of tremor superimposed upon rigidity but there is some disagreement about this. There is a tendency for the patient eventually to develop more rigidity in the flexor muscle groups, which results in what is called flexion dystonia. The patient adopts a generally flexed posture. In parkinsonian rigidity, deep tendon reflexes do not show clonus and tendon jerks are within normal limits. However, there is an increased response to stimulation of the tonic vibration reflex. It is thought that although both alpha and gamma motoneuron hyperactivity are present in the early stages, alpha motoneuron hyperactivity is probably dominant at a later stage. However, whether rigidity is of primarily alpha or gamma origin is a controversial point (Denny-Brown 1968, Steg 1972, Andrews, Burke and Lance 1972, Hassler 1972 and Wallin, Hongwell and Hagbarth 1973).

Where rigidity is present as an exaggeration of spasticity, the patient's movement problems will be similar to those described for spasticity. However, the patient with parkinsonian rigidity, in which the lesion is in the substantia nigra and its connections, demonstrates movement problems which are in part due to rigidity and in part to bradykinesia. Clinically therefore the patient's movement problems will be different. The reader will find them described in Chapter 7.

Dystonia

As we have seen, this term is used qualitatively to describe severe manifestations of hypertonus. Used clinically, the term seems to imply a relatively fixed and abnormal posture resulting from an inappropriate contraction of muscle groups antagonistic to each other. Flexion dystonia describes the flexed posture of advanced Parkinson's disease. Lance and McLeod (1975) describe the spastic hemiplegic posture of a long-term stroke patient as 'dystonic'. They suggest that although fusimotor hyperactivity is a feature of early spasticity this becomes over-shadowed by skeletomotor hyperactivity as spasticity becomes established over a period of time. Dystonia also occurs in association with athetosis (see Chapter 12).

TREATMENT OF PATIENTS WITH HYPERTONUS

The treatment of hypertonus cannot be discussed in isolation, as it is necessary to consider the problems of each individual patient. Treatment for patients with hypertonus varies according to its severity, the problems it is causing, and the functional goals for each particular patient. The following illustrations may clarify this point. Immediately following a stroke, treatment goals are aimed at stimulating movement, preventing disability and helping the patient achieve maximum functional ability. Hypertonus should not present a major problem. On the other hand, in a head-injured patient with severe spasticity and contracture of, for example, the calf muscles, the immediate goal may be the inhibition of spasticity in order to allow weight-bearing. In the multiple sclerosis patient with spasms and hyperreflexia of spinal cord origin probably combined with spasticity of central origin, the goal may be relief of painful spasms to enable the patient to assume comfortable sitting and perhaps periods of standing.

Below is a brief discussion of some points to consider in the treatment of any brain-damaged patient who demonstrates increased tone.

It is the authors' opinion that in many patients following acute brain lesions, particularly those who have had a stroke, the degree of hypertonus which develops may depend a great deal on the patient's experiences following his brain damage and his experiences, of course, include his treatment. Brain-damaged patients who are untreated or not treated appropriately, tend to demonstrate a progressive increase in abnormality, which will result eventually in severe handicap, with a marked degree of hypertonus, soft tissue contracture and secondary sensory and perceptuo-motor disabilities. Some physical techniques may actually *increase* hypertonus. Techniques involving resistance, whether applied by weight resistance to particular muscles or by PNF techniques, may be responsible for setting the patient on to the cycle of effort leading to increased tone leading to effort. Ways of preventing an unnecessary build-up of spasticity include the avoidance of unnecessary muscular activity, the stimulation of balance reactions and the use of the principles of motor skill learning as described in Chapter 3.

Physical techniques which may be effective in altering muscle tone and allowing the stimulation of functional movement include reflex inhibiting movement patterns, the stimulation of balance reactions, mechanical vibration, weight-bearing inhibitory plasters, prolonged application of ice and biofeedback therapy. These techniques are described in Appendix 1. Of these techniques, emphasis should be placed on the stimulation of balance reactions as this technique not only has an inhibiting effect upon hypertonus but also, by stimulating weight shift and balance, provides the essential background to all functional movement.

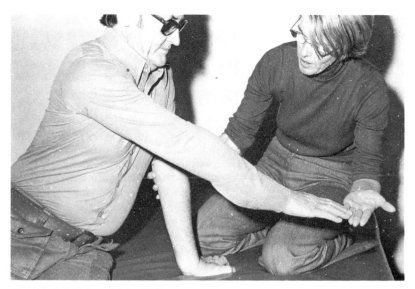

Fig. 86. *Inhibition of left-sided spasticity is gained by weight-bearing through the affected arm combined with trunk rotation.*

Inhibition is gained through *movement and weight-bearing with the body parts in normal alignment* (Fig. 86). Movement should not involve effort, and the patient should not have to struggle, using inappropriate muscle activity. Effort causes an increase in tone throughout the body because of the effect of associated movements, and it gives the patient a false idea of what is required. Normal movement, after all, usually involves little or no effort. The most important movements for the patient to recover at this stage are the automatic adjustments to changes in his centre of gravity, and the semi-automatic movements involved in ordinary everyday activities. Most everyday movements involve the head and trunk as well as the limbs, and are automatic or semi-automatic in nature, requiring the presence of normal postural adjustments. Even such a simple movement as turning the head to look around the room requires balance adjustments.

Alleviation of anxiety and stress. The patient's state of mind influences his muscle tone just as it influences the muscular tension of normal subjects. Stress causes an increase in emotional tension and in muscle tone and this should particularly be avoided in hypertonic patients. It is common for emotional tension to develop in brain-damaged patients as they strive to become more effective in their

271

activities and as they yearn for independence. The therapist, if she does not realise the effect of this, may increase the stress upon the patient, by her tone of voice, by her manner, and by vigorous stimulation. If a patient becomes tense and anxious, it may be sufficient for the therapist to point this out to him, suggesting that he take a few deep breaths with relaxed expiration. The importance of being relaxed while moving should be explained to him, as he may believe that one can only relax when lying down. There is a tendency for the patient to become more relaxed as he experiences freer movement. However, it may be necessary for the patient to be taught a particular method of relaxation and control of tension.

Relaxation of tension is closely associated with the *elimination of unnecessary muscular activity*. In treatment, the therapist not only points out to the patient his tension (demonstrated by, for example, an elevated shoulder) but also helps him to use only the necessary amount of muscle activity for the function he is performing.

An important factor in the effectiveness of treatment is *auditory feedback* to the patient which gives him information about the success or otherwise of his attempts at more normal movement. The therapist monitors his performance continually, particularly early in treatment when the patient is aware only of confused internal feedback. She tells him when he tries too hard, uses too much effort, or moves incorrectly. She monitors as far as she can his state of tone, so that he learns to recognise varying degrees of tension in his hypertonic muscles.

There are some other methods of reducing hypertonus which are used clinically by physiotherapists and physicians. Some of them have definite uses in specific cases, others have, in our opinion, little practical value, or are not suitable for brain-damaged patients because they are based on misconceptions about the nature of the disorder.

Drugs such as diazepam, and the GABA derivative baclofen are sometimes used in the care of hypertonic patients and details of their effects have been described by Sambrook (1975), Gautier-Smith (1976) and others. Unfortunately, a dosage which is sufficient to have a useful effect on hypertonus may result in a patient who is difficult to arouse or who is unable to concentrate.

Intrathecal injections of phenol are used to interrupt the stretch reflex arc where painful spasms resulting from spinal cord injury or demyelination of the cord are causing contracture and preventing the patient from sitting in his chair or standing.

Surgery is sometimes recommended, in the form of neurectomy or tenotomy. It is possible that in all but a very small percentage of adult patients, the gains are outweighed by the losses in terms of function.

Sometimes surgery merely changes the situation rather than improves it. Obturator neurectomy may result in dramatic release of adductor spasticity of the lower limb but the result may be a patient who can still not control movement at the hip. A partial obturator neurectomy may, however, enable a patient to walk if the surgery is followed *immediately* by treatment designed to stimulate balance in a weight-bearing position. This surgery is probably appropriate only for young cerebral palsied adults with long standing hypertonus and contracture. Division of the tendo Achilles may sometimes be necessary, and again, if it is followed by treatment in the weight-bearing position, may show an effective result. However, we suggest that a weight-bearing inhibitory plaster should be applied first, as it will in many cases make this type of surgery unnecessary.

The main problems which result following surgery frequently arise from a lack of understanding on the part of the surgeon and therapist of the neurological mechanisms involved, the tendency to view spasticity as a local phenomenon and therefore a failure to follow surgical procedures immediately by appropriate physiotherapy. Clarke (1979) describes the role of the physiotherapist following orthopaedic surgery.

Splinting. A most effective form of splinting is a *weight-bearing inhibitory plaster** which effectively and quickly inhibits hypertonus and allows functional movement to be relearned. Most forms of splinting are, however, not effective in the presence of spasticity. Splinting over one joint usually shifts the hypertonus elsewhere. An example of this is the use of short leg irons to hold a plantarflexed foot in a plantigrade position. Plantarflexion of the foot is part of the abnormal extensor synergy. The effect of such a splint is usually to increase hypertonus in the knee and hip flexors, the dorsiflexion of the foot eliciting a total flexor synergy. Alternatively, it may cause an increase in extensor hypertonus around the knee and hip by stimulating the hyperexcitable fusimotor neurons in the calf muscles.

Many forms of splinting cause an increase in tone by stimulating hyperactive stretch receptors and probably by stimulation of touch and pressure receptors. An example is the plaster or metal 'night' splint applied posteriorly to the lower leg and foot. When this method of splinting is used it is common to hear complaints from nursing staff that by morning the patient's heel has moved up out of the foot piece and is showing signs of pressure. No bandage is firm enough to hold a limb immobile in such a splint. Pressure of the splint against the ball of the foot stretches the calf muscles and therefore

* Appendix 1

stimulates the fusimotor neurons causing such a strong plantarflexion response that the heel is pushed up off the foot piece.

Proprioceptive neuromuscular facilitation techniques. Knott and Voss (1968) have described the use of local relaxation techniques (hold/relax, contract/relax, slow reversals) to facilitate the relaxation of spastic muscles, thereby allowing an increased passive range of movement or active contraction of the antagonistic muscles. In the authors' opinion, these techniques are inappropriate in the presence of hypertonus and may actually *increase* hypertonus. They involve resistance to an isometric or isotonic contraction which results in an unwanted increase in tone through associated movements in other parts of the body. These associated movements, because they are, in the brain-damaged, widespread and abnormal, are difficult to control.

Quick stretch is also recommended by Knott and Voss in order to stimulate the stretch reflex and facilitate a movement. However, Hagbarth and Eklund (1968) have suggested that stimulation of the T.V.R. has a similar and probably better inhibitory effect and requires no effort in terms of overcoming resistance on the part of the patient.

Sahrmann (1977) comments that because of the destruction of cortical cells in brain-damaged patients, the effort to elicit a maximal contraction does not produce a normal response in the motor cortex, as cortical drive is diminished. Furthermore, the patient's cortical effort to elicit a contraction stimulates the already hyperexcitable motoneuron pool. Stimulation of the stretch receptors further increases this hyperexcitability. Sahrmann concludes that the patient should not use excessive effort in treatment as the increase in stretch reflex activity will impede movement. She points out that walking is an automatic and reciprocal movement and suggests that the use of effort (for example, resistance) in walking would impede the movement.

SUMMARY

In this chapter the pathophysiology and characteristics of hypertonus of central origin are described. The differences between spasticity, rigidity and dystonia, and the need to distinguish between hypertonus of central origin and hypertonus of spinal origin, are discussed. The effects of hypertonus on movement and the treatment of problems which result from hypertonus are briefly discussed.

References

Andrews, C. J., Burke, D. and Lance, J. W. (1972) Tonic vibration reflex in spasticity, Parkinson's disease and normal subjects. *J. Neurol. Neurosurg. Psychiat.*, **35**, 477.

Ashby, P. (1973) The neurophysiology of spasticity. *Physiotherapy Canada*, **25**, 4.

Bobath, B. (1959) Observations on adult hemiplegia and suggestions for treatment. *Physiotherapy*, **45**, 279–289.

Bobath, B. (1970) *Adult Hemiplegia: Evaluation and Treatment.* London, Heinemann.

Brunnstrom, S. (1970) *Movement Therapy in Hemiplegia.* New York, Harper and Row.

Burke, D. and Lance, J. W. (1973) Studies of the reflex effects of primary and secondary spindle endings in spasticity. In *New Developments in Electromyography and Clinical Neurophysiology,* edited by J. Desmedt, **3**, 475–495. Basel, Karger.

Clarke, J. (1979) The management of the cerebral palsied child undergoing orthopaedic surgery. *Aust. J. Physiother.* In press.

Denny-Brown, D. (1968) Clinical symptomatology of diseases of the basal ganglia. In *Handbook of Clinical Neurology,* edited by P. J. Vinken and G. W. Bruyn. Vol. 6. Amsterdam, North Holland Publishing Co.

de Gail, P., Lance, J. W. and Neilson, P. D. (1966) Different effects of tonic and phasic reflex mechanisms produced by vibration of muscle in man. *J. Neurol. Neurosurg. Psychiat.*, **29**, 1.

Eklund, G. and Hagbarth, K. E. (1966) Normal variability of tonic vibration reflexes in muscle. *Exper. Neurol.*, **16**, 80–92.

Eklund, G., Hagbarth, K. E. and Steen, M. (1969) Therapeutic effects of muscle vibration in spasticity. *J. Swed. Assoc. of Regist. P. T.*, **37**, 3.

Gautier-Smith, P. G. (1976) Clinical management of spastic states. *Physiotherapy* **62**, 10. 326–328.

Gillies, J. D., Burke, D. J. and Lance, J. W. (1971) Tonic vibration reflex in the cat. *J. Neurophysiol.*, **34**, 252–261.

Granit, R. (1970) *The Basis of Motor Control.* New York, Academic Press.

Hagbarth, K. E. (1973) The effect of muscle vibration in normal man and in patients with motor disorders. In *New Developments in Electromyography and Clinical Neurophysiology,* edited by J. Desmedt. Basel, Karger.

Hagbarth, K. E. and Eklund, G. (1968) The effect of muscle vibration in spasticity, rigidity and cerebellar disorders. *J. Neurol. Neurosurg.*

Psychiat., **31**, 207–213.

Hassler, R. (1972) Physiopathology of rigidity. In *Parkinson's Disease* 1, edited by J. Siegfried. Berne, Huber.

Herman, R. and Mecomber, S. A. (1971) Vibration-elicited reflexes in normal and spastic muscles in man. *Am. J. Phys. Med.*, **50**, 4, 169–183.

Herman, R., Freedman, W. and Mayer, N. (1974) Neurophysiologic mechanisms of hemiplegic and paraplegic spasticity. Implications for therapy. *Arch. Phys. Med. Rehabil.*, **55**, 338–343.

Knott, M. and Voss, D. E. (1968) *Proprioceptive Neuromuscular Facilitation*. 2nd edition. New York, Harper and Row.

Lance, J. W. and McLeod, J. G. (1975) *A Physiological Approach to Clinical Neurology*. 2nd edition. London, Butterworths.

Norton, B. J., Bomze, H. A., Sahrmann, S. and Eliasson, S. G. (1974) Objective documentation of the relationship between spasticity and rate of passive movement. *Proc. W.C.P.T. Congress*, 416–422.

Riddock, G. and Buzzard, E. F. (1921) Reflex movements and postural reactions in quadriplegia, with special reference to those of the upper limb. *Brain*, **44**, 397.

Sahrmann, S. (1977) Therapeutic exercise: past and future. *Paper delivered at 43rd Congress of A.P.T.A.*, St. Louis, Missouri.

Sambrook, M. A. (1975) Medical management of multiple sclerosis. *Physiotherapy*, **61**, 1, 2–4.

Steg, G. (1972) Biochemical aspects of rigidity. In *Parkinson's Disease* Vol. 1, edited by J. Siegfried. Berne, Huber.

Stuart, D. G., Mosher, C. G. and Gerlach, R. L. (1971) Properties and central connections of Golgi tendon organs with special reference to locomotion. In *Symposium on Muscle and the Muscle Spindle*, edited by B. Banker. Amsterdam, Excerpta Medica.

Wallin, B. G., Hongell, A. and Hagbarth, K. E. (1973) Recordings from muscle afferents in Parkinsonian rigidity. In *New Developments in Electromyography and Human Reflexes*, edited by J. Desmedt. Berlin, Springer.

Further Reading

Basmajian, J. V. (1974) *Muscles Alive: Their Functions Revealed by Electromyography*. 3rd Edition. Baltimore, Williams and Wilkins.

Basmajian, J. V. (1976) Electromyographic investigation of spasticity and muscle spasm. *Physiotherapy*, **62**, 10, 320–322.

Lance, J. W. and Burke, D. (1974) Mechanism of spasticity. *Arch. Phys. Med. Rehabil.*, **55**, 332–337.

Chapter 12

Hypotonus

'Hypotonus' is the term which will be used in this chapter to describe decreased postural (or muscle) tone which is caused by a lesion or lesions in part of the brain and which results in an inability to move or sustain a posture against gravity. Physiologically the mechanism probably involves a loss of facilitatory influence over spinal fusimotor and skeletomotor neurons. This hypotonus may involve the whole body or be of a hemiplegic distribution. It may be transient in nature following stroke, head injury or surgery to the brain.

The meaning of the word hypotonus is unclear, both in clinical practice and in neurophysiological terminology. Hypotonus, flaccidity, flaccid paralysis, paralysis, paresis and weakness are all used interchangeably and are frequently ill-defined. All these terms refer to a low state of tone, which may occur due to lesions of either the central or the peripheral nervous systems, and they all result in difficulty with movement.

The term 'flaccidity' is often used to infer an extreme degree of hypotonus. Denny-Brown (1966) commented that the term 'flaccid' is poorly defined in clinical neurology. Eyzaguirre and Fidone (1975) suggest that 'flaccid' may be an inappropriately extreme term when related to hypotonus of central (pyramidal) origin. 'Flaccid paralysis', 'paralysis' and 'paresis' are probably more suitably used to describe the lack of muscle tone evident in a muscle denervated by peripheral nerve lesion or anterior horn cell lesion, the so-called 'lower motor neuron lesion'.

Although the authors recognize that there is a common acceptance of the term 'weakness' in discussion of both central and peripheral lesions, it must be stressed that this practice is very misleading. If weakness is used as synonymous with hypotonus, clear distinction must be made between weakness of movement due to lack of central control over movement (or cortical drive) which occurs following lesions of the brain, and weakness due to a peripheral nerve lesion in which the muscle fibres are denervated. Where 'weakness' is used without this discrimination, there is a tendency to approach all patients with hypotonus as though weakness of muscle were the major problem. The goal of treatment for a patient whose hypotonus ('weakness') is due to a peripheral lesion (of anterior horn cell or peripheral nerve) is to strengthen the remaining innervated muscle fibres or the muscle fibres whose innervation is recovering. However, the goal of treatment for a patient whose hypotonus is due to a central lesion should not be directed at strengthening muscles but at improving central control over those muscles.

Although disorders of the peripheral nervous system will not be discussed in this book, a brief outline of the manifestations of the flaccid paralysis which results may make clear the clinical differences between these peripheral lesions and disorders of a central origin.

Flaccid paralysis occurs as the result of lesions of the *anterior horn cell*, which may include the effects of infection such as poliomyelitis, of transverse myelitis, or of vascular occlusion, or be part of a slow degeneration as in motor neuron disease. It may also occur as the result of the expansion of a tube-like cavity within the *spinal cord* in syringomyelia, and immediately following spinal cord injury when it is termed 'spinal shock'.

Flaccid paralysis also occurs in disorders of the *peripheral nerve*, which may occur as a result of trauma, an anaphylactic process, an inflammatory disorder as in leprosy, in Guillain-Barré syndrome and in various deficiency disorders. The motor root of a spinal nerve may be compressed as it leaves the spinal cord by a displaced intervertebral disc, diseased vertebra or tumour.

According to Noback and Demarest (1975), flaccid paralysis in all these cases is demonstrated by muscle paralysis, areflexia (absence of reflexes), atony (absence of tone), atrophy (wasting), prolonged chronaxie (excitation time), fasciculation (spasms of fibres within the muscle) and soft and flabby muscles on palpation. However if only a percentage of muscle fibres are denervated, the patient will demonstrate muscle weakness, hyporeflexia (diminished reflexes), decreased tone and less pronounced atrophy.

CHARACTERISTICS OF HYPOTONUS OF CENTRAL ORIGIN

Hypotonus is seen as a transient state following acute injury to the brain as may occur in stroke and head injury, and following surgery to the brain. This transient state is often referred to as 'cerebral shock'. Its mechanism is not understood but it has been suggested that the excitatory state of the spinal cord is depressed. Denny-Brown (1950) considers that it represents 'depression of motor function rather than a true loss of any specific movement or the power of contraction of any particular muscle'. This hyporeflexia results from the sudden withdrawal of descending impulses from supraspinal centres in the brain (Eyzaguirre & Fidone 1975).

It is demonstrated by decreased or absent tendon reflexes and loss of movement which may last for several hours. As the effect of this cerebral shock wears off, the release phenomena associated with hypertonus become evident (see Chapter 11). A transitory hypotonus may also occur as a symptom of intermittent cerebral vascular insufficiency.

Hypotonus is also termed transient when it is seen in newborn infants as an early manifestation of cerebral palsy. This hypotonus may last for varying periods up to several months of age. Gradually the problems associated with hypertonus, athetosis, or uncommonly, ataxia, develop. Severe hypotonus from birth or the 'floppy baby syndrome' has a multiple aetiology, which includes cerebral palsy, mental retardation, cerebral degenerative disease, brain tumour, spinal muscular atrophy, myopathy and benign congenital hypotonus (Paine 1963).

Clinically it is important to remember that hypotonus, if it is transient, may mask the development of spasticity. Techniques to increase tone and postural stability must be given cautiously and the patient should be discouraged from using unnecessary activity and effort. Both indiscriminate stimulation and inappropriate effort will increase abnormal reflex activity which will be manifested by associated movements in abnormal synergies.

Hypotonus also accompanies cerebellar lesions involving the posterior lobe or neocerebellum. It is probable that the absence of fusimotor tone makes the spindle less responsive to stretch. The loss of the normal reinforcement by the cerebellum of motor activity initiated by the cerebral cortex may be the cause of the 'weakness' of movement accompanying this form of hypotonus.

Hypotonia in cerebellar disorders is demonstrated by brisk tendon reflexes, a pendular response to tendon tap, decreased resistance to passive movement and decreased postural stability. André-Thomas, Chesni and Saint-Anne Dargassies (1960) have used the terms extensibilité and passivité to distinguish the particular quality of tone demonstrated clinically in these patients.

Hypotonus may also be evident in association with *chorea* and in certain patients with *athetosis*.

Problems of Function

Hypotonus has certain obvious effects upon function. These include the inability to move against gravity (Fig. 87) and to sustain a posture,

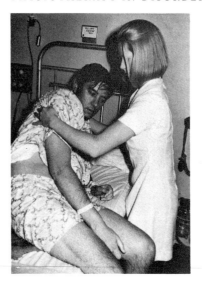 

Fig. 87 *This man with right-sided hemiplegia cannot get into sitting because he lacks lateral trunk movement and has poor lateral head movement.*

Fig. 88. *He has difficulty getting into standing because he cannot shift his weight and his body alignment is abnormal.*

difficulty shifting weight, inability to move from one position to another (Fig. 88), inability to bear weight through the limbs in normal alignment (Fig. 89) and difficulty with oral function and facial expression. Proximal stability and head and trunk righting will be poor. This interferes with movement of the head, trunk and limbs. Lack of stability around the shoulder girdle prevents effective use of the hands while lack of stability around the pelvis affects control of the pelvis on the legs in sitting and standing. Lack of head and trunk righting will interfere with balance. The patient will lack symmetry if one side of his body is affected.

METHODS OF INCREASING TONE AND STIMULATING MOVEMENT

It is not our intention to deal with the problems and management following lower motor neuron disorders or disorders arising from injury to the spinal cord. However, because of the confusion which exists in terminology, it is necessary to emphasise the differences in terms of the treatment given. For example, an important aim in the

280

Fig. 89. *This man with left-sided hemiplegia has difficulty bearing weight through his left leg with normal body alignment.*

treatment of a patient with a lesion of anterior horn cells (lower motor neuron lesion) is to hypertrophy the remaining muscle fibres. This is done by increasing the contractile protein in the remaining muscles and by sprouting of collaterals from intact neurons (Sahrmann 1977). Similarly, if the patient has a complete spinal cord transection, an essential treatment aim is to stimulate and strengthen the muscles which are still innervated from the brain and remaining spinal cord.

On the other hand, the emphasis in the treatment of a patient with a lesion of the brain, whose presenting problem is hypotonus either of a transient nature or associated with cerebellar ataxia or athetosis, is on the restoration of the 'idea' of movement. The objective is to stimulate the brain to exercise the most control possible over movement. Treatment aims to stimulate recovery in any area of the brain not functioning and to stimulate maximal adaptation of the undamaged parts of the brain. There is an important distinction between these goals and a goal which emphasises strengthening or hypertrophy of muscle.

Below is a description of some points to be considered in the treatment of patients whose low tone is transient or associated with cerebellar ataxia or athetosis. Physical techniques which increase tone and stimulate the patient to relearn functional movement include weight-bearing or approximation, the stimulation of balance reactions, vibration, brisk application of ice, pounding and tapping, biofeedback and placing and holding of a limb. These are described in detail in Appendix 1. Some of the techniques described are aimed at peripheral organs, for example, those which aim to stimulate the joint receptors. Others are aimed more centrally, influencing the vestibular and cortical mechanisms.

There are some points which should be considered in any treatment programme designed for the hypotonic patient.

The therapist uses *speech* to stimulate and to guide movement. With brain-damaged patients, all of whom have learning problems, the therapist must find the correct phrase to trigger off a motor response. This consideration of the meaning and interpretation of the *words* that are used is important in all communication. A patient may not respond to a request when it is phrased one way but may respond when it is phrased differently. For example, 'push' may not elicit a response, while 'reach up toward the ceiling' may. Push implies strong effort, and concentration on effort may actually inhibit the movement he is attempting. It seems that with each individual, certain expressions trigger off a motor response more automatically than others.

Alteration in the tone of voice may also make a difference. The patient may use his own speech (either internally or externally) to help him perform a movement (Luria 1961, Cotton 1974). This is often a very effective way of reinforcing movement, probably because it helps the patient concentrate on what he is doing, and because speech can be used to regulate movement. Speech can be used to provide *auditory feedback* to the patient, giving him information about the accuracy of the movement he is performing, and suggesting any alterations needed.

Mental practice, or the act of sitting quietly and rehearsing in one's mind what one is trying to learn is an effective means of stimulating movement for some patients. It is described in Chapter 3. Similarly, some patients who are asked to *visualise* the movement they are attempting and to think about its direction do better than other patients at relearning movement.

If the patient is encouraged to *look* at the part which he is trying to move and in the direction in which he is to move, he may be stimulated to move more effectively by the use of vision and visual feedback to reinforce his motor performance. For example, following stroke and other brain trauma, hypotonus may be so severe that movement appears to be impossible. With guidance from the therapist combined with visual stimulation, the patient should be able to attempt a small part of a particular movement or at least gradually to assist in part of the movement. For example, the patient is encouraged to look at his hand while reaching forward with his arm. This visual stimulation helps him to concentrate his attention on movement of the limb, and reinforces his sensation of where he is in space and the direction in which he is moving.

The Patient with Transient Hypotonus

A most important point to remember in the treatment of patients with transient hypotonus is that this form of hypotonus usually masks the emergence of hypertonus. Stimulation of tone without due concern for this will result in more hypertonus than would otherwise have occurred. The treatment of this patient aims not only at stimulating functional movement but also at preventing the development of unnecessary hypertonus. There seem to be *three main factors in retarding the development of severe hypertonus* in those patients who are seen by the physiotherapist immediately after an injury to their brain such as a stroke.

(a) The early stimulation of automatic balance adjustments which appears to have an inhibiting effect on hypertonus and which allows the patient to redevelop motor skills.
(b) The early relearning of the common motor skills which the patient has been practising all his life. These motor skills must be practised with particular emphasis on the appropriate body alignment and weight-bearing. This, if it commences before bad habits of movement have developed, seems to trigger off central control over movement and motivates the patient by providing recognizable and important goals. His attempts at movement seem to be directed into previously well-learned programmes of activity instead of into the abnormal synergies of spasticity.
(c) The prevention of stimulation of associated movements which are elicited by inappropriate effort, anxiety, and resisted exercise.

The use of *resistance,* other than by the force of gravity or by approximation for guidance is contra-indicated. Hypertrophy of muscles will not improve the ability of the brain-damaged patient to move. Furthermore, it is possible that resisted exercise in these patients is an important factor in the establishment of severe spasticity and actually prevents the re-learning of functional movement (see Chapter 11).

SUMMARY

In this chapter, the problems of function associated with hypotonus of central origin and methods of stimulating movement are outlined. Ways of preventing the development of spasticity following acute brain lesions are discussed.

References

André-Thomas, Chesni, Y. and Dargassies, S. A. (1960) *The Neurological Examination of the Infant.* London, Heinemann.

Cotton, E. (1974) Improvement in motor function with the use of Conductive Education. *Develop. Med. Child Neurol.,* **16,** 637–643.

Denny-Brown, D. (1950) Disintegration of motor function resulting from cerebral lesions. *J. Nerv. Ment. Dis.,* **112,** 1–45.

Denny-Brown, D. (1966) *The Cerebral Control of Movement.* Liverpool University Press.

Eyzaguirre, C. and Fidone, S. J. (1975) *Physiology of the Nervous System.* Chicago, Year Book Medical Pub.

Luria, A. R. (1961) *The Role of Speech in the Regulation of Normal and Abnormal Behaviour.* London, Pergamon.

Noback, C. R. and Demarest, R. J. (1975) *The Human Nervous System.* 2nd edition. New York, McGraw-Hill.

Paine, R. S. (1963) The future of the 'floppy infant'. *Develop. Med. Child Neurol.,* **5,** 115.

Sahrmann, S. (1977) Therapeutic exercise: past and future. *Paper Delivered at 53rd Congress of A.P.T.A.* St. Louis, Missouri.

Further Reading

Granit, R. (1970) *The Basis of Motor Control.* New York, Academic Press.

Matthews, P. B. C. (1972) *Mammalian Muscle Receptors and Their Central Actions.* Baltimore, Williams and Wilkins.

Chapter 13

Cerebellar Ataxia

Cerebellar ataxia may be defined as the inability to co-ordinate movement as a result of a lesion of the cerebellum. It affects the background to volitional and automatic movement and therefore interferes with all motor function.

The word 'ataxia' means unsteady and unco-ordinated movement. Its clinical use is sometimes confusing. For example, it is used to describe walking inco-ordination. It is linked with dyssynergia, dysmetria, intention tremor, nystagmus and hypotonus under the heading of 'cerebellar syndrome'. It is also common practice to describe patients with certain lesions of the posterior columns of the spinal cord, such as tabes dorsalis (locomotor ataxia), some cases of multiple sclerosis and subacute combined degeneration of the cord, as having 'sensory ataxia' to clarify the point that their inco-ordination has a sensory origin.

The discussion in this chapter will be confined to the problems and management of patients whose unco-ordinated movement is caused by cerebellar lesions.

The common causes of cerebellar ataxia are developmental abnormalities such as hydrocephalus, hypoxia at birth or later in life, brain trauma as a result of head injury or surgery, tumours and other space-occupying lesions, infections such as encephalitis, demyelinating diseases such as multiple sclerosis, familial and hereditary diseases such as Friedreich's ataxia, metabolic disorders such as myxoedema and Wilson's disease, vascular disease as in vertebro-basilar artery insufficiency, and intoxications by drugs or alcohol. In adults, cerebellar ataxia will be, however, most commonly seen following head injury.

Pathophysiology

The cerebellum is made up of three systems (Fig. 90) which regulate vestibular, spinal and cortical mechanisms by means of neuronal connections which are reciprocal. The cerebellum is generally described as enriching the quality of movement as it is a regulatory

285

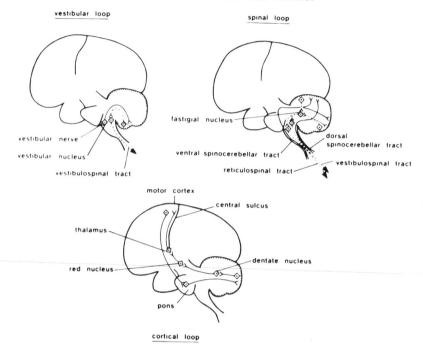

Fig. 90. *The three regulatory circuits of the cerebellum. (From Lance, J. W. and McLeod, J. G. (1975)* A Physiological Approach to Clinical Neurology. *2nd edition. London, Butterworths.)*

centre for the control of motor activity. Its involvement in the regulation of the intensity of movement through its connections in the brain stem and the cerebral cortex has been generally accepted since the work of Rademaker (1935). It receives sensory information from tactile, proprioceptive, auditory and visual receptors. It thus acts as a comparator, comparing the motor performance occurring peripherally with motor command signals from the cerebral cortex (Eyzaguirre and Fidone 1975).

When this comparator function breaks down as a result of a cerebellar lesion, corrective signals from the cerebral cortex and brain stem cease to occur automatically. Each movement tends to be broken up into its component parts and the limb overshoots or oscillates around its goal.

The problems associated with cerebellar dysfunction depend upon the area of the cerebellum involved. Disorders of the anterior lobe (palaeocerebellum) interfere with control of brain stem regulating centres, particularly those concerned with the postural mechanism. The patient may show extensor hypertonus as well as ataxia. Disorders of the posterior lobe (neocerebellum), which are much more common in man, usually result in hypotonus due to depressed fusimotor activity. Lance and McLeod (1975) suggest that the cerebellar cortex normally inhibits the activity of the medullary reticular formation and some of the cerebellar nuclei which are themselves inhibitors of tonic mechanisms. Damage to this area of the cerebellum therefore allows uncontrolled inhibition of gamma efferent activity by reticular system pathways. Disorders of the flocculonodular lobe (archicerebellum) result in a state of disequilibrium characterised by vertigo, nystagmus and ataxia.

Characteristics of Cerebellar Ataxia

Lesions of the cerebellum and subsequent release of its control over sensorimotor function through its connections in the cortex and brain stem result in identifiable problems which are seen during all movement, whether it be automatic or volitional. There is a significant loss of the normal regulated background to movement. Intelligence and the conscious appreciation of sensation are not affected as the cerebellum plays no part in these functions (Noback and Demarest 1975, Eyzaguirre and Fidone 1975).

The problems of tone and movement which occur can be summarised under the following headings

hypotonus
dyssynergia
dysmetria
intention tremor
nystagmus.

Hypotonus. André-Thomas, Chesni and Saint-Anne Darqassies (1960) have described the quality of hypotonus found in these patients in terms of what they call 'passivité' and 'extensibilité'.

As described in Chapter 12, this hypotonus is probably due to the absence of fusimotor tone or loss of the dynamic spindle response, which makes the spindle less responsive to stretch. The weakness of movement which accompanies this form of hypotonus is probably due to the loss of the normal cerebellar reinforcement to the motor activity of the cerebral cortex.

There is diminished resistance to passive movement (passivité). There is also an unnatural increase in joint range on passive movement (extensibilité). The wrist, for example, can be flexed or extended beyond its normal range. The phasic reflexes are brisk and demons-

287

trate a pendular response if the limb is unsupported. The knee jerk, for example, is followed by a series of pendular oscillations. The muscles feel flabby and tire easily. There is decreased postural stability. For example, attempts to hold a limb steady in an antigravity position result in the limb drifting downward, which becomes more pronounced when the eyes are closed. This is also demonstrated by the patient's tendency to lean against whatever or whoever offers him support.

Dyssynergia is the term used to describe the interruption of the normal, smooth control of movement of the trunk, limbs and organs of speech, through a lack of co-operation between agonist, antagonist and related muscle groups. There is a lack of fluidity and a slowness and difficulty in stopping and starting movements (Fig. 91). Dyssynergia is characterised by decomposition of movement, the rebound phenomenon, and dysdiadochokinesia.

Decomposition of movement is a gross manifestation of dyssynergia. Movement is broken up into its component parts which are performed sequentially but without flowing into each other. The *rebound phenomenon* occurs when the patient is unable to check a movement by the immediate contraction of the antagonist muscles. This can be demonstrated by asking the patient to flex his elbow against the examiner's resistance. If this resistance is suddenly released, the patient is unable to stop the movement until it is arrested by ligaments or by opposing joint surfaces, and he may hit his face unless protected. *Dysdiadochokinesia* is difficulty in performing fast, alternating and repetitive movements, such as pronation and supination of the forearm. These movements are done clumsily and slowly, and as the patient persists, the arm swings about with increasing error.

Dyssynergia of the organs involved in speech results in problems of articulation and phonation. Speech may be explosive, slurred or scanned. Scanned speech is the breaking up of words into syllables.

Dysmetria is difficulty measuring distance and range in the course of a movement (Fig. 92). This results in overshooting (hypermetria) or undershooting (hypometria) by the limb as it approaches its target. Normally the accuracy required to reach a target depends upon constant feedback and correction during the performance of a movement. This ability to correct the movement appropriately is lost in patients with cerebellar dysfunction.

Intention tremor appears on volitional movement and becomes worse at the end of the movement, the extremity oscillating as it approaches its target. It is particularly evident on fine movements involving the fingers and hand, and therefore interferes with hand

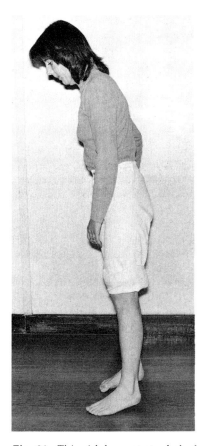

Fig. 91. *This girl demonstrates lack of smooth control over movement. She has difficulty stopping when asked.*

function. It is absent at rest. The cause of this tremor is uncertain.

Nystagmus is a disorder of the posture of the eye which is characterised by a more or less rhythmical oscillation. It may be acquired or congenital. When seen as a result of a unilateral cerebellar disorder it may be deflected towards the side of the lesion. Moderate or severe nystagmus interferes with head righting and balance.

These problems of movement regulation can be expressed as errors of rate, range, direction and force. They *affect all functional movement*, both the adjustments for balance as well as volitional movement. If

289

Fig. 92. *She demonstrates difficulty measuring distance and range and is therefore lacking in accuracy.*

the cerebellar lesion is unilateral the movement problems are seen on the ipsilateral side. The patient tends to deviate or fall toward the affected side although his head may be turned to the opposite side probably in an attempt to regain balance.

In cerebellar lesions there is a lack of postural stability which is most obvious proximally. This results in difficulty in sustaining activity, particularly against gravity, and difficulty in adapting posture to changing conditions. Instability around the shoulder interferes with control of the arm and instability around the pelvis interferes with control of the pelvis on the extended leg in weight-bearing. There is a lack of the normal subtle regulation and gradation of muscle contraction which is necessary for all movement and posture, and this results in an excess of motion on movement. Holmes (1969) suggests that the inability to control the proximal segment of the limb is one of the causes of deviations from the direct line of movement which is a feature of cerebellar ataxia.

Balance reactions are exaggerated, inappropriate (Fig. 93) and slow to be initiated. There may be constant movement in antigravity positions seen as a swaying of the body in an attempt to regain and maintain balance. These adjustments are more gross than normal,

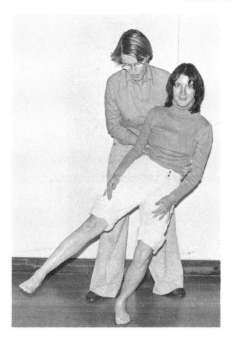

Fig. 93. *The therapist displaces her weight laterally. She loses control and her weight goes backward. Note the lack of trunk side flexion.*

and where balance is severely affected, the patient may be unable to maintain antigravity positions or move from one position to another.

Many patients cope with their disability by voluntarily restricting their movements. They decrease the amount of head and trunk movement in an effort to gain more stability. They hold themselves stiffly (Fig. 94). In turning around they take small steps rather than rotating the trunk and pivoting on the feet.

Ataxic arm movements, combined with nystagmus and voluntary restriction of head movement, result in poor visual fixation and eye-hand contact. Difficulty in regulating small ranges of movement combined with intention tremor result in clumsy hand function. Lack of control proximally makes it difficult for the patient to manipulate objects at a distance from himself. He tends to confine the use of his hands to a position close to his body. He is better able to regulate his

291

Fig. 94. *This girl has a wide base of support and holds herself stiffly in a flexed posture in order to gain more stability.*

movements in this position as it requires less control of his shoulder girdle.

Ataxia may be combined with either hypertonus or athetosis. Patients following head injury or with multiple sclerosis frequently present with a multiplicity of problems including ataxia.

Assessment of the patient with cerebellar ataxia is carried out along the lines suggested in Chapter 4. However, there is one point which it is important to make, as failure to recognise its significance will result in an inappropriate treatment plan. The ataxic patient may voluntarily restrict his movement in order to cope with his disability. If this restriction of movement is taken by the therapist as the primary problem instead of the ataxia which led to the restriction, the emphasis in treatment will be incorrect. The patient with mild or moderate ataxia may so restrict his movement that his ataxia may not be too evident unless the therapist asks him to move more slowly or more quickly, to stop in different parts of the range or to change direction. Some patients try to overcome their lack of balance by moving quickly. The true extent of their ataxia may only be evident when they are asked to move more slowly.

TREATMENT

'The execution of a voluntary movement requires a combination of sustained muscular contractions accurately controlled in force and extent and appropriately organised in space and time with relevant postural adjustments' (Garcin 1969). In general for all patients with ataxia, the objectives of treatment will be to improve the background to movement, that is, to improve proximal stability and to regulate balance adjustments, both of which are essential to movement; to regulate the interplay between related muscle groups; to enable the patient to feel controlled purposeful movement in antigravity positions; to improve visual fixation and eye-hand contact in all positions as a stimulus to stability.

Treatment of those patients who have ataxia combined with hypertonus will have to be modified according to which has the most detrimental effect on movement. Patients who have both ataxia and spasticity may demonstrate increased tone proximally and ataxia distally or vice versa.

Techniques described in Appendix 1 such as weight-bearing, approximation, alternate tapping, and placing and holding of the limb are used to improve postural stability and balance, and provide a more normal background for motor activity. Below is a description of the ways in which these techniques can be applied to some specific problems which may be seen in ataxic patients.

Problem 1. Inability to sit
Let us consider some ways of treating a patient who cannot sit unsupported. He should sit with his feet flat on the floor, his weight well forwards at the hips and his arms resting on the table in front of him. This upright position will stimulate visual fixation and orientation in space. The therapist gives approximation down through his shoulders making sure his weight remains well forward and his thoracic spine is extended. As stability improves, he is encouraged to shift his weight holding it in different positions, although always with his weight forwards, until he has enough control to be able to transfer his weight backward and forwards and from side to side without losing balance, that is, by making the appropriate adjustment of his head and trunk.

As the patient improves, treatment is progressed. If he lifts one arm, looks up and reaches out to touch an object, his centre of gravity will be altered and he will have to make some balance adjustments. Head movements and eye-hand contact are thus encouraged and he is able to achieve volitional movement on a more normal postural background. This is a matter of great reassurance for such a handicapped patient. If he is encouraged to turn his head to look around, his balance will be even more disturbed and he will need to control it. He may be able to hold a stick out in front of him while the therapist approximates through his extended arms. This approximation increases extensor tone and tone around his shoulder girdle and upper trunk, therefore improving proximal stability. The amount of approximation must be carefully graded, a matter of reciprocal response between the therapist and patient. The patient must not lean on the stick and the therapist must not approximate so firmly that she pushes him off balance. In this position he practises weight transference forwards and backwards in an increasing range, and laterally as he gains confidence. The therapist encourages him to place one hand on his knee while he still maintains sitting balance, then both hands, by which time he is sitting alone. Some stability can be stimulated by pressure down through his knees while he experiments with shifting his weight and looking around. This method of approximation can be used by the patient himself when he feels he needs more stability in sitting.

Once the patient can sit without assistance even momentarily, the therapist stimulates more automatic equilibrium reactions by displacing his weight slightly and stimulating head and trunk movement. She then gradually increases the amount of displacement, stopping him at various points and making sure he does not reach the point where his reactions become exaggerated and he loses control.

The patient's improved sitting balance is used to stimulate function in this position. His ability to transfer weight forwards at his hips with his head and trunk extended enables him to get into standing. As soon as he no longer needs his arms for support the technique of placing and holding of the arm* can be stimulated. This will prepare him for reaching out for objects in different directions, grasping and releasing them and for holding an object through a range of movement.

Saywell (1975) describes the effect of horseback riding on sitting balance. She gives the example of a child with ataxia telangiectasia previously unable to sit, who achieved this after a period of assisted

* Appendix 1

riding. Balance will not improve in a position unless the patient is given the opportunity to experience that position even if he needs outside help. The movement of the horse provides the stimulus to balance and the activity itself provides motivational stimulus.

Problem 2. Difficulty balancing in standing and walking
A common problem in most ataxic patients is instability of the pelvis on the legs. This is demonstrated by the patient's inability to balance in standing with the hips in the appropriate amount of extension. The patient tends to stand with his weight backwards, his hips slightly flexed, and his trunk leaning forward (Fig. 91). In walking, he needs a wide base because of lateral instability.

Basmajian (1977) has pointed out that physiologists and kinesiologists do not appreciate that each and every muscle has several (sometimes many) component parts which are recruited in different functions at different times'. Treatment should therefore concentrate on gaining stability, that is, muscular control, in the particular specific position in which it is lacking. The hip extensors and abductors for example, must be stimulated in the particular positions in which they are required to act. It is important that the patient gets the feeling of how to extend his hips thus gaining this normal alignment. He will learn to do this by practising the movement and therefore getting the feeling of moving his pelvis on his legs. It is fine control in a very small range of movement that he needs, so the therapist should prevent him from making gross adjustments. Pounding over the hip abductors may also be effective in gaining lateral stability of the pelvis.

The patient's ability to maintain and regain balance in the upright position is stimulated by alternate tapping* sideways, forwards and backward with feet together as well as in a walking position. As in all situations which require balance the patient must have the opportunity to practise making the necessary adjustments in the position in which he has difficulty, in other words at the point where he has insufficient control. Therefore he should not stand with his feet wide apart (Fig. 95).

With the patient's hands on her shoulders the therapist may guide weight transference while stimulating stability by approximation down through his hips on the side of the weight-bearing leg (Fig. 96). She may approximate with her hands through the patient's extended arms as he walks (Fig. 42). The amount of approximation needs to be properly graded. It should be sufficient to increase stability yet not so much that the patient has to struggle against resistance as this will

* Appendix 1

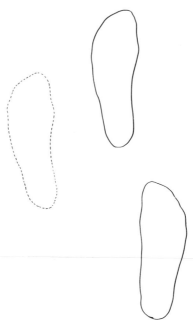

Fig. 95. *The continuous outline indicates a normal step forward. The dotted outline represents an abnormally wide-based step.*

result in altered alignment of his pelvis on his legs. Similarly, he should not be allowed to lean passively on the therapist. Walking requires the ability to balance, not only on a narrow base (Figs. 97 and 98), but also on one leg while taking a step with the other.

The patient needs to experience rhythmical, well-timed walking with even steps. Footsteps marked on the floor may help to improve symmetry in walking and are an added stimulus to reducing his wide base. Counting, the use of the words 'right-left' and facilitation of walking from the shoulders will help to achieve. this. Luria (1971) has emphasised that speech is a regulator of movement and can be used to reinforce it. The therapist encourages the patient to combine speech and movement by using counting as a regulator of his walking rhythm. This also improves symmetry of movement.

As the patient improves he can practise walking around obstacles and stepping over them. His centre of gravity can be altered by getting him to bend down to pick up objects, or to reach up for

Fig. 96. *Stimulation of walking on a more narrow base. The therapist guides the movement by alternately approximating down through the pelvis.*

objects. He can practise stepping over the rungs of a ladder laid horizontally.

The approach described in the example above can be applied to other problems of function. For example, it is necessary to improve the patient's ability to get from one position to another as the ataxic patient has difficulty maintaining sufficient stability while moving. He must be able to roll on to his side and bear weight through his arms in order to push himself up into sitting from lying. He may also need to bear weight through his arms in order to stand up from sitting (Fig. 99). It is important that he knows ways of improving stability on his own. For example, by approximating down through his legs he improves his stability and control in standing up from sitting.

Some General Points in Treatment

Some techniques recommended for increasing tone and stimulating movement are contra-indicated in the presence of ataxia. Hagbarth

297

Fig. 97. *Stimulation of the seesaw reaction. This gives the patient the idea of stepping forward with normal body alignment and an appropriately narrow base.*

and Eklund (1968) report that motor performance is adversely affected by the use of vibratory stimulation. Excitatory cold may cause a hyperactive response in patients with ataxia. Rhythmic stabilisation is sometimes suggested as part of the treatment of ataxic patients. However, this technique is more suitable for strengthening weak muscles than for improving the ataxic patient's control over movement. It involves the recruiting of additional motor units and this does not necessarily improve the subtle control over muscle activity required for normal function.

In general, movement is stimulated smoothly and steadily, in a small range initially (Fig. 100), gradually increasing the range as the patient gains more control (Fig. 101). One of the most essential aspects of movement to be improved is the regulation of balance, and balance will only be improved if the patient is in an antigravity position and with a normal base of support.

Any position can be made more stable by using pressure and

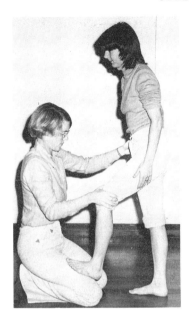

Fig. 98. *The patient practises balancing on the right leg.*

approximation and by giving the patient more than one fixed point of stability. For example, we are more stable when sitting with our feet flat on the floor than with our feet unsupported. The patient can stand with his hands against a wall giving him points of stability at his feet and hands. This enables him to concentrate on controlling one part of his body, for example, on extending his hips. The very ataxic patient who is unable to sustain *any* activity against gravity *can* therefore be controlled in an antigravity position, such as sitting or standing, by using more than one fixed point, which leaves him with only one part of his body to control. This point must be emphasised as the patient will only develop antigravity control if the therapist gives him the chance to do so.

In the treatment of an ataxic patient the therapist must respond sensitively to the patient in order to feel how much pressure and approximation is necessary to help him grade his movement and to know when to reduce or remove her control which allows the patient to see and understand that he can do something himself. It should be clear that too much approximation becomes resistance and can push the patient off balance or pin him down so he feels he cannot move.

299

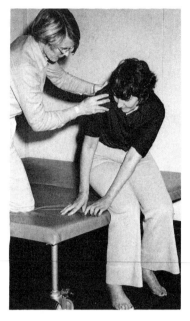

Fig. 99. *Sitting to standing with weight-bearing through the arms.*

The ataxic patient tends to lean on support and will not respond if he is held too much and not given the opportunity to regulate his movement. In other words, there has to be a balance between stimulating sufficient proximal stability to allow the patient to move and holding him so that he cannot move or does not have to try.

An important objective for the therapist in **progressing treatment** is to *withdraw her control and guidance* gradually, so that the patient is moving by himself. She may do this in several ways. She may reduce the amount of pressure and approximation or she may change her handling from proximal to more distal. This will allow the patient to take over more control himself. She may reduce the number of fixed points or introduce more movement and therefore increase the need for balance (Fig. 102). For example, the patient is encouraged to turn his head in order to see and reach for objects.

At the same time the therapist will *increase the complexity* of movement. Speed is altered from slow to fast to slow, range is altered from small to large, direction of movement is changed, the patient is asked to stop the movement and start again without losing control.

Fig. 100. *Stimulation of balance. The therapist displaces weight to the point where the girl is about to lose control. She then practises maintaining control around this point.*

Activities involving more rotation can be used. In this way the therapist alters her handling to help the patient regulate his performance so he is actually moving on his own in progressively more difficult ways.

Although *speech* is slurred, scanned and explosive it is usually intelligible. Prolonged and controlled expiration can be stimulated in an attempt to improve co-ordination between respiration and speech and to improve phonation. Expiration with overpressure can be given in a stable position, such as in sitting, to improve sentence length. It is also possible that speech will improve as general stability improves.

The use of *weights* worn by the patient is sometimes suggested as a means of improving movement control. Holmes (1939) noted that weighting of the arms in patients with cerebellar lesions improved the ability to perform rapid alternating movements of pronation and

301

Fig. 101. *Range of movement is increased as she gains more control.*

supination. Others (Chase, Cullen, Sullivan and Ommaya 1965) have investigated the effect of weights on intention tremor in cerebellar lesions.

Weights may be attached proximally, for example with a weighted belt, in order to improve trunk stability. An improvement in stability proximally often results in a decrease in errors of movement more distally. For example, a young man following head injury reported improved hand function in the workshop and improved ability to control his movement when playing snooker when he wore a weighted belt. The amount of weight worn by the patient is usually the minimum weight which improves control. The patient's own opinion of the effectiveness of the weights is important, and the therapist should record his movements on videotape or film in order to assess their effect. Weights may be useful in the transition from assisted walking to walking alone, or in order to improve a particular skill. The weights should be removed immediately if there is any increase in symptoms.

Fig. 102. *The therapist reduces the number of fixed points of stability and increases the complexity of movement by encouraging the patient to turn her head and reach for objects.*

SUMMARY

In this chapter the characteristics of cerebellar ataxia are described. Ataxia most commonly results as part of the sequelae of head injury, tumour or multiple sclerosis. Methods of stimulating control of movement and more effective function are briefly described.

References

André-Thomas, Chesni, Y. and Saint-Anne Dargassies (1960) *The Neurological Examination of the Infant*. London, Heinemann.

Basmajian, J. V. (1977) Motor learning and control: a working hypothesis. *Arch. Phys. Med. Rehabil.*, **58**, 38–41.

303

Chase, R. A., Cullen, J. K., Sullivan, S. A. and Ommaya, A. K. (1965) Modification of intention tremor in man. *Nature*, **206**, 485–487.

Eyzaguirre, C. and Fidone, S. J. (1975) *Physiology of the Nervous System*. Chicago, Year Book Medical Publishers.

Garcin, R. (1969) Co-ordination of voluntary movement. In *Handbook of Clinical Neurology*, edited by P. J. Vinken and G. W. Bryn. Amsterdam, North Holland Publishing Company.

Hagbarth, K. E. and Eklund, G. (1968) The effects of muscle vibration in spasticity, rigidity and cerebellar disorders. *J. Neurol., Neurosurg. Psychiat.*, **31**, 207–213.

Holmes, G. (1939) The cerebellum of man. *Brain*, **62**, 1–30.

Holmes, G. (1969) *Introduction to Clinical Neurology*. Edinburgh & London, Churchill Livingstone.

Lance, J. W., and McLeod, J. G. (1975) *A Physiological Approach to Clinical Neurology*. London, Butterworths.

Luria, A. R. (1971) *Speech and the Development of Mental Processes in the Child*. London, Penguin.

Noback, C. R. and Demarest, R. J. (1975) *The Human Nervous System*. New York, McGraw Hill.

Rademaker, G. C. J. (1935) *Réactions Labyrinthiques et Equilibre*. Paris, Masson.

Saywell, S. Y. (1975) Riding and ataxia. *Physiotherapy*, **61**, 11, 334.

Further Reading

Hewer, R. L., Cooper, R., and Morgan, M. H. (1972) Investigations into the value of treating intention tremor by weighting the affected limb. *Brain*, **95**, 579–590.

Marsden, C. D. (1975) The physiological basis of ataxia. *Physiotherapy*, **61**, 11, 326.

Chapter 14

Athetosis

The term athetosis is used to describe a particular type of movement inco-ordination with a dominance of random, apparently purposeless movements, which are combined with an instability of posture affecting the upper and lower limbs, the trunk, the head and the neck. The problems of athetosis and their management cannot be discussed in isolation from abnormalities of tone as they are always associated with abnormal postural tone. Athetosis is classified neurologically as an involuntary movement disorder, together with ballimus, chorea and tremor.

In its most typical form it is characterised by irregular writhing movements which tend to alternate between two extremes of posture but which are seldom seen through a complete range. These changes of posture appear to result from an intermittent build up of muscle tension in antagonistic muscle groups. They become more pronounced as the patient struggles to control his movements. They may be relatively rapid or, when associated with spasticity, slower and more obvious distally. The involuntary movements are usually more severe in the upper limbs, trunk and head than in the lower limbs.

It is not proposed to discuss the problems associated with chorea and ballismus, as they are similar to those associated with athetosis. *Chorea* is seen in rheumatic Sydenham's chorea, which usually recovers spontaneously and completely, and in Huntington's chorea, a progressive, degenerative disease of late adult life. Choreic movements in their coarsest form are identical with athetoid movements, or they appear as involuntary twitching movements. *Ballismus* usually affects one side of the body (hemiballismus) and is characterised by wild swinging movements of the limbs. The principles of physical treatment for patients with chorea are essentially the same as those for patients with athetosis.

Pathophysiology

Athetosis results from disorders of the basal ganglia which affect in particular the putamen and also the caudate nucleus (Lance and

305

McLeod 1975). It shares, in common with all lesions of the basal ganglia, problems in initiating willed movements, and disturbances of body posture. As Denny Brown (1962) stresses, the term 'athetosis' is used to describe the movements and not the postural background.

Although clinically athetosis is recognisable by fluctuations in tone, involuntary movements and tremor, the pathophysiological mechanisms involved are not understood.

Lance and McLeod (1975) describe the 'athetotic action tremor' which occurs on voluntary muscle contraction and is evident on electromyographic investigation. They point out that although it is often considered that athetosis depends on an increased sensitivity of the resting tonic stretch reflex, it is possible to decrease this reflex activity with drugs without improving the patient's motor performance. They quote Neilson (1974) who postulates that involuntary movements bear an intimate relationship to the 'action tonic stretch reflex', that is to reflex transmission during voluntary activity. It is possible that control of voluntary movement in patients with basal ganglia lesions is mediated through less direct motor pathways than normal, leading to instability of this reflex which is apparent as action tremor.

However, Harris (1971) comments that although neurologists have traditionally explained involuntary movements such as athetosis in terms of central motor mechanisms, athetoid movements may arise from defective sensory feedback from the moving limb. He sees the problem as possibly the result of a sensory disorder rather than a purely motor one, in other words, as a 'control system failure'. If this is so, faulty feedback from peripheral sense organs (joint receptors, muscle spindles, tactile receptors), which does not accurately represent actual limb position, would result in postural instability. He suggests the possibility of additional cerebellar damage and postulates that subcortical and cerebellar damage would result in diminished reticulo-spinal activity. This would allow the stretch receptors to slacken and become desensitised. There would be a lapse in time between a muscle fibre stretch or contraction and the detection of this by the receptors. Therefore, 'the athetoid limb wanders about in space unable to find a stable position because it does not know when it has gotten there'. Harris concludes that a vicious cycle would then exist, in which faulty sensory input leads to disturbed movement control which leads to more faulty input and thence to further disturbance of movement.

This latter is an interesting hypothesis. Bobath (1967) has also suggested that the chaotic sensory feedback from athetosis must interfere with the learning of movements, making repetition impossible.

Causes of Athetosis

Athetosis is most commonly seen in infancy as a result of such perinatal causes as anoxia and kernicterus resulting from haemolytic disease. Since the availability of exchange transfusion and the introduction of immunoprophylaxis against Rhesus incompatibility, kernicterus is no longer one of the commonest causes of athetosis in the perinatal period. Prior to this, many infants died or developed athetosis as a result of the effects of a high concentration of bilirubin in the blood and consequent damage to the basal ganglia. Deafness is frequently associated with the athetosis which develops from this cause.

Athetosis is also seen as a manifestation of such uncommon degenerative conditions as Wilson's disease (hepato-lenticular degeneration) and dystonia musculorum deformans (torsion spasms), and following encephalitis. It seldom develops in adult life, although it is sometimes seen as a sequel to post-anoxic encephalopathy or degenerative disease of the basal ganglia, and following trauma. Most adults who demonstrate athetosis have suffered it from birth as part of the condition known as cerebral palsy.

Classification of Athetosis

There are many different manifestations of athetosis, so many that the practical classification of these patients poses serious problems. Attempts at classification usually fail because most patients demonstrate problems which overlap from one group to another.

Athetosis may be found associated with choreiform movements when it is referred to as *choreoathetosis*. In this case postural tone is basically low with abrupt fluctuations. Integration of the functions of agonists and antagonists is lacking (Bobath 1972). The patient finds it difficult to maintain a position, and lack of proximal fixation allows ungraded large range jerky movements. Athetosis may also be *associated with intermittent tonic spasms and dystonia* in which case there are abrupt variations from hypotonus to extreme hypertonus. Tonic reflex activity is clearly seen, and the patient becomes temporarily fixed in extremes of posture. Attempts at voluntary movement cause contraction of the antagonistic muscle group. Head control is always poor, and the patient has little control over movement.

Denny Brown (1966) and Lance and McLeod (1975) describe dystonia as a condition in which part of the body or the whole body becomes fixed in an abnormal posture. Dystonia may be a manifestation of a primary degenerative disorder of the basal ganglia, such as dystonia musculorum deformans. It more commonly is seen as a secondary change in progressive disorders of the basal ganglia such as Wilson's Disease, Huntington's chorea and Parkinson's disease. Dystonia may also eventually develop in patients with athetosis with intermittent tonic spasms of the type seen in cerebral palsy and in patients who suffer from long term spasticity following stroke.

Athetosis may also be seen *associated with spasticity*, in which the stretch reflex is hyperactive and tone increased. Involuntary movements are noticeable more distally, and tonic reflex activity is not usually pronounced, although it may be present under stress.

Characteristics of Athetosis

Athetosis disappears during sleep and when the patient is in a state of complete relaxation if this can be achieved. However most patients, even in a supported position with gravity eliminated, demonstrate constant involuntary movements. The patient finds it virtually impossible to keep still. With great effort he may be able to maintain a motionless state for a short time but this is always followed by a further, and usually increased, burst of activity. Athetosis is increased and exaggerated by attempts at voluntary movement and postural adjustment, changes in emotion, anxiety, stress, speech and even by the desire to move or speak. As well as being obvious in the part of the body moving, athetosis may also be evident in another limb or in the face. For example, attempts at reaching out with one arm which itself demonstrates athetoid movement, may be accompanied by involuntary movement of the other arm, of the legs and perhaps the face. These associated movements (Twitchell 1959), are particularly obvious in the upper limb and frequently mirror the movements of the other arm.

Tone may fluctuate from very low to very high in sudden unpredictable changes, which are influenced by the presence of tonic reflex activity (tonic neck reflexes and tonic labyrinthine reflex*). These tonic reflexes may be induced by passive movement of the head or by active or involuntary alterations in the posture of the head by the patient himself, or in the case of the tonic labyrinthine reflex, by the assumption of the prone or supine position. Tonic reflexes may not necessarily be seen as movements but may be merely tonus changes which can be felt as resistance to passive movement. The asymmetrical tonic neck reflex is usually stronger on one side than the other and results in the asymmetry frequently seen in athetoid patients. In some patients, attempts at movement appear to be composed almost entirely of fluctuations of tone with a combination of tonic neck and

* Glossary

tonic labyrinthine activity, retained primitive reflexes such as the Moro, avoiding reactions (Twitchell 1959), and total patterns of flexion and extension. There tends to be hypermobility of joints in patients whose tone is basically low with a poor ability to grade reciprocal innervation.

There are considerable difficulties describing the *athetoid movements* which are so readily recognisable to the eye. Nevertheless, there are certain abnormal combinations of movements which are commonly seen (Fig. 103). For example, flexion of the wrist and pronation of the

Fig. 103. *Poor body alignment, difficulty sustaining a posture.*

forearm are frequently accompanied by extension and abduction of the fingers, and adduction and extension of the thumb. This movement may be followed by supination of the forearm and flexion and adduction of the fingers and thumb. Sometimes certain fingers may spontaneously flex while others extend (Fig. 104). Examples of typical athetoid movements in the lower limb include eversion and plantar-flexion of the foot with toe abduction, which may accompany flexion, adduction and internal rotation of the leg. Many patients find it

309

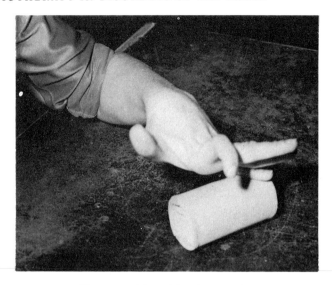

Fig. 104. *Athetoid hand movement.*

impossible to bear weight through their feet. When this is attempted, the patient makes mock stepping movements which give the impression that he is walking on hot coals. These continual stepping movements may be partly the result of a tactile sensitivity of the soles of the feet.

Other patients, when their feet are brought into contact with the floor, develop a severe extensor spasm with the feet in plantarflexion or they collapse into flexion. Extensor spasms may be utilised by the patient in his attempt to maintain an erect antigravity posture. This may be the only way in which he can build up sufficient extensor tone to become antigravity. The tendency for this extensor spasm to be followed by a complete collapse into flexion probably illustrates the patient's basically low postural tone.

These problems may be demonstrated functionally by difficulty in sustaining a posture, by asymmetry and by difficulty in keeping the head, hands and eyes in the midline. The head, trunk and limbs are therefore poorly aligned. There will be difficulty in using the arms for weight-bearing and therefore in changing from one position to another, difficulty keeping the feet on the floor, the arms forward, and the weight forward at the hips to balance in sitting or standing. The patient has difficulty moving his eyes independently of his head, his head independently of his body, and his arms independently of his head. He may be able to balance momentarily in sitting but rotation of his head to one side may initiate an asymmetrical tonic neck reflex and flexion or extension of his head may initiate a flexor or extensor spasm, all of which will cause him to lose balance.

Reaching for an object with the eyes and the hand may be impossible because of the difficulty bringing the arm and the head to the midline. There may be difficulty in reaching for an object because of lack of sitting balance, and lack of proximal fixation at the trunk and shoulder girdle. Twitchell (1959) considers that there is an element of ataxia in all athetoid movements, and certainly attempts to extend the arm to reach for an object are accompanied by errors in rate, force, direction and range. The patient may approach the object with his fingers extended but may be unable to flex his fingers in order to grasp it. Denny Brown (1962) and Twitchell (1959) refer to this as an 'avoiding reaction'. They consider that athetosis is demonstrated by a loss of equilibrium or a lack of integration between grasping and avoiding reactions, or groping and withdrawal responses, with the grasping reaction usually the strongest.

Attempts at grasping may result in flexion of the wrist and elbow prematurely and the patient pulls his arm away before he has grasped the object. Alternatively, he may flex his fingers before he gets to the object and then be unable to extend his wrist and fingers in order to grasp it. Should the patient succeed in grasping and holding on to the object, he may not be able to sustain the grasp while moving his arm, and he may not be able to release it. He may be unable to regulate the strength of his grasp. He may be unable to keep one arm still and maintain both his visual grasp and his manual grasp on an object while moving the other arm, that is, he may be unable to use one hand independently of either his head or his other arm.

Visual fixation, particularly as an aid to prehension, is difficult because of lack of head control and because of difficulty controlling eye movement and position. Eye movement may be influenced by asymmetrical reflex activity which makes it difficult to move the eyes to the midline and keep them there. Alternatively, the patient may be unable to move his eyes independently of his head. He may be unable to combine visual fixation with arm movement and will strike out at an object without looking at it. Twitchell (1959) calls this a 'visual avoiding response'.

Oro-facial function. Many examples of involuntary movement are seen in the face and mouth. The jaw may strongly deviate to one side and/or thrust downwards. This latter movement is usually associated with extensor hyperactivity, while a strong biting action may be associated with flexor spasms. Poor lip and jaw closure are frequently associated with extensor hypertonus. The lips may retract, 'grin', purse or protrude. The tongue may protrude or move uncontrolled around the mouth, constantly at risk of being bitten, or it may be tense and immobile.

Difficulty with swallowing and poor lip and jaw closure may result in severe drooling. Eating problems are common with most athetoid patients for a combination of reasons, which include poor sitting balance, inability to stabilise the head, asymmetry, difficulty getting the food to the mouth, poor lip and jaw closure, unco-ordinated tongue movements and difficulty in swallowing. The presence of a strong biting action prevents the patient chewing and interferes with mouth opening.

Facial expression is in many patients asymmetrical and often grimacing, with muscles or groups of muscles contracting strongly and distorting facial features. In other patients facial expression is merely inappropriate.

Communication is a major problem when the patient has dysarthria, which is due to inco-ordination between tongue, lips and soft palate, poor co-ordination between respiration and speech, difficulty sustaining the expiration necessary to express a phrase or sentence, and reduced vital capacity. Speech is very slow to develop in athetoid children, and the adult with cerebral palsy may never have mastered understandable speech.

It is not within the scope of this book to discuss the problems, assessment and treatment of the infant and young child with athetoid cerebral palsy. However, therapists who treat adult athetoid patients will find it helpful to understand the abnormal development of the athetoid infant. The reader is referred to Bobath and Bobath (1975) for a description of this. Finnie (1974), Shepherd (1979), Ellis (1967) and Bobath & Bobath (1975) describe the handling and treatment of athetoid infants and small children.

The problems of the adolescent and adult who have had athetosis since birth will depend on a number of factors including how early treatment was commenced, how appropriate and effective this treatment was, how much his development was affected by his problems, the severity of the initial brain damage, the presence of secondary problems such as delayed cognitive and social development, soft tissue contractures and deformities. The most common deformities are scoliosis and dislocation of the hip and temporo-mandibular joints. The problems of the patient who develops athetosis in later childhood or adult life will depend also on whether it is a result of a progressive, degenerative disorder or whether it is in combination with other neurological dysfunction.

312

TREATMENT

The behaviour of these patients is often very bizarre and the therapist will need to ensure that her assessment enables her to pick out the main problems of function underlying the athetoid movements.

The therapist's overall approach to treatment will be to help the patient organise and regulate his movements in order to function more effectively. She should help the patient to learn movements he can relate to his functional needs, whether it be sitting in a classroom or an office, working on an assembly line or looking after himself. Most patients who have had athetosis since early childhood have devised methods of functioning which are effective even though not normal in appearance. It is up to the therapist to work with this person in finding out ways of further improving his function.

The athetoid patient experiences chaotic feedback, particularly proprioceptive feedback, in his attempts at functional movement. Some of the motor problems experienced by the athetoid cerebral palsied adult are secondary and result from long term abnormal or faulty feedback which cuts down the patient's ability to repeat the necessary movements and to learn motor skills.

It follows from this hypothesis that therapy must give him the experience of functional movement even if such movement must be controlled at first by the therapist. The functional movements practised must involve tasks which the patient understands to be relevant to his problems. He should know when he has accomplished the task correctly as this knowledge of success will reinforce learning. Similarly, he must know when the movement goes wrong and why, so that his next attempt will be directed towards a more appropriate movement.

If athetoid movements are the result of a defective monitoring system with inappropriate feedback which does not accurately represent the position of the limb, trunk or head (Harris 1971), then the therapist must devise ways of reinforcing the patient's awareness of the actual position of the part.

The acquisition of some degree of *head control* is essential to the learning and execution of most functions. Stability of head position is vital for communication, eating, visual fixation, manual activities, and all activities requiring balance including walking. As well as the ability to maintain a steady head position, the athetoid person must learn to move his eyes independently of his head and his head independently of his body and arms. Approximation through the head or shoulders with the patient in sitting or lying will stimulate the joint receptors in the cervical and thoracic spine and this may help the

313

patient gain some control. This should be done with the patient in a symmetrical position.

Treatment should particularly aim for *symmetry of posture and movement* as this seems to help the patient organise himself and gives him a more natural position from which to initiate movement (Fig. 105). Joint approximation and guidance given throughout movement

Fig. 105. *Elevation of his arm encourages more normal body alignment as he takes a step forwards.*

will usually help the organisation of that movement. This effect may be due in part to the increased awareness given to the patient of the position of that part of him in space.

It is usually easier for the patient to gain control of one part of his body at a time. He may, for example, be able to gain control over his head in sitting with his feet on the floor if he holds on to a rail in front of him. In this case his body is fixed at two points, at his shoulders and his hips, leaving him to concentrate only on moving and controlling his head. Once he can do this he can go on to moving another part of himself at the same time as controlling his head, for example, moving one arm while he holds on with the other.

The ability to *fixate visually* is often a difficult skill to develop in the adult who has up until now managed without this skill. The therapist should encourage the patient to look at what he is doing and to look at the person to whom he is talking. In many adult patients, not attempting to look at what they are doing becomes so much a part of the patient's activities that it requires much concentration and considerable motivation for this skill to be acquired.

Some head control is essential for the acquisition of *balance*, as head and optical righting are essential components of equilibrium reactions, and the ability to maintain and regain balance is essential for all activities in which gravity has an effect. To improve standing balance, for example, the patient must experience and practise how to control and regulate his own movements by keeping his feet on the floor, his weight forwards at the hips, his arms forwards, his head in the midline and aligned with his trunk to prevent flexor or extensor or asymmetrical spasms.

He may develop sitting balance by practising the specific movements involved in regaining balance. The therapist stimulates equilibrium reactions by slowly altering his centre of gravity which facilitates adjustments of head, trunk and limbs. She guides his responses ensuring that they remain controlled and appropriate and she prevents sudden and uncontrolled reactions. By encouraging slow responses in small ranges around the midline to begin with, she gives the patient time to appreciate a more organised feedback, which should enable the response to become learned and automatic. As the patient's own control over his movements improves, the therapist uses less guidance and support, and stimulates a greater range of movement.

Many athetoid patients who have learned to walk never progress beyond walking with a wide base. As they never attempt to walk with their feet closer together, they never develop the antero-posterior balance which is essential for walking with a narrow base. Practise of weight transference in walk standing will enable balance in standing to develop further. Approximation through the trunk to increase extension against gravity and improve stability is followed by alternate tapping* to the trunk in walk standing, practice of stepping backward and forwards with the arms fixed, and eventually activities which are more balance-threatening. These will usually lead to improvement in walking balance. Care must be taken not to allow the

* Appendix 1

patient to lose control over his stability by giving excessive and ungraded stimulation.

Some patients reach adult life without ever learning to stand or walk. The problems in standing found in the adult may include the following. There may be difficulty keeping the feet flat on the floor, the weight may be too far backwards, fluctuating tone may cause instability, there may be no effective ability to maintain and regain balance, and a lack of head control may make balancing in standing impossible.

Artificial proprioceptors giving information about position in space may enable some patients to learn to walk. *Electronic head control devices*, for example, have been found to initiate the development of independent walking in some children (Harris, Spelman and Hymer 1974).

Some adult patients are resigned to life in a wheelchair, having given up the struggle to walk because of the extreme effort involved. These people should be helped to stand for a short period each day, and be able to stand briefly in order to get from chair to lavatory and from chair to bed.

Attempts to improve *hand function* should aim at stimulating wrist extension during grasp and release, grasp and release close to the body and at arm's length, the ability to maintain grasp of an object while moving the arm, and control over grading of grasp. Wrist extension can also be stimulated automatically by eliciting protective reactions (Fig. 106).

Many athetoid adults are capable of improving this function. For example, treatment to improve the function of grasp and release in a patient whose hands were held in an extreme posture of flexion at the wrists and pronation of the forearms commenced with stimulation of wrist extension in a more normal radially-orientated position. She found she could actively grasp and maintain that grasp with guidance. Treatment concentrated upon getting grasp and release, with the wrist maintained by the therapist in an extended position (Fig. 107). Gradually the patient took over active control at the wrist. This was practised with the arms straight out in front, a position which enabled her to be symmetrical and to control her head. Wrist extension was stimulated and encouraged by direct stimulation over the wrist extensors and by the patient concentrating on the 'feeling' of where her wrist was in space. She initially practised maintaining the position gained by the therapist, then progressed to moving a small way into flexion and back into the original position. Eventually treatment concentrated on helping her to control her wrist position with different types of grasp and while she reached out in different directions with her arm.

Fig. 106. *Wrist and finger extension is encouraged if the therapist stimulates automatic protective reactions. The patient must be off balance for this response to occur.*

Techniques for improving *oro-facial function* are described in Chapter 15. The oro-facial problems associated with athetosis cannot be separated from general problems of tone and movement. It is easier, for example, to stimulate more effective oro-facial function when the patient is symmetrical, has head control and is in a position which minimises fluctuations of tone.

One of the most serious problems because it is both unpleasant for the patient and socially unacceptable is *drooling*. Lake (1979) describes a behaviour modification programme for controlling drooling in a group of athetoid adolescents.

Rhythmic intention. Many of the ideas of Petö* can be applied to the patient with athetosis to encourage his participation in the acquisition of skill and to discourage the therapist from wanting to

* Appendix 2

317

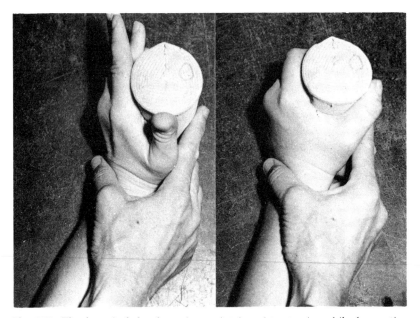

Fig. 107. *The therapist helps the patient maintain wrist extension while she practises grasp and release.*

exercise too great a restrictive, manual control over the patient's involuntary movements.

Biofeedback Therapy. Harris (1971), in discussing the necessity for improving feedback from the limbs and trunk, suggests that biomedical engineering in the form of artificial limb position detectors may be able to provide accurate feedback for the athetoid patient whose own feedback function is defective. A later article (Harris, Spelman and Hymer 1974) describes a programme involving the design of artificial sense organs which provide information for head and limb position control, their incorporation into substitute feedback systems and the use of such sensory aids in treatment programmes.

Biofeedback therapy may be used in other ways to help the patient monitor his behaviour. Macpherson (1967) describes the treatment of a sixty year old woman with Huntington's chorea, who received conditioning with biofeedback therapy to help her control her involuntary movements. In this case biofeedback was used to help the patient overcome anxiety and stress which are usually noted to increase the severity of involuntary movements. After she was shown

318

relaxation techniques, along the lines described by Jacobson (1938), wire electrodes were implanted under the skin over muscles which had involuntary contractions. The wires were connected to earphones. She was instructed to try to relax her muscles as soon as she heard the auditory signal. As a result of this therapy she was able to perform movements with less interference from involuntary movements than before. The author stresses that the effects of this approach are purely symptomatic, and that further investigation needs to be carried out into the contribution of the various parts of this treatment programme to the functional improvement noticed by the patient.

Recreational activities such as horse riding and Halliwick swimming (Reid 1976) may enable the person with athetosis to develop more control over posture and movement and provide enjoyment. Golf and skiing are two other activities to consider.

SUMMARY

This chapter describes the movement problems associated with athetosis. Despite the difficult problems with which the person, who has probably suffered from athetosis since birth, presents, physical treatment should help him gain some of the motor skills important for effective function. Some general points in treatment are described.

References

Bobath, B. (1967) The very early treatment of cerebral palsy. *Develop. Med. Child Neurol.*, **9,** 4.

Bobath, B. and Bobath, K. (1972) Diagnosis and assessment of cerebral palsy. In *Physical Therapy Services in the Developmental Disabilities*, edited by P. H. Pearson and C. E. Williams. Illinois, Thomas.

Bobath, B. and Bobath, K. (1975) *Motor Development in the Different Types of Cerebral Palsy*. London, Heinemann.

Denny-Brown, D. (1962) *The Basal Ganglia and their Relation to Disorders of Movement*. London, Oxford University Press.

Denny-Brown, D. (1966) *The Cerebral Control of Movement*. Liverpool, Liverpool University Press.

Ellis, E. (1967) *The Physical Management of Developmental Disorders*. London, Heinemann.

Finnie, N. (1974) *Handling the Young Cerebral Palsied Child at Home*. London, Heinemann.

Harris, F. A. (1971) Inapproprioception: a possible sensory basis for athetoid movements. *J. Amer. P. T. Assoc.*, **51**, 7, 761–770.

Harris, F. A., Spelman, F. A. and Hyman, J. W. (1974) Electronic sensory aids as treatment for cerebral-palsied children. *Phys. Ther.*, **54**, 4, 354–365.

Jacobson, E. (1938) *Progressive Relaxation*. Chicago, University of Chicago Press.

Lake, B. (1979) Dribbling control programme. *Aust. J. Physiother.* In press.

Lance, J. W. and McLeod, J. G. (1975) *A Physiological Approach to Clinical Neurology*. London, Butterworths.

MacPherson, E. L. R. (1967) Control of involuntary movement. *Behav. Res. Ther.*, **5**, 143–145.

Neilson, P. D. (1974) Measurement of involuntary arm movement in athetotic patients. *J. Neurol. Neurosurg. Psychiat.*, **37**, 171–177.

Reid, M. (1976) *Handling the Disabled Child in Water*. Birmingham, Association of Paediatric Chartered Physiotherapists.

Shepherd, R. B. (1979) *Physiotherapy in Paediatrics*. 2nd edition. London, Heinemann.

Twitchell, T. E. (1959) On the motor deficit in congenital bilateral athetosis. *J. Nervous and Mental Disease*, **129**, 2, 105–132.

Further Reading

Halpern, D. *et al.* (1970) Training of control of head posture in children with cerebral palsy. *Develop. Med. Child Neurol.*, **12**, 291–305.

Haskin, M. R., Erdman, W. J., Bream, J. and MacAvoy, C. G. (1974) Therapeutic horseback riding for the handicapped. *Arch. Phys. Med. Rehabil.*, **55**, 473–474.

Langworthy, O. R. (1970) *The Sensory Control of Posture and Movement. A Review of the Studies of Derek Denny-Brown*. Baltimore, Williams & Wilkins.

Yahr, M. D. (1972) Involuntary movements. In *Scientific Foundations of Neurology*, edited by M. Critchley, J. O'Leary, and G. Jennett. London, Heinemann.

Chapter 15

Oro-facial Dysfunction

Adults with disorders of the central nervous system frequently demonstrate the involvement of speech and breathing mechanisms, of articulation, language, facial expression, eating and gesture. Speech and language depend upon movement and human contact, along with adequate stimulation from the environment. If this environment is not provided for the patient who is unable or slow to respond, he is deprived of the stimulation which is necessary to enable him to communicate and socialise.

The organs of eating, speech and respiration are to a large extent the same and normal function of these organs is essential for ventilation, nutrition, speech and socialisation, all of which lead to physical and emotional well-being.

NORMAL ORO-FACIAL FUNCTION

To understand normal oro-facial function in adults it is necessary to study the various organs involved in eating, speaking and facial expression and their relationships to each other.

The *lips* are sensitive to touch, temperature and pressure, thus preventing the entrance into the mouth of any unsuitable food, such as food that is too hot. Lip closure is necessary for taking food and particularly liquids into the mouth, for retaining them and for preventing dribbling of saliva. They are normally closed during swallowing. In speech, they aid in the formation of consonants and vowels.

The *tongue* is a muscular organ made up of small intrinsic muscles by which it changes shape, and larger extrinsic muscles which move it about the mouth, protrude it and retract it back again. Its functions are both sensory and motor, and it is capable of a variety of very complex movements, and of a wide range of sensory discrimination. It moves the food around the mouth, mixes it with salivary secretions, and assists chewing by placing the food in the proper place. It forms the food into a mass called the bolus and transports it to the back of the oral cavity for swallowing. It helps to remove the food left between the teeth and gums. Its taste buds, along with the sensation of smell, identify the flavour of food, and its nerve endings are sensitive to texture and temperature.

The *cheeks* enclose the food. The muscles which comprise the cheek aid the tongue in mixing the food bolus with moistening and digestive secretions. They push the food back on to the teeth when the action of chewing tends to push it sideways.

The *teeth* bite, tear or cut the food. The molars are used for grinding the food into small enough pieces for swallowing. The *jaw* has a hinge-like movement used in tearing, and a lateral movement used in chewing. Chewing movements are adapted to particular foods. The jaw is also capable of performing the fine complex movements which are required for speech. The muscles controlling the jaw, therefore, are capable of producing both powerful sustained movement and small complex adjustments.

The *pharynx* can be divided into three sections – the nasal pharynx (epipharynx), the oral pharynx and the laryngeal pharynx (hypopharynx). It is a muscular membranous tube which is attached to the base of the skull and extends to the level of the cricoid cartilage at the lower margin of the sixth cervical vertebra. At this point it

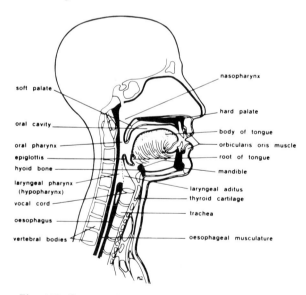

Fig. 108. *Cross-section of the head and neck showing the relationship between the structures involved in oral function.*

becomes continuous with the oesophagus. Its anterior wall is incomplete because of its communications with the nasal, oral and laryngeal cavities. It is also connected to the ears by the Eustachian tubes. The nasal pharynx normally has a purely respiratory function. The oral pharynx extends from where the mouth communicates with the pharynx to the pharyngeal-epiglottal folds. In this part of the pharynx the pathways of food and air cross each other. The laryngeal pharynx lies posterior to the larynx and becomes progressively smaller as it descends towards the oesophagus (Fig. 108).

The *larynx* forms the anterior wall of the pharynx. It is made up of cartilage and vocal cords which are moved by sensitive muscles. It is suspended from the hyoid bone and the skull and is continuous with the trachea below. It protects the respiratory tract from invasion of food by acting as a sphincter valve. The lower portion is largely involved in phonation. The larynx also plays a part in maintaining an open airway.

The *gag reflex* is the only oral reflex found in adults. It is present at birth and is relatively hyperactive. It gradually modifies as the infant's swallowing matures, and remains throughout life as a protective reflex. It is elicited by tactile stimulation to the back of the tongue and soft palate, which causes the muscles of the pharynx to constrict.

Mechanism of Eating and Drinking

Swallowing or deglutition is a highly integrated function. The initial preparation of the food bolus is under voluntary control, but once the bolus is in position for swallowing its sets up a chain of reflexes. A similar situation exists in the presence of saliva.

The sequence of eating can be divided into four parts, each of which overlaps:

movements necessary to take food or liquid into the mouth,
chewing,
preparation of the bolus,
swallowing.

Food is taken into the mouth with the lips and is bitten, torn or cut by the front teeth. The tongue moves the food on to the molars which are especially shaped for grinding, and mixes it with salivary secretions. The cheeks enclose the food and also assist in moving it on to the molars. Chewing further stimulates taste by breaking up the food and this increases the flow of saliva and gastric juices. Food has to be moistened sufficiently before it can be swallowed.

The tongue selects the food which is ready for swallowing and forms it into the bolus. The bolus is placed on the dorsum of the tongue, the tip of the tongue touches the hard palate just behind the teeth, and the bolus is squeezed backward by upward and forward pressure of the tongue on the hard palate. Ardran and Kemp (1951) describe the passage of the bolus as being 'like toothpaste being pressed from a tube'. 'Humping' of the tongue is the term sometimes used to describe the elevation of the posterior third of the tongue immediately prior to swallowing.

In preparation for swallowing, the hyoid bone is brought forwards into a position of moderate elevation through the movements of the tongue. The teeth are occluded, the lips and jaw closed, the soft palate and uvula made tense and raised to seal off the nasopharynx, and the bolus, pushed backward by the raising of the back of the tongue, penetrates the pharynx. The larynx is pulled upward behind the hyoid bone and towards the back of the tongue. This narrows the lumen of the larynx which helps to protect the respiratory tract. As the bolus reaches the epiglottis, some of it spills sideways descending on one or both sides of the larynx into the oesophagus (Ardran and Kemp 1951). Only very big food masses spill over the epiglottis. The pharynx is also pulled upwards over the bolus, propelling it a short distance into the oesophagus.

The contact of the bolus with the mucosa of parts of the mouth and pharynx acts as a stimulus to the reflexes which make up the action of swallowing, thereby ensuring that the bolus descends to the oesophagus. During this phase of swallowing, respiration is inhibited momentarily, more often during expiration than inspiration. Aspiration of foods and liquids is prevented by fine co-ordination between the mechanism of swallowing and the mechanism of respiration. When the bolus enters the oesophagus it continues downward by peristaltic action. Gravity plays a large part in the swallowing of liquids during which the surface of the tongue is grooved by the elevation of its lateral margins. This forms a tubular space with the palate. The fluid within this tunnel is squirted into the oral part of the pharynx by the dorsum of the tongue (Lockhart, Hamilton and Fyfe 1959).

There appears to be a marked difference in solicited and unsolicited swallowing. Kydd & Toda (1962) using strain gauges in the palate found that the tongue exerted twice as much pressure with command swallowing compared with spontaneous swallowing.

There are other factors in normal eating which should be considered. These include good sitting balance and the ability to move the head independently of the trunk, the ability to move the jaw, lips and tongue independently of the head, eye-hand contact and the ability to take food to the mouth. Salivation, chewing and swallowing are stimulated by the palatability of food, which is interpreted through sensations of vision, smell, taste, touch, texture and temperature.

Mechanism of Speech

Speech is an intrinsic part of normal life. It is ultimately related to thought and there should be no differentiation made between these two processes (Luria 1970).

Speech as a means of communication depends upon many senses but particularly upon hearing. Speech is delivered and received with gestures and facial expression. Socially it originated in primitive man as a means of improved communication. So complex is this remarkable ability that physiologically and anatomically it is little understood. Articulation is the mechanism of language the result of which is the spoken word. Articulation involves the structures of the mouth and larynx, but the sound that is uttered is also dependent upon the passage of air.

During speech the regular rhythm of inspiration and expiration is interrupted. Inspiration occurs rapidly at the ends of sentences or at pauses. Speech takes place during the expiratory phase which is prolonged to last from pause to pause. The volume of speech (its degree of softness or loudness) is controlled by altering the pressure of expired air. Speech also requires co-ordination of the movements of the mouth, lips and tongue, and the possibility of making sounds without undue effort. The tongue, lips and teeth act as devices to vary the quality of consonants and vowels.

ORO-FACIAL DYSFUNCTION

Oro-facial dysfunction occurs as a result of lesions in certain cranial nerves (V, VII, IX, X, XII) and their nuclei, and in the cerebral cortex and its connections.

Traumatic injury to the brain stem may injure the cranial nerves or interfere with the swallowing centre in the medulla. Cranial nerve fibres, such as those of the facial nerve, may be damaged along their route causing muscle weakness or paralysis. The higher centres of the brain which control eating and speech may be damaged following head injury or stroke. Intracranial tumours and degenerative diseases such as multiple sclerosis may also cause dysfunction by involving the relevant parts of the nervous system. Lesions involving the basal ganglia, such as idiopathic Parkinson's disease, will cause oro-facial dysfunction.

As a result of trauma to the brain, speech and language problems of any degree of severity can be found, varying from total aphasia with inability to speak and very poor comprehension, to slight difficulty with articulation, occasional failure to comprehend, or a minor difficulty in naming objects and finding words. Reading and writing are written speech and can also be affected. Non-verbal functions of gnosis* (knowledge) and praxis* (action) are necessary components of speech processes. These, together with inner speech, 'the abbreviated schema of speech which precedes the speech act itself' (Luria 1970), can also be affected.

The problems associated with oro-facial dysfunction should not be considered in isolation as they may affect other parts of the body and other functions. The dangerous effects of aspiration of food or saliva can be cited as an example of this, as can the effect of a swallowing difficulty on nutrition. Abnormal tone throughout the body influences oro-facial function, and conversely the desire to speak or the effort required to speak can cause a generalised increase in tone.

Abnormalities of tone such as hypertonus, hypotonus or fluctuating tone affect the ability to open and close the mouth. Poor head control and lack of stability cause difficulty in moving the lips, jaw and tongue independently of the head and in the co-ordinated way necessary for speech and eating. The inability to balance in a sitting position makes eating mechanically difficult as well as socially unacceptable. In certain patients, with, for example, severe spastic quadriplegia following head injury, generalised extension hyperactivity is frequently associated with jaw extension. Generalised flexor hyperactivity is frequently associated with jaw closure. The presence of an asymmetrical tonic neck reflex or persistent head turning will result in an asymmetrical head position, making eye contact difficult, interfering with normal communication, and resulting in the inability to take food to the mouth in an organised manner.

Abnormalities of tone will cause *alterations in facial expression*. These may result in overactivity, which may be seen as fleeting facial grimacing, or in immobility which may be associated with Parkinsonism. Asymmetrical loss of facial expression in the lower part of the face is seen in the early stage following stroke, associated with hypotonus. The effects may be exaggerated by overactivity of facial movement on the unaffected side. All these problems will be associ-

* Glossary

ated with poor lip and jaw closure, difficulty in swallowing and in many cases constant drooling.

Hypotonus of the cheek combined with a relatively immobile tongue allows food to collect between the cheek and gum, and prevents it from being placed between the teeth for chewing, and from being collected into a bolus for swallowing.

Lack of facial expression or inappropriate expression, plus the inability to react with gestures and therefore express emotions, needs and fears, may result in a lack of stimulation from other people which is necessary for the re-establishment of non-verbal as well as verbal communication. Unfortunately an unexpressive, drooling face may give the appearance of disorientation or slowness of intellect when neither exist.

Sensations of taste, smell, touch, texture, pressure and temperature have all been described as necessary for eating, for stimulation of saliva production to moisten the food, and for stimulation of the swallowing reflex. A person who is deprived of these sensations through specific sensory loss, continued nasogastric tube feeding, or through an extended period of eating pureed food, will be reluctant to try to eat. *Diminished sensitivity* may cause the patient to burn himself or bite his cheek, and will result in inco-ordinated chewing and swallowing. A patient may have difficulty keeping his false teeth in place because of poor sensory feedback. Alternatively, he may demonstrate *hypersensitivity* of the oral area associated with an exaggerated response to tactile stimulation of lips, tongue, cheek or soft palate and an exaggerated gag reflex.

The patient may demonstrate *abnormal reflex activity* such as hyper- or hypoactive gag reflex. A hyperactive gag reflex may cause him to gag whenever anything goes near his mouth. A hypoactive gag reflex is potentially dangerous because of the risk of aspiration, particularly if combined with a depressed cough reflex. Severely brain-damaged patients may show some evidence of released primitive reflexes such as a positive bite reflex which results in the patient biting vertically on anything that goes near the mouth. This makes handling the oral area very difficult and the patient may not be able to tolerate food in his mouth. Hypersensitivity and abnormal reflex activity are sometimes seen following prolonged nasogastric tube feeding.

Lesions of the brain may result in shallow and irregular respirations which cause a *lack of co-ordination between breathing and speech,* and *breathing and swallowing.* This inco-ordination increases the tendency to aspiration of food and saliva, adds to difficulties with articulation and phonation, and may result in either explosive or whispering speech. Patients with hypertonus may demonstrate tense and

327

retracted abdominal muscles with poor expansion of the thorax. This may result in weak vocal tone and a tendency to speak on inspiration.

Problems Associated with Eating

Below is a summary of the particular problems which may interfere with eating and drinking. These are:-

Difficulty swallowing. He may not be able to close his lips because of weak and poorly co-ordinated lip closure; he may not be able to close his jaw; the position of his head may be interfering with his ability to close his mouth; he may have an immobile inactive tongue, in particular inability to elevate the posterior third effectively and inability to elevate the lateral borders.

Hypersensitive mouth.

Abnormal reflex activity.

Diminished sensation.

Poor co-ordination between respiration and swallowing.

The patient and his relatives will be distressed by these problems which are magnified for the patient by fear of choking and the physical discomfort of aspiration. Meal-times may become even more difficult if nursing staff do not realise the importance of the influence of the patient's position on swallowing. For example, the semi-supine position increases the risk of aspiration and it is not normally a position in which we attempt to eat.

It is unfortunate that eating problems in brain-damaged patients are frequently left untreated, with the result that nasogastric tube feeding is instituted or prolonged. This leads to irritation of the mucus membrane, poor nutrition, lack of sensory stimulation to the mouth and oropharynx, lack of stimulus to chew, move the tongue and swallow. The presence of the tube also predisposes to oesophageal reflux (Larsen 1972). Hence a cycle is established in which the untreated oro-facial problems result in emergency measures which in turn perpetuate and in some cases increase the original problems.

Problems Associated with Speech

Emotional lability, or difficulty in controlling emotions resulting in inappropriate outbursts of laughing and crying, is often associated with loss of speech and language. This is very distressing for the patient and for those around him. If he is not helped to control his emotions this lability will interfere considerably with his treatment programme. Other problems may arise including frustration, anxiety, fear of the future, or fear of failure, all of which may lead to depression or anger. The patient may withdraw from contact, or he may pretend to understand and nod encouragingly at everything that is said to him.

Auditory attention span may be short in patients with certain speech problems and concentration in general may also be very poor. It is wise to remember that most brain-damaged patients understand a great deal more than they are capable of expressing verbally, provided there is no dementia or mental retardation.

Although the specific problems of speech disability are the responsibility of the speech pathologist, a brief description of the various forms of speech disability with which the physiotherapist may be confronted in patients with brain damage is outlined below.

Aphasia

Aphasia is a disorder of the use of language which may affect the ability to speak, read, write, calculate or comprehend what is heard. It is a disturbance of those higher functions of the brain by which meanings are expressed or comprehended. The word dysphasia is frequently used synonymously.

Trousseau in 1861 applied the term aphasia to the loss of speech due to a cerebral lesion exclusive of that due to paralysis of the muscles concerned with speech and exclusive of dementia (Nielsen 1965). Broca, in the same period, localised damage to a limited area of the brain which resulted in destruction or damage to the motor aspect of speech, and Wernicke in 1874 applied this idea of localisation to the sensory aspect of speech. Luria (1970) has pointed out that it is naïve to attempt to localise function, and that damage to any part of the cerebral cortex which plays a role in the integration of one or another form of cerebral activity inevitably affects the overall psychophysiological process. Reference to the categorisation of aphasia into sensory (receptive) and motor (expressive) is useful in a discussion of the problems associated with speech but it must be remembered that mixed forms are more common. The term 'global aphasia' is sometimes used to describe the presence of both sensory and motor aphasia.

Sensory or receptive aphasia is the loss of comprehension of what is being said and written. The patient often speaks volubly and may be euphoric. He will be unable to understand that his language is unintelligible to others.

Motor or expressive aphasia is the loss of expression in speech and writing with relative comprehension of language. The motor aphasic person may have retained a few words and the ability to utter spontaneous exclamations, for example, swearing or repeating the same phrase over and over again. Sometimes he will be embarrassed by his own mistakes when attempting to speak, because he knows what he wants to say.

The term *paraphrasia* is used to describe misuse of words. When speech is so jumbled as to be unintelligible, it is called jargon. *Nominal aphasia*, sometimes called amnesic aphasia, involves difficulty in naming objects and remembering words.

Automatic speech is the ability to count or recite something familiar that does not involve thought mechanisms. This type of speech will often return more quickly than propositional speech, and can be confusing for relatives and nursing staff if they do not understand.

Dysarthria

This term describes a disorder of the motor mechanism of articulation. It is usually associated with difficulty swallowing and asymmetrical or distorted facial expression. Speech may be explosive, monotonous, slurred, slow or scanned, and can be further distorted by irregular breathing and poor phonation.

ASSESSMENT OF ORO-FACIAL FUNCTION

Physical assessment of oro-facial function (Fig. 109) in preparation for the development of a treatment programme for a brain-damaged patient must be part of the patient's overall evaluation, which will include assessment of facial expression, sitting balance, ability to move the head independently of the body, hand usage, communication, eye-hand control and general behaviour. Specific assessment of the oral area is essential and consists of digital examination, inside and outside the mouth, of the tone of the lips, tongue and cheek.

The tongue is examined to determine its tone, its response to stimulation, its position in the mouth, its symmetry and its ability to assume different shapes in the mouth. A hypotonic tongue feels soft, looks too big for the mouth and is easily moved. A hypertonic tongue is retracted, feels tense and is difficult to move.

If the bite reflex is present it will be easily elicited by pressure on the teeth. The gag reflex is tested by observation and by walking a finger gently and slowly backward towards the posterior third of the tongue. A patient with a hyperactive gag reflex may gag as soon as the tongue is touched. A patient with a hypoactive gag reflex will have a very high threshold to tactile stimulation. Examination of the gag reflex is often suggested to evaluate oral function but the

ASSESSMENT OF ORO-FACIAL FUNCTION			
FACIAL EXPRESSION & SYMMETRY			
LIP and JAW CLOSURE			
TONGUE (appearance, position)			
SPONTANEOUS SWALLOWING			
SENSITIVITY (of face and mouth)			
CO-ORDINATION of RESPIRATION with SWALLOWING			
ABNORMAL REFLEX ACTIVITY			
GAG REFLEX	Present	Hypoactive	Hyperactive
BITE REFLEX	Present	Absent	
EATING and DRINKING			
Summary of main problems:			

Fig. 109. *An assessment chart.*

response between normal individuals varies so greatly that only asymmetrical responses are of value. For example, although the soft palate may elevate when the gag reflex is elicited, during swallowing it may fail to elevate, causing closure of the nasopharynx to be ineffective.

It is preferable to use a finger to assess tone in the oral region and for intra-oral treatment. It gives a discriminating sensory impression, an accurate 'feeling' of the quality of tone, and the sensation is familiar and acceptable to the patient. A spatula recommended by some therapists has none of these advantages.

The therapist will observe the patient's breathing control and his ability to co-ordinate breathing with speech and swallowing and his lip and jaw closure. Assessment is preceded or accompanied by a discussion with the patient of what he considers to be his difficulties in eating, drinking and speech.

Asymmetry of the face, grimacing or lack of expression will indicate abnormality of tone. Facial expression is noted as the patient speaks, eats and is at rest. The degree of mobility of facial expression is noted, as well as any unnatural mouth postures, drooling, and control over eye closure.

Eating and drinking are difficult to evaluate with accuracy as the functions within the mouth cannot be easily seen. However, the therapist should note how the patient copes with solids and fluids, whether he can chew, whether he can keep his mouth closed and retain the food within it, whether he can co-ordinate breathing with eating, whether he pushes food out of his mouth with his tongue, and, if he wears false teeth, whether he can control them.

If the patient is being fed by nasogastric tube, the therapist should determine the reason for this. It may be the only way he can be fed without danger of aspiration, but on the other hand it may also be due to an oral problem which is easily amenable to treatment.

The evaluation of speech and language problems will be carried out by the speech pathologist and will include assessment of expression, comprehension, inner language, reading and writing skills, ability to cope with numbers, money, date and time. This assessment will include evaluation of sensory and perceptual function. In the dysarthric patient she will observe the function of lips, tongue and soft palate, breathing co-ordination, phonation, articulation, rhythm and intonation. In the aphasic patient she will assess hearing and visual perception, as well as the more specific tests.

Following this evaluation she will then be able to give particular help and guidance to relatives and to all those responsible for the patient's care, to enable them to understand better his problems, and how to communicate with him and provide stimulus. It is important that the patient is referred early to the speech pathologist for evaluation and treatment. He will benefit very much from the reassurance of finding someone who understands and has some insight into his problems, who is prepared to talk about them with him, and who can explain them to his relatives.

TREATMENT OF ORO-FACIAL DYSFUNCTION

A favourable environment and good relationships are basic to communication and to the re-establishment of a normal relaxed routine of eating and drinking. The social aspects of family and friends eating and drinking together must be considered in a treatment programme as well as the details of the mechanisms of these functions.

Positioning
The best position in which to relearn more effective eating is in sitting, the position in which we normally eat. The patient should sit with his weight well forwards at his hips and with his feet on the floor. He may be supported on pillows as in Fig. 72 if he cannot sit alone. This will enable him to gain some control over head position.

Fig. 110. *Stimulation of lip and jaw closure.*

333

Fig. 111. *Gentle shaking to the inside of the cheek. Note the uncontrolled extension of the jaw indicating oral hypersensitivity.*

The head should be flexed slightly at the atlanto-occipital joint in order to facilitate the passage of food or saliva into the oesophagus. It is difficult to swallow with the head extended. Head position can be controlled from the jaw (Fig. 110). If the patient has marked hypertonus the assumption of the sitting position may require preparation (Figs. 71 and 72).

Techniques for specific problems

Poor lip and jaw closure. The jaw is held closed and the perioral area is stimulated firmly in the direction of closure (Fig. 110.). If the patient's lip closure is asymmetrical, stimulation should concentrate on the affected side. If tightness of the cheek is interfering with lip closure, the index finger is placed inside the cheek which is shaken in the direction of closure (Fig. 111). It is important to stimulate lip and jaw closure when required throughout his entire treatment. The patient can also be encouraged to do this himself. If it is difficult

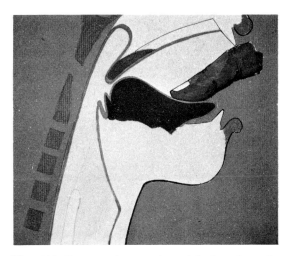

Fig. 112. *Pressure downwards and backward on the anterior third of the tongue.*

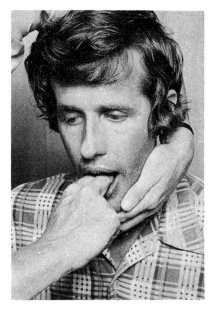

Fig. 113. *Lateral vibration to the tongue.*

335

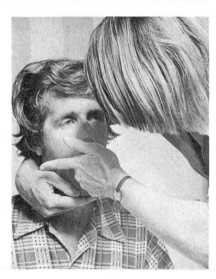

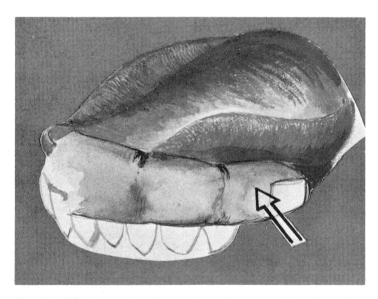

Fig. 114. *Vibration to the inferior surface of the tongue. Note the position of the therapist's arm. It should be in this alignment in order to vibrate at the correct angle (see arrow).*

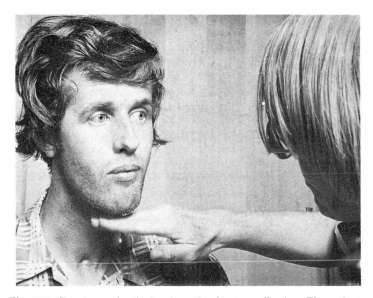

Fig. 115. *Tapping under the jaw is a stimulus to swallowing. The patient must be able to control jaw closure, otherwise he may bite his tongue.*

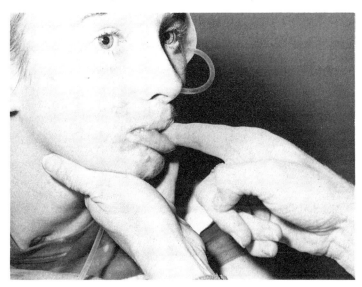

Fig. 116. *Stroking the external surface of the gums. This increases sensory awareness. Firm stroking desensitises a positive bite reflex.*

337

stimulating jaw closure, the patient's sitting position may need altering, for example, his hips may need more flexion although his thoracic spine must remain extended.

Poor tongue movement and swallowing. One of the most important movements of the tongue is the ability to elevate the posterior third in preparation for swallowing. Pressure of the index finger downward and backward on the anterior third of the tongue (Fig. 112) stimulates elevation of the posterior third and closure of the posterior oral cavity. Digital vibration (Mueller 1977) given laterally on the anterior half of the tongue with firm pressure downward (Fig. 113) stimulates contraction of the small muscles of the tongue, causing it to be more mobile and more readily assume the shapes necessary for preparation of the bolus and swallowing. It is also useful if the tongue is too far forward in the mouth.

A third technique to stimulate tongue activity is digital vibration in a diagonal direction with the middle finger under the lateral border of the tongue (Fig. 114). This stimulates elevation of the lateral border, an important part of the sequence of swallowing.

These techniques are repeated several times. The therapist should intersperse digital stimulation with stimulation of lip and jaw closure otherwise the patient will not have a chance to swallow and it is the promotion of an effective swallow that is the therapist's main objective. An added stimulus to swallowing can be given by firm pressure to the base of the tongue and by tapping (Fig. 115) with the back of the hand under the jaw (Mueller 1977).

Diminished sensation. Sensory awareness can be improved by stroking the external surface of the gums (Fig. 116), the inside of the cheek and by vibration to the tongue. These techniques must be done in a stimulating way. Sensory stimulation, by making the patient more aware of his mouth, will stimulate tongue movement and swallowing and will also enable him to keep his false teeth in position.

A hypersensitive mouth. The unpleasant response to touch is diminished by firm pressure commencing in the least sensitive area. The patient's lips are stroked in the direction of closure, with the jaw held closed. When he can tolerate this the therapist places her finger in his mouth and his gums are rubbed firmly, on the outside then on the inside. When it is possible to touch his tongue, digital vibration may have a further desensitising effect. Care should be taken that the patient has the opportunity to swallow from time to time.

Abnormal reflex activity. When the *gag reflex is hyperactive* it is necessary to increase its threshold to stimulation. This is achieved by desensitising the oral area as described above taking care not to

Fig. 117. *Stimulation of the cheek in an upward direction to stimulate facial expression.*

stimulate a gag. When the *gag reflex is hypoactive*, a more normal threshold to stimulation may be gained by the techniques of improving sensory awareness described above. The uvula and soft palate may be stimulated directly by a soft camel-hair brush or a cotton bud with the wool fluffed out. This stimulus is applied briefly and followed by stimulation of lip and jaw closure.

A positive bite reflex is desensitised by firm rubbing of the external surface of the gums. When it is difficult to open the patient's jaw, the bite reflex may be inhibited by firm stroking from the side of the nose to the mouth. Firm pressure over the temporo-mandibular joint may also release the jaw. When the patient is being fed, care is taken to avoid pressure of the spoon downward on the bottom jaw, which would elicit this reflex. Similar care should be taken when the therapist puts her finger into the mouth.

Poor facial expression. To stimulate symmetrical facial expression, the therapist strokes the inactive side of the face near the mouth in an upward direction (Fig. 117). The patient can be encouraged to do this himself. If his unaffected side is overactive, he is encouraged to relax

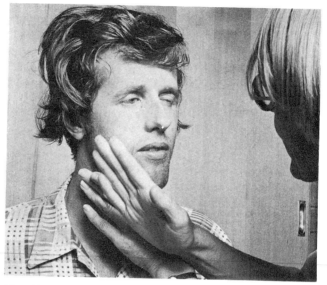

Fig. 118. *Tapping to the cheek to stimulate tone in the facial muscles.*

that side. Tapping to the cheek stimulates the facial muscles (Fig. 118). The stimulation of facial expression is of particular value in the immediate stage following stroke. Whenever the therapist is with the patient she should stimulate him to react and use facial expression to communicate with her, and this will be encouraged if she varies her own expression.

Assisted eating and drinking

Prior to meals the patient's oral function is improved by whichever techniques are appropriate to his specific problems. Food should be given to him in the midline, so he can see it, smell it and therefore anticipate it. The spoonful is placed in his mouth, firm pressure downward and backward on the anterior third of the tongue is *briefly* applied, the spoon is withdrawn *quickly*, the jaw is held closed and lip closure stimulated. His head is kept slightly flexed and he is given time to swallow or stimulated to swallow before he is given the next mouthful. The patient is encouraged to feed himself as soon as possible.

It is important that food is palatable, with a pleasant smell and appearance, and it should be selected both for its texture and for the patient's personal preference. It has already been noted that taste,

340

smell and pressure of food combine to stimulate certain areas of the tongue and oropharynx and therefore swallowing. Consistency and texture of food is very important when it is being used to retrain effective tongue movement and swallowing. Pureed foods are not stimulating to pressure receptors and may be easily aspirated. Bosma (1957) comments that thickened food is usually handled with relative safety. It should preferably be food which does not quickly become sloppy in the mouth. Larsen (1973) describes canned peaches as being of a satisfactory texture to stimulate touch and pressure senses, salivation and easy swallowing. Food is certainly less likely to be aspirated than fluid. Fluid escapes easily into the trachea when swallowing is impaired and it does not stimulate the reflex receptor endings (Larsen 1972). Chewing can be stimulated by holding a strip of lightly cooked meat between the molars (Mueller 1977).

A plastic cup with a curved lip may be the most effective way for the patient to drink. The cup is rested lightly on his lower lip with his head flexed slightly forwards at the atlanto-occipital joint. When a small amount of fluid is in his mouth, jaw and lip closure are encouraged. If he has difficulty sealing his lower lip on the cup this can be stimulated by upward pressure to the lip.

Some therapists suggest sucking on an ice block or chips of ice to improve oral function. This suggestion is not recommended as it is not specific for any particular problem. Furthermore, liquid is more easily aspirated than solids and prolonged sucking on ice will numb the oral area which will interfere with sensory awareness and movement of the tongue.

MANAGEMENT OF SPEECH PROBLEMS

Language and communication are stimulated at all ages through touch, movement, gesture and sound. Stimulating relationships are important for communication. Many authors stress that the recovery of the aphasic or dysarthric patient is aided or hindered by *all* the people with whom he is in contact from the moment he finds himself unable to speak. Their positive attitude to his problems will help him to regain his self-confidence and self-respect. Leche (1974) considers that most patients have a greater potential than is apparent.

Some form of communication must be established immediately. As the physiotherapist will often see the patient before the speech pathologist, she may need to make an assessment of his ability to communicate in order to tailor her speech to his needs.

The therapist should not assume the patient cannot understand and should give him time to respond either verbally or by some other means. It is important to establish a yes/no response. Relatives will need help to understand the particular problems and the importance of providing language stimulation. They will assist also by telling the therapist the name by which he is called, and his interests. Photographs of his family will provide stimulus to conversation.

The therapist tries to create an environment in which the patient can feel able to attempt to speak. She should not raise her voice if he does not appear to understand as this will add to his confusion, and she should avoid having conversations with other members of the staff across his bed without including him. In attempting to communicate with him the therapist can use clues, gestures and association. For example, 'are you thirsty?' may have no meaning for him. However, 'would you like some tea?' may have meaning if the therapist also points to a cup of tea. It will take away his incentive to speak if someone always finishes sentences or answers questions for him. It is important that he is not left in a situation where it is imperative that he be able to answer, for example, in a waiting room where he will be asked his name and for what he is waiting. This kind of experience will add to his frustration and can easily be avoided.

Some brain-damaged patients may revert, in the early stages, to their mother tongue despite their previous fluency in the second language, or they may confuse the two languages. The patient's ability to communicate may vary from day to day and in different situations. It is adversely influenced by tension and anxiety.

As the patient gains more confidence he is encouraged to socialise and communicate with other, non-aphasic, patients who can support and stimulate his speech. With a patient who perseverates on a word or phrase the therapist should not take these perseverations literally but try to find out what he is really trying to say.

It will help the emotionally labile patient if he is reassured that he will gain better control of his emotions as he is more able to co-ordinate his breathing with speech, and when he is better able to control his movements. The patient can be helped to gain control by concentrating on breathing more deeply through his nose. It also helps him if he knows that the therapist is not embarrassed by his tearful outbursts, and can accept them.

To improve breathing control the therapist encourages deep inspiration and sustained relaxed expiration. Expiration can be combined with sound, the patient attempting to vary the sound as he breathes out. Vibration to the thorax and gentle pounding over the spine while the patient breathes out and vocalises gives him the idea of how the sound can be altered. Breathing in and out through the nose can be practised with air held in the mouth. This encourages lip closure and elevation of the posterior one third of the tongue to seal off the posterior oral cavity, and it requires controlled and co-ordinated respiration.

SUMMARY

In this chapter the main aspects of normal oro-facial function which should be understood by the physiotherapist have been outlined. The oro-facial problems which may be seen following brain damage are described in relation to their effect upon eating, drinking and facial expression and suggestions are made for their treatment. The authors emphasise that techniques of treatment must be specific to each patient's particular problems.

References

Ardran, G. M. and Kemp, F. H. (1951) The mechanism of swallowing. *Proc. Roy. Soc. Med.,* **44,** 1038.

Bosma, J. F. (1957) Deglutition: pharyngeal stage. *Physiol. Rev.,* **37,** 3, 275.

Kydd, W. L. and Toda, J. (1962) Tongue pressure exerted on the hard palate during swallowing. *J. Amer. Dent. Ass.,* **65,** 319–330.

Larsen, G. J. (1972) Rehabilitation for dysphagia paralytica. *J. of Speech and Hearing Disorders,* **37,** 187–194.

Larsen, G. J. (1973) Conservative management for incomplete dysphagia paralytica. *Arch. Phys. Med. Rehabil.,* **54,** 4, 180–185.

Leche, P. M. (1974) The speech therapist and hemiplegia. *Physiotherapy,* **60,** 11, 346–349.

Lockhart, R. D., Hamilton, G. F. and Fyfe, F. W. (1959) *Anatomy of the Human Body.* London, Faber.

Luria, A. R. (1970) *Traumatic Aphasia.* Paris, Mouton.

Mueller, H. (1977) Personal Communication

Nielsen, J. M. (1965) *Agnosia, Apraxia, Aphasia, Their Value in Cerebral Localisation.* New York, Hafner.

Further Reading

Bosma, J. F. (1973) *Oral Sensation and Perception.* Illinois, Charles C. Thomas.

Brown, J. W. (1972) *Aphasia, Apraxia and Agnosia.* Illinois, Thomas.

Carr, J. H. (1979) Oral function in infancy. *Aust. J. Physiother.* In press.

Farrar, W. B. (1976) Using electromyographic biofeedback in treating orofacial dyskinesia. *J. Prosthet Dent.*, **35**, 4, 384–387.

Gane, G. (1972) Practical notes for nurses about to nurse patients with dysphasia. *J. Aust. Coll. Speech Therapists*, **22**, 59.

Halpern, H. (1972) *Adult Aphasia*. New York, Bobbs-Merrill.

Jenkins, J. J., Jiménez-Pabón, E., Shaw, R. E. and Sefer, J. W. (1975) *Schuell's Aphasia in Adults*. New York, Harper & Row.

Pannbacker, M. (1972) Publications for families of adult aphasics. A review of the literature. *Rehabil. Lit.*, **33**, 3, 72–79.

Appendix 1

Techniques of Treatment

STIMULATION OF BALANCE AND BODY ORIENTING MECHANISMS

Inability to relate to the effects of gravity is very common following brain-damage and is manifested by difficulty orienting the head and trunk in space, in shifting weight and regaining balance throughout each shift of weight. Even the smallest weight shift requires appropriate postural adjustments. 'A very finely regulated mechanism is in control and the slightest shift is reacted to through the nervous system by reflex postural adjustments; sometimes the motor responses are so fine they can only be detected electromyographically' (Basmajian 1974).

Certain predictable movements of the head, trunk and limbs occur when balance is threatened. These have been described in figures 27–29.

The patient who lacks one or more of these movement components may use certain strategies in an attempt to compensate for his lack of balance. He may use a wide base, externally rotate his legs in sitting, hold himself stiffly, move his feet instead of his trunk, hold his breath, take a step out to the side instead of forwards, put out his

345

hands before he needs. The observant therapist will be able to point out to the patient how these manoeuvres are preventing him from regaining balance and therefore movement.

Methods of stimulation

For balance to improve in a position, the patient must be assisted to assume that position. In other words, for balance to improve in standing, it must be stimulated in standing. The missing components are therefore stimulated with the body parts in the appropriate relationship to each other and to gravity. Man's body axis is vertical, and it is in the vertical position, that is, in sitting and standing, that he most needs the ability to withstand the effects of gravity. Peiper (1963) points out that the quadrupedal animal does not need to develop antigravity reactions in the vertical position because his body is horizontal. This observation runs counter to the suggestion made by some therapists that balance must be retrained in a sequence of positions which includes four point kneeling and kneeling.

Analysis of balance reactions and body alignment in responses to shifts of weight will identify the missing or abnormal components which require specific stimulation. For example, the regaining of balance in a lateral direction requires movement of the head laterally and movement of the trunk laterally, in particular elevation of the pelvis (Fig. 27). Any one or all of these components may be missing and must be stimulated by the therapist (Fig. 119). By triggering off these well learned adjustments the therapist enables the patient to recover a sense of balance and the ability to regain his balance. To be effective, balance must be stimulated with the patient using a normal base of support and not with his feet wide apart.

A technique devised by Bobath and described by Semans (1967), called *alternate tapping*, stimulates balance in antigravity positions. The technique is particularly effective in standing and walk standing (Fig. 120) in patients who lack the ability to make appropriate postural adjustments in order to maintain and regain their balance. Gentle taps are applied alternatively to the upper trunk with the body in normal alignment. The effect should be to displace the patient very slightly off balance in alternate directions which will stimulate the necessary adjustments. It must be stressed that the displacement should be small so as to stimulate only fine adjustments. The taps are given in quick succession at first, then, when effective responses occur, at irregular intervals and more slowly. As the patient gains more control, his stability and balance will be improved.

Stimulation of balance in the erect position appears to have several important effects. It *stimulates the body orienting mechanism* and there-

346

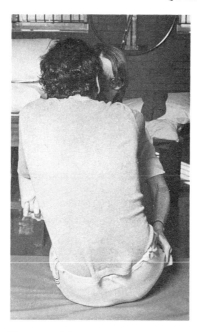

Fig. 119. *The therapist concentrates on stimulation elevation of the pelvis in order to gain lateral trunk flexion, which is lacking when the patient's weight is shifted to the left.*

fore has a positive effect on improving visual contact. The patient *becomes more alert* and is better *able to concentrate*. It allows the patient to move confidently and provides a more normal background for the re-learning of skills. The patient will not have to concentrate on balancing but on the task to be learned. It *has a motivating effect* as he is surprised to see what he can accomplish.

Early stimulation of balance is a strong factor in the *prevention of the development of spasticity* and also has an inhibiting effect on spasticity. As it stimulates symmetrical and reciprocal movement it will have an effect upon perceptual function. The physiological mechanism of the effects of stimulating balance is not entirely understood. Barlow (1961) hypothesises that since nature is concerned with the survival of the species, the structure and function of the synaptic relay centre have been moulded and shaped according to the environmental

347

Fig. 120. *Alternate tapping in walk standing to improve the ability to regain balance. Gentle taps are applied alternately in opposite directions. This patient makes the necessary adjustments which enable her to stand alone for the first time.*

demands placed on the organism and the intent of that organism to survive. He suggests that sensory information and survival value have primacy and are most readily transmitted to action centres such as those involved in righting and equilibrium.

Balance may also be stimulated over a ball (Figs. 121 & 122) or a roller, in sitting or prone. In standing, the ability to move the feet quickly and adjust to unexpected threats to balance is stimulated by ball games and by catching a roller (Fig. 123). Protective support on the hands is stimulated over a roller, against a wall (laterally and backward as well as forward) and against a table (Fig. 106).

348

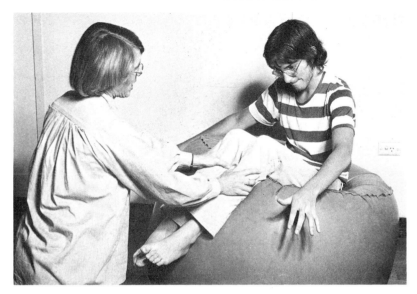

Fig. 121. *Stimulation of balance on a ball.*

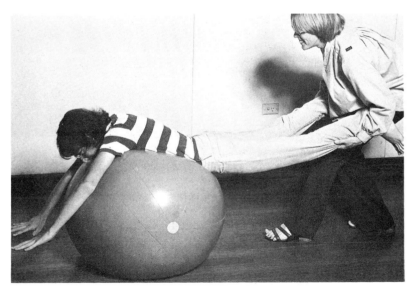

Fig. 122. *Stimulation of balance and protective extension on a ball.*

349

Fig. 123. *Stimulation of automatic responses using a light roller. This can be done from different directions and can be used to encourage the patient to move about quickly.*

References

Barlow, H. B. (1961) Possible principles underlying the transformation of sensory messages. In *Sensory Communication*, edited by W. A. Rosenblith. New York, John Wiley.

Basmajian, J. (1974) *Muscles Alive. Their Functions Revealed by Electromyography.* 3rd edition. Baltimore, Williams and Wilkins.

Peiper, A. (1963) *Cerebral Function in Infancy and Childhood.* London, Pitman.

Semans, S. (1967) The Bobath concept in treatment of neurological disorders. *Am. J. Phys. Med.*, **46**, 1, 732–785.

BIOFEEDBACK

EMG biofeedback is a developing therapeutic technique which offers interesting prospects for the future. It provides a means of monitoring the state of the patient's muscular activity. Although it should not replace the subjective monitoring by the therapist, it does offer three advantages. It is physiologically accurate about the degree of tension in muscles, it gives more immediate feedback about changes in tension and it can be used by the patient on his own.

There is a considerable amount of literature on the use of biofeedback or sensory feedback therapy in patients with *hypertonus*. Brudny, Grynbaum and Korein (1974) report the use of auditory and visual feedback training in nine cases of spasmodic torticollis. They comment that 'external sensory information, reflecting the functional state of involved muscle, can apparently augment or substitute for a defect in the servo-mechanism of patterned voluntary movement and aid in re-establishing the integration of sensory motor interaction'. In these cases, therapy was directed toward decreasing voluntarily the spasm in the involved sternomastoid and in increasing voluntarily the contraction of the contralateral muscle. The same authors in 1975 report on the use of sensory feedback therapy to another group of patients suffering either spasmodic torticollis or dystonia. Swann, Van Wieringen and Fokkema (1974) report on EMG feedback in the inhibition of undesired motor activity in hemiplegic patients.

Miniaturised EMG feedback muscle trainers have been used with encouraging results in the treatment of stroke patients (Basmajian, Kukulka, Narayan and Takebe 1975, Kukulka and Basmajian 1975). There are several reports of biofeedback training for children with cerebral palsy (Halpern *et al.* 1970, Wolpert and Wooldridge 1975).

As in the use of any treatment method, it is important that the therapeutic goals are clearly defined. The main goals, whether decrease of hypertonus during movement of the limb or contraction of poorly functioning muscles, must be clearly explained to the patient. The therapist demonstrates to him, using a normal muscle in order to help him to understand the relationship between muscle contraction and relaxation and their effects on the monitor display. One of the advantages of auditory or visual feedback is that the patient receives immediate information of success or failure. Consequently it has a motivating effect upon his endeavours. Basmajian (1974), in discussing biofeedback, comments that both patient and therapist 'receive immediate objective assessment of the functioning of the muscle; they can then work together on either recruiting or inhibiting the activity'. It has been noted that when biofeedback training has successfully decreased tone in the muscles being monitored, spasticity is also decreased throughout the body. Feedback is gradually withdrawn as the patient gains control over movement, and he is re-evaluated periodically and reinforcement sessions given where necessary.

351

Biofeedback may also be used effectively, in the *transient hypotonus stage* following stroke, to demonstrate to the patient both visually and by sound when there is activity in particular muscles, at a time when that activity is not sufficient to produce other sensory evidence. In the early stages following stroke, muscles may be working at such a low level that no detectable feedback is generated and therefore muscle contraction cannot be appreciated by the patient. The feedback monitor, by giving the patient instant information about the presence of muscle contraction, provides external feedback which gives the patient a frame of reference, making it easier for him to recognise the internal feedback needed to regain control over those muscles. He can then concentrate on attempting that movement, receiving feedback from the apparatus as to the success of his efforts, until he can recognise his own internal feedback information.

In the authors' opinion, EMG biofeedback will provide a useful adjunct to the treatment described in this book in which the emphasis is on helping the patient relearn the specific components of particular motor skills. However, it will only be useful for patients with sufficient intelligence, concentration and communication ability.

References

Basmajian, J. V. (1974) *Muscles Alive: Their Functions Revealed by Electromyography.* 3rd edition. Baltimore, Williams and Wilkins.

Basmajian, J. V., Kukulka, C. G., Narayan, N. C. and Takebe, K. (1975) Biofeeatment of foot-drop after strokes compared with standard rehabilitation techniques. Part 1. *Arch. Phys. Med.,* **56,** 231–236.

Brudny, J., Grynbaum, B. B. and Korein, J. (1974) Spasmodic torticollis: treatment by feedback display of EMG. *Arch. Phys. Med.,* **55,** 403–408.

Halpern, D., Kottke, F. J., Burrill, C., Fiterman, C., Popp, J. and Palmer, S. (1970) Training of control of head posture in children with cerebral palsy. *Develop. Med. Child Neurol.,* **12,** 290–305.

Kukulka, C. G. and Basmajian, J. V. (1975) An assessment of an audiovisual feedback device for use in motor training. *Am. J. Phys. Med.,* **54.**

Swaan, D., Van Wieringin, P. C. W. and Fokkema, S. D. (1974) Auditory electromyographic feedback therapy to inhibit undesired motor activity. *Arch. Phys. Med.,* **55,** 251–254.

Wolpert, R. and Wooldridge, C. P. (1975) The use of electromyography as biofeedback therapy in the management of cerebral palsy: a review and case study. *Physiotherapy Canada,* **27,** 1.

BRUSHING

Brushing is a method of stimulating movement which has been described by Rood (Goff 1969 and Stockmeyer 1967). Rood suggests that it causes an increase in the gamma efferent impulses to the spindle when applied to areas of skin supplied by the anterior primary rami of spinal nerves. Rood recommends that it be applied to dermatomes whose nerve root supply is the same as the muscle to be stimulated. The brushing is done with a battery-operated brush (Fig. 124) which oscillates rapidly, quick light touch with the fingertips, or

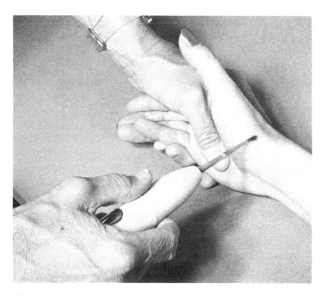

Fig. 124. *Stimulation of abduction of the thumb using a battery-operated brush.*

a paintbrush. Brushing is followed by a delay of 30 seconds before any effect on the muscle spindles is obtained. Maximal effect is said to occur up to 20 or 30 minutes later, and brushing should therefore precede other techniques of stimulation. It can be used around the lips, chin and cheeks to stimulate tone around the mouth.

Rood (Goff 1972) describes precautions in the use of brushing. She stresses that it should not be applied for longer than 30 seconds in one place but it may be repeated once or twice. It may cause a seizure in a patient who is too flaccid to make a motor response.

353

References

Goff, B. (1969) Appropriate afferent stimulation. *Physiotherapy*, **55**, 1, 9.

Goff, B. (1972) The application of recent advances in neurophysiology to Miss M. Rood's concept of neuromuscular facilitation. *Physiotherapy*, **58**, 12, 409–415.

Stockmeyer, S. A. (1967) An interpretation of the approach of Rood to the treatment of neuromuscular dysfunction. *Am. J. Phys. Med.*, **46**, 900–956.

CRYOTHERAPY

Brisk Application of Ice

The use of brisk icing as a stimulating technique has been recommended by Rood (1962) and described by Goff (1969a, 1969b) and Stockmeyer (1967).

Its effects are probably due to two factors. The patient is made more aware of the part stimulated, as the icing adds reinforcement to other methods of eliciting a controlled response. Also, by stimulating the skin, ice is said to have a reflex effect upon the excitability of the stretch receptors. It may put the muscles in a state of readiness.

It is important that brisk icing is combined with other stimulating techniques and with treatment designed to improve function. It has no purpose if unrelated to the relearning of a particular movement.

Method of application

In order to apply brisk icing most effectively, a cube of ice is firmly stroked along the skin for a brief period. The skin should then be dried. Water should not be dripped on other parts of the skin as this distracts the patient from the movement he is practising.

Rood (1962) stresses that brisk icing, to be effective in stimulating the stretch receptors, must be applied over the dermatomes whose nerve supply coincides with the muscle to be stimulated. For example, the dermatomes on the radial side of the back of the forearm correspond to the motor nerve supply to the radial wrist extensors. Icing to the radial extensors can precede or be combined with practice of grasping and releasing, making it easier for the patient to relearn these functions, since wrist extension is an essential component of grasp and release. Ice stimulation of the finger tips on their palmar surface may also improve the patient's ability to grasp and release for fine function and can follow the stimulation of wrist extension.

Goff (1969b) suggests that brisk icing over the vasti muscles (L3 & 4) will stimulate knee stability, and over the anconeus muscle (C7) will stimulate elbow stability. This technique should be accompanied in these examples by movement of the limb in a weight-bearing position.

Care must be exercised in the use of brisk icing as unwanted effects can result from a failure to understand the response to stimulation of certain dermatomes. For example, the dermatomes of the spinal nerves L1 and 2 over the front and side of the trunk do not correspond to the muscles underlying them, and icing of this area will initiate an emptying of the bladder.

There are some contra-indications to icing which have been described by Rood (Goff 1969a, 1969b), which include the sudden lowering of blood pressure if ice is applied behind the ear, and a strong emotional response if it is applied to the sole of the foot or palm of the hand in a person who is emotionally unstable. Brisk icing increases spasticity, especially if given over the sole of the foot or palm of the hand.

Prolonged Application of Ice

Prolonged application of ice will temporarily aid in the reduction of hypertonus. It raises the threshold of the muscle spindle to excitation and it induces changes directly or indirectly in nerve and muscle transmission and in skin receptors. It is applied by means of immersion, wet cold towels or cold packs.

Eldred, Lindsley and Buchwald (1960) state that local muscle cooling reduces the discharge rate for the muscle spindle afferents. It is considered unlikely that cold influences the muscle spindle directly since in many experiments cooling takes place in a period of time which is insufficient for muscle cooling to have taken place (Miglietta 1962).

Hartviksen (1962) considered that the decreased Achilles tendon reflex which occurred following cutaneous cooling of the gastrocnemius was due at first to decreased activity in the cutaneous receptors, followed after 20 to 30 minutes by a decrease in muscle activity as the muscle became cooler. It appears that cooling may inhibit some sensory input from the skin which has an inhibitory effect on motoneuron activity.

There has been much discussion over the the last few years on the effects of cooling upon hypertonus, whether it be spasticity or spasm due to spinal or cerebral lesion, or spasm as a protective response to pain. Many experiments have been described on the reduction of

355

spasticity by the use of cold in spinal cord injured patients (Claus-Walker *et al.* 1974, Lightfoot and Verrier 1976) and in patients with cerebral lesions (Lee and Warren 1974).

There is a subjective evidence in which patients describe relief of pain and hypertonus following cryotherapy (Chambers 1969, Levine, Kabat, Knott and Voss 1954). However, there have been some conflicting reports of effectiveness, with some writers (Urbscheit and Bishop 1970) reporting that alpha motoneurons were facilitated, or that hypertonus increased (Knutsson 1970, Knutsson, Lindblom and Martensson 1973).

Despite all this investigation, the mode of action of ice, which undoubtedly does have a short-lived effect on hypertonus, is still largely unknown. It is possible that further investigations of the effects of cooling may add to the understanding of the relationship between the temperature regulating areas of the brain and the tone regulating areas.

Prolonged icing is a passive procedure for the patient and it is difficult to combine it with stimulation of active movement. Other methods of reducing hypertonus in patients whose spasticity is of central origin are more effective than cryotherapy as they involve patient participation and can be combined more readily with methods of stimulating movement. For these reasons the authors prefer to confine the use of cold to those patients whose spinal cord injury or multiple sclerosis cause spasms which cannot otherwise be relieved.

Method of application
One method of application is the immersion of thick (Turkish) towels into water and flaked ice. They are wrung out to eliminate excess moisture, then applied to the belly of the spastic muscle over its entire length for a sufficient period of time to have the required effect of diminution of hypertonus. The towels probably need to be changed after approximately one to three minutes or before the cold effect wears off. The water temperature as described in the literature on the subject ranges from approximately 7°C (Miglietta 1973) to 18°C (Knott 1969). Too brief an application will result in an increase in hypertonus (Eldred and Hagbarth 1957). Boynton, Garramone and Buca (1959) describe the use of a cool (26·7°C) Hubbard tank for the treatment of multiple sclerosis patients, which resulted in an improvement in co-ordination and walking ability. Knott (1969) also describes immersion in cold water for approximately four minutes followed by a brisk rubbing dry to prevent chilling.

Certain contra-indications to the administration of cold have been described, and these are the presence of Raynaud's disease, cold allergy (Mead and Knott 1966), post-sympathectomy and causalgia (Knutsson 1970). Some patients have an aversion to this form of treatment and would probably gain little from it.

References

Boynton, B. L., Garramone, P. M. and Buca, J. T. (1959) Observations of the effects of cool baths for patients with multiple sclerosis. *Phys. Ther. Rev.* **39,** 297–299.

Chambers, R. (1969) Clinical uses of cryotherapy. *Phys. Ther.,* **49,** 3.

Claus-Walker, J., Halstead, L S., Carter, R. E., Campos, R. J., Spencer, W. A., Canzoneri, J. (1974) Physiological responses to cold stress in healthy subjects and in subjects with cervical cord injuries. *Arch. Phys. Med. Rehabil.,* **55,** 485.

Eldred, E. and Hagbarth, K. E. (1957) Facilitation and inhibition of gamma efferents by stimulation of certain skin areas. *J. Neurophysiol.,* **77,** 59–67.

Eldred, E., Lindsley, D. F. and Buchwald, J. S. (1960) The effect of cooling on mammalian muscle spindles. *Exp. Neurol.,* **2,** 144–157.

Goff, B. (1969a) Appropriate afferent stimulation. *Physiotherapy,* **55,** 1, 9.

Goff, B. (1969b) Excitatory cold. *Physiotherapy,* **55,** 11, 467.

Hartviksen, K. (1962) Ice therapy in spasticity. *Acta Neurol. Scand.* Suppl. 3, **38,** 79–84.

Knott, M. (1969) Some suggestions for reducing spasticity in neurological conditions. *J. Swed. Assoc. P.T.,* **27,** 3, 7–8.

Knutsson, E. (1970) Topical cryotherapy in spasticity. *Scand. J. Rehab. Med.,* **2,** 159–163.

Knutsson, E., Lindblom, U. and Martensson, A. (1973) Differences in effects in gamma and alpha spasticity induced by the GABA derivative Baclofen (Lioresal). *Brain,* **96,** 29–46.

Lee, J. M. and Warren, M. P. (1974) Ice, relaxation and exercise in reduction of muscle spasticity. *Physiotherapy,* **60,** 10, 296–302.

Levine, J. C., Kabat, H., Knott, M. and Voss, D. E. (1954) Relaxation of spasticity by physiological techniques. *Arch. Phys. Med.,* **35,** 214–223.

Lightfoot, E. and Verrier, M. (1976) Neurophysiological effects of prolonged cooling of the calf in patients with complete spinal cord transection. *Physiotherapy,* **62,** 4.

Mead, S. and Knott, M. (1966) Topical cryotherapy. Use for relief of pain and spasticity. *Calif. Med.,* 105–179.

Migletta, O. (1962) Evaluation of cold in spasticity. *Amer. J. Phys. Med.,* **41,** 148–151.

Migletta, O. (1973) Action of cold on spasticity. *Am. J. Phys. Med.*, **52**, 4, 198–205.

Rood, M. (1962) The use of sensory receptors to activate, facilitate, and inhibit motor response, autonomic and somatic, in developmental sequence. In *Study Course V1. Approaches to the Treatment of Patients with Neuromuscular Dysfunction*, edited by C. Sattely. Dubuque, Iowa, Brown & Co.

Stockmeyer, S. A. (1967) An interpretation of the approach of Rood to the treatment of neuromuscular dysfunction. *Am. J. Phys. Med.*, **46**, 900–956.

Urbscheit, N. and Bishop, B. (1970) Effects of cooling on the ankle jerk and H response. *Phys. Ther.*, **50**, 1041.

STIMULATION OF HAND FUNCTION

In the rehabilitation of hand function, 'hand exercises' are inappropriate to benefit either the severely handicapped or the relatively mildly handicapped brain-damaged person.

This latter patient's main problems in manipulation, as well as arising from poor fine muscular control, may stem from disabilities which are so minor in comparison with those the therapist usually sees that the patient may find himself discharged before he has reached his potential recovery. Assessment of function is difficult at this stage, partly because of difficulty in understanding the complexities of normal hand function, and partly because there is a tendency to concentrate treatment on those patients whose disabilities are more obvious. This relative neglect of the mildly handicapped is unfortunate. These patients, with appropriate treatment, are capable of returning to a normal life.

Example: A man with mild residual hemiplegia demonstrated good hand function, but his poor appreciation of the compressibility of objects made him clumsy when he picked them up between thumb and forefinger. This interfered with his ability to write which he felt was his major residual problem. On assessment, he demonstrated an inability to control the position of his thumb at the carpo-metacarpal joint when the thumb was abducted in different positions (Fig. 125), and he had slightly diminished sensibility over the palmar surfaces of thumb and index fingers.

Treatment consisted of direct stimulation to the short abductor of the thumb with the wrist in different positions of flexion and extension, using a small vibrator, plus small movements of the thumb around the abducted position (Fig. 126). It is important in this situation that the patient practises only those specific parts of a

Fig. 125. *Assessment of hand function. Inability to control the position of the carpo-metacarpal joint in abduction which interferes with pincer grasp.*

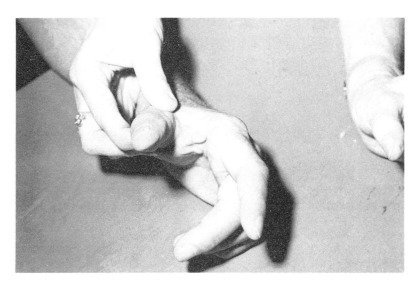

Fig. 126. *The therapist demonstrates the movement and encourages the patient to concentrate on the fine muscular control required.*

359

movement which he finds difficult to control. He should not practise what he can already do. With this patient, the therapist found that only at one particular point of abduction did he lack control, and so she encouraged him to practise fine variations of this position. This approach to hand function requires from the therapist a very specific assessment and an explanation to the patient of exactly what he must relearn.

The palmar surface of his thumb and fingertips was stimulated by brushing and vibration, and the patient practised picking up small objects of different textures, shapes and densities with his vision obstructed, naming them as he picked them up. Objects were placed in sand or in soapy water to give different sensory experiences. He practised colouring small spaces with thick crayon and paintbrush so the movement required had to be subtly controlled, and drew pictures with a pen. He reported more awareness of his hand, particularly on the radial side, his writing became less laboured and steadier, and his clumsiness diminished.

Hand function in the severely handicapped person should also not be neglected. Even if he has no functional movement of his hand, experience of weight-bearing through it with his arm in different positions, develops his sensory awareness and prevents contracture of the wrist and finger flexors which can be a great handicap to eventual recovery of some prehensive ability. The first functions to

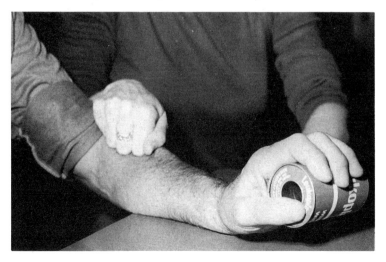

Fig. 127. *Wrist extension is stimulated with the patient holding different sized objects.*

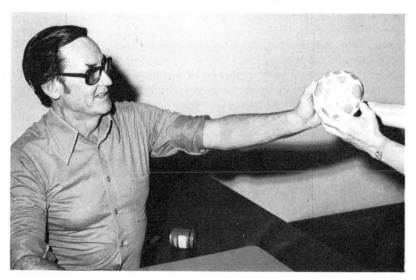

Fig. 128. *Practice of hand function away from the body.*

Fig. 129. *This hemiplegic man practises holding an object while he moves his arms. Note the bimanual nature of the task.*

361

concentrate on are wrist extension and radial deviation with the patient holding objects of different sizes (Fig. 127), grasp and release of objects with the wrist in extension, and forward abduction of the carpo-metacarpal joint. Direct stimulation using ice, vibration, light tapping or pressure over particular muscle groups may be used to help the patient develop awareness of the movement required.

Treatment should consist of stimulation and practice of hand function away from the body (Fig. 128) as well as close to it. The ability to hold an object while the arm moves about (Fig. 129 & 130), to grasp and release with the arm in different positions, and to grasp appropriately objects of different degrees of compressibility. Mental practice of hand functions and biofeedback may help the patient who can concentrate sufficiently.

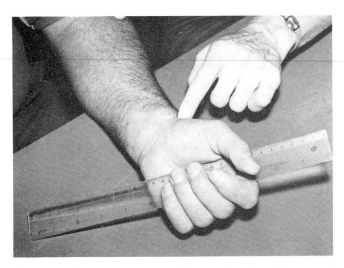

Fig. 130. *This patient practises holding an object through a range of supination and pronation. This also requires him to control his elbow in various degrees of flexion.*

PLACING AND HOLDING

This method of stimulation (Bobath and Bobath 1972) is useful both for the assessment of tone and for the stimulation of control of a limb (Fig. 131). It is particularly effective when applied to the upper limb in a patient whose inability to control a movement is combined with hypotonus.

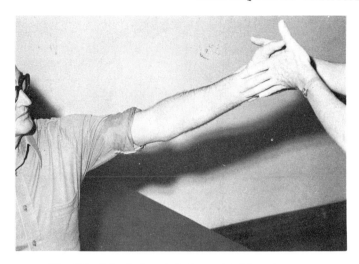

Fig. 131. *Stimulation of placing and holding the arm.*

The therapist moves the limb in the direction in which she wants movement, or to the position which she requires the patient to hold. When she feels the patient has control she gradually takes her hand away, although she keeps close enough to be able to guide the limb if the patient is having difficulty maintaining the position. Placing and holding the limb may be used in combination with tapping, in which case the limb is tapped to the point where the patient begins to gain control, or with approximation, the patient attempting to hold the limb steady while the therapist approximates through the length of the limb. Even an apparently very hypotonic patient may be able to maintain a position with his arm and move it in a small range. This technique is usually most effective with the arm in elevation or at an angle of 90° to the body in supine. It is also useful in demonstrating to the patient that he has some control over his apparently useless arm.

To illustrate the use of placing and holding of the lower limb, we will take the same example as given under *Pounding and Tapping*. If the patient in taking a step is unable to flex his knee with the hip extended and maintain the flexion while he takes his leg forward, this particular component of walking may be stimulated in prone by heel pounding and tapping combined with placing and holding of the limb (Fig. 134). The patient gains control over his knee position through the different parts of the range required for taking a step forwards and during both concentric and eccentric movement. These

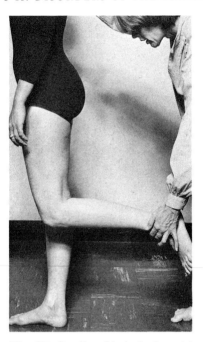

Fig. 132. *Practice of knee flexion with the hip extended prior to taking a step forwards. The therapist controls the patient's balance at the opposite shoulder. This may follow pounding the heel in prone.*

techniques should be followed immediately by practice of taking a step forwards and the therapist can reinforce the movement required with the patient in the standing position (Fig. 132).

Reference

Bobath, B. and Bobath, K. (1972) Diagnosis and assessment of cerebral palsy, in *Physical Therapy Services for the Developmentally Disabled*, edited by P. H. Pearson and C. E. Williams. Springfield, Thomson.

POUNDING AND TAPPING

These terms (Semans 1967) describe two methods of giving sensory

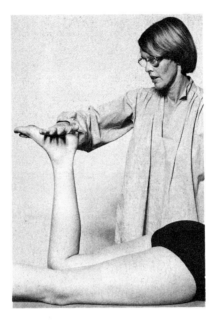

Fig. 133. *Pounding the heel to stimulate knee flexion with the hip in extension.*

stimulation to increase tone and stimulate movement. They are particularly useful in patients whose difficulty initiating or controlling movement is combined with hypotonus.

Pounding the heel with the patient prone and with his knee flexed to a right-angle will stimulate knee flexion and foot dorsiflexion (Fig. 133). The patient is asked to try to keep his knee bent while his hip remains in the extended position. This is an important component of walking. As the patient gains control the therapist encourages him to maintain this control during movement. He is asked to try to straighten his knee a little, to hold it in different parts of the range and to reverse the movement. The therapist stimulates his ability to hold at certain points by pounding the heel. Tapping to the dorsum of the foot will have a similar effect. If the leg tends to fall into internal or external rotation brisk tapping to the lower leg towards the vertical position will help the patient regain control (Fig. 134).

If the patient has some degree of extensor hypertonus in the lower limb, the technique must be modified. The therapist pounds the heel with the knee in at least 90° of flexion making sure that the hip is

365

Fig. 134. *Tapping to the lower leg towards the vertical position.*

extended. Only gradually does she encourage the patient to move his knee into a more extended position.

Pounding, as described in the example above, has an interesting effect when performed on a normal subject. The subject is asked to stand up and walk after a suitable period of stimulation. He usually reports an augmented awareness of the stimulated leg, and its position in space. As he takes a step he is observed to bend his knee more on the stimulated side compared with the other.

Tapping may be applied to the head very gently to stimulate appropriate head movements and to give the patient an awareness of where his head should be in space. This can be done with the patient in any position in which he lacks head control. It is particularly useful in the early treatment of head-injured and stroke patients who lack head and trunk righting. Tapping is applied with the finger tips in the direction in which movement is required.

Light tapping can also be applied by the finger tips over a particular muscle group which is to be stimulated, for example, over the wrist extensors to stimulate the maintenance of wrist extension during activities to improve hand function (Fig. 127).

The reason for the effectiveness of these techniques is uncertain. It is probably a combination of factors, with the pressure and tactile receptors, stretch receptors and joint receptors all involved in the stimulation effect.

Reference

Semans, S. (1967) The Bobath concept in treatment of neurological disorders. *Am. J. Phys. Med.*, **46**, 1, 732–785.

REFLEX INHIBITING MOVEMENT PATTERNS

These are movements which have been found to have an effect upon hypertonus, particularly spasticity following cerebral lesions (Bobath 1970). They are movements which alter tone by altering the abnormal postures and movements seen as a result of loss of central control over brain stem reflex activity.

Sherrington in 1947 described how a change in body position can result in a changed reflex response. There have been several attempts to explain the effectiveness of these movements. Hagbarth and Eklund (1969) suggest that the gradual decrease in spasticity which occurs as the patient adjusts to the more normal alignment of his body may depend on a stretch-induced, tonic, autogenic inhibition from Golgi and secondary spindle endings, which, at a certain degree of muscle stretch, tend to take over from the primary spindle endings. They go on to say that according to the law of reciprocal innervation, this change of reflex dominance 'results in facilitation of the antagonists to the spastic muscle groups which helps to unlock the abnormal postural set, therefore improving the patient's ability to move'.

The important relationship between inhibition and movement is pointed out by Semans (1967), who suggests that 'rerouting of nerve impulses is facilitated by stimulation at the first possible moment of either an automatic or a voluntary pattern of movement which had previously been inhibited by abnormal tonic patterns'. She points out the importance of combining stimulation of balance and protective responses with reflex inhibiting movements, both in inhibiting hypertonus and in stimulating an increase in tone.

Reflex inhibiting movement patterns represent partial reversals of the patient's initial abnormal patterns of spasticity. Inhibition of spasticity seems to be most effective when these movements are

367

concentrated on proximal parts of the body. The position of the head is important because head movement is an important component in most movements and because of the influence of the tonic neck reflexes. The total body position is important because of the influence of the tonic labyrinthine reflex. In other words, in a patient with an asymmetrical tonic neck reflex, maintenance of a face forward, symmetrical head position will inhibit the effect of the reflex and allow the patient to move in a more symmetrical manner. In a patient with evidence of a tonic labyrinthine reflex, inhibition of this reflex by avoiding at first the prone and supine positions, will also allow more effective attempts at movement.

Originally Bobath (1955) called these movement patterns 'postures', but as they were misinterpreted as passive positioning, the term was changed to 'movement patterns' in order to stress that these patterns are, in effect, movements. Nevertheless, they are often misunderstood. Kottke (1975), for example, describes them as 'techniques for stretching procedures', and goes on to say that Bobath points out 'that prolonged stretching may be necessary to obtain complete relaxation'. Bobath (1967), however, has insisted that complete relaxation is *not* required because the therapeutic goal is function.

This method of gaining movement is effective, particularly in the early stages of hypertonus before the stereotyped patterns of spasticity become established. Combined with balance stimulation and practice of normal movements it is effective in preventing the progressive increase in spasticity which otherwise occurs following stroke or head injury. However, although this technique is relatively simple to perform, it requires from the therapist a sensitivity of handling and an ability to understand and evaluate movement. With poor handling, reflex inhibiting movement patterns degenerate into painful, ineffective, passive stretching, or passive posturing of the patient, which does not make movement any easier for him, and which will probably cause an increase in spasticity.

It is possible that reflex inhibiting patterns combined with the early stimulation of automatic reactions and guidance in the performance of normal movements is effective because the mature brain is pre-programmed in regard to the way in which movement is performed. By stimulating the patient in this way, particularly by concentrating on body alignment, the therapist triggers off the programme most appropriate to the function to be regained.

Below is a list of reflex inhibiting movement patterns which have been related to certain problems. These are intended as examples only. They would have to be modified for particular patients depending on the distribution and degree of hypertonus. Although they will often involve the trunk, head and limbs, sometimes inhibition need only be directed to one part of a limb. However, inhibition applied proximally to the trunk, pelvis and shoulder girdle will usually inhibit hypertonus throughout the body.

The effective use of these techniques requires that the therapist knows what she is aiming for, how hypertonus interferes with this functional goal and appreciates how essential it is to gain movement. The inhibitory effect of rotation, both of the trunk and the limbs, needs to be stressed, as it is an important part of these movement patterns.

For example, in sitting, if the leg is internally rotated it is difficult for the spastic patient to transfer weight on to it in order to stand up. Some external rotation of the leg allows this movement to occur. Trunk rotation inhibits both flexor and extensor spasticity when it is incorporated into a functional movement (Fig. 72).

As we have seen, hypertonus is always associated with asymmetry because it causes malalignment of the body parts in their relationships with each other. On the whole, inhibition is directed towards restoring normal alignment of the body and therefore symmetry. Sometimes such restoration of alignment alone is sufficent to gain inhibition. Conversely, no inhibition will be effective unless it involves more normal alignment of the head, trunk and limbs.

There are a few key areas at which alignment can be most effectively adjusted. The shoulder and the pelvis are two of these. Elevation of a depressed shoulder inhibits hypertonus and stimulates weight transference and more normal weight-bearing through that side. An important factor in more normal weight-bearing alignment in standing is the extended position of the hip which brings the body weight into correct alignment over the foot. This enables the patient to gain control over his knee, an important area of instability in many patients.

Movement with rotation and with the body in more normal alignment is probably the most important element in this form of inhibition. The patient is not held in any position for a period of time but is moved, if necessary passively by the therapist, around the point where control is required, and stimulated in such a way that he must respond by moving or by making small adjustments. As soon as possible the patient performs functional movement with only minimal guidance from the therapist. In other words, the therapist gradually decreases her amount of handling as the patient controls his own movement. Local stimulating techniques are used to stimulate control of a particular joint.

There are certain basic reflex inhibiting movement patterns but

369

these will always need modification and variation. The patterns listed below would never be performed like this, but would be incorporated into particular movements as described in the five examples of treatment which follow.

For the spastic flexor synergy of the upper limb
Elevation and protraction of the shoulder girdle, abduction and external rotation of the shoulder, extension of the elbow, wrist and fingers, supination of the forearm, abduction of the thumb.

For the spastic extensor synergy of the lower limb
External rotation, abduction and extension of the hip, dorsiflexion and eversion of the foot and extension of the toes.

The following examples illustrate how these reflex inhibiting movement patterns may be applied in the presence of certain problems. The reader should note that inhibition in each case is

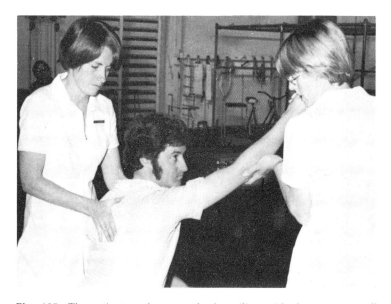

Fig. 135. *The patient reaches towards the ceiling with the arm externally rotated, the shoulder elevated and protracted. The second therapist is holding the thorax to enable him to feel how to isolate the movement. She gradually reduces her control. In this situation a relative or the occupational therapist may work with the physiotherapist.*

370

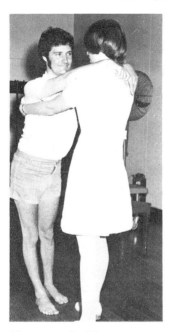

Fig. 136. *Inability to bear weight in normal alignment because of extensor spasticity.*

gained by movement, passive initially if necessary, more automatic and goal-directed as soon as possible. There is no advantage to the patient if his hypertonus is decreased without a resultant increase in ease and effectiveness of movement.

Problem Inability to balance in sitting because of extensor spasticity preventing weight transference forwards at the hips (Fig. 71).

Treatment Trunk rotation with arms elevated and externally rotated, legs abducted and externally rotated with feet flat on the floor (Fig. 72). Weight transference forwards and backward at the hips, extension of the thoracic spine and head righting. Progress to stimulating shifting of weight sideways and to stimulating balance reactions.

Problem Inability to bear weight through the arm because of flexor spasticity, particularly of elbow, wrist and fingers.

Treatment In sitting, elevation of the shoulder girdle, external rotation and abduction of the arm, extension of the elbow and wrist, abduction of the thumb, extension and rotation of the trunk. Patient

371

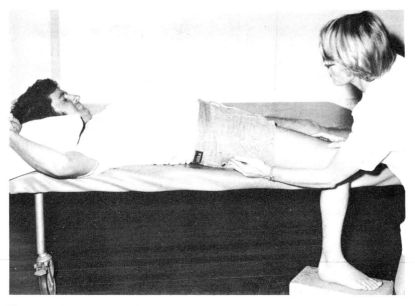

Fig. 137. *Stimulation of more normal extension of the hip. The patient's toes and foot may need to be held in dorsiflexion to inhibit the extensor spasticity.*

attempts to reach towards the ceiling (Fig. 135). Progress to weight-bearing through the extended arm, rotation of the trunk to reach out with the other arm (Fig. 86).

Problem Inability to bear weight in standing because of extensor spasticity (Fig. 136).

Treatment Lying supine with the hip extended and slightly externally rotated, knee flexed over the side of the bed, foot and toes dorsiflexed, trunk and upper limbs symmetrical. Patient extends the hip (Fig. 137) by gently pushing the heel down to the floor. The foot is kept in the dorsiflexed position and the knee is flexed at approximately a right angle. Progress to weight-bearing in standing with the pelvis over the leg in normal alignment, to weight transference sideways and to stepping forwards with the other leg (Fig. 138). Dorsiflexion of the toes with the leg slightly externally rotated is often sufficient to continue the inhibitory effect in standing.

Problem Difficulty transferring weight in standing because of extensor spasticity and poor alignment of head, trunk and limbs.

Treatment Elevation of the shoulder on the spastic side, pelvis forward over weight-bearing leg, that is, hip extended, external

372

Fig. 138. *The patient is now able to bear weight in normal alignment and practises stepping forwards and backwards with his other leg.*

rotation of the leg, dorsiflexion of the toes (Fig. 139). Weight transference sideways on to this leg. Progress to stepping sideways then to facilitated walking.

Problem Difficulty taking a step forwards because of retracted pelvis and shoulder on the right side.

Treatment Lying on the left side, right leg externally rotated and in some abduction, foot dorsiflexed, right arm protracted, small pillow under the waist. Forward rotation of the right side of the pelvis, with extension of the right hip (Fig. 140). Progress to transferring weight backward and forwards in standing in normal alignment, and then to walking. The therapist guides the movement and maintains inhibition by transferring weight on to the heel with the leg externally rotated and foot dorsiflexed. The shoulder may need to be elevated to maintain inhibition of trunk spasticity.

373

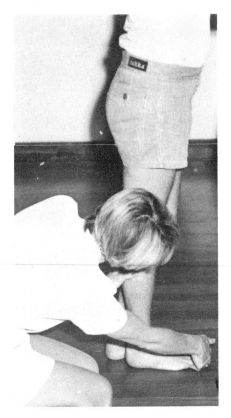

Fig. 139. *Dorsiflexion of the toes and normal alignment of the limb and trunk allows weight shift in standing. The patient is now able to take a step with the left leg.*

References

Bobath, B. (1955) The treatment of motor disorders of pyramidal and extra-pyramidal origin by reflex inhibition and facilitation of movements. *Physiotherapy*, **61**, 146–153.

Bobath, B. (1967) Personal communication.

Bobath, B. (1970) *Adult Hemiplegia: Evaluation and Treatment.* London, Heinemann.

Hagbarth, K. E. and Eklund, G. (1969) The muscle vibrator – a useful

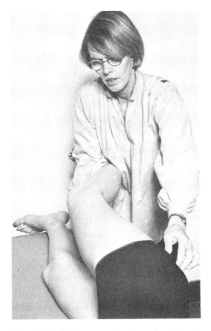

Fig. 140. *Hip extension is gained by forward movement of the pelvis. Note the leg is supported so as to prevent adduction and internal rotation. The therapist may need to keep the foot dorsiflexed.*

tool in neurological therapeutic work. *Scand. J. Rehab. Med.*, **1**, 26–34.

Kottke, F. J. (1975) Neurophysiologic therapy for stroke. In *Stroke and its Rehabilitation*, edited by S. Licht. New Haven, Licht.

Semans, S. (1967) The Bobath concept in treatment of neurological disorders. *Am. J. Phys. Med.*, **46**, 1, 732–785.

Sherrington, C. S. (1947) *The Integrative Action of the Nervous System.* 2nd Edition. New Haven, Yale University Press.

TREATMENT OF SENSORY DISORDERS

If we consider the sensory disabilities which may interfere with function, we must include tactile disorders, tactile aversion, astereognosis, and inability to discriminate two points touched simultaneously, proprioceptive disorders including difficulty perceiving

375

the sensation of movement and position of a limb or part of a limb in space, disorders of motor planning (apraxia or dyspraxia) and disorders of body image or body schema.

Theoretically therefore, sensory disabilities could be said to fall into one of two categories, those which result from failure of sensory information to reach the brain and those which result from a failure of the brain to interpret correctly the information received and convert it to effective motor function. In practice, such a distinction is sometimes difficult to make in the brain-damaged patient.

Treatment to improve motor function as outlined in this book will affect the sensory system as well. For example, treatment which emphasises body parts and their relationships will stimulate body awareness and prevent the secondary development of agnosia. However, it is necessary to consider treatment which is specifically for certain sensory disorders.

Proprioceptive sensation is stimulated by many treatment techniques described in this book. In the patient who has difficulty recognising the position of a limb in space, for example, the therapist, as well as stimulating tactile and proprioceptive receptors, reinforces these sensations in several ways. She encourages the patient to concentrate on the feeling of where his limb is, varies tactile stimuli to increase his awareness of having moved, questions him about the position of his limb, and encourages the use of visual control. Always she feeds back to him immediate information about his accuracy.

Poor *tactile discrimination*, particularly with regard to the hand, is seen at different levels of severity. Some patients, for example those with a relatively mild residual hemiplegia following stroke, find the main handicap to more skilled hand function is poor tactile discrimination. Treatment to improve hand function should therefore include activities which will stimulate stereognosis and two point discrimination, as well as direct tactile stimulation techniques using ice, brushing or vibration to increase sensory awareness wherever it is diminished, and no matter how slightly. Fox (1964) described improved tactile stimulation in patients with hemiplegia through the use of touch pressure stimuli. Tests for stereognosis and two point discrimination, which have been described on page 115, can be adapted into activities which will enable the patient to practise these skills and improve them. As mentioned before, it is important that the patient knows when he is right in his recognition of the object and when he is wrong. Abercrombie (1968) reports improvement of two point discrimination after a few hours of training. Inglis, Sproule, Leicht, Donald and Campbell (1976) describe improvement in touch sensation, two point discrimination and possible movement sense following EMG biofeedback.

376

Tactile aversion is a relatively common problem in mentally retarded children, in some cerebral palsied children and in some with minimal cerebral dysfunction. It may also be present in brain-damaged adults, particularly those who have suffered a recent head injury, although it is also sometimes seen following stroke. Ayres (1964) describes what she calls 'tactile defensiveness', as consisting of 'feelings of discomfort and a desire to escape the situation when certain types of tactile stimuli are experienced'. Some patients respond aversively to a light touch of the therapist's hand, others to pressure exerted by the therapist to the limb. The patient who pulls away from the therapist, avoiding touch with an expression of distaste on his face, is probably demonstrating this reaction. He may express his dislike of treatment, and, in certain circumstances, tactile stimulation may cause rage or hyperactive behaviour. Similarly, the patient who does not want to put his foot to the floor may be demonstrating the same reaction.

Desensitising treatment involves conditioning the patient to accept stimulation to the area involved by introducing stimuli which are acceptable, gradually changing them and moving toward the less well accepted stimuli. Stimulation will also start away from the most sensitive area and gradually move toward it.

In many cases, desensitisation can be commenced with a vibrator, which is usually very well tolerated. Rubbing of the skin firmly with a thick rough towel helps the patient to become accustomed to tactile stimulation. Following a period of desensitisation, he should be able to tolerate increased handling and weight-bearing, and treatment to stimulate movement can be commenced.

Poor *motor planning or apraxia* is characterised by clumsiness and hesitancy in movement and perseveration on particular movements. Some severely affected patients may have an almost complete loss of the ability to plan movements, and are able to act only at a very automatic level. For example, a patient may be unable to roll over when asked, but will roll over quite normally in order to get out of bed.

Ayres (1966) emphasises the importance of tactile and proprioceptive stimulation followed by purposeful skilled motor tasks which require planning, in the treatment of patients who have difficulty in planning and carrying out movements. Tactile and proprioceptive stimulation and movement will help the apraxic patient re-establish his body image and this will help him recover the ability to motor plan. In these patients movement should begin with motor activities which involve balance reactions and progress as the patient improves to actions which require finer skills.

Patients with perceptuo-motor dysfunction benefit from treatment which helps them to sort out their relationship with the environment, particularly spatial relationships and relationships with gravity. Hence, experience of movement is essential, and passive static experience should be avoided.

We must stress at this point that although it is necessary with certain patients to isolate and treat specific areas of sensory dysfunction, all patients with lesions of the brain have some degree of sensory disability. This may be a local diminution of sensory receptivity, or abnormal feedback from a spastic limb or from a generalised rigidity which makes all movement stiff and awkward. In the early stages following acute brain injury, many patients have perceptuo-motor dysfunction, which may include various degrees of apraxia and agnosia.

All treatment must therefore have as goals the improvement of awareness of body parts and of various sensory experiences, the stimulation of more normal balance reactions, of symmetrical and reciprocal movement and of functional motor skills. This will give the patient the experiences he needs in order to re-establish sensory integrative function and therefore develop more effective movement.

References

Abercrombie, M. L. J. (1968) Some notes on spatial disability: movement, intelligence quotient and attentiveness. *Develop. Med. Child Neurol.*, **10,** 206–213.

Ayres, A. J. (1964) Tactile functions: their relation to hyperactive and perceptual behaviour. *Am. J. Occup. Ther.*, **18,** 19.

Ayres, A. J. (1966) Interrelation of perception, function and treatment. *J. Amer. P.T. Assoc.*, **46,** 741–744.

Fox, J. V. D. (1964) Cutaneous stimulation effects on selected tests of perception. *Am. J. Occup. Ther.*, **18,** 53–55.

Inglis, J., Sproule, M., Leicht, M., Donald, M. W. and Campbell, D. (1976) Electromyographic biofeedback treatment of residual neuromuscular disabilities after cerebrovascular accident. *Physiotherapy Canada*, **28,** 5, 260–264.

VIBRATION

High frequency vibration applied mechanically over a skeletal muscle (Fig. 141) induces a reflex contraction of the muscle vibrated and simultaneous relaxation of its antagonist. It appears to restore a more

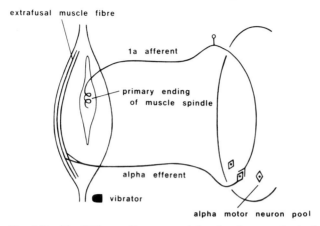

extrafusal muscle fibre

1a afferent

primary ending
of muscle spindle

alpha efferent

vibrator

alpha motor neuron pool

Fig. 141. *The TVR uses the same peripheral pathway and spinal neural components as the monosynaptic phasic reflex. Not shown in this diagram is the essential control over the TVR exercised by higher brain mechanisms.*

normal balance between the tonic stretch reflexes of opposing muscle groups. Eklund and Hagbarth (1966) called this reflex response the tonic vibration reflex (TVR), and pointed out that it can be demonstrated in all skeletal muscles in healthy adults. In 1969, they wrote 'Vibratory muscle stimulation in man imitates the effect of fusimotor activation of the primary spindle . . . a type of activation which does not normally occur unless the subject actively contracts the muscle'.

The development over recent years of the technique of muscle vibration indicates that it has some therapeutic applications in the inhibition of spasticity and in the stimulation of movement.

In the treatment of *spastic* patients, vibration is applied over the muscles antagonistic to the spastic group. This stimulates a response in these muscles and causes reciprocal inhibition of the spastic group. However, if vibration is applied directly over the spastic muscles, it enhances the hypertonicity not only of the muscles vibrated but also in the other muscles which form part of the spastic synergy (Hagbarth and Eklund 1969).

Hagbarth and Eklund (1968) have suggested that the technique of vibration has definite advantages in patients with upper motor neuron lesions as compared with the quick stretch and resistance recommended by Kabat and Knott (1953) because vibration reinforces voluntary motion more effectively.

Vibration is probably most effective in those patients whose apparent weakness of movement is the result either of inhibition of certain muscles caused by spasticity in the opposing muscle groups or of lack of cortical drive. Vibration of these apparently 'weak' muscles is particularly effective in combination with methods of stimulating active goal-directed functional movement. Even if no actual muscle contraction occurs there will be reciprocal inhibition of hypertonus in the spastic antagonists, and it can be assumed with certainty that the motoneuron pool is receiving excitatory impulses via the monosynaptic arc (Bishop 1975).

Vibration is also effective in increasing facilitatory impulses to the less excitable motoneurons innervating hyptonic muscles in patients with *transient hypotonus* following stroke or head injury. For example, vibration is an effective way of stimulating antigravity muscles in order to help the patient maintain the standing position. In this case, the vibrator may be applied proximally first to the hip extensors, for example, in order to help the patient gain control of his trunk and his legs.

The perceptual effects of vibration are very interesting. Improved ability to recognise affected limbs and an increased urge to move have been reported in children with perceptual impairments of spatial orientation and body image (Hagbarth and Eklund 1969). Eklund (1969) describes the effect on the subject's perception of his position in space during vibration of the calf and anterior tibial muscles in the standing position. Tilting movements are stimulated which displace the subject's balance, as the vibration has apparently given false proprioceptive advice to the equilibrium centres of the brain. In other words, the vibrated muscles have reported, inaccurately, a forward or a backward displacement of the body and the brain has made the appropriate motor response causing the stimulated muscles to contract, therefore supposedly restoring balance. In fact, this is inappropriate as no displacement has actually occurred.

Certain other interesting effects of vibration have been reported which have therapeutic relevance. If a muscle is free to shorten isotonically against gravity, joint movement occurs as an increasing number of motor units are recruited. If extra load is applied which tends to stretch the muscle, the muscle contraction increases (Hagbarth 1973). The tonic vibration reflex develops more quickly, however, when the muscle is only allowed to contract isometrically. Blindfolded subjects have reported the illusion of slow joint movement during this isometric contraction.

Method of application

The small vibrators recommended by Hagbarth and Eklund (1969) and Hagbarth (1973) comprise cylindrical direct current motors which

380

are compact enough to be attached transversely over a muscle or tendon and held in place by a rubber band. They vibrate at 150 Hz. 100 to 200 Hz is recommended as the most effective with an amplitude of 1 to 2 mm although Stillman (1970) used vibration at 50 Hz for his clinical studies, with an amplitude of approximately 1 to 2 mm. Vibration when given by hand held apparatus is usually given for approximately two minutes, as after this time the build-up of heat and friction may be unpleasant for the patient (Bishop 1975). It appears that a facilitatory effect remains after vibration is discontinued, with a second period of vibration resulting in a more rapid rise in muscle tension. The response is influenced by the position of the head and by cooling. In many cases application of the vibrator is most effective over the muscle tendon or at the musculo-tendinous junction.

Bishop (1975) considers it takes several hours practice on normal subjects before the therapist is sufficiently skilled to apply vibration to patients. The actual mode of use, that is, the muscle to which the vibrator should be applied in order to stimulate a particular function, will be worked out by the therapist with each particular patient.

Although the controlling effect of vibration may be essential in helping the patient to regain cortical control of his movements in the presence of spasticity, this technique is not used in isolation but in combination with other methods of altering tone and stimulating movement, which will enable the patient to appreciate the sensation of movement, regain the automatic background to movement (righting and equilibrium reactions) and regain functional movement. For example, in the spastic patient with hypertonic elbow flexors as part of the abnormal pattern of flexion in the upper limb, vibration of the elbow extensors will help him overcome his flexor spasticity and extend his arm. This may be combined with weight-bearing through the arm.

Hagbarth and Eklund (1969) report that the combination of vibration and reflex inhibiting movement patterns makes it easier for the patient to break away from his abnormal postural set. They stress that it is important that stimulation of functional movement should be closely related to the time of vibration. The effect of vibration is felt for thirty minutes or more.

Long-term improvement of motor control has been reported by Eklund and Steen (1969) in a group of children with cerebral palsy. Patients have subjectively reported greater feelings of relaxation and less handicap resulting from spasticity (Hagbarth 1973).

There are some contra-indications to the use of vibration. Hagbarth and Eklund (1968) report that motor performance is adversely

381

affected by vibration in some patients with rigidity and with cerebellar syndromes. Rigidity may show a very marked increase (Hagbarth and Eklund 1969, Hagbarth 1973). Parkinsonian tremor may also increase. Vibration may induce clonus. It may stimulate intense spasms in athetoid and dystonic patients (Bishop 1975), and choreoathetoid movements may be exaggerated. For all these patients, and any other patient in whom it accentuates the motor handicap, vibration is contra-indicated. In addition, special care needs to be taken not to prolong the time of stimulation in patients with poor tactile sensation as damage to the skin may result. It should be noted that drugs such as barbiturates and diazepam cause a suppression of the tonic vibration reflex (De Gail, Lance and Neilson 1966).

References

Bishop, B. (1975) Vibratory stimulation. Part 3. *Phys. Ther.*, **55**, 2, 139–143.

de Gail, P., Lance, J. W. and Neilson, P. G. (1966) Differential effects of tonic and phasic reflex mechanisms produced by vibration of muscle in man. *J. Neurol. Neurosurg. Psychiat.*, **29**, 1.

Eklund, G. (1969) Influence of muscle vibration on balance in man. *Acta Soc. Med. Uppsala*, **74**, 113–117.

Eklund, G. and Hagbarth, K. E. (1966) Normal variability of tonic vibration reflexes in muscle. *Exper. Neurol.*, **16**, 80–92.

Eklund, G. and Steen, M. (1969) Muscle vibration therapy in children with cerebral palsy. *Scand. J. Rehabil. Med.*, **1**, 35–37.

Hagbarth, K. E. (1973) The effect of muscle vibration in normal man and in patients with motor disorders. In *New Developments in Electromyography and Clinical Neurophysiology,* edited by J. Desmedt. Basel, Karger.

Hagbarth, K. E., and Eklund, G. (1968) The effect of muscle vibration in spasticity, rigidity and cerebellar disorders. *J. Neurol. Neurosurg. Psychiat.*, **31**, 207–213.

Hagbarth, K. E. (1969) The muscle vibrator – a useful tool in neurological therapeutic work. *Scand. J. Rehab. Med.*, **1**, 26–34.

Kabat, H. and Knott, M. (1953) Proprioceptive facilitation technics for treatment of paralysis, *Phys. Ther. Rev.*, **33**, 53–64.

Stillman, B. C. (1970) Vibratory motor stimulation – a preliminary report. *Aust. J. Physiother.*, **16**, 3, 118–123.

WALKING FACILITATION

Walking facilitation, as described by Bobath (1970), is a good example of a technique which can be used to trigger off the semi-automatic movements which make up walking. The therapist transfers the patient's weight laterally and forwards from the shoulders and the trunk is rotated away from the weight-bearing leg (Fig. 142). This

Fig. 142. *Facilitation of walking. The therapist transfers the patient's weight laterally and forwards from the shoulders and rotates the trunk away from the weight-bearing leg.*

transference of weight and rotation will stimulate the patient to take a step with the free leg, but only if he is not held too firmly by the therapist. The patient's response occurs because the therapist has caused him to lose balance, thus facilitating an automatic equilibrium reaction. To be effective as a device for relearning more normal movement, the patient's postural 'set', that is, the alignment of his body, has to be correct (Fig. 143). Perhaps the two most important aspects of normal alignment are the following. The therapist, when

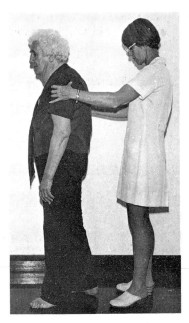

Fig. 143. *The patient must be normally aligned on the weight-bearing side, that is, the hip should not be in flexion.*

transferring weight forwards must ensure that the hip is in fact extending, and in transferring weight laterally she must ensure that the degree of displacement is appropriate.

Walking facilitation can also be done with the therapist standing behind the patient on a slow-moving treadmill. This encourages the patient to move his legs in a reciprocal, rhythmical manner.

Facilitation of walking sideways is a useful way of gaining weight transference laterally and control around the weight-bearing hip. It may therefore be used in preparation for walking forwards. The principle is the same as above.

The therapist transfers the patient's weight on to the right leg, for example, which elicits head and trunk side flexion to the left and slight abduction of the left leg. The weight is then transferred to the left with head and trunk side flexion to the right. The right leg will adduct and take its place next to the left if slight pressure is given downward through the left shoulder. No rotation of the trunk is required for this movement, and the therapist should ensure that she transfers the patient's weight by shifting his whole trunk laterally and not by depressing one shoulder.

Reference

Bobath, B. (1970) *Adult Hemiplegia: Evaluation and Treatment* London, Heinemann.

WEIGHT-BEARING—APPROXIMATION—COMPRESSION

These words are used synonymously to describe methods of stimulating joint and pressure receptors in order to elicit functional movement.

Weight-bearing through a limb improves stability in that limb and a general increase in postural tone against gravity may occur throughout the rest of the body.

Approximation or compression is used by the therapist to augment

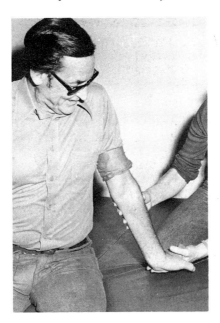

Fig. 144. *This man is practising taking weight through the heel of his hand.*

385

or substitute for the effect of weight-bearing. It can be applied, for example, in antigravity positions, by the therapist pressing downwards through a limb or through the head or trunk. It must be stressed that to be effective it is given with the limb in the appropriate weight-bearing alignment. For example, if extension is required in the standing position, approximation is applied in standing. If sufficient extension cannot be gained in this position, approximation may be applied in supine or prone in preparation for standing.

Movement in a weight-bearing position or while approximation is being applied, seems to improve the patient's ability to gain control (Fig. 144). In sitting, for example, pressure at the shoulder downwards through the weight-bearing arm will stimulate extension of the arm. If the patient attempts to bend and straighten his elbow in a small range with the therapist's guidance and assistance, movement plus approximation increases his *feeling* of weight-bearing through the arm and helps him to *learn* how to control his arm in this position. This can be done also with the arm forwards or laterally in a horizontal position, with weight being taken against a wall.

In patients whose hypotonus results in severe instability, or where instability is most marked in one particular area, approximation may

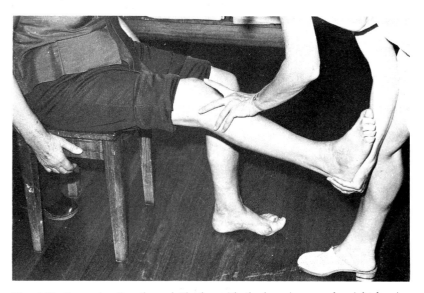

Fig. 145. *Approximation through the leg with the knee in normal weight-bearing alignment. The patient practises bending her knee and straightening it in the small range necessary for controlled weight-bearing in standing.*

386

be applied in a non weight-bearing position in preparation for weight-bearing. The limb should again be in normal alignment. For example, approximation through the lower limb in supine or sitting is used for stimulating tone, and therefore control, around the knee. The therapist applies pressure through the heel, thus approximating through the entire leg, while the patient attempts to flex and extend his knee in a small (5° to 10°) range (Fig. 145), holding the movement at various parts of the range. This is an effective way of gaining control at the knee for weight-bearing particularly with stroke and head-injured patients, when a major problem in standing and walking is instability of the knee, which is held either hyperextended or flexed. The patients frequently comment, when they assume the standing position immediately following this technique, that they are more aware of the position of the knee, and that it feels more stable. Their increased confidence is usually demonstrated by their lack of hesitancy in taking a step with the other leg.

Approximation downwards through the lower leg may be given with the patient in sitting in preparation for standing up. This approximation improves the patient's ability to bear weight through that limb, encourages more symmetry, particularly if he is hemiplegic, and improves his awareness of the position of his foot. As another example, manual pressure can be given through the heel of the hand in preparation for weight-bearing through the hand (Fig. 144).

In hypotonic patients who are athetoid or ataxic, movements in weight-bearing positions or with approximation should be in a small range at first in order that the muscular activity which occurs should not develop into an uncontrolled response. The extent of movement can be gradually increased as necessary for particular functions as the patient's control improves.

These techniques are demonstrated clinically to be effective, but the mechanism of their effect is uncertain. It is probable that the pressure receptors in skin and subcutaneous tissues and the receptors in the joints themselves are stimulated, and that this stimulation is conveyed to the muscle spindles either directly or via the sensory receptive areas of the brain.

Rood (Goff 1970) and Bobath (1967) have described techniques utilising weight-bearing, approximation and compression.

References

Bobath, B. (1967) Techniques of proprioceptive and tactile stimulation. Lecture notes from Western Cerebral Palsy Centre, London.

Goff, B. (1972) The application of recent advances in neurophysiology to Miss M. Rood's concept of neuromuscular facilitation. *Physiotherapy*, **58**, 12, 409–415.

WEIGHT-BEARING INHIBITORY PLASTERS

This technique involves the application of a skin tight plaster of Paris splint to the entire limb which is held in an inhibited position. It has been described by Hayes and Burns (1970) for reduction of hyper-tonus in the lower limb.

The essential elements causing inhibition seem to be (1) the maintenance of dorsiflexion of the foot and toes with no possibility of moving out of this position, and (2) weight-bearing while in the splint with the body in normal weight-bearing alignment. It is essential that the patient experiences weight-bearing and stimulation of weight shift and balance in standing. This form of splinting seems to have an inhibitory effect on hypertonus throughout the body.

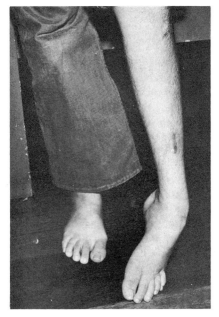

Fig. 146. *Severe contracture of the calf muscles following head injury.*

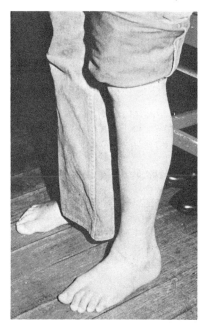

Fig. 147. *The same patient three weeks later, following below knee weight-bearing inhibitory plasters.*

Method of application

Felt padding is applied over particular bony points such as the malleoli and the head of the fibula. The splint is applied with the foot in as much dorsiflexion as possible, with the toes held on a platform in a fully dorsiflexed position and slightly abducted. Prone, with the leg flexed at the knee may be the best position in which to apply the plaster. A thick piece of felt is applied to the bottom of the plaster so the patient can commence weight-bearing as soon as the plaster is dry. The plaster is changed as soon as the toes are moving freely indicating inhibition of plantarflexion and inversion. This should occur a few days after application. Several plasters may need to be applied until the required effect is gained (Figs. 146 & 147). This may take up to three weeks, depending on the severity of the hypertonus and contracture.

This technique is useful for any patient who cannot be assisted to bear weight and balance in standing with his foot in a plantigrade

389

position and his hip in the normally extended weight-bearing alignment.

Hayes and Burns describe a long leg plaster. However, a short leg plaster is effective for adults. When the plaster ends below the knee, it is particularly important that whenever the patient bears weight he does so with his leg in normal alignment, that is with his hip extended. This will control the tendency to hyperextend the knee.

This method of inhibitory plastering can be applied to other joints.

Reference

Hayes, N. K. and Burns, Y. R. (1970) Discussion on the use of weight-bearing plasters in the reduction of hypertonicity. *Aust. J. Physiother.*, **16**, 3, 108–117.

Appendix 2

Conductive Education

Petö, with his development of Conductive Education (Cotton 1965, Hari 1968, Clarke and Evans 1973) and the method of learning called rhythmic intention, has presented the therapist with new ideas for teaching movement. Many of these ideas, based on the work of Pavlov and Luria, make a contribution to the treatment of patients with brain damage.

The physiologist Pavlov, considered that learning takes place by the formation of conditioned reflexes. The optimum conditions for learning require a quiet atmosphere, allowing concentration on the task, and repetition. The neuropsychologist Luria (1961) emphasises the importance of speech as a regulator of movement. He observes that initially a child's behaviour is regulated by the spoken instruction of adults, but it is not totally regulated because the child is not always able to act on the instructions of an adult, for example, inhibit a task once started. At about three to four years of age, the child uses his own language to regulate his motor behaviour and he can be heard describing aloud exactly what he is doing. By four and a half to five years this language is internalised and has become a strong force in the regulation of his behaviour. From this time onwards, the child is able to use internal language when learning a new skill. Similarly adults often use internal language to reinforce and regulate motor performance in learning a new skill.

The method Petö has devised for the learning of tasks is called *rhythmic intention*. The following example describes the meaning and use of the term. The therapist says 'I am going to put my hands together in front of me'. The patient repeats or attempts to repeat this phrase with the therapist. This is the *intention*. The patient then practises the task while counting to five. This gives the *rhythm* for the movement. The counting continues slowly and rhythmically until the task is completed. This rhythmic intention enables the patient to concentrate on what he is doing, to use speech to organise his movements, to speak while moving, and to learn about the position of his body parts in space. A completed task enables him to

391

experience success which will increase his confidence and prepare him for attempting other more difficult tasks.

Every task is broken down into its component parts and each part is practised until ultimately it is all put together to achieve that task. For example, to put on a pair of socks the patient has to be able to reach forwards towards his foot, he has to lift one foot off the floor while keeping his balance and keeping the other foot on the floor. He has to hold the sock open with two hands, place his foot inside, move his foot about while maintaining his sitting position and his knee in flexion. Each component of this task which is difficult for the patient will need to be practised separately.

Rhythmic intention involves the patient's motor, linguistic, cognitive and perceptual abilities. Speech acts as a conditioning stimulus and guides the movement. It is not always necessary for the patient to externalise speech. He may progress to the use of internal speech or key words as a conditioning stimulus or a reinforcer.

Petö's use of the group situation stresses motivation and the importance of the group in learning. The patient is stimulated by the others to overcome similar difficulties in order to arrive at the solution of a particular task. Success within the group provides further motivation, therefore each task must be organised so it can be fulfilled. The tasks must not be so difficult as to lead to frustration or so easy as to lead to boredom, but they should extend the patient without providing stress.

References

Clarke, J. and Evans, E. (1973) Rhythmical intention as a method of treatment for the cerebral palsied patient. *Aust. J. Physiother.* **19,** 2, 57–64.

Cotton, E. (1965) The institute of movement therapy and school for 'conductors', Budapest, Hungary. *Dev. Med. Child Neurol.*, **7,** 4, 437–446.

Hari, M. (1968) Address given at Castle Priory College, Wallingford, Berks., England.

Luria, A. R. (1961) *The Role of Speech in the Regulation of Normal and Abnormal Behaviour,* edited by J. Tizard. London, Pergamon Press.

Further Reading

Cotton, E. (1970) Integration of treatment and education in cerebral palsy. *Physiotherapy,* **56,** 4, 143–147.

Cotton, E. (1974) Improvement in motor function with the use of conductive education. *Develop. Med. Child Neurol.,* **16,** 637–643.

Cotton, E. and Parnwell, M. (1967) From Hungary: The Peto Method. *Special Ed.*, **56,** 4, 7–11.

Glossary

Agnosia is the loss or impairment of recognition even though the primary sensory pathway is intact. *Auditory* agnosia is the failure to recognise sound although hearing is intact. *Visual* agnosia is the failure to recognise common objects although vision is intact.

Anosognosia is the rejection or denial of bodily disease or dysfunction despite dense hemiplegia and inability to move. The patient shows little concern about his problems and their implications. He will look away from his hemiplegic side and even deny that it belongs to him or that there is anything the matter with it.

Autolysis is the self digestion of tissues occurring within the body as a result of a pathological condition. The disintegration of tissue is caused by the action of an enzyme peculiar to it.

Autotopagnosia, or unilateral neglect, is an unawareness of one side of the body and neglect of objects on that side. The patient may neglect this side during shaving, bathing and combing his hair, for example.

Body image or body schema is an awareness of the body, the relationship of its parts to each other and its relationship to the environment. This concept of our body results from the integration of a stream of impulses from the special senses, and from touch and proprioception. It is a mental image of the body's physical and aesthetic characteristics and includes imagery and memory.

Cerebral angiography. Radio-opaque material is introduced into the arterial or venous blood stream allowing radiographic visualisation of the cerebral blood stream. The test is used to detect various abnormalities of the cerebral circulation.

Computerised tomography (EMI scan). A computerised device moves an x-ray tube around the patient's head in an arc of 180°. It scans the brain with a pencil-thin beam of x-rays giving multiple readings during each traverse. It differentiates the densities of the tissues it encounters. The computer memorises the results of all the probes and builds a three dimensional picture which can be recorded on film.

Dementia is a progressive, irreversible, intellectual deterioration

395

without clouding of consciousness. The signs and symptoms may include forgetfulness, emotional instability, failing intellect, changing personality and behaviour with little insight into shortcomings. The word dementia is only used when impairment of intellectual function seems to be irreversible.

Diplopia or double vision may be caused by disease or weakness of the muscles themselves or a lesion of cranial nuclei 3, 4 and 6 in the brain stem or their peripheral pathways.

Echoencephalography. An 'echo' is produced by the transmission of pulsed ultra-sound alternatively through each side of the skull. When the waves meet structures of differing densities or elasticity some are reflected back to the transducer, changed into electrical impulses and displayed on an oscilloscope. The test is used to check for a space occupying lesion.

Exploratory burr holes are performed to allow the surgeon to determine the nature of a localised mass within the cranium or to relieve intracranial pressure.

Gnosis (Gr: knowledge) is the ability to recognise and identify the nature and significance of objects based upon the reception and interpretation of visual, auditory and tactile stimuli.

Isotope brain scan. The isotope is injected intravenously. Scanning of the brain is used to localise an intracranial lesion such as a tumour.

Kernig's sign is a sign of meningeal irritation. It is said to be positive when pain and spasm of the hamstrings restrict passive extension of the knee with the hip fully flexed. It is accompanied by neck stiffness. The test is of value only when tone in the limbs is not increased by any other disorder.

Lumbar puncture. A needle is introduced into the lumbar subarachnoid space. This test is performed to measure the pressure of the CSF, to collect a specimen of CSF for cytological and chemical tests, or to introduce air or an opaque medium into the subarachnoid space for radiography. The patient is usually nursed flat for 24 hours afterwards.

Palmarmental reflex. Pressure on the palm or thenar eminence causes opening of the mouth in the newborn. It may also be seen in pathogenic cerebral conditions.

Papilloedema results from increased intracranial pressure. It is observed through an ophthalmoscope. As the subarachnoid space surrounds the optic nerve, changes in the cerebrospinal fluid pressure may be registered in the optic disc. A high cerebrospinal fluid pressure, such as one caused by a space occupying lesion, whether blood, pus or tumour, exerts a force which is transmitted to the optic nerve, resulting in a swollen disc.

Post-traumatic amnesia (PTA) may be present following recovery of consciousness after head injury. The patient has no recollection of events since his accident.

Praxis (Gr: action) is the performance of a purposeful act or skilled movement.

Pseudobulbar palsy imitates bulbar palsy. It is a bilateral disturbance of the upper motor neuron pathway above the brain stem resulting in difficulty swallowing and articulating. It may be seen in arteriosclerotic Parkinsonism in which case it is usually associated with emotional incontinence. Bulbar paralysis is weakness of the muscles supplied by the cranial nerves which arise in the medulla oblongata.

Ptosis is the drooping or dropping of the upper eyelid due to weakness or paralysis.

Retrograde amnesia is a period of memory loss for events immediately preceding the accident. It is always associated with concussion.

Romberg's sign. This sign is said to be present when the patient demonstrates marked swaying or falling when he stands with his feet together and eyes closed. It is indicative of loss of appreciation of position sense in the lower limbs and is found in tabes dorsalis, subacute combined ˙degeneration of the cord and sensory neuropathies.

Scotoma, or blind spot, is a small area within the visual field in which vision is depressed or abolished.

Tentorial herniation. Any expanding lesion within the cranium may cause brain shift and herniation because of the limited confines of the skull. Part of the brain shifts from where pressure is rising to a compartment where it is lower. For example, a mass above the tentorium may push the brain stem and part of the cerebral hemisphere down through the tentorial hiatus. This causes compression, ischaemia, and oedema of the midbrain and results in ischaemia and further oedema of the hemisphere. If the third cranial nerve is stretched the pupil will become dilated on the same side. Lesions involving the posterior fossa may push the cerebellum and midbrain upwards through the tentorial notch and the cerebellar tonsils down through the foramen magnum causing compression of the brain stem. Involvement of the reticular system results in impaired alertness which may progress to unconsciousness and decerebrate posturing.

Tonic labyrinthine reflex is demonstrated in supine by increased tone in the extensor muscles, in prone by increased tone in the flexor muscles.

Tonic neck reflexes The *asymmetrical* TNR is elicited by rotation of the head. The limbs on the face side extend or show an increase in tone in the extensors. The limbs on the occiput side flex or show an increase in tone in the flexors. The *symmetrical* TNR is elicited by flexion or extension of the head. Flexion brings about an increase in extensor tone in the lower limbs and flexor tone in the upper limbs. Extension brings about an increase in extensor tone in the upper limbs and flexor tone in the lower limbs.

Index